JACK LEMMON

BILLY WILDER

"SOME LIKE IT HOT"

PAT
O'BRIEN · JOE E. BROWN · SCREEN PLAY BY BILLY WILDER and I.A.L. D...

romance!
WONDERFUL
is the word for

Sabrina

with
WALTER HAMPDEN · JOHN WILLIAMS
MARTHA HYER · JOAN VOHS
Written for the Screen by BILLY WILDER,
SAMUEL TAYLOR and ERNEST LEHMAN
From the play by SAMUEL TAYLOR

HO

☆☆

the Spirit of St. Louis

...NG PERSONAL ADVENTURE OF OUR TIME!

...as the
world
held its
breath--

BASED ON THE PULITZER PRIZE WINNING BOOK BY CHARLES A. LINDBERGH

...ND WARNERCOLOR   SCREEN PLAY BY BILLY WILDER AND WENDELL MAYES   MUSIC COMPOSED AND CONDUCTED BY FRANZ WAXMAN
PRODUCED BY LELAND HAYWARD   DIRECTED BY BILLY WILDER   PRESENTED BY WARNER BROS.

Stalag 17

STARRING
WILLIAM HOLDEN · DON TAYLOR · OTTO PREMINGER
PRODUCED AND DIRECTED BY BILLY WILDER   WRITTEN FOR THE SCREEN BY BILLY WILDER AND EDWIN BLUM

...CE
...LIER

"LOVE IN THE AFTERNOON"

AN
ALLIED
ARTISTS
PICTURE

Produced and Directed by BILLY WILDER
WITH JOHN McGIVER · Screenplay by BILLY WILDER and I. A. L. DIAMOND · Based on Novel by CLAUDE ANET · Musical Adaptation by FRANZ WAXMAN

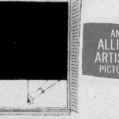

CONVERSATIONS WITH

ALFRED A. KNOPF   NEW YORK   2001

WILDER

BY CAMERON CROWE

KAREN LERNER, EDITORIAL CONSULTANT

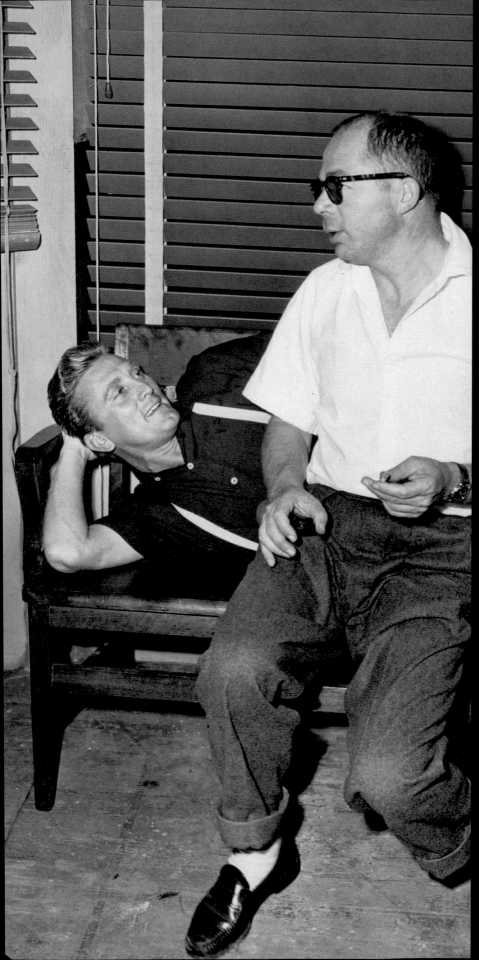

THIS IS A BORZOI BOOK
PUBLISHED BY
ALFRED A. KNOPF

www.randomhouse.com

Knopf, Borzoi Books, and the colophon are
registered trademarks of Random House,
Inc.

Library of Congress Cataloging-in-
Publication Data
Wilder, Billy.
Conversations with Wilder / by Cameron
Crowe. — 1st ed.
p.   cm.
Includes indexes.
ISBN 0-375-40660-3 (hc.)
1. Wilder, Billy, 1906–   Interviews.
2. Motion picture producers and
directors—United States Interviews.
I. Crowe, Cameron, 1957–   .
II. Title.
PN1998.3.W56A5   1999   99-31104
791.43'0233'092—dc21   CIP

Manufactured in
the United States of America
Published November 10, 1999
Reprinted Twice
Fourth Printing, June 2001

(Previous page) Billy Wilder and, across
the table, Charles Brackett, his collaborator, playing "the word game" with other
writers at the Paramount commissary

For Buddy

CONTENTS

For additional editorial assistance and research, my thanks to Scott M. Martin.

Special thanks to: Audrey Wilder, Karen Lerner, Nancy Wilson, Alice Crowe, James A. Crowe, Robert Bookman, Kathy Robbins, Gary Salt, Leonard Gershe, Tom Cruise, Bonnie Hunt, Shannon Maguire, Kathy Rivkin, David Halpern, Graydon Carter, Ann Schneider, Howard Kaminsky, Chip Kidd, Kapo Ng, Melissa Goldstein, Donald Kraus, Stratton Young, Klaus Whitley, Michael Chow, Art and Rex Cavrera, Richard and Barbara Cohen, Jerry and Ann Moss, Shelley Wanger, and the man who brought us all together—Mr. Billy Wilder.

INTRODUCTION

"Do you have a good ending for this thing?" asks Billy Wilder, the greatest living writer-director.

It is the spring of 1998, and too much has been made of the rains of El Niño, so we will not mention the torrential downpour that has blanketed California on this strangely wet and strangely humid afternoon. We have just met outside his office tucked away on a Beverly Hills side street, and walked up the single flight of stairs to the room that serves as his quiet work space. He jingles the keys, finding the right one, and looks down to see that the laces of his left shoe have come untied. Another step might well mean a fall, so he stays frozen in the hallway. He is ninety-one, and bending down from a full stand has been a physical impossibility for a number of years. He does not look over to me, nor I to him. There is some embarrassment involved here for both of us, so I bend down to quickly tie his laces, and neither of us mentions it. We enter his office and sit down for the last of our conversations, a series of interviews that have stretched on for well over a year.

Imagine for a moment a party, a somewhat elegant affair, populated solely by characters from the films of Billy Wilder.

Over there at the piano, swirling a drink, is the doomed Walter Neff from *Double Indemnity*. He's trying not to stare at the effervescent Sugar from *Some Like It Hot*. Fran Kubelik and C. C. Baxter from *The Apartment* dance closely to some postmodern jazz in another room, while Norma Desmond from *Sunset Boulevard* descends the main staircase to join the flinty and ambitious Chuck Tatum from *Ace in the Hole*. And outside, hiding in a tree on this moonlit night, yearning for a glimpse of David Larrabee, studying every movement in this full house of wildly different characters, crouches the lovesick Sabrina.

What an evening it would be. And yet chances are the host wouldn't stick around to take many bows for himself. Billy Wilder, master of the screen story, isn't much for the collecting of compliments. His life of the last ten years has often been about the dutiful collecting of awards and accolades, but the truth is even more Wilderesque. The very same industry icons honoring him could have better spent their time employing the great Wilder to direct new movies. Physically, the Wilder of today moves deliberately, sometimes with a cane. Yet he shows up at his Beverly Hills office almost daily, reading, tending to his relationships in the art world, and still staying in touch with the supercharged and, sadly, often character-deprived film fare of today.

Billy Wilder's work is a treasure trove of flesh-and-blood individuals, all wonderfully alive. In his canon of work are fall-down-laughing comedies, stinging character studies, social satire, true suspense, aching romance . . . the best in life, the sad and the giddy, the ironic and harrowing all have equal weight in his work. The great Ernst Lubitsch taught him the joys of directing, but it is perhaps Wilder's background as a journalist that gave him the gift of knowing what truth looks and sounds like. Perhaps that is why, years later, more than that of any of his contemporaries, Billy Wilder's work stands today as a portrait of the way people *are*. At a 1997 Directors Guild of America symposium featuring the DGA

Award–nominated filmmakers, the four nominees present were asked to name the individuals who had lit their own creative fuses. All agreed on only one name: Wilder.

A few fast details on a rich and well-traveled life. Wilder was born June 22, 1906, in the town of Sucha, in an area of Poland that was then part of Austria. His name was Samuel but his mother always called him Billie; his older brother, Wilhelm, called Willie, was born in 1904. The Wilders moved to Vienna a few years later, and what happened after has been amplified and overhyped and is best explained by Wilder himself in our conversations. "Much of what has been written is false," he says today. "In the old days, they made this stuff up."

What is part of indisputable public record is a creative life that began when Wilder took on a job as a newspaper reporter in Vienna. He flourished in the role and built a quick reputation for dogged pursuit of his subjects. Wilder traveled to Berlin in June of 1926 at the invitation of jazz musician Paul Whiteman. He stayed. His newspaper work—his life—grew more colorful and chaotic. For one series of articles, Wilder even posed as a dancing gigolo and wrote about the experience. His imagination soon led him to screenwriting and he became a ghostwriter for the growing German film industry. Before long Wilder was a credited writer, and his work grew in stature as wartime approached. Escaping to Paris, and later to America, Wilder turned up in Los Angeles and fell in with other refugees from Europe who would change film history. Ernst Lubitsch had arrived previously, and soon Wilder would link up with his hero to cowrite *Bluebeard's Eighth Wife* in 1938 and, a year later, the seminal *Ninotchka.* Wilder began directing in 1942 with *The Major and the Minor,* from a script written with his first great collabo-

rator, Charles Brackett. His most recent film is 1981's *Buddy Buddy*, written with another landmark collaborator, I. A. L. Diamond.

Wilder's talent for taking the darkness in men and skewering it with illuminating humor arrived early. "I was beaten in the home," he says matter-of-factly, with a characteristic lack of self-pity. But the details of his childhood have gone largely unexplored in his interviews. Asked pointedly about these years, Wilder can be detached and uncommunicative. A new subject and a joke cannot be far behind.

In 1928, Wilder's father died in Berlin, where he was visiting Billy on a stopover from a trip to America. Wilder's mother died in the concentration camps of Auschwitz. He battled the horrible memory with career perseverance and an unparalleled wit. Wilder flourished in Hollywood, the world capital of a brutal business, making films and building a reputation as a creative genius, a director of simple brilliance, and a world-class humorist by whom others are still measured. His persona is mighty, hard to crack. There have been years where he was called vulgar, and years where his later work was savaged. It is the ride every innovator takes, in full public view. Today, there are few filmmakers who don't crave to be compared with him. His is a tough-minded romanticism and elegance. His work has survived because of a lack of trend hopping or tub thumping. The lack of sentimentality has left him forever relevant as an artist. As an assessor of his own work, he can be a clear-eyed and sometimes cruel father. He has won every award, received every accolade. And he is still alive. A magnificent life, perfectly written and performed, and one can't help wondering: Perhaps the greatest character creation of young Billie Wilder . . . is Billy Wilder himself.

In 1995, I had two movies under my belt and years of inspiration from Billy Wilder's work. Like many up-and-coming directors, I made the pilgrimage to his office. He had no idea of my own work, and I didn't expect him to. I brought a poster from *The Apartment* and a head full of questions. I had pressed hard for our appointment, which had been made through my agent, Robert Bookman at CAA, a casual acquaintance of Wilder's. I arrived several minutes early at his Beverly Hills office, hidden in a nondescript building behind a gift shop on Brighton Way. There was no sound within. I looked through the mail slot and saw a sliver of the two darkened rooms, unadorned with memorabilia, just a number of books and a desk filled with paperwork.

For the next two hours I took walks around the block, killing time and calling his answering machine from the corner pay phone. Finally, the very second I had decided to leave and taken my first step toward the car, keys in hand, Wilder appeared from the alley across the street. He looked quintessentially Wilder, a compact man smartly dressed in tweed jacket and cap, and he was heading right toward me. I approached him delicately, in the overly formal manner of someone with no friends or close relatives who had lived to this age. I introduced myself. There was absolutely no spark—zero recognition. He shook my hand politely, routinely, with a sharp snap, and reached for the manila envelope in my hand. He thought I was a messenger.

I mentioned our eleven a.m. appointment, and Wilder looked surprised. He was instantly apologetic. He had been unaware of the meeting, he said, and invited me up the staircase. "Come on up, and I'll sign that thing."

As I walked up the steps with him, he filed through the week's appointments in his mind. No, no meeting planned for a Cameron Crowe. He opened the office and beckoned me inside. A photo of Marlene Dietrich was tacked to a bulletin board. A photographic collage by David Hockney of Wilder and his

wife, Audrey, hung on the wall. A portrait of Einstein; a framed photo of Wilder with Akira Kurosawa and Federico Fellini. And above the door, the famous sign I had read about, designed by Saul Steinberg, reading: HOW WOULD LUBITSCH DO IT?

He listened to a few phone messages while I took a seat across from him. He hadn't reached my messages yet. He was listening to a call from a writer for the *Los Angeles Times,* who in a fast and colorless tone explained that he had a question for an Oscar-themed issue, and his deadline was *now.* The caller then rattled off his phone number, which Wilder at first gamely tried to copy. He gave up after three digits, and put down his pen. "I will not be calling you back," he addressed the answering machine. He turned to me. "What can I do for you?"

Wilder patiently listened as I told him of my appreciation for his work. At first brusquely, then more animatedly, and soon hilariously, he answered most of my questions. He told stories that sounded like secrets even when they weren't, and spent the better part of an hour discussing his directing and casting techniques. Wilder stressed the importance of casting—citing the case of Cary Grant, his favorite missed opportunity as an actor. He had wanted him for *Sabrina* and later for *Love in the Afternoon* but hadn't been able to land him. Finally Wilder picked up the pen to sign my one-sheet. Wilder regarded the poster like an old friend. "*The Apartment,*" he said. "Good picture."

"My favorite," I said.

"Mine too," he said, as if the decision was now final. "We had the right actors. It worked." He paused dryly. "And I cannot think of anything funny to write on your poster." He signed his name and dated it. As he walked me to the door, I told him I would like him to play a small part in my third movie, *Jerry Maguire,* the script of which was just about finished. He suggested I call him when filming approached. He said he was not an actor. "It's just a small part," I said, "but it's important. It's Jerry Maguire's mentor, the original sports agent, Dicky Fox."

"*Small* part?" he noted. "Then I *definitely* won't do it!"

He walked to the bathroom, just down the hall, and as I was leaving, he specifically mentioned that I should call him again about the acting part. As he stood in the door to the bathroom, he said, "Cameron. That's a good name. In Germany, they have only two names. Hans . . . and *Helmut.* Good afternoon." A pleasant crack, delivered with style. He disappeared into the can. I left, strapped to a creative rocket.

For months I told friends that I had begun discussions with Billy Wilder to play a part in my film. I had even scheduled it as the first shot of the production. Wilder would be my good-luck charm.

Only one problem—I now could not reach him. I called his agent, who seemed to recall that

Wilder had mentioned the acting offer. But he had not heard back from Wilder. As we neared production, I finally positioned an intern outside the doorway of his office building. The assignment—call when you spot the master.

It was now late 1995, the first day of rehearsals with Tom Cruise, Cuba Gooding Jr., and Bonnie Hunt, all of whom were now cast in *Jerry Maguire*. The call came. Wilder was in his office. I tried the number, and he answered after a single ring.

"Mr. Wilder, this is Cameron Crowe. We discussed you acting in my movie."

"Leave me alone!" he roared. "I am an old man. I am not an actor and I will not appear in your picture." The great Billy Wilder then hung up on me.

Within a few moments, I was splashing through the rainy streets of Beverly Hills with Tom Cruise. Our mission was to drop in on Wilder in person. Armed with the star of the film, we would make this offer face-to-face.

Wilder answered the door to his office and expressed dismay that we had come without an appointment. Still, he invited us in. For close to an hour, as we pled the case for the part and discussed the movie with him, he still said no. ("I know what I can do and I know what I cannot do. . . . I will just fuck up your movie. It will be bad. Pick somebody else. I am awkward. I am not myself.") Cruise leaned forward, turning on the high beams, and explained that Wilder's participation was essential. He still said no. I reminded him of his own disappointment with Cary Grant, explaining that I was reluctant to give up on this dream casting. Wilder looked at me—or more accurately, right through me. I felt like a brownnoser, a bullshitter, and the sad fact was, I meant every word.

He chatted with Cruise about *Sabrina, Ninotchka,* and *Sunset Boulevard,* mathematically dissected the plot of our movie, and then finally turned to me to ask a personal question.

"Is this your first movie?"

"Third."

"Do you ever think about giving up?"

"Yes," I said, utterly honest, embracing the personal question.

He nodded. I had answered incorrectly, of course, and knew it instantly. I had flunked out of a one-question boot camp for directors. Or maybe this was an elegant insult. Or hey, it's Billy Wilder, it's gotta

be *all of the above*. He blinked at me, as if to say, "Directing is a tough business. . . . Hamlet belongs on a stage, for God's sake." He never quite looked at me again. Immovable and charming, tough without slickness. . . . "Tough"—that was the key description for this gentleman, who did not recall meeting me earlier and who now felt no qualms about telling me and the future Jerry Maguire no with great flourish. Finally we stood up to leave.

"Nice to meet you, and nice to meet you," he said in a courtly fashion. His gaze passed across me and stopped on Tom Cruise. "*Especially* you."

I left his office and got inside the car with Cruise. I had just introduced one of the biggest stars in the world to something he had not experienced much: failure. Not quite the accomplishment I had in mind for the first day of rehearsal. We drove back in silence, continued rehearsals, and made the movie, mentioning Wilder every few weeks. The force of his rejection was still humbling months later, a black joke between Cruise and me. Sometimes I would repeat the bitingly funny, Wilderesque goodbye from that failed meeting. "Nice to meet you, nice to meet you . . . *especially* you." We always laughed. Painfully.

In February of 1997, *Jerry Maguire* had been in release for several months. A journal had been published in *Rolling Stone* magazine detailing the episode with Wilder and the making of the film. A fax came to the office from Karen Lerner, a longtime friend of Billy and Audrey Wilder's. Lerner had first met the Wilders in the early sixties, as a journalist from *Newsweek;* she would later marry Alan Jay Lerner. Karen's relationship with Billy and Audrey had stayed strong over the years. She was a regular visitor and dinner companion as well as a Wilder aficionado. She had read my journal in *Rolling Stone.* Would I be interested in a book idea, a volume of new interviews with Billy Wilder, not unlike *Hitchcock* by François Truffaut? Of course the idea was intriguing, but I called her and described what I felt would be the problem. Wilder and I had not quite clicked. I did not want to push the issue. Heroes usually belong at arm's length—on a bookshelf, in a record collection. At a heroic distance. I did not wish to continue the flogging.

Lerner persisted, telling me that Wilder too had read my journal and enjoyed it. Wilder had offered to do a magazine interview with me—he wasn't doing many interviews these days—and Karen suggested we see if the chemistry worked. If it did, perhaps the interviews would turn into a book. I would be meeting him back at the site of our previous disaster, and we could begin by discussing a couple of pictures that Wilder had fond memories of—*Double Indemnity* and *The Apartment*. Everything in me sensed an exercise in masochism. I had a new script to begin. There was no time. Best to file this one away as an odd turn of events, an ironic twist, a surprising invitation from the master that I would smartly have to turn down.

Of course I made immediate plans to meet Wilder.

"You seem taller," he said, upon opening the door to his office. "You have grown with your success." Wilder wore a suit, with suspenders and tasseled loafers. He motioned me into the same small room where I had first met him. Shortly after greeting me, he was off and running with conversation of the upcoming Academy Awards, suggesting that *Jerry Maguire*'s five nominations, including Best Picture, and particularly the Best Actor nomination for Cruise, were a great boon for the appreciation of film comedy and comedic acting. "And I liked the guy who played my part," he added.

I fumbled with my tape recorder, testing the microphone, but as usual Wilder was off and running. He was then ninety, and I was already hustling to keep up with him. And yet, as in Wilder's own best work, there was a twist, early in the first act. As I would now find out, the road to this interview-book project was littered with bodies of those who had attempted it before me.

Wilder did not want another book published about him. He had been dissatisfied with other books written about him—he found them inaccurate and, worse, boring. A recent attempt with a German author had resulted in a volume published only in Germany. He did not deem it of interest to an American audience. Earlier attempts at a Q-and-A volume had been denied over the years, and few journalists have caught his voice in print—the rich mix of middle-European phrasing, American slang, and deadly dry wit. There are few things as funny as the poker-faced Wilder himself, rarely laughing at his own jokes, but watching *your* laughter with the pleased look of a contented craftsman. And yet, at ninety, Wilder was not interested in "putting myself up as a role model." Again and again he stressed our first interview was an attempt to end our relationship on a pleasant and helpful note. "This is for your magazine," he said. "This is for your column."

Column? I *had* no column.

He reached onto his desk, put on a new pair of glasses. Carefully, with long, smooth fingers, one bent abruptly to the side with arthritis, he adjusted a small clear box of Tic Tacs before him. The desk was filled with paper—letters from all over the globe, invitations to film festivals, phone numbers—and, just off to the side, the answering machine, and the telephone he answers himself when at the office.

A half hour into our first interview, I was experiencing a strange case of déjà vu. I had read all the previous books on Wilder, and many of his interviews. But the tone of this conversation had a beautiful arc to it, a life's perspective that added a new layer to his always sharply funny observations. The valuable presence of Karen Lerner on our first round of interviews helped to loosen the atmosphere. Our talks began with many anecdotes, some of them familiar, but my journalism background was whispering very loudly for me to dig deeper—to get that interview Wilder has never truly given. Such was the Wilderesque twist of this afternoon. When I should have been home writing a new project, I was now on another quest to talk Wilder into a project he firmly wanted no part of. I sat across from Billy Wilder on the sunny afternoon, discussing some of the greatest lives of modern times—lives born in the heart and mind of Billy Wilder—and saw our talk as a poignant link to the future.

Of all his contemporaries from the earlier part of the century, Billy Wilder is the last one still stand-

ing, still swinging. His memory is clear, and in our conversations he would rarely use the lack of it as an excuse. He is still shaping, rethinking his own movies, still experiencing the grief of lost speeches or opportunities. It is remarkable, and a glimpse of what the job really is. Become a director and you, too, in the best-case scenario, will still be obsessing over minutiae sixty years from now. At this writing, he is nearly ninety-two. He is also still a wry observer of film and film business—although he rarely uses the words "film" or "cinema"—keeping up on most of the current pictures, usually at the home screening room of his friends Richard and Barbara Cohen (Richard Cohen passed away in May 1999). "Pictures" is Wilder's term of choice for the celluloid storytelling that has consumed most of his professional life. Wilder's lack of self-importance is positively rare in these over-media-ized and attention-grabbing times.

I watched as he popped white Tic Tacs, politely and sometimes warily addressing my many pages of detailed questions. I knew it would not be easy. He is not given to emotional extravagance. He would not always understand my slang, and I would sometimes be lost as he flicked from era to era, over nearly a century of work. He was, after all, a dancer. And there would always be a tendency for him to run for cover within those famous anecdotes, well honed from years of audiences of one or two or four enthralled dinner guests. My goal was to dig beneath those sparkling recitations of his best stories, his greatest hits. Some questions would have to be asked a number of times; eluding them was too much fun for Wilder. In a flash, he can turn your earnest question into a straight line. If wit is your greatest weapon, why not use it often? He does. Wilder himself is his own greatest character. What truly went into the writing and *living* of such a character? Trying to get those answers from a ninety-year-old Billy Wilder might just be a full-time job. And this was only the beginning.

—*Cameron Crowe*
May 26, 1998

A foreign affair

in AVANTI!

Buddy Buddy

DOUBLE INDEMNITY

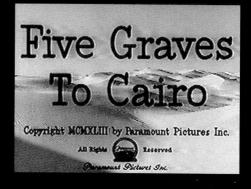

FEDORA

Five Graves To Cairo

THE FRONT PAGE

IRMA LA DOUCE

The Lost Weekend

From the Novel by CHARLES R. JACKSON

Love in the Afternoon

THE PRIVATE LIFE OF SHERLOCK HOLMES

SUNSET BLVD.

SABRINA

The Apartment

SOME LIKE IT HOT

The Fortune Cookie

"The Spirit of St. Louis"

Witness For The Prosecution

STALAG 17

The Major and the Minor

RITA JOHNS

CONVERSATIONS

WITH WILDER

Billie Wilder (standing on table) with his family in Poland

1

CAMERON CROWE: You've written women characters so well over the years. You had no sisters. Is there a character who resembles your mother in any of the movies?

BILLY WILDER: No. My mother was different. No, you see, we were not a family of readers, of collectors, of theatergoers. My father was a man who dabbled in many directions. He was an owner of a string of railroad restaurants. In those days we didn't have diners, I am talking about the Austro-Hungarian monarchy. So he had restaurants at various stations, where the trains stopped. The guy came with the bell, "We are staying here for forty-five minutes!" People are stuck there. The menus are all printed already. They ate there.

CC: Did you ever feel the desire to do an autobiographical movie, about your childhood?

BW: No. I graduated from the worst high school in Vienna. The students were either retarded, or they were crazy geniuses, absolutely. And the sad thing was that when I came to Vienna the last time, three years ago, I told the newspaper people, "*Please* write, *anybody* who went to school with me, please call me, I am at the Bristol Hotel." Not one called me all day. Five years before that, when I was in Vienna, I had a big lunch, and I told the concierge, "If somebody asks for me, I'm not here. I'm going to bed." Fifteen minutes later, the phone rings, and he says, "I'm very sorry, Mr. Wilder, but there is a man who went to school with you—his name is Martini." And I said, "Martini, of *course!* Martini! Have him come up!" Then the guy comes there. Bowed forward. Bald-headed. "Hello, Mr. Wilder." And I say, "Martini! Do you remember this guy, this professor? . . . Do you remember these things!?" [*Quietly:*] And he looks at me and says, "I think you are talking about my father. He died four years ago." He had the son that looked like him. So the guys are gone, you know.

    This is ninety years old. If somebody would have come to me when I was twenty, and said, "How would you like to get to be seventy?" I would have said, "You've got a deal! Seventy!" Now I am twenty and a half years older than that, and nobody will make that bet anymore. [*Laughs.*]

CC: Did you have a sense that you would live a long life?

BW: Not at all. No. I've had so many crazy things happen in my life. But it would not have ended by suicide. It would not have been being caught with somebody's wife, or something like that. This is not my style. I'm too clever for that. I wrote that too often.

CC: It's interesting, because when I first became a director, somebody said to me, "Well, you know, your life expectancy just went down, because the average age of a director is fifty-eight."

BW: Don't tell anybody my age. Shhhhhh.

CC: You think to yourself, I could be a dentist and live twenty years longer.

BW: I believe it. A director—a serious director, not a director of television, or something like that—it *eats you* inside. You just have to absorb so much. And the thing is that you have to swallow so much shit from people. It's a very, very simple formula. You've got to *live* with them, once you've started with them. Because if the picture is half-finished, if there's anything wrong, they're gonna throw *me* out, not one of the actors.

CC: I had that thought when Tom Cruise signed on for *Jerry Maguire*. My first thought was that if there were a serious problem, I would be gone and he would still be there. I would wake up on a desert island, someone would put a drink with an umbrella in my hand, and I would say, "Excuse me, but wasn't I directing a movie with Tom Cruise yesterday?" [*We laugh.*]

Wilder (seated front row, second from right) with his classmates in Vienna

BW: But that did not happen. He is a thinking actor. He makes it look effortless. For example, *Rain Man.* It took several years for everyone to realize that the roles could have been switched. That is a movie I would have liked to have seen—the crazy guy is the *good-looking one.* The ease in which he handles the hardest roles . . . Tom Cruise, he's like Cary Grant. He makes the hard things look simple. On film, Cary Grant could walk into the room and say "Tennis anyone?" like no one else. You don't value the skill until you see a less skilled actor try the same thing. It's pure gold.

CC: There is a story about a great king who was in power many years. And as he was dying, he was asked how many days of pure bliss he really had in all those years of power. And the king answered, "Maybe one." Maybe one day of pure bliss.

BW: Yeah. That's it. And you know it the day you *come back* to the studio, the day after a disastrous preview. The policeman does not know you. He looks the other way. You get the feeling you don't belong there anymore.

CC: Was happiness ever a goal? Have you been happy in all these years of great activity?

BW: Yeah, I mean, compared with other people's lives. I had a good life. Yes. A very good life. I had forty-some years' marriage with my wife, whom I love. I had a good career. It kind of . . . I just know that it has to end sometime. I *still* have a very good time. Still have very good thoughts. No no, no bad memories, nor no people that I hate. [*He pauses, as if giving away the secret of how to conduct a peaceful retirement in Hollywood.*] They don't come near me, because I run away like a weasel from people that give me displeasure. And I've been healthy. Ninety is pretty good. I would have liked to have made a few of the great pictures that somebody else made . . . there are some wonderful, wonderful pictures that I wish I would have made. I am ambitious, but I will not do anything that smells badly, even if I got ten times my salary. I would not do that. I mean well; I wish my co-directors, and my directors who were before me, and directors who are now very successful, I wish them well and I root for them all. If you can say that when you're ninety, you know, you've had a good life.

CC: Let's talk about one of your favorite actors, one who truly brought your words and your style to life—Jack Lemmon. How did you first hear about him?

BW: I knew he was around. He had played Mr. Pulver, and won an Academy Award, in *Mister Roberts* [1955]. He was screamingly funny, and he was brand-

Jack Lemmon and Shirley MacLaine in *The Apartment* (1960)

new. He was under contract to Columbia, making three or four pictures, and I liked him. I liked his quality.

His first day on a sound stage [*It Should Happen to You*, 1954], with George Cukor directing, he's all revved up. He rattles down half a page of dialogue, *rararaaumphrara,* and then there's "Cut," and he looks at Cukor. Cukor comes up to him and says, "It was just wonderful, you're going to be a big, big star. However . . . when it comes to that big speech, please, please, a little less, a little bit less. You know, in the theater, we're back in a long shot, and you have to pour it on. But in *film,* you cut to a close-up and you cannot be that *strong.*" So he does it again, less. And again Cukor says, "Wonderful! Absolutely marvelous, now let's do it again, a *little bit* less." Now after ten or eleven times, Mr. Cukor admonishing him "a little less," Mr. Lemmon says, "Mr. Cukor, for God's sake, you know pretty soon *I won't be acting at all.*" Cukor says, "Now you're getting the idea." [*Laughter.*]

CC: There's a lot of pleasure to be had in studying the details of your films, starting with the character names. How much time did you put into coming up with names?

BW: [*Smiles.*] There was one name, one man that I had in three or four pictures. Always the same type of character. It was a name that I liked, you know. The name was Sheldrake. It has little vibes there. It had *profile.* It's not like Mr. Jones or Mr. Weber or something—although Mr. Lloyd Webber cleverly put two *b*'s in there. But we always had little jokes with the names. For instance, Marilyn Monroe in *Some Like It Hot* [1959], we called her Sugar Kane. Kubelik—that was Shirley MacLaine in *The Apartment* [1960]. Fran Kubelik. [Jan] Kubelik was a very, very famous violinist in my day, when I went to school. C. C. Baxter came from my first assistant director, C. C. Coleman—"Buddy" Coleman we called him. I just remember names of real people. Sheldrake was a real person too. He was a basketball player at UCLA.

CC: It's also a fun name to say. Is that an important part of it?

BW: Yeah, a good name has a certain strength. Yeah, names are fun, you know. Everything is fun except writing the script itself. The things before and after are fun. In writing, you always say to yourself, "We'll find a solution for that later," but I cannot go on to a new scene until everything is okay.

CC: Hard to do. The language and rhythms of your scripts are so specific, did you often give actors line readings?

Jack Lemmon and Judy Holliday in a scene from *It Should Happen to You* (1954), directed by George Cukor. Wilder had loved Lemmon in *Mister Roberts* (1955)—"He was screamingly funny"—for which he won an Academy Award.

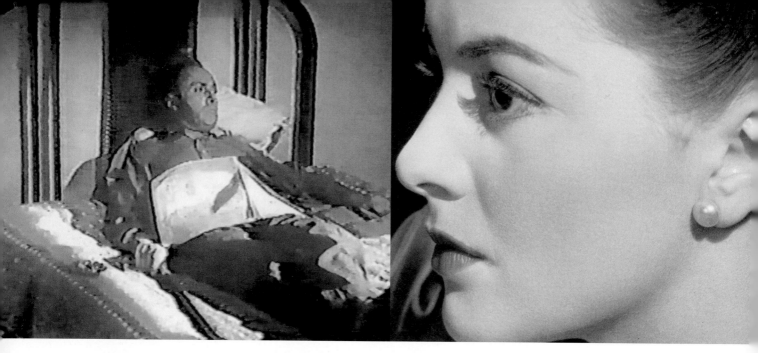

A director is born: This historic non-moment from *Hold Back the Dawn* (1941), in which Charles Boyer did not perform Wilder and Brackett's scripted speech to a cockroach, is responsible for the creation of some of the finest films in history. Not a bad trade-off. "Without the speech," Wilder recalls, "the scene became flat, nothing." At that moment, Wilder vowed to become a director.

BW: We sat around in a circle and we read. Is that what you mean?

CC: No—let's say the performance wasn't right on a line, wasn't the way you heard it in your head. Would you perform the line for the actor, the way you wanted to hear it?

BW: Yeah, but I am not a Strasberg man. I am not an actor. I'm not even a born director. I became a director because so many of our scripts had been screwed up.

The idea was that we [Wilder and collaborator Charles Brackett] were under contract to Paramount, and had to deliver eleven pages every Thursday, on yellow paper. Eleven pages. Why *eleven,* I do not know. And then the script. We were not allowed to be on the set. We were supposed to be upstairs on the fourth floor writing the script. So they would chase us off, and [Mitchell] Leisen was the worst one. Mitch Leisen.

I remember one episode. Leisen was directing *Hold Back the Dawn* [1941]. We were already writing the next script, and not allowed on the set. Policemen! Policemen were on the set to say, "No, no, no!" That was the situation we had then. In pictures, in those days, they didn't even let you watch what you wrote.

So we had written a scene in *Hold Back the Dawn* where the hero—actually, he's a gigolo—Charles Boyer, is lying there in that dirty Hotel Esperanza, across the border. It was for the first third of the picture, he's stranded in Mexico. He hasn't got the papers to get in, but he would like to get to America. He lies there in bed all dressed, and there is a *cockroach* that is crawling up the wall and the cockroach wants to get onto the broken, dirty mirror. And Boyer was to imitate a border guard, with a stick in his hand, and say to the cockroach [*officiously*], "Hey, where you going? What are you doing? Have you got a visa? . . . What, *no visa?!* How can you travel without a passport!! You can't!" That was the scene, meant to appear in the first act. They are shooting the picture, and Brackett and I were going for lunch to Lucy's—that was the restaurant across the street from Paramount. Now we are finished with lunch, and

we passed a table where Mr. Boyer had a nice French lunch with the napkin tucked in here, and a little bottle of red wine. "Hi, Charles, how are you?" "How are you boys?" "What are you shooting today?" "We are shooting the scene with the cockroach." "Oh, yeah, that's a good scene, isn't it?" He says, "We *changed* it a little bit." [*Wilder's eyes widen.*] "What do you mean, you changed it?" He says, "We changed it because it's idiotic—why would I *talk* to a cockroach if a cockroach can't answer me?" I say, "Yeah yeah yeah, but just the same, we would like you to do it." "No no no," says Boyer, "we talked and I convinced Mr. Leisen, I'm not talking to a cockroach." So it was nothing. The scene became flat, nothing.

So now we were upstairs writing the end to this picture, *Hold Back the Dawn,* the last ten pages. I say to Brackett, "If that son of a bitch doesn't talk to a cockroach, he ain't talking to nobody! Cross out his dialogue!" [*Laughs.*] We won . . . kind of. We should have had the whole script filmed. . . . But what were we talking about?

CC: Line readings.

BW: Line readings. Well, naturally, it happens with the reading, you know. Sometimes somebody hits a note that is so wonderful that you cannot believe you did not think of it. Other times you have to insist on the right reading. Then I would take the actor to the side and I would say, "Could you just do this one line again?" Maybe as a wild line that I could just slip in there. But it is not a sin to give an actor a line reading . . . the nerves sometimes give way, you know. And you just say, "This is the way, *da-da-da-da.*" I didn't do it very well, you know, because it is not my language. A *look* I can do. But I get along very, very well with actors, except when I work with sons-of-bitches like Mr. [Humphrey] Bogart. Bogart, who was a Warner Bros. man. He suddenly became available, he wanted a picture, and I had one, something called *Sabrina* [1954]. But I wanted Cary Grant. I would always say, "Well, let's get Cary Grant."

I had Cary Grant in mind for four of my pictures. He was a friend of mine, and I liked him enormously, and he liked me. But he was apprehensive; he did not want to be in new hands. He always played almost the same part. He had to because, you know . . . Clark Gable, if he's not *Clark Gable,* if he has a beard and he does that Irish Republican picture, *Parnell* [1937], nobody wants to see it. You see? You did not even know there was such a picture. Gable always has to be Gable. He must be Gable. Just the situations are different, the characters a little bit different. Same with Cary Grant, who slipped through my net every time.

So [after Grant pulled out] I just said, "Look, take somebody that is older than [William] Holden, and not so pretty." He's the businessman of the two, and he doesn't give a damn for his brother, who's a drunkard, and who has got all the dames, including Audrey Hepburn, the daughter of the chauffeur. Now, I said, "It would be nice if we had somebody who is absolutely the wrong guy for that—*he* falls in love too." Sam Cohn, the agent who suggested it to Bogart, said, "There's a nice part in this picture with Audrey Hepburn." But Bogart was used to having most of the pictures directed by [John] Huston, and they were drinking all the time. He did not like me, because in the very beginning, after the shooting, there was a little bit of drinking, like two or three martinis, in Holden's dressing room. I forgot to invite him. He was all by himself, in the dressing room with the hairdresser who had to put that hairpiece on there. He was not part of the crowd. I finally went to invite him and he said, "No, thank you very much." I rewrote [the role] for him. I would have a little rewrite. I would bring him the scene. He looks at it and says, "How old is your daughter?" I said, "My daughter is about seven." "Did *she* write that?" But very loud, you know. And he wanted a big laugh. He was new at Paramount. I was an old hand. He didn't get a laugh, because everybody was on my side. He was a shit. Because he knew that I wanted to have Cary Grant. And also, because I did not invite him with a big flask of gin. He probably would not have come if I'd asked him, but the fact that I did not ask him, he never forgot.

So now, Mr. Bogart. When we were finished with the shooting, we had a little party there. He did not come. Then I hear that he's got cancer, and then I hear from his wife, Lauren Bacall, that he would like to see me. I rushed over, and he was wonderful, absolutely wonderful, and he begged my pardon. And I said, "Forget it, this is not a British court ceremonial that we have. I fight with a lot of people." It's not true [*shrugs and laughs*]—but I told him that. And he had that incurable cancer, and he was going very quickly, and the last memory of Bogart I have is, he was a terrific guy, because that's the way I saw him last. He was very good, better than he thought he was. He liked to play the hero, and in the end, he was.

I remember, the cameraman took me to the side and said, "You have to do something about the lights, because Bogart spits when he speaks. So don't have the lights in the back there. The back light is terrible. So I just warned the wardrobe woman who took care of Audrey Hepburn to be ready with a towel every time. But to do it discreetly.

irected by
ard winner
"The Lost
Stalag 17."
LY
ER

Sabrina

. . . the chauffeur's daughter who learned her stuff in Paris!

with

ER HAMPDEN · JOHN WILLIAMS · MARTHA HYER · JOAN VOHS

en for the Screen by BILLY WILDER, SAMUEL TAYLOR and ERNEST LEHMAN
From the play by SAMUEL TAYLOR · A PARAMOUNT PICTURE

Humphrey Bogart (opposite) in *Sabrina* (1954). Wilder had wanted Cary Grant for this part and felt that not getting him set up tension between them.

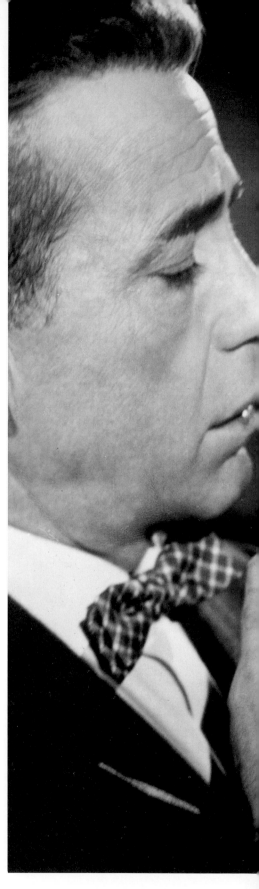

CC: I have a question about Cary Grant, your friend. In the books I've read about you, I find that you can really *fight* for an actor that you want. For example, Fred MacMurray—

BW: That too was an ersatz, but I will tell you about that later.

CC: Right. But Cary Grant was so right for your material. Why didn't you fight harder to get him?

BW: As a matter of fact, Bogart was even better casting than Cary Grant, because Cary Grant young could have played the part of Bill Holden. Bogart was a businessman. You don't think that this guy is all business, but he was.

But yeah, with this Cary Grant. I always wanted to work with him. It started with a picture on which I was but a writer. "But a writer"?! [*Laughs at himself.*] I was very proud of it, *Ninotchka* [1939]. We wanted to have Cary Grant. We wanted Cary Grant to play the part that Melvyn Douglas played.

CC: How great that would have been, to see Cary Grant doing those scenes with Greta Garbo.

BW: No, no such luck. I wanted him to play the part that Gary Cooper played in *Love in the Afternoon* [1957]. It would have been wonderful, right? "Cannot do it . . . please don't. Don't persist. Look, I like you, Wilder, but I cannot explain it. I just . . . the wrong signals come up in me."

CC: Did you feel he loved your movies?

BW: Yeah. He loved my movies. He called me after *Some Like It Hot* and congratulated me that Curtis had done a wonderful imitation. No, he was very nice, he was absolutely great. But he was a very, very peculiar man, and he was very stingy. Stingy, Mr. Cary Grant. We had a dinner party at our apartment, and then after dinner we went to my den, where I have my radio and my television. I started playing for him a recording by a German composer, a medieval hymn of instruments and of voices. Orff was the name of the composer. [The piece was *Carmina burana.*] It was very, very strong and very loud. So he sits there, and he says, "How much is your loudspeaker? How much is your phonograph?" So, knowing how stingy he is, I say, "A hundred and eleven dollars." So he calls his wife, "Barbara! This machine here! We are crazy, we are crazy. We paid two hundred and fifteen!" [*Laughter.*]

CC: I don't want to let you off the hook here. Why didn't you fight harder? You had to be disappointed when Cary Grant would turn you down.

BW: When he turned me down? No, not at all. He was a very good friend. My disappointment was professional disappointment, never personal. I was expecting that. The first two or three times, I sent him the script, it just did not work. A lot of other actors knew this, they were standing in line.

Now, just to finish the story about the phonograph. He says, "Now, tell me, those two loudspeakers. Tell me, are they included in the hundred and eleven dollars?" And I say, "No, they were extra." He says, "How much?" "Six-fifty apiece." "*Barbara!!! Barbara!!!*" [*Laughter.*] He was absolutely . . . [*shakes head with wonder*]. I've never seen it, but I understand he had a room in the basement that was filled with gold cigarette cases. He would buy them and throw them down there. A pile of gold. Very, very nice guy otherwise.

CC: Did you feel as if you knew Cary Grant very well?

BW: I did not know him very well, but I saw him all the time. The two of us were on the board of directors of the Pasadena museum of Mr. Norton Simon. We would go there for the meeting and have lunch. He only came there for the lunch. Mr. Simon would go through the various paragraphs he had cooked up, *blah-blah-blah.* "All those in favor, aye!" None of us had any time to say even no, to ask a question. Then we had a wonderful lunch and he didn't have to pay for it. [*Laughs.*] It's all right. On him it was becoming, it went with his character. If he had also been very generous, then that would kind of disturb me. Too perfect.

CC: He is now generally regarded as the king of light comedy. Do you agree?

BW: He was very, very good. He didn't miss a trick, you know. Never got the [Academy] Award. He got the "special" award. . . . But look, it's so stupid, you know, because the guys, the leading men, who get awards have to walk with a limp or act retarded.

They don't notice the guy who does all the hard work, who is making it look easy. You can't just open a drawer beautifully and take out a tie and put on a jacket. You have to take out a gun! You have to be afflicted. Then they notice you. Those are the rules that govern the forty-five hundred members of the Academy. I don't know, they're just . . . You know very well that Mr. [Dustin] Hoffman is gonna get the award if he plays the guy who is autistic in *Rain Man* [1988]. He sweated so much, he worked so hard, so many things to remember. Bullshit.

CC: I think it's much harder to spot the delicate balance that Lemmon finds in *The Apartment* [1960]. One inch to the right or to the left and the movie is lost in pathos or sweetness.

BW: That's right. That's why he was nominated for an award for *Days of Wine and Roses* [1962] . . . because he played a drunk.

CC: So it's always been like that.

BW: Sure. Mr. Ray Milland, surely not an Academy Award–worthy actor—won the Oscar for *Lost Weekend*. He's dead now, so I can say it . . . It's just kind of . . . yeah . . . Academy Awards, *phhttt*. [*Laughs.*]

Wilder directing Pamela Tiffin and
James Cagney in *One Two Three* (1961)

Anybody who plays a hunchback has got better chances than a handsome leading man. That is the revenge of the voters, you know, that they don't get the girls.

CC: I want to show you some photos. Here's one from *The Apartment*. It looks like the studio commissary, a picture of you and Jack Lemmon and Shirley MacLaine and I. A. L. Diamond. A great team, and you all look like you're having fun. Was that the situation making the movie?

BW: Not with everybody. That was a very lucky and happy picture, *The Apartment*. Also, at one time, halfway through, Aud, my wife, came on the set. She never comes on the set, but she came, so Shirley MacLaine takes her on the side and says, "Does Billy really think this is going to be good?" She was not sure at first.
[*He laughs and goes on to another photo.*]
Now you have here a shot of James Cagney in *One Two Three*. Cagney and I, we just did not even get along. Not anything mean was said, not anything demeaning, not any question with the script. But he was a very peculiar, peculiar man. He was a Republican, way to the right. He had a farm somewhere in New England. Wonderful actor, wonderful actor. He danced beautifully, kind of his own style—you

always had the feeling he's gonna fall flat on his face. He was always standing there in this fashion [*puts his hand at a 45-degree angle*]. I would invite him to a restaurant in Munich or Berlin, wherever we were. No, he would rather be with his wife. I would say, "Your wife comes along too." But he would say *blah-blah-blah*. We said goodbye on very good terms. But it was a big distance of thinking between us. We were just not especially designed for each other. I did not socialize with him, no, but that was not the purpose of our time together.

[*He returns to the previous photo.*]

CC: So *The Apartment* was a fun shooting experience.

BW: It was always fun. But if I have fun, I have it in the first half of the picture. Because if I have a feeling, you know, that it's not going to work, I still have to finish it. Then it was kind of—not sad . . . but I would spruce it up a little bit with jokes or something. But it's the sons of bitches the playwrights, they have a won-derful situation going. (A)

They are in the theater during the rehearsals. They can say no to any change that the actor wants. Can you imagine having that in pictures! [*Laughs.*] Thank God I am also the producer now, or was the producer. (B) If you write a play, and you try it out somewhere in New England, and it does not work, you rewrite it all night long and you take it to another place . . . to Pittsburgh, and it doesn't work again. The third time, it doesn't work again, no matter what you do, you bury it, you forget about it. It never comes to New York.

But a picture, no matter how dreadful it is, no matter how it stinks, you have to squeeze the last dollar. The picture must be released! To the world! [*Laughs.*] So that picture is playing, whether you like it or not, forever. The shame lives forever! There are quite a few pictures where I say, "Oh, don't don't don't, *don't show it!* I would like to please talk to the people who buy it for television." But there is a big difference with movies. A big difference. [George] Kaufman and [Moss] Hart, they buried ten or fifteen plays. This is like killing an ugly child. [*Laughs.*] Nobody knows about it. There's no police there. They are the lucky ones, the playwrights.

[*It is nearing lunchtime, and Wilder eyes my tape recorder.*]

We can talk during lunch, but not with that thing. Because nothing is worth immortalizing. A few more questions, then we'll go and eat.

CC: Okay. Who wrote the last line in *The Apartment*—"Shut up and deal"— you or I. A. L. Diamond?

BW: [*Famously cagey on the subject of which collaborator wrote which lines, Wilder eyes me evenly.*] "Shut up and deal"? I don't remember. Could have been Iz. Could have been me. [*Pause.*] We had that gin game in the plot—when she's recovering from her suicide attempt, they played gin, and the game's not finished—and we didn't want to have a kiss, and we didn't want to have something too sweet. But we had a very good stepping stone for the last scene. We had planted somewhere that he once attempted suicide, with a gun, but he did not quite know how to handle it and shot himself in the knee. So we knew that he had a gun. Then we also planted there that it's in his luggage which he's packing up because he's going back to Cincinnati, or wherever. We also planted there that Dr. Dreyfuss brings him a bottle of champagne. So we had *that thing*, you remember, it was at midnight, the lights go out. It's New Year's Eve. Mr. Fred MacMurray, by this time, is divorced. He's popped the question to Shirley MacLaine, finally, finally, finally. Then when the

lights go on, she's gone. We used that trick that at midnight all the lights go out. Now, she's running, she's running and running and running to the apartment. And we know that it's . . . that could be the ending, right?

CC: Right—

BW: He could be standing in the window and wave at her, or he opens the door and she kisses him. We didn't want to have that ending, that kiss ending. We had that good idea of, she's running, and now she hears a *shot*. And now, we don't know yet, but she thinks, "My God, he wanted to commit suicide on account of another girl, but maybe this time he's not gonna hit his knee!" So she hurries up much more, and she's faster and faster, and she gets to his door, and she knocks. He opens it and he's got the bottle of champagne foaming over [*grinning*], which it always does when you shake it. So, "Oh God, thank God," but still no kiss. But he wants to ask her, "What's the matter?" "Nothing, let's finish the gin game." They've got the cards there, still down on the table. And he asks her something amorous.

CC: He says, "I love you, Miss Kubelik."

BW: "I love you." Then she says, "Shut up and deal." And he deals the whole deck, you know, not just ten cards.

CC: The kiss would have been too romantic, too sweet.

Horst Buchholz (lower left), Pamela Tiffin and Arlene Francis (middle), and James Cagney (top right) in *One Two Three*

Ernst Lubitsch as a comedy actor playing a shoe salesman in *Schuhpalast Pinkus* (1916)

BW: Yeah. It's not an ending like "Nobody's perfect." But then again, at least it was not too schmaltzy.

CC: The champagne-popping device worked for you once before, in *Ninotchka*. When Melvyn Douglas pops the champagne and Garbo crumbles behind his back, as if she's been shot.

BW: Yeah, she crumbles, she is blindfolded. There were three of us on that script [Wilder, Brackett, and Walter Reisch]. And the fourth one was Lubitsch. He never took credit, but he did a lot of wonderful writing, or offered suggestions. He was absolutely the best when it comes to that kind of picture. He didn't do any comedies in Germany, he did great big expensive historical pictures. Just great big pictures, they were locomotives—showmanship pictures like *Madame Du Barry*. . . . He himself was a comedy actor in two-reelers. *Schuhpalast Pinkus* [1916] was the name [of one] . . . a shoe palace where he was one of the guys who sold shoes. It was all very funny and very solid. It never occurred to him that there was gold to be mined in directing comedy, because he did not make out-and-out elegant comedies in Berlin. He arrived in Hollywood in the early twenties with an avalanche of European people, actors, directors.

They came because they were searched out by Mr. Louis B. Mayer, who had gone to Europe to look at talent. Whereas I came here because I didn't want to be in an oven.

I came here with nothing. Lubitsch was then making his first American picture. He just did not know what they wanted him to do. And in his bewilderment, he made *Rosita* [1923], a picture with Mary Pickford. A serious picture, not very good, and he left Hollywood right away. He had a contract with Warner Bros., I think. It was then that he saw a picture by Mauritz Stiller, a Swedish director, and this is where he got his style. This is where Lubitsch saw that his future was in comedy, silent as it is. Sound came later. The first or second sound musical, he made, *The Love Parade* [1929]. But he was already searching for comedy subjects. And he did them gloriously. He realized that if you say two and two, the audience does not have to be told it's four. The audience will find it themselves; let the audience find the joke. There was always an innuendo, in setting up situations, and you were rewarded by the laugh of the people who added it up. And it was a whole new technique. That was in the Swedish picture too. Mauritz Stiller did it. I never saw it. And this was where Lubitsch became Lubitsch. This was where he discovered the "Lubitsch touch." He was absolutely astonished, and thought, "My God, what things you can do by innuendo!" It changed his life; it was the beginning of the Lubitsch touch. And the next picture he made [after *Rosita*] had it—*The Marriage Circle* [1924]. And the emotions of his work got sharper and sharper and sharper.

From then on, he made only comedies, if you call *The Shop Around the Corner* [1940] a comedy, which I think it was. His favorite was a picture called *Trouble in Paradise* [1932]. He told me so himself. It stars [Herbert] Marshall as a thief. He acts the part of a doctor and he places something [chemically treated] over the mouth of his patients that puts them out. And then he and his girlfriend commit thievery. I remember the third act was that Marshall goes to a party. And he sees Edward Everett Horton, who he had robbed, and who then tries to remember, where did he see that man before? Every time he passes him, he looks. Then ultimately, he smokes a cigarette and he uses an ashtray, which is a metal gondola. And the gondola reminds him, because it happened in Venice. The Lubitsch touch [*marvels*]. It was his favorite picture; he liked it better than any other that he did, including *Ninotchka*. But the beginning of it all was this picture made by Mauritz Stiller. I never saw it, and I cannot remember the name. [*Wilder invites me to seek out the title.*] I was still a schoolboy and had not graduated high school. But something in it created Lubitsch.

And to this I must say, Mauritz Stiller was a very, very fine director. Swedish pictures were then not as popular as American. But Swedish, French pictures, Polish pictures, Argentinian pictures, it did not matter . . . they were silent pictures, you had only to translate the titles, that was all. Lubitsch. He made one big bombastic picture about Ivan the Terrible [*The Patriot*, 1928], that was a silent picture with Emil Jannings and Lewis Stone, who played the doctor at the Grand Hotel.

[*A moviegoer's rapture sets in, and he pauses.*]

But, you see, I am a great admirer of Mr. Lubitsch. I really loved the man, as a human being, and as an artist—way ahead of his time. But I, you know, I am all over the place—every category of pictures I have made, good, bad, or indifferent. I could not make, like Hitchcock did, one Hitchcock picture after another. But he was very smart, because the husband says to the wife and kids, "Hey, there's a new Hitchcock picture—that means there's gonna be suspense, it's gonna be *rah-rah-rah*, there's gonna be one corpse, or more corpses, and then a super-solution. Let's go to that!" He did that very well. I don't have to worry about Mr. Hitchcock, no more.

I wanted to do a Hitchcock picture, so I did *Witness for the Prosecution* [1958], then I was bored with it, so I moved on. As a matter of fact, whenever I am very miserable, I do a comedy. And whenever I'm in a wonderful mood, then I make a serious picture. I make a serious picture, a film noir, but then it gets boring, so I go back to a comedy.

CC: Was *The Maltese Falcon* [1941] an inspiration for *Double Indemnity* [1944]?

BW: No. Has it got any similarities?

CC: The genre. Film noir.

BW: In the genre, yeah, it's very, very good. *The Maltese Falcon* was a wonderful picture; I loved it. What else can I tell you that may be of any interest to you?

CC: Here's an observation that has been made about many great writers. There is sometimes a central event or a theme in their lives that they keep revisiting, reworking, and examining. Is that true of you?

BW: [*Shifts in chair.*] No. Maybe some similar situation, or maybe the beginning of a situation, which I then developed in the picture.

CC: I just wondered if there was a key event in your life that continued to inspire you.

BW: To do something better than I did the last time. [*Pause.*] But my life was kind of . . . Except for the fact that three-quarters of my family was extinguished in Auschwitz, I don't really think that . . .
    [*Wilder considers this, the first inescapably personal question of our interviews. He decides to keep it at arm's length.*]
    Oh, there were a lot of incidents that I dramatized, incidents in the I. A. L. Diamond stuff that we did, or Brackett, you know, but no . . . You mean, if there was an occurrence that was funny, or an occurrence that was tragic? Yeah, maybe there was, but I, subconsciously I just kind of . . . [*Shakes head.*] No. My only ambition was to entertain, this way or that way. To entertain and not to repeat myself and to make as few mistakes as possible. There are so many mistakes. I remember, I lived at 704 Beverly Drive, and the way to the studio, to Paramount, is a ride of about fifteen or eighteen minutes. I mapped out in my mind where, on the way back, on the corner of La Cienega and Melrose, I always hit my leg, my thigh, and I said, "Goddamm it, *that's* the way I should have done it!" But most of the time it's too late. Too late, because the picture is cut and the actor's in Yugoslavia and the sets are down. If you do a picture like George Stevens— he did that very famous picture *A Place in the Sun* [1951]. Now, there is a district attorney in that picture who limps. I talked to somebody and said, "It's a very fine picture, but he did not have to make justice itself limp." That was too allegorical. That was not good. Because it was just a wonderful picture. And I just told him, "Look, if that was in the theater, you go backstage, and you tell the actor who plays the district attorney, 'Tonight, no cane.' " But "Tonight, no cane" in a picture, you have to remake 80 percent of the picture!

CC: I wanted to ask you about *Schindler's List*. I've read that you wanted to make this your last picture, but Spielberg already had the rights.

The Lubitsch touch: a telling detail from *Trouble in Paradise* (1932). Lubitsch told Wilder this was his favorite film. The gondola ashtray tips off thief Herbert Marshall about where he has seen Edward Everett Horton, whom he has robbed, before.

BW: Yeah, that made him take it. [*Laughs.*] I wanted to do it. We spoke about it. He was a gentleman, of course, and we acknowledged each other's strong desires. In the end, he could not give it up. He had to do it. I would have done it differently—not necessarily better. I wanted to do it as a kind of memorial to my mother and my grandmother and my stepfather. Spielberg was always a wonderful director. When he was twelve years old he was a wonderful director. Especially pictures that were for children. I think there were a lot of things in *E.T.* that were very, very funny, especially when E.T. gets drunk. But *Schindler's List*—it would have been something of my heart, you know.

CC: Your most personal picture?

BW: Yeah.

CC: You've never spoken about your family much, particularly your mother. How well do you remember your mother?

BW: I remember my mother very well. I saw her in 1936 when I went back to Europe. I saw my mother there, and then I came back [to America], and she got married. I don't know anything about how she ended up in the camp. I just know that it was Auschwitz because everybody from Vienna, where she lived, went there. I did not know that they had concentration camps. You know, it was kept quiet. Roosevelt did not tell us about it. Roosevelt was a very, very curious case of a career man. There was a boat, a German boat, crammed full with Jews who were escaping. The boat was taking them to Cuba, a German boat. They had no passports, no visas. Then they notified Washington—"Please." There was a book written about this event, I read it. [There was also a movie based on the event, *Voyage of the Damned* (1976).] Mrs. Roosevelt, she was on her knees, begging him. One word, and they could land here. No way, because the elections were coming up. No way. So now, this is the sad, sad ending of the story. The German captain took the boat to Antwerp. Some passengers went to Belgium, some to France, and some to the Netherlands. But these countries were soon in the hands of the Nazis and half of the passengers ended up in camps. This is a fact which I am telling you now.

I would have been very, very careful with *Schindler's List*. Because just to execute, that's not the picture. The picture was much deeper than that. It was a very, very good picture. I tip my hat. But if you give it to ten directors, ten directors would have made it differently. Very, very good, and I liked the ending, which is in color, and they're putting on stones—very moving. And you know, I went to the very first performance of that picture. It was in that movie house on Wilshire Boulevard, kind of half-full, and the ads had just come out. Then I stayed behind and watched the people that were coming out. And there was almost everybody crying, with tears in their eyes, young kids who you'd think wouldn't go to see a picture like that. After *Saturday Night Fever* [1977], I felt the young audience changed. They wanted to see a different kind of picture. But there they were for *Schindler's List*, with tears. A very important picture.

Wilder, Karen Lerner, and I head off for lunch, across the street, to the restaurant at the top of Armani's Beverly Hills store. Lunch for Wilder is not to be delayed or dismissed. It is the dividing point of his day, and he

chooses his companions carefully. Leaving the office, he moves deliberately, with his cane. The closer to lunch, the lighter his spirit.

We arrive at the restaurant. The young hostess guides her celebrated guest to a seat in the corner of the bar area, where it is quieter. His mood is now almost jolly, and I'm anxious to continue our conversation with the tape recorder very much still on.

BW: I sit there. You sit here, that's my good ear.

CC: [*I discuss the recent Directors Guild of America Awards. This year's recipient of the distinguished D. W. Griffith Award, which Wilder received in 1986, had been Stanley Kubrick. In what would be the last public statement before his death in 1999, Kubrick sent a video from England, where he was working on* Eyes Wide Shut. *It began with Kubrick's recalling the story of Griffith himself, who was shunned in his later career after attempting several ambitious but commercially doomed projects. Kubrick intertwined this story with the retelling of the myth of Icarus, who flew too close to the sun and melted his wax wings. . . .]*

. . . And he said, like Icarus, D. W. Griffith flew high, and his wings melted. But people don't talk about that now. Then what, Kubrick asked, is the moral of Icarus? Is it "Don't fly too close to the sun?" Or is it, as Kubrick said he chooses to believe, "Build better wings"? He then said thank you and good night.

Ninotchka: Wilder wanted Cary Grant for the part Melvyn Douglas (opposite) played; (right) an ad for the movie

BW: [*After a respectful silence, as one storyteller regards another:*] That's good. That's very good.

I was at his house once, nice man. But a very strange man, he will not fly. *The Shining* [1980]—very smooth . . . and then there's that labyrinth. I love all his movies. Kubrick, he was a wonderful director, but sometimes . . . for instance I could never understand—and I cannot discuss it with anybody, because people have not seen that picture, that costume picture, *Barry Lyndon* [1975] . . .

CC: What about it?

BW: He worked like six months trying to find a way to photograph somebody by candlelight, not artificial light. And nobody really gives a shit whether it is by candlelight or not. What are the jokes? What is the story? I did not like it. That's the only Kubrick picture that I did not like, but look, what's the last one that he made?

CC: *Full Metal Jacket* [1987].

BW: The first half of *Full Metal Jacket* was the best picture I ever saw. Where the guy sits on the toilet and blows his head off? Terrific. Then he lost himself with the girl guerrilla. The second half, down a little. It's still a wonderful picture. You know, if he does a thing, he really *does* it. But this is . . . this is a career to discuss. Every picture, he trumps the trump. These are all pictures any director would be proud to be associated with, much less make. At a picture like *The Bicycle Thief* [1947], you forget that this is your profession. You just get lost in the picture.

CC: What did you think of *Dr. Strangelove* [1964]?

BW: Oh, I love that. That's one of my favorite pictures, *Dr. Strangelove.* I was bewildered, but then I put some order in it, as I thought about it, and as I saw it again. It was a wonderful picture, but so was *Lolita* [1962]. She was a little too old. He had to make a little sacrifice there. I hear they've remade it again, getting the characters' ages closer to the book. [*Pause.*] I'm ninety-one—*I'm* the right age. [*Laughs.*] But I don't know, except for *Spartacus* [1960], he did very good.

    [*He shakes his head at the magic of these movies. Food arrives. Wilder is a careful eater, inspecting and evaluating everything before beginning. He enjoys a meal.*]

CC: What were the first previews like for *The Apartment*? What was it like showing that picture to the public for the first time? Because now, you know, you have these long questionnaires that the studios

give audiences to fill out: Do you like this character? How *much* do you like them? Was it like previewing a movie then?

BW: [*Pause.*] I'll tell you my best story, which has something to do with previews. We were previewing *Ninotchka,* and Lubitsch took the writers along too, in Long Beach. And they are outside in the lobby there, a stack of cards, with the audience invited to put down their thoughts. So the picture starts playing, and it plays very well. Now Lubitsch takes the cards, a heap of the cards, doesn't let anybody else touch them. We get into the big MGM limousine. We turn the light up. Now, so, he takes the preview cards and he starts reading. " 'Very good' . . . 'brilliant' . . ." Twenty cards. But when he comes to the twenty-first card, he starts laughing as hard as I ever saw him laugh, and we say, "What is it?" He keeps the cards to himself; he does not let anybody even look. Then, finally, he calms down a little and starts reading. And what he read was—I have the card—"Funniest picture I ever saw. So funny that I peed in my girlfriend's hand." [*Laughs.*]

CC: What were the preview questionnaires like then?

BW: Just a card. A cardboard card. Half a card, just nothing. Just "Did you like it?—Yes, No." And then "Other advice you'd like to give us?"

CC: Today they use both sides of the card, analyzing every aspect of a movie, and that is how studios determine the final cuts of most films.

BW: Well, that's when you let them.

CC: Did you learn much from previews of your films?

BW: I didn't. My ear will tell me. I know by the laughter. And I know somebody is going to do something if it's too slow or something is wrong; it's always a wise guy in the audience.

CC: *Pulp Fiction* [1994] was one of the more important pictures of the last few years. Did you see it?

BW: [*Simply:*] Yes. I saw it.

CC: [*Prompting:*] Quentin Tarantino . . .

BW: I forgot it. What did that man do since?

Wilder admitted Dietrich (left and center) was afraid of playing a Nazi. She liked playing a murderess, but was embarrassed by the love scenes, in *Witness for the Prosecution;* Charles Laughton (opposite, bottom) in the Old Bailey

CC: He's producing, acting, and writing, and recently directed a short film within a four-segment piece called *Four Rooms* [1995]. He hasn't made another full-length movie yet.

BW: There's an absolute, 100 percent truth. If you don't make a picture, how can it fail?

CC: If someone was to look over all your films, what would be the more personal ones? Is there one that stands out to you, the one that really felt closest to your heart?

BW: You know, I make a picture, and then I forget about it. I don't have a print, I don't have a cassette. I have a script at the office, in case I would like to look. Which is the best picture I have ever seen? My answer always is *Battleship Potemkin,* by Eisenstein [1925].

CC: How about a best picture of yours?

BW: I used to say "The next one." [*Laughs.*] I'm not doing any more.

EDWARD SMALL presents

TYRONE POWER
MARLENE DIETRICH
CHARLES LAUGHTON
in
WITNESS FOR THE PROSECUTION

ARTHUR HORNBLOW'S
AGATHA CHRISTIE'S

CC: [*Pressing:*] But I wondered if there was one. You said earlier that if you had made *Schindler's List* it would have been very personal for you. Of the movies that you *did* make, which one feels the most complete? Which one feels the closest to who you are?

BW: The picture maybe that has the fewest faults, obvious faults, would be *The Apartment.* But I like the end result in *Some Like It Hot.* It was a very successful picture. Or maybe, this and *Sunset Boulevard.* It really caught them unaware. Nobody expected a picture like it. And it's very difficult to make a picture in Hollywood about Hollywood. Because they really scrutinize you.

CC: A couple years ago, I heard a rumor that you'd finished a new screenplay.

BW: No, I had many, many runs on the typewriter, but it all fizzled out. Since Diamond died, there is nothing really that is worth talking about. I'm used to the old studio system. I never wrote anything on

spec. I agree to make two or three pictures, and then I have a little whip behind me. It's now a world I don't know, a new world without any heads of a studio. You know, anybody could laugh about Mr. Goldwyn, but there was somebody *there.* Selznick, Thalberg . . . Thalberg, who never had his name on the screen.

CC: Beyond being successful money-men, which of these gentlemen had a real gut feeling for movies?

BW: Mr. Goldwyn, who was not a brilliant student of language or anything else, knew what was working, what was not working. . . . Two or three times in his life, he pawned his wife's jewelry to finish a scene, or reshoot a scene that he thought needed it. He could not explain it, what he wanted; but when he saw it, he

knew it. Selznick was another producer who was much more versed, much better spoken. He had a trick. Whenever he started a picture, after God knows how many hundreds of notes have been written to the writers, back and forth, back and forth, he had two or three or sometimes even four directors start a picture. Then he had somebody entirely different finish it, so that it never was any direc-

Witness for the Prosecution (1958): Wilder (left) directing Charles Laughton and Elsa Lanchester—"Laughton was my favorite." Wilder (below) working with Laughton

tor's picture; it was always Selznick's picture.

CC: Let's attack some of the Wilder myths. You can just say yes or no to some of these. I heard that you were recently preparing a project about the famous "farteur"—Le Pétomane.

BW: Le Pétomane [*slightly embarrassed*]. No . . . it was something I was fooling around with. Either it could have been a smash hit or it could have been a total disaster. [*Smiles.*] Yeah. I was fooling around with Le Pétomane. He was a very elegant man. He wore silk; he could fart the French national anthem. An actor for Le Pétomane? Can you imagine the readings I would get? [*Laughs.*] Yeah, read for me a line! It needs a little push . . . to make me write.

CC: Let me try a few more rumors, which you can endorse or dismiss. Here's one. In your period posing as a "gigolo" in Berlin, you did more than just dance with your partners.

BW: No. No.

CC: So the evening ended with dinner?

BW: Oh, absolutely, because they would come with their husbands. Sure. And the ladies were corpulent ladies, elderly ladies. I was not the best dancer, but I had the best *dialogue* with the ladies I was dancing

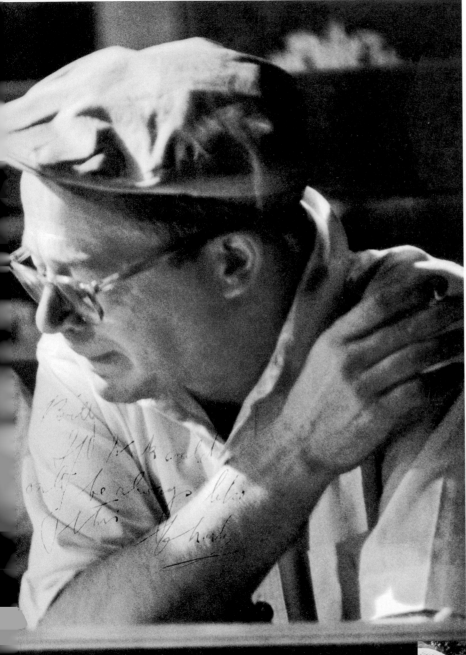

with. I wore a dark suit in the afternoon, and in the evening a tuxedo. There was cocktail dancing between five and seven, and then evening dancing after eight-thirty. I remember one day I was complaining, I was talking about the wear and tear on my shoes. And next day I come, and the concierge, there's a package left there, there are twelve pair of old shoes of her husband. [*Smiles.*] They were much too large for me anyway. But you know, I always ask myself, "Would I have done that had I not been a newspaperman, knowing that I'm going to do a series of articles on it?" I don't know anymore, but it was brand-new. I had a girlfriend, an American girlfriend, who brought over with her a new dance called the Charleston. It was the twenties, you know, and I gave lessons in Charleston.

CC: Did an actor ever move you to tears while you were filming? While you were watching a scene? That happened to me a couple of times on *Jerry Maguire*—there was a performance so surprising that I got caught up in it, it made me cry.

Wilder on location for *Love in the Afternoon* (1957)

BW: I don't know whether it's to tears, but sometimes it just moves me. I was taken aback with the greatest actor that ever lived, Mr. Charles Laughton.

CC: Why Charles Laughton?

BW: When he was at the Old Bailey, and he came forward with his theories in *Witness for the Prosecution* . . . screaming, then very low, for a page and a half, one take. I wanted to hear it again, and I did. And [Edward G.] Robinson, a wonderful actor.

CC: Yes.

BW: But I cannot let myself be seen there directing, and crying over somebody's performance, with all the other performers there too. No. Then it's "He never cried for *me,* the son of a bitch!"

CC: Good point.

BW: Laughton was everything that you can dream of, times ten. We would stop shooting at six o'clock, and we would go up to my office and would be preparing for next day's shooting. There were twenty versions of the way he could do a scene, and I would say, "That's it! All right!" And then the next day, on the set, he comes and he says, "I thought of something else." And that was version number twenty-one. Better and better all the time. He was a tremendous presence. Tremendous presence, and a wonderful instrument, wonderful vocal instrument. When he spoke to the audience, they were very quiet, because they knew. He did not just speak. He *said something.* And the sum total of it was a great performance. He only got one [Academy] Award, for *The Private Life of Henry the VIII* [1933]. But he was an absolute marvel.

Then I had him for another picture. I wanted him to play the bartender in *Irma La Douce* [1963], and he said, "Look, I've got cancer, but I'm gonna get better. Instead of starting in April, maybe you could start late summer." Late summer came, and I got a call, and he says, "Come over to our house, and I'll show you how well I am." And I went there. It was one of those side streets off Hollywood Boulevard, west between La Brea and Fairfax, you know. This is where the stars then lived. He lived there, with his wife. And he would call me at midnight. There's a certain flower that opens at midnight, and he would say, "Come, get dressed and come over, immediately!" And I got dressed, and Aud too, and we went there immediately because the flower was open. Now, he said, "Look, I've done everything the doctors told me to do, and I have now male nurses with me all the time, and I'm gonna be ready, ready, ready in September. Come over and see for yourself!"

So I took the car, we went there, and he was sitting at the pool, all dressed, and made up a little, and there was a male nurse sitting there. And he said, "Now watch me." And he got up and he went around the outside of the swimming pool, you know, but he could not quite make it—the last two or three steps were very hard on him. . . . He had lost about sixty pounds. So I knew that he was not well. But I said, "That's very good, keep doing it. September, we will start!" And a week later he was dead. But he was . . . [*Shakes head, doesn't finish sentence.*]

One summer, Tyrone Power, Laughton, and I, after *Witness for the Prosecution*—I left my wife at home—took a trip to Europe. We went to Paris, we went to Vienna, we went to where you take the famous cures, Badgastein, and we were marching through the forest, and everything was terrific, we had very, very successful previews, but I just kind of was wondering, Is he going to make even a slight move towards Tyrone Power? He didn't, he didn't. [*Laughs.*] And he was a wonderful, wonderful, very, very learned man. Whether it was Shakespeare, whether it was wines, Bordeaux . . . We went to Burgundy and we tasted the wines, we had the most wonderful time. And then Mr. Tyrone Power died, young as he was, of a heart attack. In Madrid—he was shooting a picture. And then Laughton died. It was very sad, very sad. Very wonderful people to work with.

CC: The Masked Marvel was another idea you had for Laughton.

BW: The Masked Marvel. Yes. He was a wrestler who wrestled in the provinces, not too far from where he lived. He wore a mask when he wrestled—he was an English lord. And he did not unmask himself when he wrestled. But each week he would wrestle and take that three hundred dollars and drive off. . . . In verity, in truth, he was the minister of a church, and there were insects eating away at the furniture. He needed the money to keep the church going. This part of his life was all without the mask.

CC: Did it ever get to script form?

BW: No. Never got to script form.

CC: Good idea, though.

BW: Yes. It was a good idea, the first one I brought to him. We had Laughton masquerading as an English lord who had lost his fortune. Some of his fights were fixed, some he won. He wrestled under the name of "the Lord," which people called him, not knowing that he was in fact wrestling *for* the Lord. He liked the idea, but later I brought him *Witness*, and that we did together.

"He was my Everyman": Wilder with Jack Lemmon

CC: This is a little bit of an odd question—

BW: We live to answer odd questions, or to withdraw and say, "Please take that back."

CC: You certainly have inspired a lot of romantic feelings in audiences. Many people, early in their relationship, will watch a movie like *Sabrina* or *Love in the Afternoon* together. It inspires romance. But I wonder—and again this is a romantic notion—but I just wonder, as you talk about Laughton, or you talk about Izzy Diamond, for example, do you ever think that you'll meet these people again in some form?

BW: [*Wilder again eyes me, well aware that I am casting into personal waters.*] I cannot, because I have a very, very short time to live. I'm ninety. Those relationships develop over the years, you know.

CC: I mean metaphysically. Maybe your romantic notions don't go this far. But I just wonder, as I listen to you talk about Laughton or Izzy Diamond, do you believe there's a hereafter where you might see someone like Izzy again?

BW: I hope not, because there are so many shits that I've met in my life, I don't want to meet them again. [*Laughs.*] Yeah, miserable people. And I say to myself, God almighty, am I glad I don't have to run into this guy again!

CC: It's been analyzed quite a bit by others, but what was "the Lubitsch touch" to you?

BW: It was the elegant use of the Superjoke. You had a joke, and you felt satisfied, and then there was one more big joke on top of it. The joke you didn't expect. That was the Lubitsch touch. To think as he did, that is a goal worth having. Collaborating with him, he would have many questions. "What are you going to do with this story point?" "Let's find some way to say this differently."

CC: How can one contemporize the Lubitsch style?

BW: Find some new way to tell your story. That was the magic of Lubitsch. He is eternally essential to me.

CC: There's a great story you told once, and it is about the very nature of collaboration. I heard that when you were writing *Ninotchka,* you and Charles Brackett were stuck on just how to accomplish her eventual love affair with capitalism. You'd written pages and pages—

BW: Yeah, pages. We needed a thing to prove in a short, in an abrupt, version that she too fell under the spell of capitalism, that she too is vulnerable.

CC: And you were all stuck on this story point. And Lubitsch didn't like anything you'd written. Then Lubitsch goes to the can, emerges after a minute, and says, "It's the hat."

BW: "The hat." And we said, "What hat?" He said, "We build the hat into the beginning!" Brackett and I looked at each other—this is Lubitsch. The story of the hat has three acts. Ninotchka first sees it in a shop window as she enters the Ritz Hotel with her three Bolshevik accomplices. This absolutely crazy hat is the symbol of capitalism to her. She gives it a disgusted look and says, "How can a civilization survive which allows women to wear this on their heads?" Then the second time she goes by the hat and makes a noise—*tch-tch-tch.* The third time, she is finally alone, she has gotten rid of her Bolshevik accomplices, opens a drawer and pulls it out. And now she wears it. Working with Lubitsch, ideas like this were in the air.

CC: Did Brackett love Lubitsch as much as you did?

BW: I don't know whether he did like him, but he certainly admired him greatly. A first-class man who deserved to be the first name on the list of the writers, but he did not want to be a writer. He said, "I stay the director and producer." And he was so grateful when you brought him something, it was fun. It was tough, but it was fun. It was tough because we were there for days trying to find a way to show how she begins to melt towards capitalism. And he—he just said it, he brought the solution.

CC: What was Lubitsch's body language when he had a good idea? Would he just say "This is it," or would he get excited with his ideas?

BW: He got pleased. The better the idea, the more pleased he was. But he was not jumping around. Not, no jumping on the couches, no dancing on the table, "Oh God, we have it, we have it!" No. He just hoped it's gonna work. And if it works, it's fine.

CC: Did Brackett support you as a director? Or did your success as a director mean he might be losing you as a writing partner?

BW: He wanted me to be a director, because he wanted what I wanted.

"SOME LIKE

Wilder teaches Joe E. Brown the rudimentary aspects of the tango in preparation for the memorable rose-switching moment with "Daphne" (Jack Lemmon) in *Some Like It Hot* (1959). Nearly forgotten after a career of low-budget farces in the thirties and forties, Brown was plucked out of retirement to play the loopy millionaire Osgood Fielding. Wilder spotted him by chance at the festivities before a Dodgers game. "I thought, *That's our guy!* He was an absolute surprise to young people because they had never seen him."

CC: How did it end with Brackett?

BW: I always used to say, the surface of the matchbook had worn down. We were having a discussion one day in a car, parked at the studio. Nothing to do with pictures—a personal discussion about his grandson, I think. Then it turned. He kind of flew off the handle. He just . . . [*Pauses, admits thoughtfully:*] I kind of made him dismiss me. And that was how it ended. Then he came back, and I was already with someone else, collaborating. But it ended with a discussion in my car that had grown loud. We spoke after, we were friends. He always wanted to come back. Then he was sick—he had a stroke—and we never came back together. But it ended on a discussion of something personal.

CC: So you didn't really want to get to know your actors, and learn about the people in their lives, and what they were going through. It was, do the work, let's know each other while we're filming, and that's it. That's what you liked best.

BW: Yeah, that's what I liked best. There are very few actors that are my personal friends. And, I don't know, actors in my life? Jack Lemmon, because we were neighbors at the beach when I had the beach house, and we saw each other. Now, he makes twelve pictures a year, small parts, big parts. I love him, as I love Walter Matthau. One of the handful of great actors. He even got his way into [Kenneth Branagh's] *Hamlet* [1996].

CC: Do you laugh sometimes when you the see the grand legends that come up around people that you knew?

BW: A lot of things they have backwards. A lot of things they tell you backwards.

CC: "When the legend is more interesting than the truth, print the legend."

BW: True.

CC: Something I noticed in my time as a music journalist, before I was a director . . . I used to write about a lot of rock musicians. Many of them have died and gone on to become these monolithic legends. And the legend is just very different from the people that I knew and wrote about. You have to wonder sometimes, how much of what passes for history is just "legend"?

BW: That's the way they want it.

CC: Do you feel that you need to protect the legend, in the case of Monroe, for example?

BW: No, but it's very difficult to talk seriously about Monroe, because she was so glitzy, you know. She escaped the seriousness somehow; she changed the subject. Except she was very tough to work with. But what you had, by hook or crook, once you saw it on the screen, it was just amazing. Amazing, the radiation that came out. And she was, believe it or not, an excellent dialogue actress. She knew where the laugh was. She knew. But then again, we would have three hundred extras, Miss Monroe is called for nine o'clock, and she would appear at five in the afternoon. And she would stand there and say, "I'm sorry, but I lost my way to the studio." She had been under contract there for *seven years!* I'm sure that Cruise is a very, very serious actor. He comes there and is prepared.

CC: First to arrive, and often last to leave. Very, very professional, and inspired it in all the other actors.

BW: Good.

CC: But I can see how it would work the other way. If your leading man or leading lady doesn't show up until noon, the other actors begin to wonder, "Why should I get there early?"

BW: Yeah, yeah.

CC: Do you remember your last conversation with Monroe?

BW: Whenever I saw her, I always forgave her. The last time I saw her, she was pregnant, and she was breaking up with [Arthur] Miller. She was with Yves Montand. She came to a party at Romanoff's, after a screening of *The Apartment*. She was shooting a picture with George Cukor [*Let's Make Love,* 1960], as nice a man as you can find. But [Monroe and I] never had any great or close personal relations. I did not bend, you know, to her whims. I was there. I was there and she was not there. I would send somebody for her, to knock on the door to her dressing room, the second assistant, "Miss Monroe, we're ready." "Oh, fuck off!" [*Laughs.*] I did not want to expose my first assistant, or myself. She was a . . . I don't know, she was just a continuous puzzle, without any solution.

After *Seven Year Itch* [1955], I said, "I'll never work with her again." But then I was delighted when I heard that she had read the script and she would like to do *Some Like It Hot*. It's wonderful that Monroe wanted to do the part. We had a big, big bomb there in that cannon that we could shoot off. We would not have had that sex thing. And, you know, those are the funny things that happen, where you stumble onto something that not everybody would have thought of.

CC: And it makes the movie.

BW: And you get very, very proud of yourself, and that was the case. There was, for instance, the situation where Tony Curtis steals the clothes of the guy, and plays now Mr. Shell. The Shell family, do you remember? And he now gets also the boat of Mr. Joe E. Brown, who is dancing somewhere with Mr. Lemmon. You have two things going there. Now Joe E. Brown, dancing a tango with Lemmon, that's going to be good, I knew that. We had that cold, the dips, and the rose in the teeth, you know.

CC: Is that the kind of moment you'd already acted out in the room, writing with Izzy?

BW: [*Shakes his head immediately.*] No, we just knew it. Now, when we were writing, we got a very good idea, a very important part of the picture. The idea was that he, Curtis, invites Monroe back to the boat of Mr. Shell. And it's all set up, they're alone. Now there's going to be sex, right? I woke up in the middle of the night, thinking, this is no good, this is expected. But what we will do is that [*sparkle in his eye*] he

Wilder and Raymond
Chandler did not get along
while collaborating on *Double
Indemnity* (1944). "If I did not
work with a writer twice,"
says Wilder, "that's a clue";
Ernst Lubitsch directing Gary
Cooper and Claudette
Colbert in *Bluebeard's Eighth
Wife* (1938); I. A. L. Diamond
and Wilder on the set of
*The Private Life of Sherlock
Holmes* (1970)

plays it impotent! And *she* suggests the sex. And she fucks *him*—that *has* to be better. It *must* be better to be subdued, seduced, and screwed by Marilyn Monroe—what could be better? So we switched this thing around. And we had the scene, right? I came in the morning before we filmed. I just said, "Look—we are now at the situation where he takes her to the boat. There's nothing new here. But how about *this*?"

Now, we set it up, it was just like picking oranges, you know. Because it was just all there. And now we can say what his family spent a fortune on, trying to *cure* him. "We tried Javanese dancers with bells on, we had every goddamn thing, and every doctor—it doesn't work." [*Laughs.*] And she says, "May I try?" And then they try. And you know his real feelings by what happens to his leg, as it goes up, the leg goes up, and she's kissing him. "How is that?" she says. "I don't know," he says. And up goes the leg. She says, "Let me give it another try, just one more thing." Now we lose them and we know what happens. So the idea, that made that scene. Because otherwise it's just too flat. [*Wilder still marvels at the scene.*] She's kissing him, and Curtis is laying there on the couch. Kissing him, with the camera *here,* and now you see the leg coming up, in back of her. Wonderful!

CC: And the leg is so important, it's the final touch.

BW: Absolutely, yes.

CC: The leg is everything. And did that come in the rehearsals, or was that part of the idea?

BW: That was part of the writing. It was easy. It just came. What are you going to do with these pages and pages of drivel of mine?

A conversation ensues about our desire to expand the conversation into a book.

BW: A book? I enjoy talking, but I don't enjoy seeing it printed in a book. I was hoping it's not gonna be that. In a magazine, you can print it. [*Across the restaurant, a man waves insistently at Wilder.*]

CC: Is that a friend of yours?

BW: No. I don't have friends that have shirts like that.

Conversation resumes as I suggest a new generation of filmmakers are just now discovering his films. He cuts me off quickly.

BW: [*Nodding:*] That's wonderful. Pretty soon I will be crawling around. I will be in a wheelchair. You know, it's very difficult. But it fills me with joy that the four directors at the DGA [symposium] mentioned me. . . . Maybe that's when they thought pictures started, there were no people before. [*Laughs.*]

I hate to run into kids, you know, who've heard about me, and who expect that there are going to be pearls coming out of my mouth every time I open it. But you know, people come up to me, they say, "Mr. Wilder? I would like to shake your hand . . ." or "You made my month, you made my week . . . I'm running this picture, and that. . . ." That's very nice, it's very good to hear, you know. Then you just feel like getting up in the morning. But I don't want to . . . [*He shakes his head, spoons some sugar into his coffee.*] I don't want sugar. What's the matter with me? I'm nervous.

CC: [*Laughing.*] I remember when I first came to your office. I gave you a poster to sign, and you paused and said, "I'm not going to write something funny." And you signed, "Best, Billy Wilder." And I realized the pressure you must sometimes feel to be Wilderesque.

BW: Yeah, but there's no "Wilderesque." It's just . . . stuff. [*But before he knows it, he looks at the espresso that has been served to Karen Lerner and offers an observation that could only be called Wilderesque.*] You asked for espresso, and you got it *expressly*!

CC: But what about Diamond?

BW: [*Laughs.*] I was with Iz Diamond for twenty, twenty-five years. We never talked about personal things. That was the beauty of it. I came in the morning; he came in the morning. He gets the *Hollywood Reporter,* and I get the *Variety.* Then we exchanged the trade papers, and then we said, "Now where are we?" "Oh yes . . ." And then it goes on. He was a unique man, so unique.

It was not a collaboration like with Brackett, where he told me who his dentist is, kind of things that don't belong, you know. But Iz Diamond was a very taciturn guy, my partner. It was wonderful to talk about dialogue, or about structure. He was always on the set with me.

CC: And you liked it that way. . . .

BW: I liked it that way because there was . . . you know, the peculiar thing about Iz Diamond, whom I liked very much, like a younger brother, was his discretion. He was a very, very correct man. I am an accumulator, I am a collector. I cannot be in London, for instance, or Paris, for a day without buying something, be it an antique little piece, or shoes, or something. So I would be walking down the Burlington Arcade, and I would not even ask him anymore, "I'm going in here for a minute, would you like to come?" He would say, "No no no no, I stay outside." [*Laughs.*] Now of course it's not a minute, it's an hour. And he waited outside. Then I come out with two big paper bags full of stuff. And he never did ask me, "What did you buy?"! Nothing. [*Laughs.*] Absolutely never asked me. [*He grins, still marveling.*]

CC: How would you describe your first screenwriting partner, Charles Brackett?

BW: Brackett was a very loquacious man. He was kind of a member of the Algonquin Round Table. That was his milieu. (A) He was a Republican, a rabid Republican. (B) He was in the forefront of writers of the class of Hemingway, of Scott Fitzgerald—those were the people that he knew. And he learned very quickly, because he wrote some short stories for the *Saturday Evening Post,* and that's how he got into movies. And he was just kind of hanging around Paramount and did not know what the hell to do.

Manny Wolf, the man who was the head of the writing department, he got the two of us together. Introduced me and said, "Now you two go and talk to Mr. Lubitsch, and see whether he likes you." So we talked, and we go to Lubitsch, and about half an hour later we had the job of *Bluebeard's Eighth Wife.* It was not a very good picture, but it was kind of all right. And then he wanted us again for *Ninotchka.*

But with Brackett . . . we had nothing in common except writing. Also, he told me many stories,

Riding crop in hand, Wilder working with Brackett in their office at Paramount, 1944

and I told him many stories. It was not like Mr. Raymond Chandler. We did get along. We just never saw each other, or very rarely, after the shooting or after the writing, for dinner. We never did that.

cc: Your published screenplays are extremely lively and readable, and though you always work with a collaborator, the scripts all have a single, idiosyncratic voice. For example, in the screenplay of *Some Like It Hot*, the last line of narrative reads: "And that's the end of the story, or at least what the public can see." Or in the script of *The Apartment*, the final line is, "And that's about it. Story-wise."

bw: Yes.

cc: Is that something you dictated to Izzy Diamond? Or did Diamond write the narrative?

bw: [*Quickly:*] I . . . I don't know. All I know is that I'm standing there, like a conductor, you know. And I have my yellow tablet, and I write, and he types. And we compare. Then we agree on something, then we go back and forth. Most of the writing happened in one room, at the Goldwyn office, a great place. I lived there. I had a kitchen, a bed, a shower, and a bathroom. Iz would show me pages and I would correct them, we would work on them. And off they went.

Most of the time we were still working on the third act. The last half of the third act we have on paper, but we still . . . we don't show it . . . we are still writing and fiddling around with it because the actors don't always work out the way you wrote them. An actor would be good for one line, not good for the other line. Or he would be running, not walking. So we corrected those things as we went.

The final scene of *Some Like It Hot,* we wrote on a weekend in the studio. We just did not have it. We had the guys escaping, jumping into the motorboat of Mr. Joe E. Brown. And a little dialogue between Marilyn Monroe and Tony Curtis. And then we came to the unmasking, when Jack Lemmon says, "You know I cannot marry you because . . . I smoke." And finally he takes that wig off and says, "Look, I'm a *man*." Now we needed a line for Joe E. Brown and could not find it. But somewhere in the beginning of our discussion, Iz said, "Nobody's perfect." And I said, "Look, let's go back to your line, 'Nobody's perfect.' Let's send it to the mimeograph department so that they have something, and then we're going to *really* sit down and make a *real* funny last line."

We never found the line, so we went with "Nobody's perfect." The audience just exploded at the preview in Westwood. This was also very funny, how you make pictures. We wrote it on Sunday, we shot it on Monday.

Nobody thought of Joe E. Brown. I had seen him in some silent pictures, but I did not know that he was around, and we were starting to cast. And Aud and I and Iz and his wife were there at the opening-day ceremonies for the Dodgers at the coliseum. There was a loudspeaker on the field behind home plate, and people talking, and now comes the next speaker and it's Joe E. Brown. And I said, "That's our guy. *That's the guy!*" Nobody ever thought of him.

So I asked him, "Would you like to read?" "*Would I?* Of course I would." He did the part and was an absolute surprise to people, to young people, because they'd never *seen* him. He had the biggest mouth in the *world*. He was the nicest guy. You have to be alert, you know? You have to sit there, always, and say, "Is that the best I can do?"

It's always very difficult for me to say, "This is mine and this is his," always, except of course I have to give him credit for "Nobody's perfect." Because that's the thing they jump on, and I say, "That was a temporary line, suggested by Mr. Diamond." And it wound up to be our funniest last line. I was asked by many people, "What is going to happen *now*? What happens now to Lemmon, what happens to his husband?" And I always said, "I have no idea." "Nobody's perfect." Leave it up there on the screen. You cannot top that.

cc: It does feel like a *single* voice, and maybe that's the beauty of your collaboration.

bw: Whenever I collaborated with somebody, and I always collaborated with somebody, because if you think that I am speaking lousy English now, you should have heard it *then*. I felt I had to have a collaborator [because of language]. And also, because I liked to keep strict hours, there was a responsibility if I had a collaborator. But whenever you see me collaborating with somebody *once*, only once, that means I didn't like him. [*Laughs.*] Yeah, for instance, Edwin Blum, he's dead now—I worked with him on a script of a very good picture, *Stalag 17* [1953], but I never worked with him again, because he did not *add*. It was just a very difficult situation.

Whenever I worked with somebody *more* than once, that tells you. I worked with Brackett twenty years, with Diamond twenty years, twenty-five . . . it was all very very peaceful. There was no jumping around on tables and couches, "Hahahahaha, that's great! They're just gonna die!!" No. It was very quiet. [*Pause.*] Sometimes I would leave the office in an angry mood, but in the morning, it's all forgotten. Or I knew when he said, "I'm going to go to the library"—when Diamond was upset, he went to the Beverly Hills library. He was a fine man, an absolute jewel. He was a gentleman.

cc: Were your best relationships like that? Including your wife, Audrey?

BW: Oh yeah. But my wife, there's no relationship. She's my slave. [*Wilder gives a look that indicates the opposite might be true.*]

CC: So there's not a lot of jumping and screaming. . . .

BW: No, no jumping. No jumping on each other *or* on furniture. [*Smiles.*] No no no, it's absolutely a bourgeois life. The lower level of the bourgeois. [*Laughs.*] She's a very fine girl. [*Smiles.*] She's terrific.

"Nobody's perfect": Wilder and Diamond's funniest last line

Wilder convinced director Cecil B. DeMille (above) to play himself in *Sunset Boulevard* (1950).

2

CC: Is *Sunset Boulevard* a black comedy?

BW: No. Just a picture.

CC: What was the initial inspiration behind *Sunset Boulevard?*

BW: I wanted to make things a little harder for myself, I wanted to do that thing which never quite works—a picture about Hollywood. Originally it was a comedy, possibly for Mae West. The picture became about a silent star and a writer. And we could not find the person to play the great silent star. Mae West did not want to do it. Mary Pickford, no. We were about to sign or not sign Pola Negri for the movie. Then we came upon the idea of Gloria Swanson. It might have been George Cukor who first suggested her. She had already been abandoned; she was a death knell—she had lost a lot of money on the Paramount lot. But I insisted on her. A wonderful idea, that carried with it the great value that she had *been* a silent star, and had made a picture with Erich von Stroheim called *Queen Kelly* [1928], which we could also use on the projection screen in her home. We did a screen test, she did a few lines, where an angry Swanson maintains that she's still the greatest. Now we had a picture. She got a minimal salary, $150,000, less than Holden. And it was a wonderful thing that I also had Stroheim. He had two ideas for the film, one of which I used—the writing of the fan letters himself. The other was, he wished to be seen washing her underwear. [*He demonstrates Stroheim lovingly washing the garments.*] Stroheim! Montgomery Clift was to play the writer. Three days before, he pulled out.

CC: How did you find out? Did Clift call himself?

BW: A lady agent called me. At that time Brackett was the producer. It was the last picture we did. And she talked to Brackett. It so happens Mr. Clift had had an affair with an older woman in New York [Libby Holman]. And he did not want to make his first big picture, playing the lead, the story of a man being kept by a very rich woman twice his age. He did not want Hollywood talk. He was a New York actor, and he did not want to start his career that way.

CC: Did you get angry?

BW: What is angry? Angry is not good, you know. It's just, "Who do we take?" Leading men at that time were all under contract to the studios. And I have to start shooting on Monday, right? So I went through the list Paramount had at that time. And they had a young actor by the name of William Holden. Beedle was his name really, and he had changed it. He made a picture I enjoyed, it was very good, *Golden Boy* [1939]. I gave the script to Holden at one o'clock, and at three he was at my house, and he said, "Absolutely,

Wilder (opposite) dancing with Gloria Swanson on the set of *Sunset Boulevard;* and directing *Sabrina:* "Audrey Hepburn had just returned from Paris in the picture, and she was wearing that dress, which was a killer. I was telling her something very simple. Show *love* . . . just show love."

I want to do it." And people underestimated him, you know, because he was very good. He was a very good actor. And I made other pictures, like *Stalag 17,* with him, and *Sabrina.* It was kind of like what I had with Lemmon later on, you know.

He died, unfortunately. He was a drunk. We had a date with him at his new house in Palm Springs. We were to go there Saturday morning, and we were all packed, and then we called the house in Palm Springs, we are on the way, and the guy said he never showed up. So now, other people were wondering too. They opened the door to that apartment there, Pacific Boulevard or whatever. He was drunk, terribly drunk, and he fell, and he hit his head on the corner of a table there. And there was nobody around, and he bled to death. When that happened, when somebody told me Holden is dead, I thought it could be only two things: either he died in a helicopter crash in Hong Kong, where he had an apartment, or he was trampled to death by a rhinoceros in Africa, where he also had a house. But that he's gonna die through a small little thing?

When I did *Double Indemnity,* I tried every leading man in town. I went about as low as George Raft, that's pretty low. [*Laughs.*] He had somebody read the script for him, because he could not read. Could not write and could not read. So somebody read the script, and then halfway through, he came over to the studio and said, "I'm halfway through that script, and where comes the lapel?" And I said, "The lapel?" "You know what I mean— when does he show that he's an FBI man? The lapel!" [*He demonstrates turning the lapel of a coat over, showing an FBI badge.*] "There's no lapel," I tell him. "I really *am* a murderer!? I wouldn't do that! I wouldn't touch it, for God's sake!" But Stanwyck knew that it was good stuff, and she grabbed it.

CC: Do you remember the direction you gave Barbara Stanwyck on *Double Indemnity* for that silent shot on her face while the murder is occurring in the backseat? It's almost sexual, that buzz she gets in her eyes.

BW: When he shoots the husband in the backseat. Yes. Sure, that was a highly intelligent actress, Miss Stanwyck. I questioned the wig, but it was proper, because it was a phony wig. It was an obviously phony wig. And the anklet—the equipment of a woman, you know, that is married to this kind of man. They scream for murder.

Yeah, naturally we rehearsed this thing. But I rehearsed it with her once or twice, that's the maximum, and it was not that much different from the way she would have done it. She was just an extraordinary woman. She took the script, loved it, right from the word go, didn't have the agent come and say, "Look, she's to play a murderess, she must get more money, because she's never going to work again."

With Stanwyck, I had absolutely no difficulties at all. And she knew the script, *everybody's* lines. You could wake her up in the middle of the night and she'd know the scene. Never a fault, never a mistake—just a wonderful brain she had.

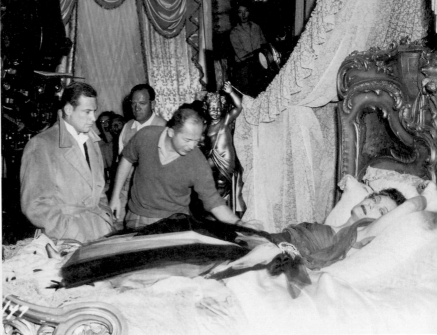

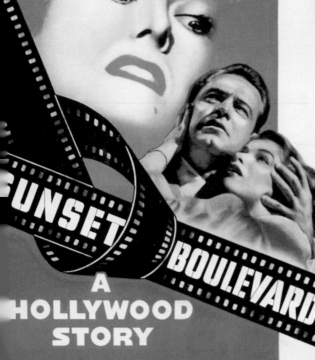

CC: Did you write the part for Barbara Stanwyck?

BW: Yeah. And then there was an actor by the name of Fred MacMurray at Paramount, and he played comedies. Small dramatic parts, big parts in comedies. I let him read it, and he said, "I can't do that." And I said, "Why can't you?" He said, "It requires acting!" [*Laughs.*] I said, "Look, you have now arrived in comedy, you're at a certain point where you either have to stop, or you have to jump over the river and start something new." He said, "Will you tell me when I'm no good?" [*He nods: a partnership is born.*] And he was wonderful because it's odd casting.

(Opposite) "This is Sydney Skolsky, a journalist for the *Citizen News* in Hollywood. I had him playing a newspaperman. And then I took somebody else." Did it help to court the press in this way? "No, he wrote bad things about the picture." (Above) *Sunset Boulevard:* William Holden looks on as Wilder makes adjustments to Swanson; (right) Wilder got Erich von Stroheim to play Max, the butler who used to be a well-known film director.

The same thing happened with *The Apartment.* Everything was cast, including the guy who's the boss of the insurance company. The boss who then takes the key himself, Sheldrake, was Paul Douglas. He would have been perfect. But Paul Douglas died, at breakfast, just before he was to take the plane or train to start shooting. And there again was Fred MacMurray. And he said, "No no no, don't you come near me, please. I'm under contract, lifelong contract, at Disney [doing films like *The Shaggy Dog* (1959)]. You know, for the kids. If they find out that I'm having an affair with my telephone operator, that's impossible. I cannot do it. *Absolutely not.*" And Monday morning, he was on the set.

CC: I love the hipster dialogue that you occasionally give Fred MacMurray in both movies. Especially in *The Apartment,* where he wants the key, and tells Baxter, "It takes only thirty seconds for you to be out on the street again . . . *you dig?*" It's a such a beatnik moment.

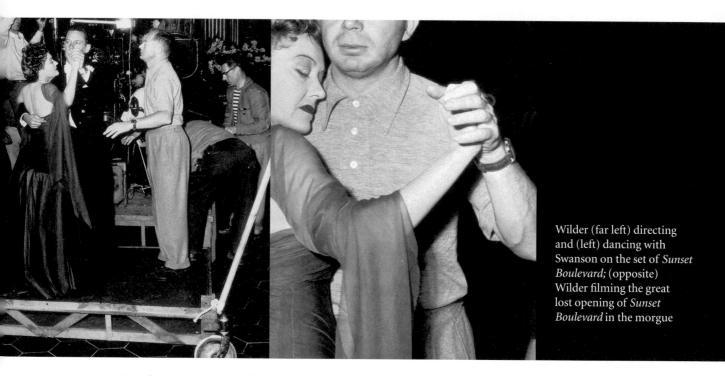

Wilder (far left) directing and (left) dancing with Swanson on the set of *Sunset Boulevard;* (opposite) Wilder filming the great lost opening of *Sunset Boulevard* in the morgue

BW: For those days, yeah. Thirty-five years ago. [*Smiles.*]

I'll tell you a very funny story about him, the last story that I tell you with Mr. Fred MacMurray, who was a very stingy man. I loved it. I loved the man and I loved his stinginess too. It amused me. There was a scene in *The Apartment* before he comes into his office. He has his shoes shined by a black man. And then, from his suit, he gets out a quarter and he flips a tip to the shoeshine guy. And now, we're shooting it, and we're shooting it, and he *cannot* do it. And I say, "That's all right, it's too small, let's do it with a fifty-cent piece, it's bigger." And MacMurray says, "I would never give him fifty cents—I cannot play this scene." [*Laughs.*]

[*The bill arrives.*] Give it to me, please.

CC: No. It would be my honor. You get it next time.

BW: *Next time?*

CC: I once heard this advice. When directing a romance, or a romantic comedy, a director must fall in love with his leading lady through the lens. "If *you* don't, no one else will." How did it feel to direct Audrey Hepburn? Did you fall in love with her, through the lens?

BW: Of course. There was so much inside her, a feeling that communicated. But was she "sexy"? Off camera, she was just an actress. She was very thin, a good person, sometimes standing on the set she disappeared. But there was something very likable about her, just absolutely adorable about her. You trusted her, this tiny person. When she stood before the cameras, she became Miss Audrey Hepburn. And she could put it on a little bit, the sexiness, and the effect was really something. For instance, in *Sabrina*, when she came back from Paris with the dress.

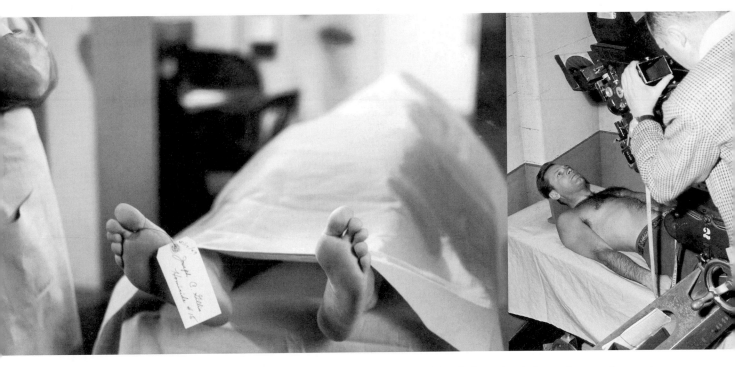

There was gold in that picture. For instance, the character of the father, the father who smokes and drinks and has to do it in the closet so his wife does not see him. And the scene where Sabrina, Audrey Hepburn, is in love with blond, handsome Mr. Holden, but she knows it's not going to work, and there's a garage with sixteen cars, so she decides to commit suicide, and she turns on the gas in every car, and sits there and waits. And it is the brother, the Bogart part, who wakes her up and grabs her and takes her up. It's a very good scene there, with the twelve cars shaking there, and the girl sitting there in the middle, the gas is coming. I asked a very talented director, Sydney Pollack, why it was not in the remake. He said, "The picture was too long." How can it be too long? *The picture is the picture.* [*Laughs.*]

CC: Every year, it seems, somebody is heralded as the new Audrey Hepburn. Every new young actress is called the "next" Audrey Hepburn.

BW: Again, that's the element X that people have, or don't have. You can meet somebody and you can be enchanted, and then you photograph them and it's nothing. But she had it. And there will not be another. She exists forever, in her time. You cannot duplicate her, or take her out of her era. If the element X could be distilled, you could make all the Monroes you wanted, and all the Hepburns . . . like that sheep they cloned. But you can't. And she was something entirely different on the screen than she was in life. Not that she was vulgar; she wasn't. But she started something new, she started something classy. She, and the other Hepburn, Katharine, at a different time. She was absolutely wonderful. Today, there is Julia Roberts. She is quite capable, very funny . . . I loved her instantly in *Pretty Woman* [1990]. But no actress should be expected to be Audrey Hepburn. That dress by Mr. Givenchy has already been filled.

Sabrina was a difficult time for me. This was a picture that was still being written and shaped as we went. There were sleepless nights. My back troubled me. The script was not quite finished, and we were falling behind in the writing. She had a big scene with Bogart, when she visits him in his conference room and he tells her to go to Paris, and it did not quite work. So I arrived at the studio and I had only a page and a half, and I had to fill the entire day. I cannot go to the front office and say, "Look I've run out of script." It was Friday; we had Saturday and Sunday to write. We had to stall. So I went to her and I told her the problem. "Look, you have to fumble a line, you have to misread the line. I'm terribly sorry, you have to help me, we cannot shoot more than a page and a half. That's all." And she said, "I'll do it." And she did it.

She said, "Oh, I have a *terrible* headache, let me lie down a little bit." And then she was fifteen minutes, an hour, so I just barely ran out of stuff, the page and a half, by six o'clock. Then, on Saturday and Sunday we rewrote *that thing*. Then I was ready. But she was helping me. That's a wonderful thing. Because she may have appeared difficult that day, she did not want to have the reputation that she had holes in her brain. But she did not care. She just did it.

Are we off? Because we could be here for dinner.

Our conversation resumes several days later at Wilder's Brighton Way office, with Karen Lerner again accompanying me. The director has granted another session for clarifications, but the idea of an extended book of interviews is still very much in doubt.

CC: I have a question about the look and the art direction of your movies. Just below the

(Center and bottom) Wilder with Barbara Stanwyck on the set of *Double Indemnity* (1944)

surface of the scripts and the acting is a very rich layer of visual detail. When you head into a picture like *The Apartment* or *Double Indemnity,* do you have a painter in mind whose work has inspired you? What kind of specific vision do you give to your production designer?

BW: [*Warming instantly:*] Not actually a painter, but sometimes houses. Like for instance, *Double Indemnity.* I had to find a house that is typical for a guy like the husband of Barbara Stanwyck. Two stories I wanted, because I wanted to photograph her coming down the steps with the anklet. The art director lived in a house like this, and what I wanted, what I was trying for with my cameraman, John Seitz—he was a very old man. [*Smiles.*] Only fifty-one at the time and had done pictures with Valentino—was a very specific thing. I told him that whenever I come into a house like this, whenever I opened the door and the sun was coming in, there was always dust in the air. Because they never dusted it. And I asked him, "Could you get that effect?" And he could.

CC: How did you arrive at the visual style of the movie?

BW: We had to be realistic. You had to believe the situation and the characters, or all was lost. I insisted on black-and-white, of course, and in making operattas I'd learned that sometimes one technical shot destroyed a picture. You could say that *Double Indemnity* was based on the principal of *M* [Fritz Lang, 1931], the very good picture starring Peter Lorre. I had a feeling, something in my head, *M* was on my mind. I tried for a very realistic picture—a few little tricks, but not very tricky. *M* was the look of the picture. It was a picture that looked like a newsreel. You never realized it was staged. But like a newsreel, you look to grab a moment of truth, and exploit it.

CC: But the lighting was sometimes very dramatic. Were you influenced by the German expressionist films?

BW: No. There was *some* dramatic lighting, yes, but it was newsreel lighting. That was the ideal. I'm not saying that every shot was a masterpiece, but sometimes even in a newsreel you get a masterpiece shot. That was the approach. No phony setups. I had a few shots in mind between MacMurray and Edward G. Robinson, and they happened at the beginning and the end, when the two were together in that room. That was it. Everything was meant to support the realism of the story. I had worked with the cameraman before and I trusted him. We used a little *mezzo* light in the apartment when Stanwyck comes to see MacMurray in the apartment—this is when he makes up his mind to commit murder. That's it. I always had a good friendship with my cameramen. Fritz Lang told me early in my career, "Look for the good shooters, there are some special ones." He was right, and I was very lucky. They were good, very fun. They did what was asked. Sometimes they wanted to do a little move . . . and held back. [*Smiles.*]

CC: Some still wonder about that door in the apartment hallway in *Double Indemnity*. In the great scene where Stanwyck comes to visit Neff (MacMurray), she hides behind the door as Keyes (Robinson) exits. Yet apartment doors always open in, and this one opens out.

BW: Yeah, that was a mistake that we made and I did not want to correct it. We'd already shot it. It worked and I did not want to reshoot it.

CC: The film compositions in *Sabrina* are particularly artful, very painterly. Was that part of your original plan?

BW: No. We just went ahead as usual. I mean, I didn't suddenly become an idiot. The sets were always very, very good, and very true. For instance, in *The Apartment*, it was just there—it's just next door to the doctor. Simple and true. In *Sabrina*, it was the only time I ever did anything that lush. Anything that kind of portrayed a little bit the money that the family was living on. The only other time was *The*

Scenes from *Double Indemnity* (1944) including (opposite left) the silent shot of Stanwyck's face as the murder of her husband is occurring in the back seat of the car

Emperor Waltz [1948]—but I would not mention it. Just say the only time I worked with money was *Sabrina*. It worked out fine, I enjoyed that.

In *Sunset Boulevard*, they were very good, because I told the man, the architect who designed it, one line: "early Wallace Beery." It was a kind of Spanish house, with a staircase. A little rich, but not too much. Have you seen that thing on stage [in the Andrew Lloyd Webber musical version]? It was like a *palace*? [*Shakes head.*] It's all right. In the picture, the whole width of the thing was one living room.

In those years when we made the picture [1944], there were few modern houses, so we went to the Los Feliz district and we found a house like this with a corner where kids could play ball or something, some action there. I don't know how it is now in the new print or the old print. John Seitz took some magnesium and he kind of made it into dust and then he blew it up there, and that's when we were shooting, before it settled. So we got that effect.

But, you know, whenever I write a script, the thing is to give the reader the impression without going into details. Only what is necessary. For example, in *Sunset Boulevard*. I looked at the script recently. The house was nothing like the one on the stage. On the stage it's kind of a Taj Mahal, he had a big stage to fill. There was no such thing in those days. We got the house on a loan, we paid for it, we got it from an early wife of Paul Getty. She conducted a school for acting there; she did not live there. And it was on the corner of Irving and Wilshire Boulevard. We needed a swimming pool, and we said we would like to rent that thing and we will build the swimming pool. So while we were building the swimming pool, she did not want it connected with the real water. She wanted to put the earth in there and flatten it out again when we were finished—idiotic. But now the house has been destroyed altogether, because the Tidewater Oil Company, which Mr. Getty also owned, took the place of this two-story house. I used to hang around quite a bit while we built the little touches, looking at the plans. Sad that it is gone. I would have liked to make the house even smaller, more compact, more corny. But we had to make room for all the photos.

When we did *The Apartment,* I went around Central Park West and I looked at various apartments. We just made a combination of things. Except that then I started collecting Thonet furniture. It's an Austrian firm that specialized in bentwood. This guy Mr. Thonet and his brothers, they found out that with certain trees, you can bend and put them in a press and leave them there for a week or so, and when you take the press off, it's a bentwood chair. This, for instance, is bentwood, and they gave it to me as a present, as a joke. [*He proudly indicates one of the chairs in his office. One of the chair legs is curved around itself in a knot.*] So you see I made the whole apartment bentwood—even the bed was bentwood.

CC: So even the rooms have a back story. The effect is subliminal, of course, but a film can't help but soak up that kind of rich detail. In *The Apartment,* I keep trying to make out what that painting is on the back of Baxter's apartment wall.

BW: It was a print from the Museum of Modern Art. He kind of tacked it up.

Sabrina (1954): (clockwise from opposite top) Audrey Hepburn at the train station; performance, behavior, shot, and costume all come together in the giddy second-act conference-room scene; lunch break on the set, with cameraman Charles Lang on the end; Sabrina attempting suicide in the garage with sixteen cars. "It's a very good scene, with the twelve cars shaking . . . and the girl sitting there in the middle, the gas is coming I asked a very talented director, Sydney Pollack, why it was not in the remake. He said, 'The picture was too long.' How can it be too long? *The picture is the picture.*"

CC: Right. That makes sense. He has bachelor tastes. He buys a print, and there's no one around to say, "Maybe you should frame it."

BW: Oh yes, it was very much like the guy, Baxter, would have done it. What else would he do with himself when the apartment was busy? Especially on holidays, they would call him, it goes on all the time. . . . So he would go to the museum and he would look at the paintings and get some of those posters. [*Laughs.*] And so, that was his apartment.

CC: The idea of a little man in a big office is pervasive. Was that the purpose of those playful Kafkaesque shots of Baxter at the insurance company?

BW: Yeah, that I did with my friend [production designer] Alexander Trauner, who was Hungarian-French. A guy who was a genius. I did that whole set of all the desks. I did it on stage number 4 at Goldwyn Studios, which is not a large stage, but what we did there, we put in the front row [of the office], then the second, then the third. Then we got smaller and smaller desks, and smaller and smaller extras, and ultimately we had cutouts, people just like this [*makes tiny gesture with his hands*], and we had little cars there going outside, as if it were from up above.

CC: So that's the secret. And the perspective changes you can accomplish with models makes the space even more "modern."

BW: Perspective, yes. We put some lighting fixtures in there, and that was it. We just *did it,* the whole set there, did it in one day, a day and a half. It was just the invention of doing the perspective. Trauner got the Oscar for it, but it was nothing bombastic. It just kind of looked right.

CC: The way you shot *The Apartment* seemed very specific, a lot of wider shots and masters. By doing that, C. C. Baxter always seems very alive, struggling against the bigger world of business. Was that the visual concept?

BW: Yes. The idea behind shooting it is getting everything that is written on the screen. Everything, making it clear. I did not shoot a face like this, and like *that,* and then over again, from other angles. No.

(Clockwise from right) Holden walking away from his garage apartment in *Sunset Boulevard:* "When we made the picture, there were few modern houses so we went to the Los Feliz district and we found a house"; Wilder filming *The Apartment;* Shirley MacLaine and Jack Lemmon playing cards in *The Apartment*

I just shot it once. And that was about forty-some-odd years ago. I did not endlessly try to find any specific good angle. I just tried to be good, careful that one thing led into the other thing. One close-up here, another there . . . never too many, only when necessary. And when I'm through with a picture, there's only about a thousand feet left on the floor of the cutting room. We did *The Apartment* in fifty days and edited it in less than a week. We had three feet of unused film. That was good.

The story was good, our ideas worked. For example, we had the dame, a broad with Lemmon, coming back into the apartment. And he was dancing around, and making fun, and suddenly he sees the girl, Shirley MacLaine, asleep in his bed, but he cannot wake her up. That's why, in structuring it, we invented a doctor who lives next door, Dr. Dreyfuss.

CC: The mensch who helps save her and teaches Baxter how to live a better life.

BW: Yeah. We never went into the apartment [of the doctor]. No time for that. We only went into the doorway.

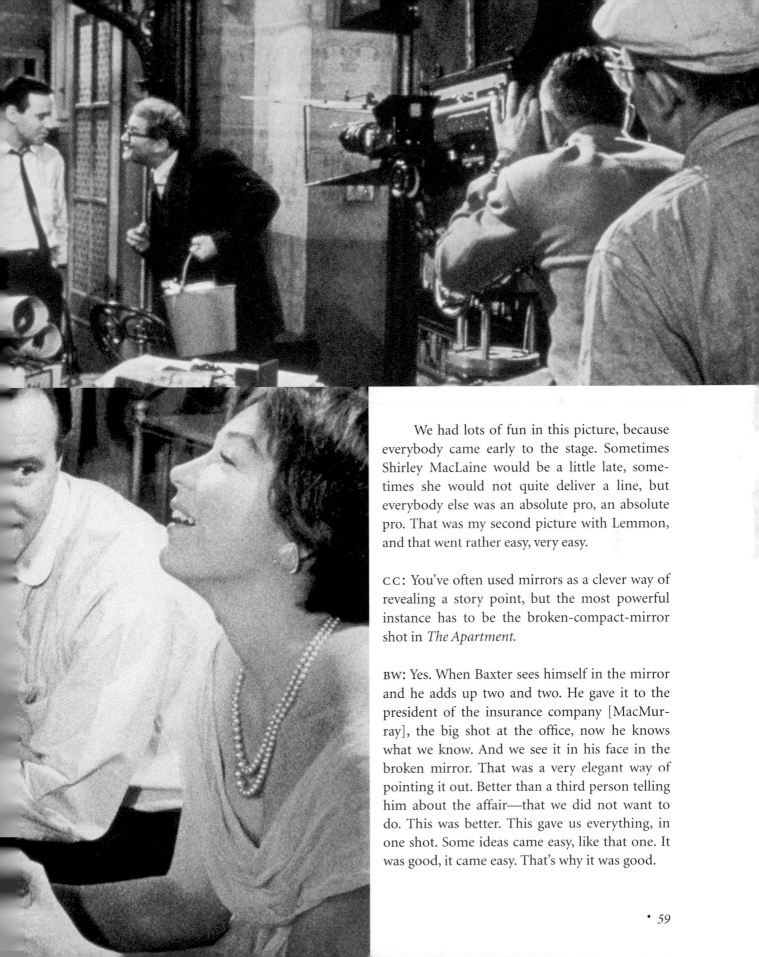

We had lots of fun in this picture, because everybody came early to the stage. Sometimes Shirley MacLaine would be a little late, sometimes she would not quite deliver a line, but everybody else was an absolute pro, an absolute pro. That was my second picture with Lemmon, and that went rather easy, very easy.

CC: You've often used mirrors as a clever way of revealing a story point, but the most powerful instance has to be the broken-compact-mirror shot in *The Apartment.*

BW: Yes. When Baxter sees himself in the mirror and he adds up two and two. He gave it to the president of the insurance company [MacMurray], the big shot at the office, now he knows what we know. And we see it in his face in the broken mirror. That was a very elegant way of pointing it out. Better than a third person telling him about the affair—that we did not want to do. This was better. This gave us everything, in one shot. Some ideas came easy, like that one. It was good, it came easy. That's why it was good.

CC: From what I gather, the spaghetti-strained-through-the-tennis-racket idea in *The Apartment* began with an innocent comment by Izzy Diamond: "Women love seeing a man trying to cook in the kitchen."

BW: Yes.

CC: So then you both set about trying to find the perfect situation that shows—

BW: —how a man tackles a problem with a missing kitchen object. It was obvious that it was his apartment—you know, he just never cooked. Or he just bought himself a sandwich or something, on the way home. But there I did not have a sieve, you know. So I don't know whether it was [Diamond] or it was me, but it came kind of spontaneously. For macaroni or spaghetti, we need a sieve. So I said, "Let's have a tennis racket."

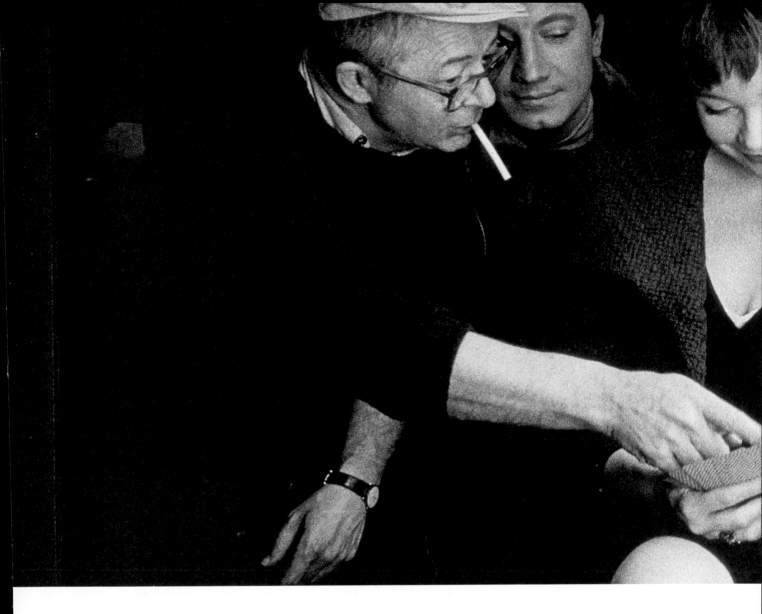

CC: Shirley MacLaine has said *The Apartment* was written as you filmed. She had only forty pages of script when you began.

BW: That's all we gave her. But sure, we had most of the script. We always knew where we were going, always. Sometimes you leave yourself open, you want to see how the actors will play it, you adapt to what shows up in the rehearsing and the filming. We always knew our destination.

CC: There's a wonderful glow about Shirley MacLaine as she's running back to Lemmon at the end of the movie. The right lens, the right lighting . . . there's such a beautiful, complete, glowing look about her.

BW: Yes. I only had three houses behind her, so I kept repeating them in various shots. I just kept reshooting so I could prolong it. She was running past the same house three times.

Wilder directing Shirley MacLaine on the card game in *The Apartment;* (inset) MacLaine and Lemmon in the elevator scene

CC: So there's no special lighting treatment on Shirley MacLaine?

BW: No. Just sometimes, only sometimes did I do a special shot.

CC: Joseph LaShelle, your cinematographer on the movie, was one of your great collaborators. You used him for many years, and then switched before *The Private Life of Sherlock Holmes* [1970]. Was it time for a new look?

BW: No, but he was an elderly man, you know. He was kind of on the verge of retiring, and I got him for other pictures. He was not a young man, he was an *experienced* man. And at that time, you know, I was doing mostly pictures in black-and-white. I like black-and-white very much. And black-and-white is much more difficult to shoot than color pictures, because you have the discrepancy of the depths of the color. You have to do it artificially with a lot of lights, in black-and-white, the shadows. You can paint it a little bit darker, you can paint it a little bit lighter.

When Monroe came on the set and saw the first day's rushes on *Some Like It Hot,* she said, "I am very disappointed, I thought the picture's going to be in color. I'm at my best in color." And I said to her, "Well, we were fooling around with it, I tested it." I lied to her. "You know, when we make the men up as women, we will need much more makeup and much more powder not to have the skin of the man with the beard growing as they're shooting, so we had to do it in black-and-white."

CC: And she bought it?

BW: She bought it. [*Laughs.*]

CC: But why was it *really* in black-and-white?

BW: Because I liked it in black-and-white. I was then one of the last guys still doing it. But when I run

into people—you know, as a test—they say, "I saw *Some Like It Hot*, it was wonderful, wonderful," and I say, "How did you like the color photography?" They say, "It was great, it was absolutely great." People forget, they don't remember. It's less important than the content of the picture, you know. After five minutes they forget about it.

CC: Was there a special technique you had for shooting Marlene Dietrich? Her close-ups have a glow—she pops off the screen.

BW: I had a joke with her. I always said to her, "*You* light this scene, *you* light it." She always thought that she was a great cameraman, because of her relation with [Josef] von Sternberg. She made many pictures with Sternberg, the first one being *The Blue Angel* [1930]. She'd say, "God, they're so stupid, they don't have the key light on me." She stood in the key light, always. No, I just shot her. She was neither good nor bad—she was Dietrich. And that worked for the picture, to have her play the Nazi girl, for instance, in *A Foreign Affair* [1948].

CC: So you didn't change your lighting style for Dietrich?

BW: No, I did not change. I just told her to light it herself. And she lit herself.

The phone rings, and Wilder bends down to answer. His face stays angled near the cradle; the cord is tangled; he stays close to hanging up for most of the call. He is busy, he says, but the caller is insistent about making an appointment with him. "Yeah. . . . Yes, sure, I didn't get it yet, but I will sign it. . . . Okay, I will sign it the moment I get it. . . . Not so good, I'm getting old. I'm an old man and I can't pee, and I asked the doctor

The broken compact mirror in *The Apartment:* "When Baxter sees himself in the mirror . . . he adds up two and two. Better than a third person telling him about the affair—that we did not want to do. This gave us everything, in one shot."

about it, and the doctor asked me how old am I, and I said ninety, and he said, 'You've pissed enough.'" Wilder pauses briefly to accommodate the laugh of his caller, then continues, sprightly. "Yeah. Okay. . . . Okay, I'll call you. . . . A week? I hope that I'm gonna live for a week! I will sign it, and I will keep you informed about my urinary progress. Goodbye."

Days later, after waiting through a lengthy ceremony to accept a Lifetime Achievement Award from the Producers Guild of America, Wilder would abandon his prepared speech and simply tell this joke. It brings down the house. Captured on video and included in the American Masters film on his career, this riotous moment is the one Wilder promises to be his last public appearance. "I cannot take these functions anymore," he says. "They are ridiculous and too long. However, I'm happy to accept anything sent to my home."

CC: [Laughs.] Do you sometimes feel that, having made all these movies, you threw a party for others that you were unable to attend yourself? Were you ever able to enjoy the movies as much as everybody else?

Lemmon (left) in *The Apartment;* Wilder and William Holden (above) on the famous staircase of *Sunset Boulevard*

BW: I guess not. I have a preview. I have a second preview. And then I may look at it, once more, maybe get a cassette, get a disc there, and put it away. I never like to look at old pictures of mine. But I know it—I did not feel that I was part of that event. I just always thought *I* was the event.

CC: You worked very consistently for many years, almost a movie a year. Every once in a while you took a year off. You had three films in 1957, which was an amazing feat. Then *The Apartment* in '60, *One Two Three* in 1961, and then you took a little bit of a break. Did you ever feel, as Moss Hart whispered to you when you were up on the stage receiving the second of your three Academy Awards for *The Apartment*, "It's time to—"

BW: Quit? [*Wilder considers the word for a long beat. Hart's actual comment was "Billy, it's time to stop."*]

CC: Looking back, did you ever reach that creative peak of *The Apartment* again?

BW: [*Soberly:*] No, I never could, and I tried, but I failed in that. It is a tremendous drop, because I got a little bit confused. I wanted to, after one or two failures . . . I wanted to give them—United Artists, Mirisch Company—a picture that is going to make some money for them.
    I don't know, actors [began to] get sick on me. Like Peter Sellers—he had a heart attack after the first week of shooting *Kiss Me Stupid* [1964]. Matthau, for him we had to wait three months in the middle of *The Fortune Cookie* [1966]. He too had a heart attack. I waited for him. But for Sellers I could not wait. I only had one week's shooting there. But I like Matthau. I had half the picture, the character and everything, so I waited for him. Then on another picture [*Buddy Buddy*, 1981], Mr. Matthau jumped out

of the window, for no reason at all, one story, but fell on asphalt. I told him, "Look, you guys are going to go down the chute, but I have two gymnasts that are going to go out here, and down below there's going to be a mountain of mattresses, and there are going to be some stunt men," but then I turn around and I hear a scream. He just jumped out of the window—I have no idea why. And then I wait another two months. It was just incredible.

CC: Were you the kind of director who knew all the crew members' names?

BW: Yeah, I always did. My first assistant for many pictures was C. C. Coleman. I got the C. C. for Baxter from him. He fell off the roof of a house that he was building or rebuilding in Lake Arrowhead, and he killed himself. [*Fondly:*] He was a real, real, real idiot. He was very, very good in his profession, but beyond it he was an idiot. For years and years he was the assistant director of [Frank] Capra, and then he came to Paramount, and he was absolutely illiterate. For instance, we were going to Europe, I was going to shoot a picture there, in Paris I think, and we were on a boat. I was stretched out there on one of those deck chairs, and he's next to me, and just to give you an idea, he turns to me and says, "There's a lot of fucking water in this world," and I said, "Uh-huh." And after a little pause he says, "And we only see the *top* of it." That's a Buddy Coleman line. Everything kind of backward. But he was a very, very good assistant.

CC: I once read an interview with Truffaut that I found very helpful. He felt that in the filming and the acting of a script, the movie always gets more serious. So if you put more comedy than you want in the script, you'll end up with the right mix of comedy and drama.

BW: [*Agreeing:*] Because they're not gonna laugh at some things.

CC: Is that something you've found to be true?

BW: Yeah, well . . . I do the joke if the joke is germane to the whole story, to the picture. But not if I have to squeeze it in artificially, with a shoehorn. I don't do that. I never overestimate the audience, nor do I *underestimate* them. I just have a very rational idea as to who we're dealing with, and that we're not making a picture for Harvard Law School, we're making a picture for middle-class people, the people that you see on the subway, or the people that you see in a restaurant. Just normal people. And I hope that they're gonna like it. If I have a good scene, a good situation with the characters, then we fool around

with it and explore it. That is the fun. Because there are many versions that you can do. You find the theme of the situation, find the joke, find the high point, and end the scene on the high point. I don't let it dribble on.

Like, for instance, one of the big laughs in *Some Like It Hot*. There was a scene that played about three or four minutes. That's very long. That was the scene where Mr. Tony Curtis climbs up the back of the hotel, goes in the room, and there is Jack Lemmon with the maracas. He's still singing the tune [from his evening with Joe E. Brown], and the maracas were very important. They were very important because I could *time the jokes* there. In other words, I say something, you say something, now I needed some kind of an *action* that helped time the joke. For instance, Tony Curtis comes up. He says, "Well, what's new here?" [*Does Lemmon:*] "Well, you'll be surprised, a little news here, I'm engaged." *Ya-dup-pap-pap-pap* [*shaking imaginary maracas*]. Now I knew, when I cut back, I knew how long the laugh was gonna be . . . then I put in the other straight line, then comes another joke. But I timed it so that not one straight line is lost. Because sometimes you have a straight line and the straight line *gets the laugh*. So now you're really dead, because they will not hear the payoff. They laughed over the straight line. And then they hear the top of the next joke already, without hearing the preparation. The rhythm is off. You have to be very, very careful.

That was the whole secret of the Marx Brothers: they tried it out in the theater first. There you can time it. "Let's wait until the laugh subsides." You do anything, you light a cigarette . . . you do anything as you wait for the laughs to die down, then you come in with the next joke. How are you gonna do it in films? So what [Irving] Thalberg thought of—he was a very inventive man—he had three routines from, let's say, *A Day at the Races* [1937] or *A Night at the Opera* [1935]. He took the three routines, gave it to the guys, and sent them on a tour of live vaudeville acts. Thalberg knew that the difficulty with the Marx Brothers was, they started with a joke. Then there's a big laugh, then comes another straight line. But what are we going to do in case there is no laugh? Or if the laugh is twice as long as we thought? They're going to be stepping on the feed line, which would ruin the next joke. So he took the Marx Brothers and he sent them all around America, into vaudeville places. And he tested the strength of the laughs. Was the joke a ten, was it a three, or what? In about twenty theaters they tried it out. Then they knew what they had. I stole that, the method of timing the laughs. They had it timed, with a clock.

CC: That's brilliant.

BW: So nothing got lost. In silent pictures of course it was wonderful. That was a helluva wonderful thing, because Chaplin and Buster Keaton, the more laughs the better, because they didn't even have titles then. That's wonderful. But you have to kind of find a happy medium in pictures. Of a hundred jokes, you always lose *thirty*.

CC: After all the work you'd put into a script, did it rip you up inside when you'd see some of your lines blown by the actor you'd hired?

BW: [*Quickly:*] Yeah, that happens. When I was a young director, there was a bigger chance of ripping my innards out, but then you get used to it and you settle down and you say, "Well, this worked; this did not work quite as well." Some pictures play wonderfully to a room of eight people. I don't go for that. I go for the masses. I go for the end effect. [*Laughs.*]

CC: I want to ask you about some of the pictures we haven't talked about.

Bing Crosby in *The Emperor Waltz* (1948)

BW: That was on purpose. Because they were no good.

CC: But it's interesting that you generally talk about the movies that are loved by the most people.

BW: Yeah, sure, why talk about something that did not come off? [*Pause.*] I will talk, I will talk.

CC: Good, because I think some people have some real favorites among your—

BW: Failures. [*Laughs.*] Sure. Sure. Of course. Go ahead. Now comes the painful part. Okay . . .

CC: Just give me your basic feeling, the feeling that comes to mind. Let's talk about *The Emperor Waltz* [1948], Bing Crosby.

BW: I did that after I came over from the war, from Germany, where I was stationed in Frankfurt. That was 1946, right?

CC: 1948.

BW: It came out in '48. We held it back as long as we could. We shot it in 1946. Because I know that we were in the Canadian Alps, where I shot a lot of the stuff, and we were celebrating my fortieth birthday. And I had made two grim pictures, *Double Indemnity* and *Lost Weekend*. *Double Indemnity* was so grim, by the way, that Brackett kind of ducked out. He says, "No, it's too grim for me." So that's how I got [Raymond] Chandler. Mr. Raymond Chandler, from whom I learned in the very beginning, you know, what real dialogue is. Because that's all he could write. That, and descriptions. "Out of his ears grew hair long enough to catch a moth" . . . or the other one I loved: "Nothing is as empty as an empty swimming pool." But he could not *construct*.

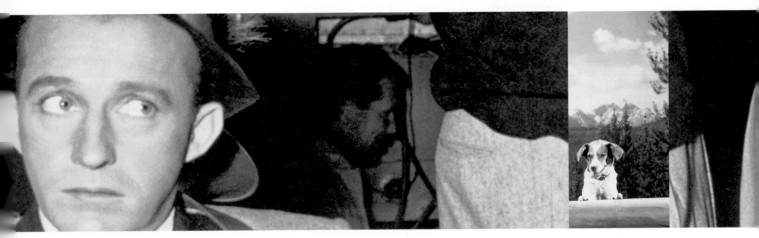

He was about sixty when we worked together. He was a dilettante. He did not like the structure of a screenplay, wasn't used to it. He was a mess, but he could write a beautiful sentence. "There is nothing as empty as an empty swimming pool." That is a great line, a great one. After a while I was able to write like Chandler. . . . I would take what he wrote, and structure it, and we would work on it. He hated James Cain. I loved the story, but he did not care for Cain. I tried to get Cain, but he was busy making a movie. Chandler also did not care for Agatha Christie. But each had what the other lacked. Christie, she knew structure. Sometimes the plot was very high-schoolish. She had structure, but she lacked poetry. Very underrated, Christie. She is not discussed enough.

CC: Over the years, it appears you've upgraded your estimations of [Mitchell] Leisen and Chandler.

BW: Sure, the anger gets washed, gets watery. You know, you forget about it. That's a very good thing. That's the only thing. Sure. I cannot forgive Mr. Hitler, but I certainly can forgive Mr. Leisen or Mr. Chandler. That's a different story. [*Pause.*] But then . . . there was a lot of Hitler in Chandler.

CC: [*Laughs.*] In what way?

BW: In the way he talked behind my back. And the way he quit writing with me and then came back the same day. Because I had told him to close that window, a Venetian blind in the office, and I didn't say "please."

CC: You had the stick too, right? The riding crop. And you said, "Shut the window."

BW: Yeah, I had the stick. I had the stick, and I had three martinis before lunch, and I called girls—six girls. One of them took fifteen minutes for me to get off the phone . . . and he was just outraged. He just could not take it, because he was impotent, I guess. And he had a wife who was much older than he was, and he was in AA, Alcoholics Anonymous—an unnecessary thing, because he got to be a drunkard again when we finished. [*Wilder is poker-faced.*]

CC: So it must have driven him crazy to see you having a martini.

BW: Yes, and I had one more martini than I should have had . . . because of him! But to hell with that. I'm back talking about the successful pictures. You asked me about *Emperor Waltz.* I kind of thought it would be fun to make a musical. I have no talent for a musical, because I can't get it into my head that people break into a song for no reason whatsoever. But they did it, they do it. For instance, *Singin' in the Rain* [1952], which is wonderful—they had a little help there because they were shooting a picture [within the film]. So I was handicapped there; I was not up to making a musical. I don't know, I should have gone to a hospital or something, after being in Germany and cutting an hour-and-a-half documentary about the concentration camps in London.

CC: You've never really discussed *Death Mills,* the documentary you made after the war. What specific memories do you have of the experience?

A technicolor tribute to the Austro-Hungarian Empire: Vienna and the world of Franz Josef in *The Emperor Waltz* (1948)

BW: I didn't make it. I just cut it. It was filmed in the concentration camps, the day after the troops came in. All of it. That was cut, only cut. There's not one shot that I made. I just cut it.

CC: Some people have written that you directed it.

BW: There was nothing to direct. It had to be a natural thing that happened that they were just able to photograph. You cannot have corpses built up in a little funeral pyre. No. And there was that one shot that I really loved, a shot that they took in a concentration camp, either Dachau or Auschwitz. There was a field of corpses, a *field,* and one corpse was not quite dead. And he looked and he saw the camera, did not know what it was, and he walked to the corpses, on top of the corpses, and sat down, ultimately, on dead corpses, and stared at us. That was the shot. I was not there when they photographed it. But that was the shot, and I used the whole shot.

So I was kind of very eager to do something on the more frivolous side. But *The Emperor Waltz* just was no good, it just did not come off. And I never even attempted to make a musical. As a matter of fact, nobody makes musicals anymore. Ever since Fred Astaire and Gene Kelly died, there's been nothing.

CC: Is *Emperor Waltz* an homage to Lubitsch?

BW: If it is any homage, if there is any feeling of an homage, that's wonderful. But I did not think of it. I just wanted to make a musical.

Wilder in Berlin during the filming of *A Foreign Affair* (1948)

3

CC: What are your memories of *A Foreign Affair* [1948]? It's one of your best films, I think, and one that shows all your strengths. All the characters are strong, and there's that wildly funny dialogue throughout.

BW: *Foreign Affair* I regard as one of my better pictures. I just had a new leading man, John Lund, who I think was very good. The casting worked. Jean Arthur, that was the leading lady, right? She and Marlene [Dietrich].

Jean Arthur did not get along with me at all. She would come with her husband—he was also a little bit in pictures. They came at midnight to my house. We were shooting that picture. At midnight,

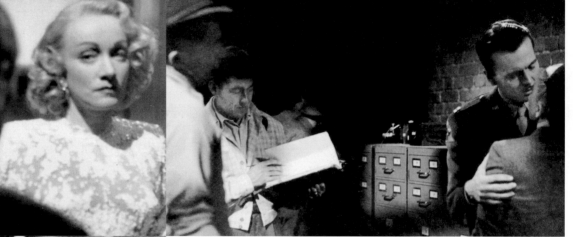

there's a knock on the door, I'm being awakened, and there is Jean Arthur, there's her husband—[Frank] Ross I think was his name—and he says, "My wife tells me something very unpleasant." And I said, "What is it, what happened?" And he said, "There was a close-up, and she was absolutely gorgeously beautiful, just terrific, and then I came to the studio to pick her up, and we asked to see the rushes, and then that close-up disappeared, and so we now have to assume that you were favoring Miss Dietrich." He thought we would destroy the beautiful close-up of his wife so as not to step on the toes of Dietrich. I said, "This is absolute madness, that I would destroy something." She was very unpleasant, but then she got a little bit better. When the last shot was done, the little humor she put in, she says, "Was this my last shot? Was there a hair in the aperture?" I said, "No. . . ." Then I said, "All right. We're going to see the cut in two weeks," and she said, "No thank you," and she left.

Then, about forty years later, there's a call from Carmel, up north, and it's Jean Arthur. I recognized her voice, she had a very unique voice, and she says, "Billy Wilder, I saw the picture," "What picture?" I said, and she said, "Well, you know, that thing when I'm the congresswoman. I saw it. Somebody showed it to me, and it's wonderful. I'm so sorry that I put you through those things." Then two years later, she died . . . because she was nice to me. [*Laughs.*]

CC: Did you often find that to be the case? You had to fight hard to get the actor's strongest quality on screen?

BW: Not often. I don't know, it's very difficult to say, she seemed to be very, very proper and very accurately cast, Miss Jean Arthur.

I had a stronger version that I dreamt up, and I tried it on Brackett. What I wanted to do was that not only is Captain Pringle in the American army, he also was Jewish. *That* is going to really *cement* it, you know. The American lieutenant with whom Dietrich is having the affair, and is going to marry, is Jewish. "What? She's going to marry a . . . !" That picture I would have loved to make. But then we chickened out. [*Smiles.*] And we just made him American. But the trick was good, it held water. I don't think it was a failure. The failures come later.

CC: I want to make the case for John Lund, who played Captain Pringle, as one of your upper-tier leading men. He had only a few

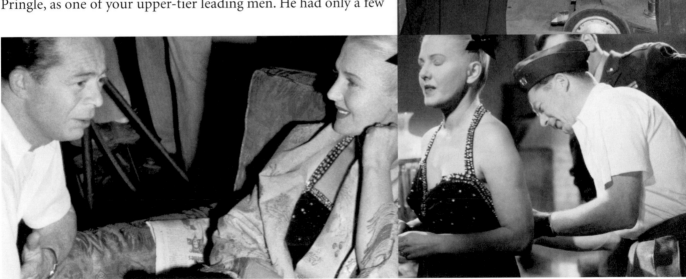

film credits before *Foreign Affair,* yet he gives you a performance that lifts him into the realm of a Lemmon or Matthau or Holden. He has that extra twinkle—he delights in your words.

A Foreign Affair: (opposite above left) One of Marlene Dietrich's great "looks"; (opposite above right) at work on the file-cabinet scene: As the script supervisor looks on, Wilder examines the clutch between John Lund and Jean Arthur. The scene is one of his most dramatically lit, and the movie rested on the romantic tension it would create. "That was a good sequence, right?"; (opposite) directing John Lund; (above) on the set with Jean Arthur

BW: I agree with you. He was a very intelligent man. He spoke in the picture like he spoke in life. He just was on top of the situation . . . except with the audience. I don't know if he was not handsome enough, or what. He just did not work as a popular leading man. He didn't do too much after I was through with him. Somehow, he was not strong in other people's pictures. He was a very, very funny guy. He was not an actor. He was too good to be an actor. He would invent lines, like for instance when he gets a cake—

CC: —from "Dusty," the girl back home.

BW: Yeah. The girl back home gives the cake to the congresswoman to bring to him in Germany. Jean Arthur gives it to him, and he takes immediately the cake and he swaps it to the black market in Berlin for a mattress, because [he and Dietrich] have to fuck on the bare floor. I remember that they were just kind of tossing lines around, we were rehearsing it. He kisses her, a little sexual byplay, and then suddenly he came up with the line "Gently, baby, it's Mother's Day." It was a great line! It was not even Mother's Day.

CC: Pringle had a crackling relationship with Erika von Schlütow [Dietrich] in *Foreign Affair*. Especially when he's saying those lines like—it's great soldier talk, I guess—"Why don't I choke you a little, break you in two, build a fire under you, you blond witch!" You had to be laughing behind the camera, hearing him do this stuff.

BW: [*Still impressed:*] Yeah, sure. And he had the right reading, but it was *not* the right reading. I don't know. I thought he would have used *A Foreign Affair* as a kind of stepping stone, and he would go on from there. But there were so many leading men. If you went to them for Clark Gable, and he was half-

"Gently, baby, it's Mother's Day." One of Wilder's favorite lines from his movies was a rare bit of actor improvisation that he kept and used. The line came from John Lund during rehearsals for a spicy scene with Marlene Dietrich in *A Foreign Affair*. Years later, it popped up as the name of a failed song written by Ray Walston's character in *Kiss Me Stupid*. Berlin (opposite) as it looked during the shooting of *A Foreign Affair*

finished with a picture, then it's, "All right, let's take Spencer Tracy." Everything was there in that big basin of stars, "more stars than there are in heaven." William Powell, Spencer Tracy, Franchot Tone—there were so many leading men that you had to have the best. Spencer Tracy was pretty good there. They had Fredric March, more then in one studio than all together now in Hollywood. We took Lund because he was a newcomer to Paramount and they wanted to launch him.

CC: Would you have rather had Gable for the part?

BW: Yeah, but Gable was not to be had.

CC: There's a powerful introduction of Dietrich in the film. Not unlike the arrival of Marilyn Monroe in *Some Like It Hot,* she enters with a band. Dietrich's brushing her teeth, in the bathroom, swishing the toothpaste. She looks at Lund. The look is everything. And I wondered, was it hard to talk Dietrich into being introduced in a film with her mouth full of toothpaste?

BW: Sure, sure, sure. She would do anything, absolutely anything, that I wanted her to do. Then she brushes, and opens the mouth full of mouthwash. Now, she lets go a little bit. They didn't want me to do that. They just said, "Oh my God, a woman spitting, no." She's not spitting. It's mouth water.

CC: There are some great sidelong glances and looks in *Foreign Affair.* When Lund, for example, is talking to Jean Arthur. He's got this cake from Dusty, and he's pretending like it's his "girl" back home, when he's got fifty girls back home. I've asked you about line readings. Did you ever do *look* readings? When you'd say to an actor, "Give me a look just like *this*"?

BW: Oh, sure. It depends as to what kind of a look I want to give. [*He offers a trademark character look.*] The I Would Like to Fuck You look. [*And now the pièce de résistance: His eyes widen; he looks truly taken aback.*] There's the Astonished look. I just do it automatically. But "the look" is good, because you're cutting to a close-up. And if you're cutting to a look, it has to be a *look.* It has to register.

CC: There's another great look I want to mention. It's also from *Foreign Affair,* and it's the piano player when Dietrich is singing "Black Market."

BW: Yeah. The composer played that, [Frederick] Hollander.

CC: He's got the cigarette; he gives it to Dietrich. She gives him the cigarette back. And the look he gives her at that point, I don't know if you intended this—you probably did—but the look he gives her says, "We've had sex." They've had a relationship; he's the ex-lover from a year ago. But he's still there playing the piano. Happily.

BW: Yeah. I was going for that, I guess. I think so, but—[*He offers a look: Who am I to argue?*]
     That was Frederick Hollander. He was a lyric writer, he was a composer. The best lyrics in Germany. He wrote the entire score, the music, the lyrics for *Blue Angel* [1930]. He was big, then he was. He was playing the piano, and the American soldiers were rushing toward him.

CC: Did the musical numbers go quickly for you, or were they laborious?

BW: Very quickly. Just, they did it two or three times. Maybe part of the song, I knew I would cut away. Look, it was not Maria Callas—but Dietrich sold a song very well.

CC: A bit about the production design in *Foreign Affair.* The detail work is very passionate in this movie. The file-cabinet sequence especially.

BW: Yeah, it's good. [*Pause.*] It was not a big hit, this picture.

CC: Well, that file-cabinet sequence is a killer. And also, the production design in Dietrich's bombed-out apartment was perfect. You're very careful with your close-ups in that file-cabinet sequence. You give Lund that close-up: "During the war we couldn't go fast enough. One day the war was over. Well, everybody can't just stop like that. You crash into a wall, you bash your fender, and you scrape your fine shiny ideals." You gave him the close-up for that, a great speech. Generally, do you know when you're going to give the guy a close-up?

BW: It's very funny that you analyze that picture. Nobody ever talked to me about this picture.

CC: It also seemed a little autobiographical when you write in the context of a speech about German women: "The Germans have to be gracious. They're too poor to not be gracious." What a wonderful line. True, I guess.

BW: Yes, sure.

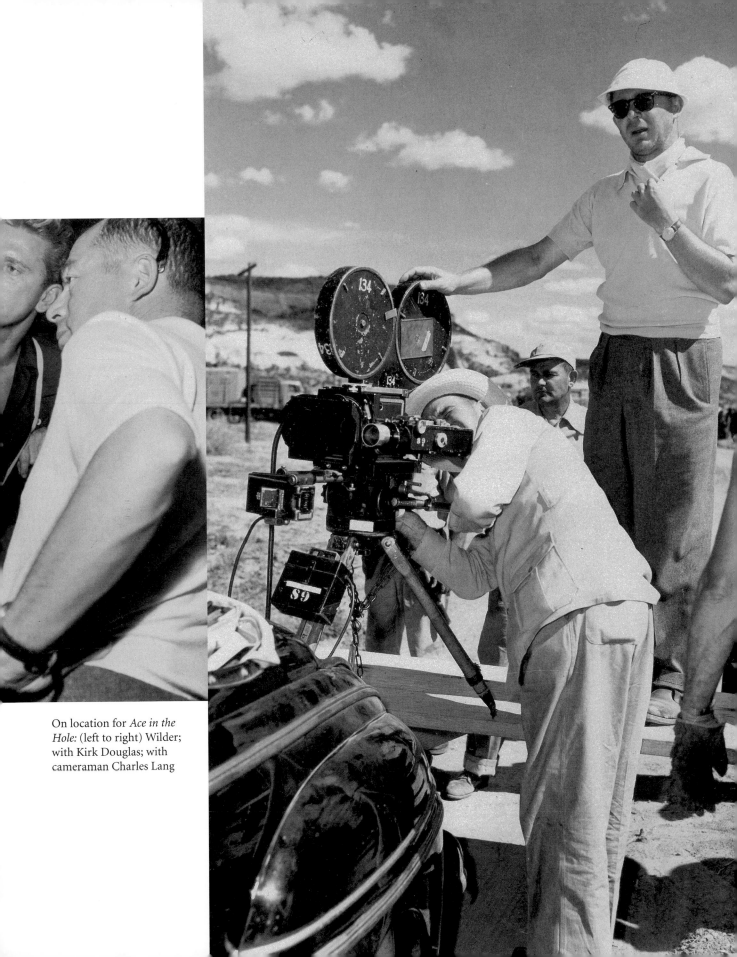

On location for *Ace in the Hole:* (left to right) Wilder; with Kirk Douglas; with cameraman Charles Lang

CC: As a scriptwriter, did you worry about keeping Lund's tough-loverboy character sympathetic?

BW: Yeah, I wanted him to be a grown-up man, with pros and with cons, not goody-goody, and then not a guy who fucks *everybody,* but just a human being. With errors, with faults, with wonderful things.

CC: [*Laughing:*] So he only sleeps with the women he likes. As opposed to just anybody.

BW: Yes.

CC: There's a telling shot in *A Foreign Affair,* right before the "Ioway (That's Where the Tall Corn Grows)" song. The two actresses are finally in the same shot. And it's like two different movies coming together. It's so odd to see them standing in one frame, they're both so different. They're like magnets. You can see sparks flying between them, even in that shot.

BW: It's just the two women, the way they were, coming together, meeting at a certain moment. They don't belong in the same picture, because it's an odd picture to do—about a congresswoman who goes to Berlin. And Berlin is kind of a very dangerous town, with people smoking pot then. But she is of course a congresswoman from Iowa, and it's just not being done, you know. It was a completely different world.

CC: But comparing the close-ups in the film, you did seem to put special care into Dietrich's close shots. Maybe that was her knowledge of the lighting and the camera, but it seems that it would be hard in a way to not fall in love with Dietrich, looking through the lens?

BW: I was not. I do not fuck a star. That's a primary rule of mine. Because I'm so busy with the picture. Because I'm so worried about the picture. If I did have a real yen for that thing . . . then I fuck the stand-in. I go to the Valley, where the stand-in lives.

CC: [*Laughter.*] There is a quote floating around attributed to Dietrich, where she said "Acting with John Lund was like acting with petrified wood."

BW: I didn't hear that. But he was not. He was good, but he was not *great.* He was an intelligent, keen, learned man . . . he did not want to be a leading man, but we sort of pushed him into *that thing.*

CC: People have often wondered which of the Billy Wilder films are most personal to you. I pick this one. *Foreign Affair.*

BW: Yes.

CC: From the opening shots overlooking Berlin—

BW: It was absolute ashes, Berlin. I did that shot from a plane, a long shot. Rubble, rubble, rubble. All rebuilt, and *badly.*

The toothbrush scene in *A Foreign Affair*: "She would do anything, absolutely anything that I wanted her to do . . . She brushes, and opens the mouth full of mouthwash. Now, she lets go a little bit. They didn't want me to do that. They just said, 'Oh my God, a woman spitting, no.' "

CC: *Ace in the Hole* [1951]?

BW: *Ace in the Hole* was a very peculiar thing. I was *very* fond of the picture—I got wonderful, wonderful reactions to it from more serious people. But for some reason or other, people did not want to see that *grim* a picture, that boasted the guy in the hole there, and the reporter, Mr. Kirk Douglas. It was very somber. It was one of my most somber pictures. And they did not believe me that when somebody's a newspaperman, they are *capable* of that behavior.

CC: Very much ahead of its time.

BW: [*Shrugs.*] Yeah.

CC: In this current age of tabloid culture, *Ace in the Hole* has never felt more up-to-the-minute. Is it amusing to you, how this film has held up?

BW: Yeah, that's very funny, I must say. It was a complete failure. It was just . . . I don't know. I just changed my mind about the audience. I just think that if you do something very fine, that they will get to the core of the thing, what it's about, what it's really about. But they never, at the time, they never gave it a chance. Somebody in an editorial, I think, in *Life* magazine said that "Mr. Wilder should be deported." I felt that I was not with it anymore. That I wrote against the audience, the people who paid, in those days, a dollar fifty, two dollars. They felt robbed. They wanted to be entertained, entertained in a serious way, but not *too* serious a way. I don't know. Then again, they did go for *Double Indemnity*. You can

(Opposite) On Dietrich's singing: "It was not Maria Callas—but [she] sold a song very well." (Left) Wilder, Lund, Dietrich, Arthur

never, never, never predict an audience's reaction. You never know how it's going to affect them. But I hear about *Ace in the Hole* quite a bit these days.

CC: It's no surprise that Spike Lee recently wanted to remake it.

BW: He wanted to remake it? Spike Lee came one day to the office. He wanted to have some autographs, he brought some pictures, I said, "To whom?" He said, "To Spike Lee," and I said, "You're Spike Lee?" I did not know him. I never saw a picture of him. But I don't know whether *I* would have gone to see *Ace in the Hole*. And then one day Mr. Y. Frank Freeman, the head of Paramount—and as the joke goes, "Why Frank Freeman?" "A question nobody can answer"—he decided that the title was bad, *Ace in the Hole*. So he gave it a new title, *The Big Carnival*. Idiot. It was an unpleasant picture, I grant you that.

CC: *Ace in the Hole* is one of the few times you didn't help yourself out by casting a sympathetic actor to play a louse. It seems you didn't want to do that on this picture. Kirk Douglas is much more serious than many of your leading men.

BW: Yeah, a little serious, yeah. But that was the story. And my wife gave me the best line in the picture. It's on a Sunday, in that little town in New Mexico where Douglas asks the wife of the man who's down in the hole, Jan Sterling—she was then married to Mr. Paul Douglas—"It's Sunday, aren't you going to church?" [*With a connoisseur's appreciation of the line:*] "I never go to church," she says, "because kneeling bags my nylons." That was Audrey's line.

CC: I remember when I came to visit you with Tom Cruise, and we asked you to act in *Jerry Maguire*. You asked what the story of our movie was. We told you, briefly, and you replied, "How will you make

this man sympathetic?" Was this a question you asked yourself about your own movies, particularly *Ace in the Hole*?

BW: Yeah. I did not make him sympathetic, but I made him, I hope, interesting. I made him kind of riveting, as close to riveting as I could. So that you're just in the laboratory of a potential killer, which he turns out to be. But he does not have to be sympathetic. That was the plan for the film.

CC: Now you say that you usually will go against your own feelings when you direct. If you're feeling angry, you'll do a romantic comedy, and vice-versa. Is it safe to say that you were in a good mood when you made *Ace in the Hole*?

BW: I was in a good mood, yes. I was in a good mood, and I took Aud along with me. We stayed in Gallup, and we had a wonderful, wonderful Mexican restaurant there. We just made the picture, but it was kind of . . . more or less rejected by the audience. [*Pause.*] I thought, It's gonna be an interesting thing if I make him a killer. Not a killer, but he was a newspaperman and an attacking guy, because he had been rejected. Because he lost face in New York. So he wanted to come back with something big, and he made it big.

CC: *The Seven Year Itch* [1955]?

BW: *Seven Year Itch* was just a play. I was angry there, I was on a loan to Fox. I was angry because I was going to New York and I was going to test a man who had promise. I'd seen Marilyn Monroe, but I could

not get Monroe to do a test. So I took an actress who knew that she's not going to play it, but just to help us, Gena Rowlands. Anyway, the guy we tested, I've never seen a guy like this, he was absolutely terrific. I was so excited—and then I came back and they said, "Let's go safe, let's do it the way the play was, and let's take the actor from the play, Tom Ewell." And the guy that I was testing was *Mr. Matthau.* And he would have been tremendous there, because he was brand new, he was never on the screen before. And I was talked out of it by Mr. [Charles] Feldman, the producer who was in on *that thing,* and Mr. [Darryl] Zanuck. Tom Ewell was not right. He wasn't a bad actor. [*Simply:*] He was Tom Ewell. But the wrong casting, the wrong actor. . . . Plus, I didn't have the scene I *wanted.* All I needed was a hairpin . . . second act, third act . . . the maid finds the pin in Tom Ewell's bed. And you know then that they have committed the act.

But I thought, if nothing else, the picture was good for the invention of that girl, The Girl who is always hot, you know. She's got no air conditioning. But she says, "Let me just change my clothes. I've got to run up to my icebox." He says, "You *what?* You—" "Yeah, I keep my underwear in my icebox, why *not?*" It leaves you kind of really astonished, my God. Then they go to see that movie [*Creature from the Black Lagoon*], and then they walk back, and she stands there over the grille, where the cold wind is coming, and her skirt blows up. [*Aside:*] I had guys fighting as to who was going to put the ventilator on, in the shaft there, below the grille.

CC: So you knew at the time that it was going to be a famous sequence.

BW: Yeah, I *did* know, I did know, and it played very well. But then again I was so stupid, because we were looking for a representative ad [for the movie], and it did not occur to me that this thing, where she's kind of trying to keep the dress down, that this is it! They copied it. They made little figurines and sold it. We had some noninteresting ad for the movie. We had all sorts of ideas for the advertisements except that one. [*Pause.*] But it was a play, you know. It was not much, but I don't think it was a failure. People had a good time, it was a success.

CC: Years later, do you think Arthur Miller was out of line to make such a fuss over your treatment of Marilyn Monroe on *Some Like It Hot*? He famously took you on for the so-called "exploiting" of his wife?

BW: He was an idiot. He came to me one day toward the end of *Some Like It Hot*—we were at the Coronado. He takes me aside and he says, "Marilyn is pregnant, so please, don't make her *work* before, let's say, eleven o'clock. Don't have her come up there." I say, "Before eleven o'clock? She's *never* on the set before eleven o'clock! I wish you would be directing it—you would be tearing out your hair, you would slit your own throat, because she's never there!" One day, as I told you, she came at five o'clock in the afternoon because she lost her way to the studio, she said. She was either a maniac or she was very, very soft and gentle, and she plays a three-page dialogue scene on the beach without a fault. "I would be *delighted* if she came after lunch. Every day after lunch? *Please*, I would be delighted to have her."

But there's a very good joke about Marilyn Monroe when she married Arthur Miller. They were engaged then. He said, "I would like you to meet my mother, she would like to see you. So I thought we'd go to her little apartment in the Bronx, we'll have a little dinner, and she'll get to know you." And Marilyn said, "Wonderful, wonderful." So they go there, to that tiny little apartment, with a kind of very flimsy door between the living room and the toilet. They're having a very good time, they get along great, and then Marilyn Monroe says she's got to go to the WC, the toilet. And she goes, and because the walls are thin, she turns on all the faucets so they would not hear it in the next room. Now she comes out, and everything's beautiful, kiss, kiss, kiss. Next day Arthur calls the mother and says, "How did you like her?" And the mother says, "She's sweet, a wonderful, wonderful, wonderful girl, but she pisses like a horse!"

CC: *Irma la Douce* [1963] was a hit movie for you in America. A bright performance from Shirley MacLaine. What's your assessment?

BW: It was a little bit of a period picture, the twenties or so. Again, it was a sort of mezzo-musical. But I missed. It was too broad in certain scenes. It didn't work. There is always something wrong about people not speaking the language of the foreign country where the picture takes place. And you could not stand a Lemmon or a MacLaine speaking English with an accent, either. It's false. It just does not work.

CC: Was it true that MacLaine and Lemmon went to the Paris brothels to do their research?

BW: Yes, sure. I don't know whether they went together, or separately, but they went.

Wilder with his stars on the set of *A Foreign Affair;* Dietrich sings at the Lorelei Club.

Wilder with Brackett, his collaborator on *A Foreign Affair*, talking with Dietrich; (opposite below) filming in Berlin

CC: How about *One Two Three*?

BW: *One Two Three*, I dig. I like. [*Laughs.*] Cagney, very good, wonderful. It was the last thing that he did. He did one scene in *Ragtime* [1981], where he played the police commissioner, but he was sitting there, he couldn't get up anymore.

CC: *Kiss Me Stupid*?

BW: Failure. I have never analyzed why it is not good. I just wish I could take my pictures for previews out of town and then burn them, like they do with the plays.

CC: Did you save the Sellers footage, does that exist anywhere?

BW: There was this one scene in which he played. One scene, with the jealous husband, where he's spying on his wife. He thinks that she is doing it with the milkman. It was at the beginning of the picture.

CC: *The Spirit of St. Louis* [1957]?

BW: *Spirit of St. Louis*, I got into that. I suggested it. But I could not get in a little deeper, into Lindbergh's character. There was a wall there. We were friends, but there were many things I could not talk to him about. It was understood—the picture had to follow the book. The book was *immaculate*. It had to be about the flight only. Not about his family, about the daughter, the Hauptmann thing, what happened after the flight . . . just the flight *itself*. [*Confides:*] I heard a story from newspapermen who were there in Long Island waiting for him to take off. And the newspapermen told me a little episode that happened there, and that would have been enough to make this a real picture.
　　The episode was that Lindbergh was waiting for the clouds to disappear—the rain and the weather had to be perfect before he took off. There was a waitress in a little restaurant there. She was young, and she was very pretty. And they came to her and said, "Look, this young guy there, Lindbergh, sweet, you know, handsome. He is going to—" "Yes, I know, he is going to fly over the water." And they said, "It's going to be a flying coffin, full of gas, and he's not going to make it. But we come to you for the following reason. The guy has never been laid. Would you do us a favor, please. Just knock on the door, because the guy cannot sleep. . . ."
　　So she does it. And then, at the very end of the picture, when there's the parade down Fifth Avenue,

millions of people, and there is that girl standing there in the crowd. She's waving at him. And he doesn't see her. She waves her hand at him, during the ticker-tape parade, the confetti raining down. He never sees her. He's God now. This would be, this alone would be, enough to make the picture. Would have been a good scene. That's right—would have been a good scene. But I could not even *suggest* it to him.

CC: Couldn't you have had your producer bring it up?

BW: No. Absolutely not. They would have withdrawn the book or something. "There you go, Hollywood, *out of here!*" I don't know—very tough guy, very tough guy. I know, because I pulled jokes on him. One day when we were flying to Washington, Charles Lindbergh and I, we were going to the Smithsonian Institution to see the real *Spirit of St. Louis,* which we had duplicated. Hanging off the ceiling, it's there. And we were in a plane flying to Washington, and it's very very rough, so I turned to him and I said, "Charles, wouldn't that be fun if this plane now crashed, can you see the headlines?—LUCKY LINDY IN CRASH WITH JEWISH FRIEND!" And he said, "Oh, no no no, don't talk like this!"

CC: Did you ever think about using that character in another picture? The waitress from the early days?

BW: Sure, that can be used, yeah, but it fit there.

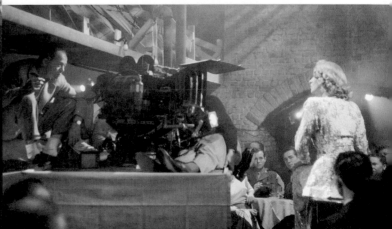

And just that girl, who we'd see again at the very end. And you fade out on that. [*Wistfully:*] That would have made the whole picture. But it was not to be, so now we had to *invent*... because I did not want to have voice-over. I had to invent a fly that finds its way into the cockpit, and Lindbergh, played by James Stewart, talks to the fly. The fly is very good, because when Lindbergh talks to the fly, he says, "Look, you're good luck, because nobody's ever seen a fly crash."

CC: When I saw the film recently, I thought, "This is the old Boyer speech to the cockroach."

BW: That's right. That's right. I just wanted a different bit of business, because we were gonna be in that cockpit for a long time. So he talks to the fly! That's good, you spotted that. I did not think of it at the time.

CC: Did you always see *Spirit of St. Louis* as a big-canvas color film? For most directors it would be a signature film, but for you it's one of the least "Wilderesque" films you've made. Yet it succeeds in a very mainstream-Hollywood way.

BW: I always saw that one in color. It was the only time I ever worked at Warner Bros. Anything to help that picture, but it did not happen.

CC: I'll go through a few more of these fine, fine films.

BW: Yeah, these are the ones that hurt! They gave me an award yesterday, but they did not talk about my bad pictures. You know, I made so many. I think that anybody in show business who bats four hundred is terrific. There's nobody that bats a thousand.

CC: *Love in the Afternoon* we've talked about a little bit. Let's discuss the casting of Gary Cooper. Again, you wanted to have Cary Grant—

BW: Yeah, I wanted to have Cary Grant. I could not get Grant, and then I got Gary Cooper, because he loved to be in Paris. The big hero, and he's a wonderful, wonderful guy. And if you compare the lives of the two people, Cary Grant and Gary Cooper, the guy in the picture was much more Gary Cooper than Grant, because Grant was pretty straight. But I think the picture was a success.

CC: Audrey Hepburn in this movie is operating at such a high level of understanding your words and your film. Rarely has an actress been as in sync with her director as the two of you in *Love in the Afternoon*.

BW: I think it was a good picture, and I think that we lost some of the audiences because they saw superimposed on that lover boy who's got the Gypsies playing while he's doing it to some female twins—superimposed, they saw a sheriff. [*Laughter.*] They could not get away from *High Noon* [1952]—you know, the sheriff with the hat and the guns. Whereas in life, he was the most elegant man that ever lived.

CC: The first time we met, we discussed this picture. You said that you were looking for someone who could play "a real *fucker,* a lover of women."

BW: Oh yes, he was one of those guys. And he learned everything the first time he went to Europe on a boat with the lady . . . she was older than he. What was her name? She was an aristocrat, she was society, Hollywood society. Dorothy di Frasso. The Countess di Frasso. The joke was "Gary Cooper went to Europe on the Countess di Frasso," as if it was the name of the boat. [*Laughter.*] She taught him how to dress, what kind of shirt to wear with what tie . . . he was a very ele-

Irma la Douce (1963): "It was a little bit of a period picture, the twenties or so. It was a sort of mezzo-musical."

gant, a terribly elegant man. Sloppily elegant, on purpose, you know, not like George Hamilton. But he was a goer, and he had that wonderful trick, you know, about how he operated with women. He let them talk. Once in a while he would throw in "Is that so?" or "Oh, I never *thought* of it that way." Just listening to her. They finally found a man who's listening to them. Not a man who's sweating under the arms because he's got to be "on" and he's got to be "successful," so he goes goes goes, and she's listening to *that guy* and she's thinking, "When is that guy gonna run out of breath?" No, Cooper just listened. As for Cary Grant—it's spilt milk. What the hell are we crying about?

CC: Some biographies have mentioned that Grant actually began rehearsals for *Sabrina* before pulling out. Is that true?

BW: Not true. It never went that far.

CC: I just don't understand what held him back from these parts. They wouldn't have been that great of a stretch for him. Was it that he no longer wanted to play the lover?

BW: No, that was one excuse, but what about the other times when we wanted him? Lubitsch, who was then the director, wanted him desperately for *Ninotchka*. I don't know, it was strange, because he was a very, very likable man and he came by the house and we were talking forever, but when it came to committing . . . [*Shrugs.*] But he made a lot of bad pictures too.

CC: Was there any actress you regret never having worked with?

BW: There was an actress married to Clark Gable . . . Carole Lombard. That was an actress I liked very much. I wanted to work with her . . . and I never even met her. Maybe some quick hello or goodbye.

CC: *Avanti!* [1972]?

Filming *The Spirit of St. Louis* (1957): (opposite) Wilder doing his own stunt; (opposite below) Wilder with his Malacca cane and the replica of *The Spirit of St. Louis*; (left) James Stewart as Lindbergh; (below) Charles Lindbergh on the set. "I could not get in a little deeper, into Lindbergh's character. There was a wall there. We were friends, but there were many things I could not talk to him about."

BW: Yeah. [*He cheerfully imitates Italian accent.*] Avanti! Avanti! [*Back down to earth; he likes the title better than the movie.*] *Avanti!* could have been better. It was also from a play by Samuel Taylor, who did *Sabrina Fair*. Very strange case with *Sabrina*. It was a play. It was first made into a movie, with all the changes, radical changes, and the play came out a year *after* the movie and was a complete flop. It did not have the same structure anymore. It just kind of kept the relation—there are two sons of a rich industrialist, and a chauffeur and a daughter.

I was surprised by the remake. I got the script from Sydney Pollack, a talented man and a very nice guy. I wanted to talk to him about it, but they were starting to shoot next Monday. They gave me the script to read—"If you have any ideas," etc. I had one good idea for that thing. That was to make it now, 1996, and the Larrabee fortune and the empire that they built was going down. Now there is a *Japanese* family, very rich, like Sony, or whatever you want . . . they have a daughter and she falls in love with Holden, so if it worked, then they get the Japanese as partners. So now Linus, the older brother, must get Sabrina away from Holden, so that Holden goes for that Japanese girl. And he falls in love with Sabrina himself.

CC: There was an excellent actress, Thandie Newton, who almost got the part as Sabrina. That would have changed things too, because she's black.

BW: For Sabrina? That is a chance. I must say, this is a big chance. No, I don't mind mixing it up, but that is too . . . it needs a little preparatory work.

CC: In *Sabrina*, the opening shot of her in the tree is one of your best character introductions. It's such a perfectly composed close-up, with Audrey Hepburn longing to be a part of the Larrabees' ball . . . it creates a spell that lasts the entire movie.

BW: Yes, yes, sure, because you felt for the girl.

You fell in love with the girl immediately, barefoot as she was. . . . [*Fond memories.*] She was just sort of kibitzing with the father who was washing the car. And she was in love. It reminded you of when *you* were in love. But in the remake, there was a cold fish in that tree. She was not right, she was not *in love.*

CC: Okay, next. *Buddy Buddy* [1981].

BW: *Buddy Buddy,* I try to forget that. Lemmon and Matthau. I don't know. It just misfired. I have this ability to forget that which I don't want to remember.

CC: *The Front Page* [1974].

BW: *The Front Page.* That's when I swore off ever to do a remake anymore. I did it because I felt people had not seen *The Front Page* [1931], the original, which had become kind of a historic hit, a landmark, and everybody thought that—"It's *The Front Page!* Every line is a laugh." It withered there. I had every joke that was in the original one. But the original is not up to people's memory of it. There was another remake: where Hildy Johnson is played by a woman, by Rosalind Russell, that is sort of a reversal of *that thing,* you know, and the chief, the Matthau part, was played by Cary Grant. Howard Hawks did it. It was a good picture—*His Girl Friday* [1940].

CC: Yes.

BW: Now take the dagger out of me.

Stalag 17 (1955): Based on a hit play, the movie starred William Holden and, with two men dancing together in the scene here, touched on the Wilderesque theme of role reversals.

CC: *Mauvaise Graine* [1933] was one of your very first pictures, made in Paris, before you came to America.

BW: *Mauvaise Graine* is a picture which was made in France [with Alexander Esway], a picture I made for $100,000, with lots of automobile chases, because it is about young automobile thieves in Paris. And I had to make all the chases out of a truck, there was no [background projected] transparency to use. No transparency for a chase—that's death. Because for a chase you would like a car to go 130 miles an hour, but I had to do it from the back of a truck, driving around Paris. It was done for no money at all. I was not shooting that picture in a studio, I was shooting that picture in a garage.

CC: *The Major and the Minor* [1942] was your first Hollywood directing job. Had you fallen in love with directing at that point? Were you enjoying the process?

BW: Yeah, I enjoyed it. I enjoyed it. It was a funny picture. The people at Paramount, they thought, "Wilder is a good writer. And we would like to keep him as a writer." And I started kind of complaining about Mitchell Leisen changing this and that, and I had not been able to watch [him filming] because I was already writing the other picture with Brackett. I made no mistakes, you know. I knew they told themselves, "Let Wilder make a small picture, he's gonna fall on his ass, then he's gonna go back to the fourth floor, he's gonna be a writer again." I knew that, so I did a *commercial* picture, as commercial as I've ever been. Just a girl, twenty-six, pretends to be fourteen. It was prematurely *Lolita.*

CC: Did you have a good relationship with Ginger Rogers?

BW: Yeah, wonderful. Yeah. But then later on she blew up like a *balloon,* it was incredible. She was finally in a wheelchair.

CC: *Five Graves to Cairo* [1943].

BW: It was a good picture, I liked it. I had [Erich von] Stroheim, and I had Franchot Tone, whom I could not stand. And I had Anne Baxter, whom I loved. Did you ever see it?

CC: It was your first picture with John Seitz, the cinematographer.

Five Graves to Cairo (1943) (below): "It was a good picture, I liked it. I had Stroheim, and I had Franchot Tone . . . And I had Anne Baxter, whom I loved"; *The Front Page* (1974) (opposite): "That's when I swore off ever to do a remake."

BW: John Seitz. That was the guy that was making black-and-white pictures with Rudolph Valentino. And he could not *stand* to watch actors acting. So when he got it all set up, he had one thing, he would kick one or two legs a little bit out, and sit down. Then he would always wear a hat, and then he would go in the *corner* of the set. I was shooting there, and he was *facing the walls*, and he was scratching his head through his hat. Could not stand actors. You meet those guys, you know. Seitz. And then, I told him when we were doing *Five Graves to Cairo*, I told him I would like to have it *night*, I would like to have it dark. I did not know myself what I was talking about; I wanted it very dark. So we go and see the rushes. All black, *completely* black. I don't know, he wanted to teach me a lesson on that.

CC: *Stalag 17.*

BW: *Stalag 17,* that's one of my favorite pictures. Isn't it nice? It was very

good. It was a commercial hit, on Broadway too, but I think that I improved it 100 percent, if I say so myself. Yeah. The whole character of Sefton—that was the character that Holden played. The idea of making him a braggart—people think a liar, and a phony—then we find out slowly that he is really a *hero*. As he pleads there with that lieutenant at the end, he tucks his head out again, from the hole they have there in the barracks, and says, "If I ever see any of you mugs again, let's just pretend that we don't know each other." And off he goes. And he only does it because the mother of the lieutenant who is captured is a rich woman, and he's gonna get ten thousand dollars. *He's no hero,* he's a black-market dealer—a good character, and wonderfully played by Holden.

CC: I've heard that they were trying to shut you down while you were making *Stalag 17,* because of the politics.

BW: I was called in by the front office, and I had a couple of guys, prisoners, I had them in dirty underwear. It was too dirty for them. They said, "We can't go on with that picture with the men being so dirty running around." I said, "Like hell I will. I will close down the picture, and you can have somebody else do it." And I did it dirty, as it was. The war was over, and what were we afraid of?

CC: But the whole idea, as in *Stalag 17*, of two men dancing together, the role reversals, the masks—these

were all elements that would come to be a part of your style.

BW: Yeah, when I saw the play, I saw the potential. And I wrote it—rewrote it, I should say. It was not one of the nominated pictures, but it hung to me as a medal. You know, maybe not a gold, maybe a silver medal.

CC: You had by this point hit such a confident stride in your directing. Could you safely say that at this point you loved being a director as much as writing?

BW: When I write, I wish I was on the stage and I was with live people I don't have to invent. I can place them better, I can make them cross a little bit more elegant, right? When I'm directing, I wish I was alone with Diamond, in my *room*. It's quiet, nice, nobody's pushing us. It works the other way. When I write, I'd like to direct. When I direct, I'd like to write.

CC: *The Private Life of Sherlock Holmes* [1970].

BW: *Sherlock Holmes* was a wonderful picture, too long. I was going to Paris to shoot a picture there and

I told the editor—I had the final cutting rights—I told him, "I trust you, you know what I would like. Cut this, cut that." And then when I came back, it was an absolute disaster, the way it was cut. The whole prologue was cut, a half-sequence was cut. I had tears in my eyes as I looked at that thing. And then some of the stuff that was cut out, the *negative* disappeared. We cannot find it. Because a lot of people have asked me, they would like to show the whole picture, the way it was. And they could find some reels with just dialogue, sound, and some reels, some tiny little reels, *without* any dialogue. But it was a very, very well-done picture. It was the most elegant picture I've ever shot. I don't shoot elegant pictures. Mr. Vincente Minnelli, *he* shot elegant pictures.

CC: I've read several books on you, and many, many interviews. But I've wondered if there's something they've always missed when they wrote about you. Something so obvious to you, but nobody else caught it. The thing that makes you think, "Why don't they ever notice *this* . . . ?"

BW: No, I believe everything I read, and I turned my character according to the prize-winning jokester who kind of belittles everything. I don't know. That's why I don't like interviews, you know, because I start *thinking* about myself, and I don't *want* to think about myself. Very boring.

CC: But you've worked so consistently for so long, though, do you ever see the guy on the street working in construction and think, "Well, there's a guy who's really lived life, while I've been in—"

BW: —in pictures. You know, when I look back, I've really done a lot of pictures. And now . . . now . . . it's slower now. Now people write on spec, fast, but they should be writing much slower. It will

take you a year to write. And file and get it smooth. But *then* you would write one script after another. I cannot live it again. I wish I could. I would make fewer pictures, and better pictures.

CC: Would you have taken more time off—to travel, for example?

BW: No, I traveled. A little time back, we went every year to Europe. Yeah. I've spent a good life, traveling and working, and sometimes very successfully. And I have here an Academy Award nominee inquiring about me. That's kind of very nice. That's very nice.

CC: Thank you. And, my last question for today. Let's say you and Izzy were doing a script on your life. Do you know how you'd end it?

BW: I don't know. Maybe some doctor would come with a new pill or injection that makes me go on until I'm 120. I don't know. Sometimes I felt, when I was more energetic, I felt like killing myself after a failure. After a waste of time. But not anymore. I'm not well. I have that problem with my balance, and I go to a [physical] therapist. I don't think I could direct anymore. If my legs hold out, I may make another picture, if they give me the money. Which they're not. But at least I could be around and hate somebody else's pictures.

The Seven Year Itch (1955) (above): "I was so stupid because we were looking for a representative ad. And it did not occur to me that this thing, where she's kind of trying to keep the dress down, that this is it! They copied it. They made little figurines and sold it. We had some noninteresting ad for the movie"; (below) scenes from *The Major and the Minor* (1942) with Ginger Rogers and Ray Milland

I turn off my tape recorder. Wilder asks me, "Now what are you going to do with this?" I tell him I'll send him a copy to proofread, as he'd requested.

BW: I'm going to read it, naturally, but I'm not going to make myself an example for other young people to follow.

CC: Well, we've been talking about doing this as a question-and-answer book.

BW: What *book*? The book is going to be like shit, because there's a lot of crap in the book.

I mention to Wilder the story of my fellow directors all citing him at the Directors Guild Awards as an example that his work is still very much in the present day. One nominated director, Joel Coen, was filming and not present, but the other four directors—Anthony Minghella, Scott Hicks, Mike Leigh, and Cameron Crowe—had all mentioned Wilder as an influence.

BW: The fifth is going to be punished.

CC: I'm sure Joel Coen would say the same thing.

BW: That's very nice. That's good enough. Even if I only made one good picture, like Mr. [Orson] Welles, but what a picture.

CC: Thank you for your time. And may I finally note that you've accomplished all this, your entire body of work, without one overly complicated shot.

BW: If it does not follow the story, why? It's phoniness. The phoniness of the director. [*Does a hushed voice:*] The *director,* the *director* . . . wearing a buttonhole here . . . the director is just another guy that helps with the making of the picture. I have a little louder voice, I've got a little more freedom, the choice

is mine, and it's fun. But many people make the movie. It's fun to make pictures because you live, actually you live five, ten, or fifteen, or *twenty* different lives. Because you're moving in different backgrounds. You're not going every day to the shop and selling hats your whole life. No. I have a hat shop, but also I am a brain surgeon, and . . . I've lived many lives. It all depends how interesting the background is. And, of course, the *character.*

[*Wilder quietly places both hands on his desk. It's now late afternoon, and nothing more need be said.*]

Billy Wilder has now read everything up until this point, and I call him one afternoon to discuss the fate of this material. He seems pleased to hear from me. "It is well written," he says. "But who wants to read it?"

Once again, I emphasize that there are several generations of Billy Wilder fans who have yet to read a volume of interviews, his words on his own movies.

"Yeah," he says impatiently. "And now I'm gonna piss ice water on you and tell you that it's of no interest, and it's not gonna sell."

We joust for a few minutes on this subject. The idea of a lengthy time commitment, a series of meetings spent dissecting and discussing the past, strikes him as a taxing and self-reverential commitment. "My blood pressure is high, I don't feel well, I'm still going to the office. I'm trying to pretend everything is okay. Who wants to read all these old stories?"

"For one, I do."

"I respectfully disagree," he says firmly. But he seems to enjoy the battle enough to agree to another interview session. Happily, I continue to avoid my own writing deadlines by further immersion into the films of Wilder. Is there any better excuse for not finishing my own screenplay?

Filming *The Seven Year Itch:* "I had guys fighting as to who was going to put the ventilator on, below the grille."

4

11:00 a.m. We meet again. When I arrive he looks fresh, seems chipper, and, as always, is dressed elegantly. He greets Karen Lerner and me at the door wearing a simple dress shirt with pants anchored by a pair of suspenders. His morning physical-therapy session already behind him, he is energized and ready. He moves back to his desk, arms crooked outward like a gunslinger, his shoes clicking across the floor.

"So what are we going to do now?" he asks briskly, turning his full attention to his visitors. He pops a white TicTac. Our familiarity has increased, almost against his will.

My opening subject is the little-seen Fedora *[1978], Wilder's last great creative effort with I. A. L. Diamond. Wilder's body language changes instantly, as it often does when one of his less-well-received works is mentioned. The transformation takes place in a flash. Gone is his often rascalish nature, now replaced by a manner not unlike that of a schoolchild brought before a headmaster to discuss misconduct. He shifts uncomfortably.*

BW: Oh, that *Fedora* thing. The basic idea of how we were going to do it was kaput the moment we started making tests in Munich. The following thing happened. The actress Marthe Keller—she's not much of an actress, but that's not her fault; or maybe it is—Marthe Keller was to play both parts, the part of the mother and the part of the young girl [the Garboesque actress Fedora]. We started to test the makeup for the old woman, and she started to scream. It turned out that Marthe Keller had been in an automobile accident, and they kind of sewed the wound up in a way so the nerves were exposed, which made it very, very difficult to put that rubber mask on her, which we had to do, to make her old.

Henry Fonda, as the President of the Motion Picture Academy of Arts and Sciences, presents an Oscar to the retired screen goddess Fedora, Marthe Keller, at her villa on a remote Greek island.

cc: You didn't recast at that point?

bw: We were already in Munich, and I'm a company man. I try to protect the [investment in a production]. Which was wrong in this case, and I said, "Well, let's take another actress to play the mother." And that did not work—that did not work at all. I just kind of . . . I wanted to stop the whole thing after we were shooting for a week or so, [but] I couldn't. . . . I mean, I could, but it would have been a loss of income, so I just finished it. It never became a sort of second *Sunset Boulevard.*

cc: Was the ghost of *Sunset Boulevard* hanging over the production?

bw: It was hanging over, and that I think was good. Because we would cash in on something, another Hollywood picture, which was completely different in content. But it just did not work.

cc: The script survives, I think. In many of the great speeches, there's a very clear sense that you and Diamond are making personal statements about what the film business felt like to you at the time, in the late seventies. For instance, when Holden's character says, "The kids with beards are running the studios."

bw: Yeah. You are right. But the lines were not as good, for example, as "I am big, it's the pictures that got small." Above everything else in *Sunset Boulevard* was the *drama* of the oncoming era of sound in pictures. That was the end of Norma Desmond. And it was always there, right in front of them—they saw it coming, that *thing*. Sound. That was the drama. We didn't have anything like that in *Fedora*. Either we didn't hit it in the script, or we did hit it, but it was too weak.

CC: Nudity and swearing crop up in some of the later films, *Fedora* and *Buddy Buddy*. At the time it was almost a betrayal to some people, who missed the days when you were sneaking around the censors. To hear Holden or Matthau say "fuck" in a Wilder film, it's surprising.

BW: Maybe it was wrong; maybe we should not have said it. But that character, I think, would have said it. Izzy and I had long discussions about it.

CC: It's almost a trap, I think, to have done such great work during a period of censorship. People have strong romantic memories about the early work.

BW: If they remember my name.

CC: There's a beautiful moment in *Fedora* when Fedora's mother, who we now know is actually Fedora, changes the music at her own "funeral." The shot lingers on the band in the upper tier as they leave, and then they come back to try another song. You watch it and you think, here is a director who loves music and the comedy of musicians too. This is the same man who brings you the string quartet in *Love in the Afternoon* and also works so delicately with "La Vie en Rose" in *Sabrina*. . . .

BW: Yes. "La Vie en Rose" had been a big hit but I felt there was still a little life left in it so I used it. But it was a period piece, *Sabrina*.

CC: I wanted to ask you about music, though. It plays an important part in many of the films, but you've talked very little about music over the years.

BW: Yeah. Because I cannot whistle, I cannot sing, I cannot play the piano. I am totally unmusical. But I am musical as far as the song or the music for a picture is concerned. In that I am very, very finicky.

CC: Did you spend much time on the scoring stages when your films were being scored?

BW: Yes, always, and then they had to play it for me so I could make sure the music was the right way. Whether it was [Frederick] Hollander, or whether it was [Franz] Waxman, or whether it was Mr. [André] Previn, who has kind of washed his hands of ever having worked in Hollywood. He would have starved to death, but you know, he said in his memoirs or his interviews, he just said he was "seduced" by Hollywood. But that is past tense; he would not talk about that. [*Laughter.*] He was forced; they would have *broken his bones* if he had not done the score to . . . I don't know *how* many pictures he did!

CC: Another aspect of your movies are the great voice-overs, from Holden in *Sunset Boulevard* to Lemmon in *The Apartment*. How much did you direct the voice-overs?

(Opposite) *Fedora* (1979) was the movie that did not become a second *Sunset Boulevard;* (above) Ernst Lubitsch directing Greta Garbo in *Ninotchka* (1939) when Wilder discovered that Garbo "had eyes in the back of her head. She saw me [on the set]. 'Throw that man out!' So they threw me out."

BW: I directed it all. The thing about voice-overs—you have to be very careful there that you don't show what they're already seeing. *Add* to what they're seeing. I think that you can, within seconds, really seconds, you can tell things that are much better to *hear* than to see, because it's an unimportant scene. I made my first voice-over in *Double Indemnity*. I did a voice-over in *Stalag 17*. I did a voice-over in *Sunset Boulevard*, where a dead man was speaking—why not? [*Laughs.*] Why not? We just did it. Nobody got up and said, "Now wait a minute, a dead man speaking, *rum-rum-rum-rah*, I don't want to see that. . . ." They listened.

CC: The voice-over opening of *The Apartment* breaks the rules of screenwriting, but it works. The opening narration is told from Lemmon's point of view, yet the movie is told from an omniscient point of view.

BW: Who wrote the rules? There are no rules. But I kind of think that in every picture, there is something which would take six to twelve pages to explain, and I can do it in six or twelve seconds by having a voice-over. There's nothing to be ashamed of.

CC: No, particularly if you've shot specifically for a voice-over. Like the beginning of *Love in the Afternoon*, where you're giving us a leisurely tour of Paris.

BW: Paris. The people kissing.

CC: Is that Maurice Chevalier doing the opening narration?

BW: No, that was Louis Jourdan. He did it, he had a little French accent, and it was very good. That's

Wilder directing Lemmon (above and opposite) in *The Fortune Cookie* (1966); Wilder on voice-overs: "Good as long as you are not describing what the audience is already seeing"; (opposite right) Audrey Hepburn's voice-over from the tree at the beginning of *Sabrina* (1954)

fine, but later on I just let it go. There's no more narration at the end of *The Apartment,* either.

CC: And the same in *One Two Three.*

BW: Voice-over is good as long as you are not describing what the audience is already seeing. You don't have to tell them what they're already looking at. Show, don't tell.

CC: And in *Sabrina*—

BW: We did it in *Sabrina.* We did it in a lot of things where we could, with one line, cover something that would have cost thousands and thousands to shoot. It is much better to ignite the interest of the audience—for example, with the voice of Sabrina herself—than to stage a whole new sequence. It costs nothing, and

we had little *things* in the voice-overs—like for instance in *Sabrina* too, she introduces the picture. She is in Long Island, and she is the daughter of a lady cook and the chauffeur, and she says, "There was an indoor and outdoor pool, *rum-rum-rum* . . . and we also had a goldfish named George." How are you going to bring George in? You don't want to do a whole scene. Instead she just says it. It's not a joke, not a joke. It just kind of puts people into a fine mood. [*Proudly:*] That was the last line of the beginning of the picture: ". . . a goldfish named George."

CC: In our first conversation you mentioned that you liked Jack Lemmon's quality. How would you describe it?

BW: He was my Everyman. And he could do everything, except carry a love interest to the extreme, to kissing and the precoitus thing. That is very difficult, because people could then laugh. He's very good. It's not a fault. It's his quality. He would surprise me too. He would come to the set in the morning, almost all made up, at 8:30 a.m. on the stage where I'm working. He was figuring out how he would do the scene. He was almost made up and he would say, "Last night, Felicia [Farr, his actress wife, who appeared in *Kiss Me Stupid*] and I were running the lines and a *wonderful* idea came up." Then he tells me the idea and I would go—[*Wilder quickly shakes his head no.*] And he would say, "I don't like it either!" And he left the stage, finished his makeup, played the scene beautifully, and never brought it up again. He did not force it in his voice, and he did not ask everyone to listen to his great idea which was not all that great. Somebody else would fight me and I would have to say, "It's no good, because it leads someplace else. . . ." Not Lemmon. There was a little bit of genius in everything he did.

CC: What were some of the other pictures you wished you'd directed? You mentioned *Battleship Potemkin.* What were some of the others that reached you in a way that you might have wanted to direct them yourself?

BW: I'm thinking back. I would have *rewritten* and then directed. . . . [*Laughter.*] I don't know. Things that I really liked . . . It doesn't mean that the picture was not good—the picture was good, I just wish I would have done it.

CC: You once described your friend William Wyler's *The Best Years of Our Lives* [1946] as "the best-directed film I've ever seen."

BW: *The Best Years of Our Lives.* For sure. It was beautifully directed. I could have done only worse. Much worse. [*Laughs.*]

CC: How about *Ninotchka*?

BW: [*Wilder sniffs at the question, which presumes he might second-guess the work of his mentor Ernst Lubitsch.*] *Ninotchka*, no.

We were just writers—that was at MGM—[and] I was on the stage one day, and Garbo was playing a love scene. So she went up to somebody, an assistant, and she came out and started rehearsing the scene, but in between, they put up a blackboard right in front of me. She had eyes in the back of her head. She saw me there. "Throw that man out!" So they threw me out. And then I met her later at a party at Salka Viertel's, the grandma of the German circuit. She was here in the twenties. I met her there, and now knew Garbo a little. Then one day years later I saw her running, exercising, up Rodeo Drive. Rodeo then had a track in the middle where you could run. So she was running up Rodeo and she was very sweaty, and I stopped her and said, "Hi, how are you? I'm Billy Wilder." And she said [*imitates her smoky accent:*] "Yes, I know you." "Would you like to have a martini, something to drink? I live right around the corner, Beverly Drive." She said, "Yes, I would like to." I lived right around the corner, so I took her home.

It was in the afternoon, and she collapsed in the chair and I said, "I will tell my wife, she is upstairs, to come and fix us a drink." And I said, "Aud, come on down, guess who we have here." She says, "Who, Otto Preminger?"—somebody like that. And I said, "No, Greta Garbo." And she said, "Oh, go on, go *fuck*

yourself!" And I said, "No, honestly." So she came down and I introduced her, and Aud fixes a martini, really strong, big, and [Garbo] had that thing in one gulp, and then another one and another one. They drink them like beer, those Swedish—martinis. She lived on Bedford Drive, the house of [Jean] Negulesco, North Beverly, across the street from the house of [MGM executive] Joe Cohen. And we started to talk about pictures and she said [*does accent*], "I would like to make a picture about a clown." I said, "Oh, that's fine." "I always am a clown, and I am wearing a mask, and I will not take the mask off. I will only be in the picture as a clown." She never made a picture again. She made one more picture after *Ninotchka*, and that was it. So she wanted to play the clown, and not show her face. A clown who grins all the time. I said, "That might be difficult."

She stayed on a while. Then she walked out. I wanted to drive her, but she said, "No no no no no no. I walk a little bit to cool off."

CC: Did you discuss *Ninotchka*?

BW: I mentioned *Ninotchka,* but she did not want to talk about the old pictures. She just said, "I would like to make another picture." That's when my ears perked up. Then she said, "I play a clown. I always play a clown [in life]. I will always be a clown in the picture." I only saw her there that one time, running. And then I saw her arm in arm with Salka Viertel, going down a street in Klosters, Switzerland. She was always there. She was a great friend of Salka Viertel. So that was my only long encounter with Garbo, that was kind of a half hour. "I will play the clown."

CC: You've talked a lot about Lubitsch and what he meant to you. What do you think he thought of you?

BW: What did Lubitsch think of me?

CC: Did he see himself in you?

BW: I don't think so. I did not solicit his opinions on my pictures. He mentioned *Double Indemnity* once, I think—"That was good work."

I was making two pictures at the same time when we met. He was shooting a picture in which he wrote the script, with Sam Raphaelson [a playwright and journalist who was a primary collaborator of Lubitsch's], I think. And he was doing another pic-

Jack Lemmon as the injured Harry Hinkle and Walter Matthau as his lawyer, "Whiplash" Willie Gingrich, in *The Fortune Cookie* ture, something called *Bluebeard's Eighth Wife* [1938]. We had just a short meeting. He never wanted to work with a German, because he did not want to get the reputation that he only works with Germans. Actually he wanted to have Brackett. That was when Brackett and I were paired together to write a picture. And then I stayed on with Brackett. Then we did three, four, five pictures with [producer Arthur] Hornblow.

In that picture, *Bluebeard's Eighth Wife,* Gary Cooper goes down the street in Nice, and what he's looking for is maybe in a shop, a big, big shop like Macy's. In the store window was information written out, FRENCH SPOKEN . . . DUTCH SPOKEN . . . ITALIAN SPOKEN . . . CZECHOSLOVAKIAN SPOKEN . . . and the last one was ENGLISH SPOKEN. The kind of thing you see in Nice. Then underneath that—this was [Lubitsch's] idea—he added one more line: AMERICAN UNDERSTOOD. That was Lubitsch. [*Laughs.*] We had no joke there before. He just added that, and said, "Go ahead and structure the picture, I'm shooting, but I'll give you an hour here and there." And we wrote that picture. Lots of Lubitsch ideas in the picture, lots of Lubitsch suggestions. My contribution was in the beginning.

CC: The pajama-buying sequence.

BW: Yeah, he only wants the top, not the bottom, because although he's a millionaire, he's very stingy. And he asks, "Can I have a pajamas, just the top, not the bottom?" And [the clerk] says, "I don't think so," goes and looks. Finds the head of that department, and he says, "I don't think so." And it goes higher and higher. Now he calls the owner of the store, now you see the head, the guy is sleeping, an elderly man, now he gets up, takes the phone. "He wanted what? . . . Absolutely not! This is crazy. He sleeps only in *this*? He is crazy." Now he hangs up, and the camera is there, and sees him going back without his pajama pants.

CC: Were you able to make Lubitsch laugh?

BW: Sure, we made him laugh, but then he corrected my telling of the joke. [*Laughter.*] Yeah, he laughed himself, and then he corrected.

We did one more picture for him, *Ninotchka,* on a loan, and then he had his heart attack. He had Preminger finish the picture, *That Lady in Ermine* [1948]. Then I moved in with him, because I was going through a divorce, and I just said, "Well, Ernst, would you like me to live with you? It's a period of time when you have to be at home and take medication." And he said, "Sure, certainly." So I just lived with

The so-called "cute meet" is a mainstay in romantic comedy, but few ever manage the sexual sizzle of Cooper and Colbert's meeting over a pair of pajamas in Lubitsch's *Bluebeard's Eighth Wife* (1938).

him for a short while, two or three weeks. I thought he was on the mend. Then he went back to the studio and worked for two more years before he died. He had another heart attack, on a Sunday during one of his sexual adventures. Because we were then shooting six days a week, Saturday also. Then Lubitsch, on a Sunday—you see, he couldn't have had it on a Saturday, because we were shooting—he had a heart attack, a postcoital heart attack, it's known as. He went into the bathroom to wash up or something, and then he died. And the lady in question was whisked out of the house by the chauffeur, Otto, and that was that, as they say. That was the end of Lubitsch, and he was fifty-five years old.

CC: The lore is that Lubitsch died in the arms of a prostitute, is that true?

BW: No. Not in the arms. After they were through. He had finished with that lady, and he had gone into the bathroom. That's when it happened. William Wyler and I were pallbearers, and when we were walking away, I said, "What a shame, no more Lubitsch." And then he said something better. He said, "And worse, no more Lubitsch *pictures.*"

    You know, this was a big loss, because many have tried to imitate or to have gotten something out of Lubitsch—the way jokes should be told, the way big jokes should be told, the way the story of a whole picture should be told. Many have tried and nobody has really succeeded. Lubitsch was never blunt, you know—it was never right *in your face.* It was something, you know, where you add it up and then it carried you. Very, very good. To still have him around would be a very fine thing.

CC: Who else made you laugh?

BW: Chaplin made me laugh. Jackie Gleason. And Steve Martin. He's very good.

CC: What do you think of modern romantic comedies?

BW: I laugh consistently—when I'm able to add up two plus two. They don't make as many comedies anymore because it's too much dialogue. They like to have action. Certain comedies, they still make them quite good. For instance, your stuff is very good. But this is an exception, that one can make a picture like this. I enjoy Robin Williams. . . . *Sleepless in Seattle* [1993] was first-rate. My favorite picture of the last few years is still *Forrest Gump* [1994].

CC: Here's a popular theory about why modern romantic comedy has suffered. In today's culture, with the reduction of class and racial distinctions, there are fewer dramatic barriers to keep couples apart. How do you create tension when there are less obstacles to romance?

BW: People are people. There are always going to be ways to keep people apart. That's . . . that's the beauty of living, which is not easy, as I am now reminded of daily. There will always be ways—it just takes a good sharp writer with a good sharp mind. You make pictures based on truth. You make pictures based on the way you feel. Of course romantic comedy is still alive, if you need to use that term.

Forty or fifty years ago, there was no such thing as a lusty comedy, a subtle comedy, a "black" film. We just did it. Brackett and I, or Diamond and I—we just said, "How would this be for a picture?" We just did the pictures the way they came. The bigger problem is that there are so few leading men now. There's no more Gable, no more Spencer Tracy, Gary Cooper . . . there used to be a *list* of leading men. Now there are only three or four. Who are you going to write for, unless it's Tom Cruise? Who are you going to write for?

CC: In my experience, it has often been difficult to talk a leading man into playing pure romantic comedy. It's hard today to find actors who want to say "I love you" on film. They're afraid of looking foolish. They'd rather have a gun. Was it similar in your day?

BW: It was not that way. (A) We had leading men and leading ladies; we had them by the dozens. (B) We didn't think in terms of "That's a comedy, that's a light picture." It was just a picture, and you made a lot of them. It's very different now, to have something with three thousand car crashes, or actors always looking up at the dinosaur. They're looking *up* all the time, these actors! [*Laughs.*] Explain to me how can you have dialogue with a dinosaur as big as the fifth floor? You can't even get them in the same shot!

CC: But getting back to the global economy, the global culture. Does this all bode poorly for comedy? I mean, there's just not a lot of specific culture to poke fun at.

Jane Wyman and Phillip Terry (opposite) confront Ray Milland in this first serious drama about alcoholism. The liquor industry offered the studio five million dollars to "bury" the film.

BW: Yeah yeah yeah. That's a good question. The popular pictures are a little heavier, a little more masculine. Why do we make a lot of futuristic pictures? Nobody's afraid of Batman anymore! [*Laughs.*] Everybody watches television now. They crave a bigger kind of entertainment. It's almost a sport, to have seen the big picture on the opening weekend: "I have seen it! I have seen it!" But it will all change, of course. The smaller story will come back.

CC: A question about the physical stress of directing. It's a tough job, and the human body seems to react to it in odd ways. A lot of directors I know get strange pains and afflictions during shooting. What about you?

BW: My back was a problem. But I'll tell you, I am a writer, basically. And I had a lot of stuff to learn before I became a director. The first three or four weeks are just very fine. I'm just very happy that I'm on the [sound] stage, that I'm not in a room with a collaborator and I have to write. . . . Then when I'm shooting three or four weeks I get the same idea, that I'm locked in to being a director. Then I think, as millions of questions are being fired at me, and I have to remember this and remember that, and tell the cameraman to make it a little darker, or a little bit lighter, or something like that . . . I remember that I am a writer. I still regard myself as a writer. But then again, Lubitsch is dead, and there are no other people that are my age.

CC: I wanted to ask you about the first time your heart was broken by a girl.

BW: Yes.

CC: I sometimes find, when I'm writing, that it's the girls who said no that you remember most clearly. And those are the ones you draw upon for the heartache. I wondered if you were the same way, if the beautiful melancholy of your romantic films was influenced by the women who denied you, or broke your heart.

BW: Not really. Because it was a different century. To kiss a girl, it was a big, big thing. Now school is coeducational, you go to all your classes with girls, right? But we did not do that; no such thing existed. So there were very few girls. It was very tough; it was very, very difficult. I remember one day I came home, this was in the seventh or eighth class—I was seventeen years old, and one more year and then I graduated. I would then have a diploma that said I could enter university, or technical high school. If you were a doctor or lawyer, if you wanted to become that, you went to the university, and then it became a structure thing, a matter of architecture. Where could you go? And then the joke was that you were fucking, if the word is permitted, standing up in doorways. You would not be seen. And very often, no girls, just fucking the doorways. [*Laughter.*]

CC: So your first kiss must have been a big deal.

BW: Yeah, that was a big deal, yes.

CC: Do you remember it?

BW: No, I don't remember it. I just know I've been in love with girls from the age of ten or twelve, but no touch. Then a little touch. Then I started to stand on my own legs and become a newspaperman. Then it was easy. It was easy because I was younger than they were. The girls were twenty-two, twenty-three, twenty-four; I was eighteen, nineteen. Then the whole thing became very popular suddenly, when I was thirty—[sex] became popular.

But girls broke my heart. There was one, she was ten and I was twelve, but nothing funny happened, just something very sad . . . she moved to another town. Those

Paramount was not enthusiastic about making *The Lost Weekend* (1945): "How can you make a picture about a drunk man who does not suddenly awake one day and say, 'I will not drink anymore.' "

were the big tragedies, you know? She moved away, to someplace else in Germany. That's the best I can remember.

CC: What was her name?

BW: Schreiber. Irka Schreiber. I-R-K-A.

CC: So this was a true love?

BW: It was a true love, just a children's love. We just played games in the park, saw each other. I couldn't wait to see her. That was very, very, very childish. We played diabolo, that's a game you play with two sticks and string. [*Demonstrates.*] This is called diabolo.

CC: When you first started going out with women and having girlfriends, do you remember what your approach was? Were you the kind of guy who would make them laugh, or would you be mysterious?

BW: No, I could never feign *mysterious*. No, I made them laugh, made them have a good time. As a young man, as a student, it was all pretty normal, and I did not know that I was funny. Just had no idea that I was funny. But I was, so they tell me.

CC: Did you ever fall in love with one of your leading ladies?

BW: Never. Never, never. I always flirted with the stand-in. That was as good [as] or better than the leading lady, because the leading lady would have to have her hair all straightened out later. You would lose time on the picture stage, waiting for that hair. [*Laughs.*] But I must say that when I'm directing, I haven't got time for it. You're suffering with or laughing at whatever you're shooting. But an actor or actress, she's got hours of time, nothing else to do.

A director is tied to the fate of the picture. Once the picture's finished, and the cuts are finished, then I give myself a little more to frivolity.

CC: And yet there was a real passion about the *look* of your leading ladies that could have only come from you. One of the great examples is Audrey Hepburn in *Sabrina.* Not many issues of *Vogue* go by without a photo of [Hepburn as] Sabrina as an example of classic, simple elegance. How much did Edith Head [celebrated, bespectacled, austere-looking head of Paramount costume design] have to do with the look?

BW: Very little, I must say. She was a good girl. [*Smiles.*] I mean, a good elderly lady. She did not take many bows. She got the Academy Award, I guess, for *Sabrina,* and for [seven] other pictures. The credit read "Costumes by Edith Head." But the dress that Hepburn wore, the five or six outfits, they were all Givenchy. Whatever they said, that was okay with me. Except once, there was too much material on something . . . but that is forgotten. The big joke was . . . something very vulgar again. Written on the wall of the studio toilet in big letters there was a line: EDITH HEAD GIVES GREAT WARDROBE.

CC: Can screen chemistry be "created"?

BW: No. Chemistry only comes naturally. It cannot be manufactured. Like Tony Curtis and Jack Lemmon, for instance. I knew it was there. You put them together, and there it is. They were like brothers.

CC: Like Lemmon and Matthau.

BW: Exactly. Matthau was an up-and-comer in New York. He was already an established theatrical performer. I took him to Hollywood, and he became a mainstay. You just know with those two, they would be funny together. They're comedians.

CC: *The Fortune Cookie* [1966], their first film together, is a movie we haven't talked about much. Again, it's Lemmon in a small room—

BW: Yeah.

CC: —and it seems to me that Lemmon in a small space is so much funnier than Lemmon in a big outdoor shot. He's best in small rooms, a caged guy. And this is the ultimate Lemmon-in-a-room part.

BW: It's just automatic with him, you know. *The Fortune Cookie* is the one where he's in a wheelchair, right?

CC: Yes, with the football player who has supposedly injured him.

BW: Yeah, the football player. I don't know, it's just what happens. I am not arty. I never make a setup that is obviously wrong. I never shoot through the flames of the fireplace in the foreground, because that is from the point of Santa Claus. That's not my racket. Just, what are the people doing to each other, how can I just make them believe that those are real walls? That this apartment really exists?

CC: Was *The Fortune Cookie* a victory for you?

BW: [*Simply:*] No, it was the beginning of my downfall.

CC: That's surprising to hear you say. It's a well-thought-of film.

I watch as Wilder shifts, his shoulders hunching slightly. He tries to outrun the memory of a supposed failure, but it catches him. The misfires are physically disappointing to him still.

BW: I don't know. [*Shrugs.*] It's not a memorable picture. It's a picture you did because you are under contract. It just sort of was *there*. I don't know, maybe I became lazy, maybe I became stupid or something. Sad, but I'm functioning with that black thing, that mood, which is another thing which makes me not want to direct anymore.

Such are the mood swings of a director. A failed project can bring out a poignant darkness, even in Wilder, years later. Only moments ago we were floating on the weightless memories of Sabrina.

CC: You said earlier you were a company man—

BW: I'm a company man in the sense of not wanting to have a cost of a million dollars swept under the carpet and *forget about it*. I am just too proud for that. In this direction I am a company man, but also in another direction . . . I and many others like me, my age. . . . Mankiewicz is dead now, but he was like this. But his pictures were first-class until he became . . . until he started off with *Cleopatra* [1963]. Then it . . . then he just didn't do anything. He got worse, but he could not prove himself, because he did not direct much again. I just kind of think that directing can be a lot of fun until you are sixty-five or seventy, so let that be a lesson to you. How old are you?

CC: Thirty-nine. I've got to get more prolific.

Billy Wilder and Charles Brackett flanking Charles Jackson, author of *The Lost Weekend*

BW: Thirty-nine? That's older than I thought. That's good. The older they get, the better I like them.

KL: You were always affiliated with the studio, yet you're such an independent spirit. It's hard to reconcile those two things.

BW: They knew that when they signed me to a contract. They knew it at United Artists. They knew it at Paramount. But as a rule, those deals don't exist anymore. There's nobody in the studio now who's writing there. We had 104 writers at Paramount under contract. The writers would always say, "I have seven years, that's great!" Seven years nothing. They've got *one* year, and the studio has an option for another six years. But they knew they were going to have an independent man there, and they went for it. They had the right to tell me, "This is a thing which we don't like, which we don't want to make into a picture." And then I would keep it and remember it and use it later. Producers don't always dictate what's in the picture. But I got along with them, and when I became a producer myself, then I had nobody above me, except the studio itself.

What they could say, for instance, was, "We read the book, and we don't want to do *The Lost Weekend*, we don't like it. How can you make a picture about a drunk man who does not suddenly awake one day and say, 'I will not drink anymore'?" He never says that, by the way, in the picture. He just says, "I'll

try. I'll try to stay away." But then when it came to casting, they said they will only give me the money to make the picture if I take an attractive man. I wanted to have José Ferrer to play the drunken guy. But then I compromised and I took Mr. Ray Milland.

CC: When I asked you about your mother earlier, all you said was, "She was different."

BW: My mother died in the concentration camp, as did my stepfather, whom I never knew, as did my grandmother. They all died in Auschwitz, as I found out. She had lived in America for a short while before I was born, with an uncle of mine, when she was a very young girl. She spoke very little English. She was funny, but it was very difficult to make her laugh. She was a very tough laugh. I mean, she got the joke, but . . . I don't know. [*He shrugs off the memory.*] I left my parents when I was eighteen years old, when I made the *Matura,* which is the exit exam, finishing high school. My father died in Berlin in 1928, and she was alone in Vienna. She got married again. I never met the husband before the war.

CC: She liked America, though, didn't she?

BW: She liked it very much. That's why my brother came here; he left high school in the third class. There are eight years of high school and four years in grammar school. My father was in America too, visiting my brother, who came here when he was fourteen years old. He came first to London; then from London he went to New York. Never finished the high school—a shame, right? [*Laughs.*] He's dead. [My brother] has been dead now for about ten years. It all goes so fast, you know—suddenly you are in your seventies, eighties, nineties, you know. It's a fast bridge you have to fill.

The phone rings. He answers, and his voice dances a little. It is Wilder's wife, Audrey, calling about his lunch appointment being canceled. He hangs up after a brief exchange.

BW: Would you like to have lunch with me?

Wilder hangs up and rises for lunch. Grabbing his cane, which is perched against the wall, he heads for the door at a fast clip. I pack the tape recorder and hurry to keep up. Wilder shuts the office door behind us, avoiding the elevator always, and we walk down two short flights of steps. He moves meticulously but deliberately. We walk to the Beverly Hills restaurant Prego, just around the corner. He moves jauntily through the flashy street traffic, picking up speed.

I ask Wilder about his great art auction in 1989. His paintings netted $32.6 million, a surprise for a man who collected only according to his own tastes. The auction brought him the fortune he never made in pictures.

CC: Have you kept track of the paintings you sold? What's happened to them?

BW: [*With a noticeable bounce in his step:*] I saw one Picasso which was recently estimated at much lower, about a million lower, than I sold it.

He is recognized. A tall gentleman in a nice suit, with an unmistakable power tie, reminds Wilder of a business discussion they once had. His cool manner cannot hide the thrill he has in chatting with the master. But the master is hungry, and Wilder doesn't dig in for much small talk. He shakes the man's hand and moves on without introducing us.

BW: I never introduce anybody to an agent.

We arrive at the restaurant, and all the tables are taken. We wait for seven minutes, during which Wilder begins singing softly, standing near the hostess's desk. We are seated. Wilder is interested in bread, which he will soon dunk in a mixture of balsamic vinegar and oil. He orders a glass of white wine. His back to the bus-

James Cagney as MacNamara, Arlene Francis as Phyllis MacNamara, and Christina Allen as Cindy MacNamara (opposite) in *One Two Three* (1961). Wilder was not interested in writing for children—in most of his movies they are more like props. Wilder's response to not being interested in "kid characters": "Dogs I could do, but kids . . . I don't know."

tle and chaos of the popular noontime restaurant, he asks me about my own projects and offers me his good ear.

CC: I want to be as productive as you were between '57 and '60. Bang-bang-bang-*bang!* Four movies in three years.

BW: Yeah, if I had the strength to do it again, I would. I just don't. Don't be stubborn. Well, you know, you have to be stubborn about one thing, you have to have the script first. You have to be stubborn about that.

CC: I have a few more true-or-false questions. Let's dispel some more rumors. True or false: Did you write part of *Casino Royale* [1967]?

BW: I just gave some ideas, but I never wrote anything. Yeah, there were five or six James Bonds, I don't know. I never suggested that. I was kibitzing on that. But the final version of the picture, with the five or six different James Bonds, that was not my idea. That was the idea of the writer who finally did it. Yeah, not good.

CC: "Children almost never appear in Wilder's movies because Wilder does not like children."

BW: [*Wilder awards this question with a long silent beat as he enjoys his lunch.*] I got my divorce after seven years. I've been married now almost fifty years. We had no children; I've never had children around me. I had a child from my first marriage, and she went with Mama. [*A male twin of the girl died in infancy.*]

CC: So there was nothing to observe.

BW: No, nothing. My only child, she's a grandmother now.

CC: Here's more proof of the "Wilder doesn't write children" theory, in *One Two Three.* Once again, it's "Little Tommy." Cagney's child is like a prop. So are the kids in *The Apartment,* when you see them around the Christmas tree in the background of Sheldrake's home—

BW: [*Slightly annoyed:*] Yeah.

CC: What is your answer to people who say, "Wilder just isn't interested in these kid characters"?

BW: Yeah, I'm not very good at it. I like children, I like them fine. I think it's wonderful, but it's not my whole life. [*Comic pause.*] The little buggers. [*Laughs.*]

CC: Dogs, however, are a different matter. Particularly the dog in *Love in the Afternoon,* who gets swatted with a vengeance.

BW: Dogs I could do. But kids, you know . . . I don't know. [*Pause.*] I just don't hit it off well with them. They always go around with me. I never . . . I had a few friends that had children that I liked. But they make me nervous.

CC: Even your own great-grandchildren?

BW: They're living in Reno, Nevada, and they come here for Christmas. And I know exactly that around the eleventh or the twelfth of December, there's gonna be little postcards from them, from the kids. "Sit down and write that thing, because you're not gonna get anything otherwise. Sit down! Sit down!" They're getting a little older now. Pretty soon they're gonna catch me. [*Wilder demonstrates the proper method of mixing balsamic vinegar with olive oil and dips bread.*]

CC: Did you like Jean Renoir's work?

BW: I didn't see enough of it, but some of it was great.

CC: You saw *The Rules of the Game* [1939]?

BW: *The Rules of the Game* and another one, *Charleston Parade* [1927]. World War I, wasn't that *The Rules of the Game*? Yeah. Very fine director. But somehow, you know, with the French dialogue, I wanted to understand it more. I promised myself, when I was in France, I would see the picture in French. [*Shrugs.*] But I like so many directors, like for instance [Luis] Buñuel. He was not French, but he made [his career] in France. The thing is, you know, that comedies are not taken seriously. Very rarely do they win an award. They're dismissed as something very trivial. Whereas other pictures win just because they're serious.

CC: And even the great directors of comedies generally lust after the opportunity to do more "serious" pictures. It's odd how the stereotype perpetuates itself. They don't even take their own great comedies seriously.

BW: No, but you see, the best picture that Capra ever did was *It Happened One Night* [1934]. [*Pause.*] He couldn't help himself. [*Laughter.*] It's the only time that Gable got the [Academy] Award, a rare thing. When he was in *Gone With the Wind* [1939], everybody got the award except Gable. [Robert] Donat got it for *Goodbye Mr. Chips.*

Suddenly Wilder regards the unwelcome guest at our lunch—my tape recorder. Do I have enough for my "column"? I again express the desire to publish a longer record of our interview. He engages briefly and sharply on the subject—no—and then pleasantly abandons the debate in the interest of lunch. My time with him is nearly over.

CC: It's interesting, the lack of good manners between most directors. Every once in a while you get a note from one of your peers, but I've mostly found that there isn't that fraternity of directors who call one another and discuss one another's films. I imagine it being a little more convivial in the forties and fifties.

BW: Yeah, that's true.

CC: When you saw a movie like *La Dolce Vita* [1960], did you call Fellini? Send him a note?

BW: I sent him a note, yes.

CC: What kind of note does Billy Wilder send to Federico Fellini?

BW: An enthusiastic one. But I knew Fellini, and I adored him, and he lost his way in some very fancy ways. It's just impossible now to make a picture in Italy, except a small comedy, you know, which is a local success. Yes, they have local pictures, but not big ones. And they are *meant* to be local pictures. And once in a while, you discover an *Il Postino* [Michael Radford, 1994]. But Fellini—he died too soon. That is a sad, sad thing. I loved *The Nights of Cabiria* [1957] and *La Dolce Vita*. Those were the only two that made sense to me. The weary journalist played by Mastroianni, that was a wonderful character. Every sequence in the picture was someone's fantasy. That was the structure, and that's why it worked.

CC: I've noticed in talking with you that you are very gracious about those you've worked with. Every once in a while, a little something, but always said with respect. I wondered if you're more comfortable keeping the secrets you knew about some of these legends.

BW: I don't know that many legends. Because I'm not a follower, you know, of "reputation." Of big stars. I never have too many friends who are in the picture business. I have a much better time with my dentist, for instance. I ask him about the real life, and he asks me about pictures.

CC: [*Laughs.*] That's great. Directing actors, were you often fooled by takes you thought were good and

"Here we are rehearsing in the Wall Street building in New York City. Just adjusting rhythms. Lemmon has not yet put on his overcoat, which he must wear in the picture because he has a cold. All that sniffling, it made you like him." Shirley MacLaine wears Audrey Wilder's coat.

turned out not to be? Or could you generally trust your gut instincts on the performances you printed on the day of filming?

BW: I trusted my gut. Usually the take you pick is the good one. [*Pause.*] Do you know what they did one day to Mr. Cukor, who was a very fine director, oldtime MGM? He always printed all the takes of a close-up, for instance. He took twelve takes of a close-up of Garbo, and he would print the first eight—now he had a choice. Now they played a gag on him: they printed one take eight times. And he sat there, watching take after take. After he saw all eight, he says, "I think number *three* is the best." Then the other guy, the cutter, says, "I like number *seven.*" "Okay, let's run it *again and again.*" Then they told him, that they'd printed one take, eight times. [*Laughs.*] Eight times.

Now, I think that with certain people you have more takes than with other people. With certain people, you have to print the first take because it's the best. It's got more life than any other. And with some people, you print [number] *two.* The best is very often number one. So you print number one and number seven. Then you take number one. It depends on the quality of the human being. If you rush something, and they put everything into take one, then take two, ten, or twelve is always a little weak. Every so often, there might be a little flub, or something like that. Print number one.

CC: And generally, the take that felt the best to you on the day of filming was the one.

BW: Absolutely. That's correct. And even though the other take is a little smoother, a little less of a misstep from the camera guys who are helping you . . . number one is usually the best.

CC: I haven't quite figured out how you were able to edit all those movies while still filming them in such quick succession.

BW: Quickly. That's the only way to cut them. There is no other way. *The Apartment* was done in a week.

CC: Were you editing as you went along? Would you go in and look at cuts at the end of the day?

BW: Yeah—what is missing, what are not necessary, what can be redone. Yeah, I go in every day, sometimes every second day, and look at the rushes. I look at the cut footage once a week. Just give them an idea as to how I wanted it. Sometimes I come back, make an additional chop, and that's it. Maybe if the set is not destroyed, I get an extra shot. But most of the time, I edit and I shoot very, very fast. Unless I have a stumbling actor who says to me, "It's only the first take! Please don't print it!" And I say, "I never print number one." And then I do.

CC: Didn't you do multiple takes with each actor, varying the emotion?

BW: Yeah, sure. But how many do you need? I was just a writing director—a writer who was also directing. Maybe we would try it another way; maybe we would omit something altogether. But there was only a small pile of celluloid left when we were through with the picture.

CC: And that was always the case, from the beginning?

BW: From the beginning. I often had the editor on the set with me. Doane Harrison was his name. [He

later became Wilder's associate producer.] He was a great help with the shooting, not the script. He would help me with unnecessary shots, or [to] get *this* shot.

CC: In one of the books, it's written that Doane was around to "give you heart."

BW: Give me heart? [*Surprised.*] No, I don't think so. He showed me in the beginning, the first pictures, where I should put the camera. Where it would go and where I'm gonna cut. And that was very, very good. But he did not mix in script things.

CC: Do you think it's good for a director to have his editor on set?

BW: Very good, yeah. From the beginning I was a very quick shooter. I was making pictures in forty-five, fifty days. *Sunset Boulevard*, maybe sixty days. But I did not pull much [many scenes] out of the movies. Nor did I cut scenes out as I shot. I took the beginning of *Sunset Boulevard* out, and the end of *Double Indemnity*. Very rarely. So those were the two major operations that I did.

CC: So the scripts were tight.

BW: Very tight. Always. Never setups, the positions of the characters, only when it was necessary. I am

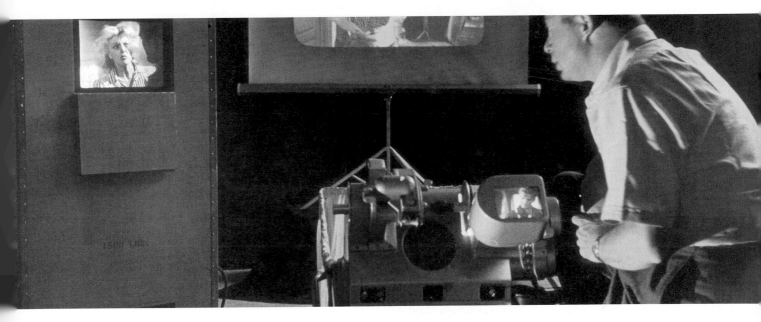

aware where they are, but I just don't *sit on it* in the script. I just touched it as lightly as possible.

CC: Did you know all your shots at the beginning of the day? Did you come prepared, or did you decide on the day?

BW: More or less. But always I sit down and I say, "All right, this scene." We read it once, and I say, "Okay, let's play this scene." The actors play the scene until they feel comfortable. And I just say, "Well, how would it be if you did not walk there, if you stayed here, and then the other character comes in . . . ?"— this and that. And then we say where the camera is going to be, and then that's it.

CC: Is a lot of the directing done in your head, as you write it?

(Opposite) Wilder looked at rushes every day or every two days and looked at cut footage once a week.
(Above) On how to edit: "Quickly. That's the only way to cut them. *The Apartment* was done in a week."

Wilder on Arthur and Dietrich: "She was alone there. You see Marlene wants to engage her in some kind of dialogue. She was a real kibitzer, you know. When an electrician had a sneeze, she would run out, barefoot in the rain, climb up the steps, and bring some aspirin. She was a great great doctor, that's what she was." (Opposite) The cockpit scene from *The Spirit of St. Louis* (1957) where Jimmy Stewart falls asleep and the plane goes into a tailspin

BW: Yeah, if I write it. I'm never stuck because I have an empty exit of a character who comes to talk to somebody sitting at the desk, and he leaves. I always have enough dialogue to cover an exit. Not a lot of dead air. There are no long explanations [in my scripts]. I just have a scene—scene 73, the scene plays in somebody's house. That's it. The last thing I do is divide it then into shots, into camera moves. The last thing I do is to figure out, where do I put the camera? First you have to have it on paper.

CC: How did you feel about adding moments of visual poetry, or putting more lyrical elements in?

BW: I was very serious about it. That's the way it had to be, that's the way it was. The words must come to life.

CC: Because there are moments, even though the scripts were all tight, there are still the moments where you let the movie breathe a little bit. Where you see the long shot of Lemmon standing outside the theater waiting for Shirley MacLaine to show up for the movie date in *The Apartment*.

BW: Yes, of course. Even that moment told part of the story—that she was not there, she didn't show up, she was with her boss. A little poetry. There must have been a reaction from Lemmon, that she didn't show up, so he was alone. Naturally that was a little bit of a heartbreak, like a normal human being would feel.

Through thick glasses, Wilder now fixes me with a curious stare. He looks down at the microphone sitting innocently near his water glass, and then back at me. We have logged a number of hours on tape, far more time than he had intended. Most of his modern biographers are routinely dismissed without as much as a returned phone call. Somehow I have traveled into no-man's land, and we both know it. "What are you going to do with all this," he asks pointedly, "now that you have it?"

Once again, Karen Lerner argues the case for this book. Wilder tolerates more than listens. A silence arrives, and I find myself blurting out the story of my own interest in him. As a beginning director in the late eighties, I had developed a powerful affinity with his work. It's an old story, of course—one writer discovers the impact of another—but Wilder's love of character and comedy arrived just in time, providing me with a map of how to proceed in the very risky world of making films. Who was this man who kept his personal writing voice so pure, and often so subversive, even in the mainstream? I wanted to know more about him, anything I could find. It wasn't easy, and it still isn't. None of the books written on Wilder were then in print. And now that we had begun these interviews, it was even clearer what was missing from bookshelves: a record of Wilder's own perspective, straight up and unfiltered.

Wilder listens to all this, blinking a little, showing no emotion. But when I put it most simply, that I selfishly want to create the book I want to read, this he understands. I know this because he nods—silently.

"Well, the fact that you're doing it makes it better," he allows, "because it's a pro, you know, who's doing it."

A breakthrough, but not without conditions. Should we continue, he says, his interviewer must log the proper time to be thorough. Many hours would be spent, hours that might take me away from my own career. And there is one important ground rule. If we are to proceed, Wilder stipulates, he wants the opportunity to readdress any subjects on which I feel he had not been clear enough. Assured of my commitment, Wilder agrees to the project. And immediately, he pitches a joke for inclusion.

BW: By the way, a crack that I once made about Marlene Dietrich. She was always looking for sick people. When she once heard an electrician, up above, sneezing . . . she would run out, barefoot in the rain, to get some medication for him. So that was her, all her life. She was a great, great doctor. That's what she was. When they were sick, she was there. She searched for sick people. When you were well, she abandoned you. [*Laughs.*] That's why I called her "Mother Teresa with better legs."

CC: There is a moment in *Fedora,* where we see Fedora, the young star, making a movie in Hollywood. She sweeps from the stage, surrounded by her entourage. A personally authentic shot, it seemed, and I wondered if that was the atmosphere around Dietrich or Monroe.

BW: Sometimes. Yes. But we must think of the finished product and forgive Marilyn for everything, you know. Since it was only once or twice in my life, you know. I said never again; but, you know, the moment where it's "Would you like to take Miss Babaloo Babalow for the part?"—that's the moment when you think, "Consider everything," and then you say, "No, I would like to have Marilyn Monroe." That's what you're up against. Even if you wait three days to get your shot. "I would like Miss Monroe." Are we finished?

CC: Yes.

BW: From here on in, it's going to be a question a day. Or "Would you phrase it better?" Or "You did not tell me this." Then we sit down, and we go over it again. That is how we should proceed. Now. With your new script, do you have your first act? Are all your problems solved?

CC: I'm still writing. There's one story problem.

BW: [*Nods.*] There's always one big problem. You work on it, you work it, you don't solve it. You think about abandoning the script. Then . . . then you *solve* it and suddenly the script is finished. It always comes down to the one big problem that you happily conquer. With *The Apartment,* I thought there had to be another woman with whom Sheldrake had an affair, and that is the telephone girl. Then one day she calls the wife . . . and we never see the wife. That was something we needed to sort out.

CC: Why didn't you show the wife?

BW: Because you don't need it. You need only the action, not the *reaction.* That you know very well. [*He reaches for his cane, and we exit. We discuss meeting again for dinner.*]

The problem appears to be my punctuality. I arrive only a few minutes late for dinner with the Wilders, at one of their favorite spots, Mr. Chow in Beverly Hills. I quickly find that they've long been seated. The Wilders like to arrive early. I join Wilder, Audrey, and Karen Lerner. Wilder has kept the seat to the right of his good ear open for me. I casually apologize for my essentially on-time, particularly for me, lateness. He regards me with a distant peevishness. Moving on, I compliment him on yesterday's interview.

"Thank you," Wilder says crisply, adjusting the container of hot sake sitting before him. "I was hoping to be rid of you by Friday."

The sting of his wit notwithstanding, dinner is a hoot. Audrey and Billy have forgotten to wear their hearing aids. Everything happens loudly, and much of the dialogue between this famously close and long-time-married couple occurs two or three times over, at various volumes.

On working with Izzy Diamond: "Sometimes we threw away eight pages or ten pages at one time. . . . Sometimes we'd write nothing in a week 'cause we were stuck."

Midway through dinner, the talk turns to Marilyn Monroe. The Wilders subscribe to no conspiracy theory regarding her death, nor do they particularly believe it to be a strict suicide. Monroe was not alone in her chemical consumption, says Audrey. Champagne and pills were a staple of many a Hollywood femme fatale's diet. "You drink, and you forget the mix." There were those who dabbled at least as much as Marilyn—there was a doctor who freely doled out pills to many of them—but it was Monroe who became the poster girl for such behavior. Wilder and Marilyn battled rather famously, sometimes splashily, even in the press, but there was always a back channel line of communication that reinforced Monroe's stated belief that Wilder was the director who best knew how to present her on the big screen. I was starting to see a key pattern in Wilder's Hollywood life. The diplomatic channel, in this matter and so many others, was always Audrey Wilder.

"I will tell you my best Marilyn Monroe story," Audrey offers in mid-meal. "We always could talk, even when she was mad at Billy, or when they were fighting. Once she called from a party in New York and we had a nice talk. Billy was never mentioned. Then, at the end of the call, she said to me"—here Audrey imitates a perfectly proper Marilyn—" 'Oh, and could you also tell Billy to go fuck himself?' " Audrey Wilder laughs. It's an infectious, wide-open, and mostly soundless laugh. Billy grins at his lively and lovely wife. Memories. And at the end of this dinner, Wilder still wishes me to know he is dubious of the entire idea. The myth of Sisyphus is on my mind as he sets another interview session for seven days later.

10:00 a.m. Wilshire Boulevard. The twelfth-floor apartment home of the Wilders. The night before today's interview I've had a conversation with Steven Spielberg about the work of Billy Wilder. Spielberg spoke eloquently about several aspects of Wilder's career, mentioning particularly a scene from The Spirit of St. Louis. *From memory, Spielberg recites every shot from the sequence when James Stewart falls asleep at the cockpit. The light reflected from a mirror above the dashboard spirals around the cockpit until it crosses Stewart's eyes and wakes him up. The random miracle saves the flight and Lindbergh's life. At the last moment, Stewart is able to correct the tailspin. Recounting this scene, rooted in which is the very magic of Spielberg's own films, the director now begins humming Franz Waxman's lush and personal score for the film, noting even Waxman's incorporation of Irish elements as Lindbergh flies over Ireland. It is a moving quotation of Wilder's work from this generation's most successful filmmaker, and I am anxious to recount it to Wilder himself.*

Today's conversation with Wilder is the first session for which I have been invited to his home. Audrey ushers me into the apartment. It's filled with artwork of all kinds, obscure and lyrical, bold and subtle; little wall space goes unused. On my way to the den to meet Wilder, Audrey shows me the collection of Oscars in the corner living-room cabinet. "Most people want to see them," she comments cheerfully. I am only a handful of minutes late this morning, but still, who can refuse an opportunity to reach past an Oscar for Lost Weekend *to heft the writing and directing awards for* The Apartment? *Not me.*

I find Wilder in his den in a white sweater-vest, finishing the New York Times. *"I am behind one week in my reading," he announces, moving the stack of papers so that I may sit next to him, on his right side. Nearby are tribal sculptures, fresh roses in a vase. He changes glasses carefully, and we begin. He is looser, more relaxed today, as I dive right in, recounting Steven Spielberg's recitation of the stunning dashboard-mirror sequence from* Spirit of St. Louis, *including his note-for-note rendition of Waxman's score. Wilder listens, utterly charmed. He enjoys the moment before commenting.*

BW: That's wonderful. I had forgotten the scene, but that's wonderful. It was not a good picture. If only I had been able to tell the story of the girl, the night before his flight.

CC: Did you ever ask Lindbergh about the incident, or request to use it?

BW: I never asked. I was not going to challenge him, or change him. I accepted him.

CC: I had a question about your collaboration with Diamond. How would he argue you *out* of an idea, and would he do that often?

BW: We never argued about anything too long. Because the argument drags on, you know? If I had something very good, he would just say, "Why not?" And if he had something very good, I would just make a face like this. [*He offers a small, satisfied nod.*] When we were writing, we never had an argument about "I told you so." If it was something very important, then I would insist on it. And when he had something very important, I would protect it, and I would say, "It's good." But his wonderful line, when he liked something, was always . . . [*A small shrug:*] "Why not?"

CC: I recently spoke with somebody who knew Mr. Diamond. They said he seemed "sad."

BW: Sad, yeah. The real humorist is always sad. You'll find that people who are truly funny never laugh about their own jokes. They just let it go, they let it pass.

CC: Now, for me, the hardest part of the process is rewriting. Jim Brooks once said this about me: "He avoids writing by writing." I hate to rewrite. For me, it's easier to start a whole new idea. Did you have a method for sticking with one idea and not giving up on it?

BW: Yeah—by enriching it. By going a little bit deeper into *that thing*. Sometimes we threw away eight pages or ten pages at one time. We'd say, you know, "That does not belong." Sometimes it's not *conducive*, inviting a joke and then getting out of a joke—the picture can live without it. That's no good, if it can live without it. Don't you find that too? Then you always find—you being alone writing it, it happens even more often—that you *repeat* yourself. You say the same thing three times.

That was Lubitsch's idea, to say two, and then say two again, after a little pause . . . and the audience will make *four* out of it. One and one and one and one is four. Or one and *three* is four. We are often repeating ourselves. He told me that; he just said it. So yeah. Sometimes we'd write ten pages a day.

Sometimes we'd write nothing in a week, 'cause we were stuck. Just something does not smell quite right. So it is good to have a censor, but a contributing censor too. It's very good to have a collaborator.

CC: Yes. Just hearing you talk about your collaborations makes me feel very lonely, writing by myself.

BW: But you insist on writing by yourself.

CC: I haven't found the perfect collaborator yet.

BW: If you find one, let me know. Whenever you see a picture of mine, and it has a new name as my collaborator, that's the one I don't like and I don't work with him again. I worked with two people and they were ideal: Diamond, of course, and Brackett, with whom I had lots of fights, but they were difficult, constructive fights. I changed them, you know—at one period of time I had like six collaborators. They either died, thank God, or they kind of . . . Yeah, whenever I started with somebody, I pursued it until the very end. I protect them. But then if I don't work with them again, that means I didn't get anything out of it, or not *enough* out of it. If they asked why we only did one picture, I would just say, "Oh, I *have* to work with this new guy—he came to me with the property."

CC: And then after Brackett you found Diamond. How and why did you hook up with Izzy Diamond as a collaborator?

BW: [*Wilder rises instantly to the subject, and recounts the following with real warmth:*] I read some of his funny stuff in the *Screenwriters Guild* magazine. Just little humorous things, small scenarios, but there was something going on there. He was trying hard, doing a little something extra. And I met him, and after I talked to him, I fell in love! He was bright and he was clever and he was just at the beginning of his career. I was sort of in the middle of my stuff. I saw one of his movies, but it was nothing important. He was beyond the stuff he was doing, and he was ready to do much more. I tried him for the next picture, which was *Love in the Afternoon*. Yes, it was a good combination.

CC: Was there always a central theme for each movie? For instance, when you got lost in the writing of a movie like *The Apartment*, were you and Izzy always able to say to each other something like, "It's a movie about a small man in a big company," or "It's the story of a nebbish who becomes a pimp who becomes a man . . ."?

BW: Yeah. We had that. We knew our theme. If we don't have a central theme, we don't even start writing. It's very difficult if you find a good opening, and a good medium kind-of-end thing, but you don't have the conflict that you need to sustain the middle. Then we just talk about it for a week or two weeks. Then we just say, "Well, it's not very good, it does not work."

CC: What was the genesis of *The Apartment*?

BW: *The Apartment* was an idea I had ten years before. Not in detail, but there was censorship then—ten years before was 1940-something, 1950. . . . Then it got to be 1960 and it was a little bit easier, and then we did it. But still people came around and said, "You did a dirty fairy tale"—[that] no such things existed. [*Laughs.*] It did not exist? It can happen anyplace.

CC: There are some conflicting stories about the origin of the project. Some suggest that it began with a treatment given to you by a newspaperman you knew. Sidney Skolsky.

BW: No, no. Skolsky? No.

CC: And Izzy Diamond once mentioned that it was inspired by the incident with Jennings Lang. [*In 1951, Jennings Lang, a well-known Hollywood agent, was shot and wounded by film producer Walter Wanger over an affair with Wanger's wife, actress Joan Bennett. Lang's trysts had supposedly happened in the apartment of an underling.*]

BW: No. The origin of *The Apartment* was my seeing the very fine picture by David Lean, *Brief Encounter* [1945]. It was the story of a man who is having an affair with a married woman and comes by train to London. They go to the apartment of a friend of his. I saw it and I said, "What about the guy who has to crawl into that warm bed . . . ?" That's an interesting character. Then I put that down, and put down some other things in my notebook. The hero of that thing was the guy who endured this, who was introduced to it all by a lie. One guy in his company needed to change his clothes, he said, and used the apartment . . . and that was it.

I picked it up again because we were just through with *Some Like It Hot* and I liked Lemmon so much. The first time we worked together was on *Some Like It Hot,* and I said, "This is the guy. This is the guy to play the leading man." A little nebbish, as we said, you take pity on him. But *The Apartment*, I had

Some Like It Hot (1959): George Raft in the famous St. Valentine's Day Massacre in the garage. Selznick, when he heard about the film, said, "They're going to walk out in *droves*."

it in mind for years and years before it was really activated. "How will it feel for the guy who crawls into that bed after the lovers have left?" That was really how it started. I thought, "It's gonna be censorable." But I kept that idea, and then when [standards] loosened up a little, we did it. I had the point of view of the insurance guy, C. C. Baxter. And I wanted to say that Lemmon is a naive guy. His superior—that guy that runs the company—wants to go to the opera, and he would like to use the apartment to change his clothes. And Lemmon says, "You can have it!" And that triggers how he becomes a servant to the head guy, the president of the insurance group, which then gets him a better job. He had to be a little shy about it for it to work. That was an important issue, the problem we had to solve—we had to find the perfect way to get that across. He does this all naively.

CC: And you slipped it in very cleverly, while Lemmon is defending himself to MacMurray, who he doesn't even realize is asking him for the apartment himself.

BW: Yes. Yes. That's how we did it. But still, in all, some people came and said it was a dirty-fairy-tale thing, and that it was not believable. And I said, "What wasn't believable?" It was believable. It could have happened anywhere in the world, except one place—Moscow. Why couldn't it happen in Moscow? Because the guy has to make the arrangement with six families that live in one apartment. [*Laughter.*] But naturally it was believable, because everybody wants to get laid, and when he's married, he just takes somebody else's apartment, he doesn't go to a motel. Or if he has *nobody,* and is just very secretive, he rents an apartment.

But that went very, very easy, in the writing. Same with *Some Like It Hot,* once we had the idea of making it in period, 1927. Because we had gangsters, we had St. Valentine's Day. It happened. Mr. Al Capone had them executed, and we said, "Let's have it in the picture." There was something slightly ridiculous about the gangsters, though. I'll grant you that.

Wilder on location shooting *Ace in the Hole* (1951)

5

CC: You are an art collector of great regard. Did you ever spend any time with Picasso?

BW: No. We were in Cannes, and he was in Vallauris. That's up above in the mountains. And I said, "Let's go see Picasso." We had common friends. Audrey and I went there, to Vallauris; it was about an hour's drive. On the piazza there was a medium statue of a shepherd who carries a lamp. I go to the house, and my hand freezes as I went to ring the bell. And I said, "I can't do it. I'm just a man from the street." Before I could even explain to him that I have friends who have great collections and they talk to him, and they would bring him cowboy hats—he was crazy about American cowboys—I just lost my nerve. *Just leave him alone.* What the hell. So we turned around and we just went back.

CC: He wasn't expecting you?

BW: No. Nothing. How can I get him on the phone? How can I get his phone number? I just said, well, the hell with it.

CC: As a young journalist in Berlin, you interviewed Freud. What was the atmosphere around him like?

BW: I did not interview him. He threw me out before I opened my mouth. I was going up to Berggasse—number 19 Berggasse. He lived there, Mountain Street. It was a middle-class neighborhood. And I came there; my only weapon was my visiting card: a reporter from *Die Stunde.* It was a piece for the Christmas issue, about "What do you think about the new political movement in Italy?" Mussolini. It was a new name. It was 1925, 1926. It was a new name to me. So I read up on him. Freud hated newspapermen, he just loathed them; they all made fun of him.

I never met any Austrian then who was analyzed. I never met *anybody* who was analyzed. It was just a kind of a secret thing there. And I pressed the bell, and the maid opened it, and she said, "The professor, Herr Professor, is having lunch." I said, "I'll wait." So I'm sitting there. Now in Europe, in Mitteleuropa, doctors have their apartments as offices. They have a combination. They have certain offices in hospitals. But for this professor, the salon was the reception room, and through the door leading to his

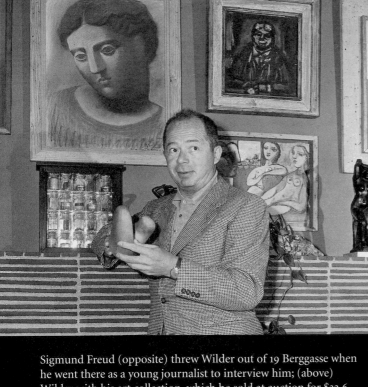

Sigmund Freud (opposite) threw Wilder out of 19 Berggasse when he went there as a young journalist to interview him; (above) Wilder with his art collection, which he sold at auction for $32.6 million; on location with Jan Sterling for *Ace in the Hole*. Wilder was accused of cynicism for this film, but, as he says, "It was the way I thought the picture should go."

study, I saw the couch. It was a very tiny little thing, about the size of this thing here. [*He indicates a small bench.*] With Turkish carpets, full of Turkish carpets, one on top of the other. And he had a collection of African and pre-Columbian art, then, in 1925 or 1926. And I was struck by how small that couch was. [*Beat.*] All his theories were based on the analysis of very short people. [*Wilder watches me contentedly: a joke well delivered, a laugh well earned.*]

He was sitting there in a chair. His chair was a kind of a little bit in back of the headpiece of the couch. And I look up, and there comes Freud. A tiny man. He had a napkin tied [around his neck], that white thing, because he got up during lunch, and he says, "A reporter?" And I said, "Yes, I have a few questions." He says, "*There is the door.*" He threw me out.

It was a high point of my career. Because people have asked me, they have traveled to ask me every detail, to tell them exactly everything that happened. But that's all that happened. Just "There's the door." And I said, "Thank you." [*Shrugs.*] Anyway, it's better than being given a state dinner by Saddam Hussein.

cc: Did he shake hands with you?

bw: Nothing.

cc: Nothing. Just—out.

bw: Just a visiting card (that I showed him). "Is this Mr. Wilder? From *Die Stunde*?" I said, "Yes." And he said, "There is the door!"

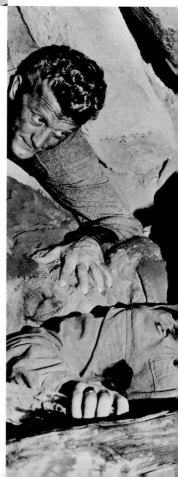

Kirk Douglas (left) as Jack Tatum, the unscrupulous reporter in *Ace in the Hole* who will do anything for a big story

CC: It's funny, reading the books written about you. They're filled with comments like William Holden's famous line—"Billy Wilder has a mind full of razor blades." You're constantly characterized as the Great Cynic. The Legendary Cynic.

BW: Yeah.

CC: Do you think your cynicism has been overrated?

BW: My cynicism? Yes. But not much. Maybe it's been overrated because I dismiss things that are not important, that are lousy. I dismiss them with a line and then go on. I am never cynical to my friends. I don't know where they get the idea that I am cynical.

CC: Ironic, maybe?

BW: Ironic, maybe, yes. Nothing, in any of my pictures . . . you know, there is no cynicism. Maybe in *Ace in the Hole.* That was the one. It was the way I thought the picture should go. There was the cynicism of the reporter who gets fired from the New York paper and then runs into that situation with the trapped man in the hole. It's cynical that he wants to use it, but then he pays for it. He pays for it because he had them there in the hole one day too long. He could have helped to get the man out. But he made a circus out of it.

But the same day that we previewed the picture, I was on Wilshire Boulevard and there was an accident. There was a woman, I think, she did not see the light, and she was thrown from the car. They took her out. Suddenly I saw a cameraman and he was taking pictures, and I said, "Somebody go and find a telephone, call the police, call an ambulance." And the cameraman says, "Not me, I've got to get the picture!" *This* is cynical.

cc: Izzy Diamond, I think, had the best description of your work. He called it a combination of "the sweet and the sour." Like life, basically.

bw: Yes, like life. That's quite true. I'm not a do-gooder. At certain moments I am good, and at certain moments I am bad. . . .

The phone rings. After a brief chat, Wilder notices his television tennis match is about to start. He hangs up. He's eager to watch the young star Martina Hingis play. Wilder monitors the muted television for the moment the match will begin. In the meantime, he invites me to continue.

cc: I found it interesting that when we first spoke about this project, you said, "Who is it for?" "Will it sell?" "Who is your audience for this project?" Was it that way with your movies? Did you always ask yourself, "Who is this movie for?"

bw: No. It's always the same audience, more or less. Except maybe the Lindbergh picture. I just always think, "Do *I* like it?" And if I like it, maybe other people will come and like it too. Maybe it's gonna get some good reviews, maybe they're gonna come. But I never . . . I never go with the wave, you know. Now it's catastrophes, right? They have floods, they have cars, they have buses. *Bah.* It's just absolutely—just no dialogue. [*Beat.*] And some are pretty good. Like, for instance, this thing *Die Hard* [1988]. It was a good picture. I liked that. But I just think, a picture has to have something new. It has to have something that they don't see every day, but recognize as the truth.

cc: So truth—truth is the key.

bw: Make it true, make it seem true. And don't have something, even in a farce like *Some Like It Hot*, that isn't true. I just imagine that there is such an idiot as Osgood Fairchild. That there is such an old fool. Then I proceed.

Wilder now sees the match is starting and unmutes the television. It is very loud in his den. He turns to me from the television, ready for another question, enthusiastically occupied on two fronts.

CC: Is it true that you were unable to get studio backing for *Fedora*?

BW: What?

CC: [*Louder:*] IS IT TRUE YOU WERE UNABLE TO GET STUDIO BACKING FOR *FEDORA*?

BW: Yeah. I think we got some help from Germans . . . I don't really know, I have no idea. I just know that we got the funding, and then I blew it.

CC: What happens in your personal life if a movie doesn't perform up to your expectations? Who or what makes you feel better?

BW: I make up my mind, "This is *good . . . this is bad.*" Nobody can talk me out of it [if] it does not work. Only once in a while did I feel that a picture, the way they emasculated it, that it deserved better, it deserved *something.* That was *Ace in the Hole.* I really felt that that was unjust. So that's when I get angry. But I don't go around with my sad story. Audrey can make me feel better, yes, but I don't talk about it. I just let it lie there. [*The television is booming.*] Go ahead. I'm listening.

CC: What are the more personal characters you've written, the ones where you felt there was a little bit of Billy Wilder in that guy or girl? You never wrote a young reporter character—

BW: A young reporter? No. Obviously, in some way, every main character, or sometimes a lesser character, reacts the way I would react.

I was a reporter. I wrote some things which are not particularly interesting. But I have experienced a lot of things, you know, in my ninety years, and when I think about a story, something in me tells me "Do it," or "Don't do it." That's the way *I* would do it. That's the way I would fall into the trap [of making the movie]. But there's very little of me. I just write a character and hope that it has a certain depth. The autobiographical details of a life . . . it's never any good, except in a biography. Only sometimes do I

Wilder's homage to Manet's *Déjeuner sur l'herbe* in *Love in the Afternoon* (1957), based on the novel *Ariane* by Claude Anet

write something which I have done before in my life. [*He settles in for the Hingis match.*] Okay, have you got any more questions?

cc: A few. I'll pepper them in as you watch. The picnic sequence in *Love in the Afternoon* is composed like an homage to Renoir. Was that the case?

bw: I was doing the picnic with the nude. Manet.

cc: Of the leading ladies in your movies, which ones were the closest to your heart?

bw: I liked working with Audrey Hepburn. . . . It was in a very bad picture [*Kiss Me Stupid*], as I mentioned, but I liked Kim Novak very much. I like all my leading ladies, except maybe Marilyn Monroe, and that was after she made me wait for her a whole day, or three days sometimes. [*Pause.*] But she was smooth when she was doing a long dialogue scene and did not make one mistake. I kind of liked her lilting way. I liked her. I just would wait for her and swallow my pride.

cc: And the characters you felt closest to?

bw: I liked William Holden in *Stalag 17*. Perfect. I liked having him around. I would maybe like to have *been* Tony Curtis in *Some Like It Hot.* [*Laughter.*] Norma Desmond, very much. And Sabrina. [*Pause.*] I liked that. It's a very, very mild picture, compared with some of the other pictures.

cc: Mild in what way?

bw: Mild in the love scenes, you know, because I don't think she exudes a long sexual history. She was *Miss Audrey Hepburn.* Now it comes out that she had love stories, secret rendezvous and stuff. I had *no idea.* I never had any desire of

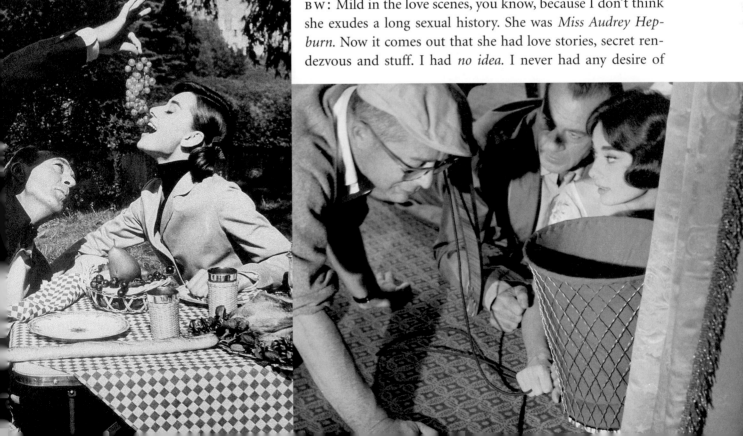

having an affair with any woman during the picture, because I'm so intrigued by the picture itself. The film does not give me any time. But sometimes your vision is altered. I was attracted to Swanson. I was attracted to Barbara Stanwyck. Yeah, they are there, these things. But that is all on the screen. You are attracted to something which is on the screen, and this just means you are doing a good job.

CC: So for you, these characters actually exist, the characters you've created—

BW: Yeah.

CC: —but they exist in the movies, and that's it. You don't overromanticize it.

BW: No. Never. For instance, Audrey Hepburn. She was the princess from *Roman Holiday* [1953] . . . or the daughter of a chauffeur. I was very, very careful not to do any suggestion of vulgarizing in the pic-

tures. I just said, "That's the way she is and that's the way she can play." Nobody [else] can play Audrey Hepburn. Nobody.

CC: But she's very risqué in *Love in the Afternoon*. There she is, running off, having an affair with Gary Cooper.

BW: Yeah, but she's not having an affair with *anybody else*.

CC: Right, which you cover by having her tell flamboyant stories of all the affairs that she's had, but we know it would never happen.

BW: Never happen. She read them all in the file of the father.

CC: There are so many touches in *Love in the Afternoon* worth pointing out. One is Audrey Hepburn's silent dance in the hallway with her cello, which is a lesson for every modern director on how to show a private character moment. Another is Gary Cooper's private string quartet, and those wonderful Hungarian Gypsy musicians. His drunk scene is one of my favorite sequences in movies. Most writers would have simply put him at a bar, talking to a bartender. But here you place him in his hotel suite, listening to a tape of Hepburn's phony list of lovers, rolling the liquor cart back and forth between rooms, with the tub overflowing, and the music playing. And *that's* when he realizes he's in love.

BW: [*Proudly:*] Yeah, he's waiting for the broads, and they're not coming, the Swedish twins, so he drinks. And now he has the Gypsies drinking with him, playing in the next room. That was a good idea, having the Gypsies, even in the Turkish bath! They were real musicians, a real Hungarian band. They fiddle around with the water coming up. That was very good.

CC: One of your few special effects.

BW: No special effects . . . we fastened the glasses to the table and rolled it back and forth. I had six people sucking with a straw to get that champagne out.

CC: You've rarely commented on the age difference between Gary Cooper and Audrey Hepburn in the movie. Were you worried about it? Cooper is often in the shadows—

BW: Yeah, sure, the age difference. Yes, it worried me a lot. I tried to make him as young as possible, and I hoped that it would work. He was in his fifties, and he died at sixty. Very soon after.

CC: Was Cooper himself troubled about the age difference?

BW: No. He could have fucked anybody he wanted. That's the guy who he was. I was also worried about the age of Humphrey Bogart in *Sabrina*. That's always a problem with the younger leading lady. In *Love*

Wilder on characters he felt closest to: "I liked Holden in *Stalag 17*" (above);
(opposite) Gary Cooper in the Turkish baths with the Gypsies in *Love in the Afternoon*

in the Afternoon, you feel it more because Audrey Hepburn is so virginal. Perhaps it's noticed, but hopefully the story sweeps you along with it.

CC: How difficult was the English language for you? How did it seem to you, as a young man?

BW: Absolutely normal. But very strange and very difficult to write it. To put it down on paper. "Though" and "tough" for example. You know, there are many pitfalls. It's easy to talk, it's difficult to write.

CC: Was it daunting, creating American heroes?

BW: Not at all. I just said, "Here is the leading man, and he behaves like *this.*" Naturally I needed help with my dialogue [in the beginning], because it was a different language. But then when I got into the rhythm of English, then it became rather simple. To talk but not to write. To write is very difficult.
    [*There's a commercial for an electric shaver on the TV.*] Only Norelco is good. Do you use it?

CC: No, I use a regular shaver.

BW: Me too. Where do you live?

CC: [*The personal question surprises me, and I answer it quickly.*] Seattle and Los Angeles. . . . What do you tell an actor who freezes during filming? Everybody is standing around, waiting. . . .

BW: If an actor freezes? And freezes and freezes? Most of the time it's all very gentle and quiet. I'm very quiet, I'm very kind, I never raise my voice on the second or third take. But if it's take *fifty* . . . [*He gives a look.*]

There's a very good story there. Preminger is directing a picture [*Margin for Error*, 1943] and he has one of the German refugees, an old man. He wants to do good, for a short part, just two speeches. And he cannot get it. He cannot get it. And Preminger gets louder, and the guy's sweating, and finally Preminger goes up to him and shouts, "RELAX!" And the guy faints. He screamed at him—"RELAX!" Later he felt sorry for the guy and made the scene work. It was very good. But this is one way of dealing with the problem. The ceiling almost came down!

CC: Did you pick out your own extras?

BW: Yeah, and I do it in the following way. I have an office on the second floor, let us say. I'm with an assistant director and then I say, "Will you go downstairs and stand the extras up against the wall?" They don't know that I'm watching.

CC: A great idea.

BW: Yeah, because if you're standing there, they give you the look, and they plead for the job. I will not give in because somebody is starving. Or can't pay the rent. No, no. I just make my picture, and then . . . I'll give them money from my own pocket.

CC: Did you know Frank Sinatra?

BW: Sure.

CC: You never worked with him.

BW: No. He's not an actor. I liked him as a singer, though to me Bing Crosby was the great stylist. Crosby was the artist. Forgotten today, but Crosby was the first.

CC: I've heard that in his day, Sinatra liked

"Action" to be called as he was walking onto the stage. No waiting.

BW: He takes no interest when people [on the set] come to him and say, "We're running longer than we thought." He has to be in Las Vegas on Thursday, and they say, "How are we going to do the scenes?" And he says, "It's very simple." He takes the pages that are not shot and tears them up. What do you do with an actor like this?

CC: Your late friend Richard Cohen says that Sinatra gave you a Picasso for your collection.

BW: He gave me the Picasso. That's right.

CC: So you were friends for a bit.

BW: I helped the writer on one of his pictures. It was a comedy, they wanted to do it like *Some Like It Hot. Ocean's Eleven* [1960].

CC: And he gave you the Picasso as a gift.

BW: Yeah, a small little thing, a watercolor. But it was a Picasso.

CC: Last question for today. The shot at the end of *Sunset Boulevard,* when Norma Desmond walks into her final close-up . . .

BW: I think I came up with this on the day. That is a good scene, because she was crazy, right? That's the easiest thing in the world—for somebody to go crazy. Why does he do it? *Because he's crazy!* But you understand why Norma Desmond is the way she is. She's half-mad already. And it was a wonderful excuse at the end. She goes crazy. That was the solution.

I had a feeling it was good if the last big shot leads into a close-up. Mr. Stroheim directing—"We are ready for the close-up." And she comes down. She mistakes Mr. Stroheim for Mr. DeMille. She

thinks she's in the studio, she thinks the makeup is real. The people around her . . . they know that Stroheim arranged it; we did not show it. She's all made up, and she's going to play that big scene. "Just one moment, Mr. DeMille. I would like to say a few words." Her voice gets louder, and she says that thing, ". . . all you wonderful people in the dark. . . ."

CC: And at the end of that shot, as she walks into the lens, the shot goes fuzzy—

BW: Yeah, little tricks, because her senses are mixed up. Where she is, she does not know. And then—in order to really nail it down, that she thinks she's in a studio—the line "I'm ready for my close-up, Mr. DeMille," and she walks into the close-up.

CC: Is it an optical effect as she gets closer and closer to the camera?

BW: The focus gets thrown out by the focus carrier. I left the camera running. I didn't know where to cut.

11:00 a.m. Wilder is in a jubilant mood this morning as I arrive with Karen Lerner. He sits at the secretarial desk of his two-room office, signing several fan-requested photos of himself. It has been years since he had a regular assistant. Wilder now processes the mail himself. His mere act of signing photos bodes well for today's conversation. Near him on the desk is a stack of vanilla-colored cards he has often sent to fans who have written for an autograph. The cards read simply: "Writers do not sign autographs. Autographs are for actors. BW." Today a lucky few will not get that card, but instead an inscribed photo from the director. I ask him about his fan mail.

BW: They ask a lot of questions. As you get older, and as people watch old television, I am very popular with them. Very popular with people who ask for an autograph. I don't know what the hell they expect me to say—that I've killed three of my wives? There's nothing new that I can say. [*He indicates tape machine.*] Is this working?

CC: Yes. Do they ask a lot of questions about the old movies?

BW: About the old movies. Sure. I grew up with the silents, and I co-wrote I don't know how many silent pictures. I wrote them black [his term for ghost-writing], without my name being on the screen. The scripts in those days, they had only twenty-five pages. There was no dialogue, all action. Twenty-five pages, that was the script. When you shot a whole day and you brought back, let's say, five minutes—that's terrific. You didn't have to do over-the-shoulders, you didn't have to have close-ups.

Close-ups, you know, that's a peculiar thing. All [actors] would like to have a close-up, whether they are extras, standbys—anybody who is in the film. People who haven't got a line to say, they would like to have a close-up. So I always set up the close-up, but I never had any celluloid in the camera. And I would—

CC: You'd actually say "Action?" And do a take?

Wilder directing "the last big shot" of *Sunset Boulevard* (1950)

BW: I would say "Action," but there was a wink between the cameraman and me, and yeah, because they would say, "You took a close-up of her, and you didn't take one of me!" [*Does himself, with rascalish enthusiasm:*] "Oh, yeah! yeah, yeah! You're so right! So right, it's a shame! Let's do a close-up!"

CC: You must have had a thrill or two, looking through the lens and composing some of those close-ups over the years.

BW: Yeah, but there were not too many. I did not have a close-up that was not a pay-off. It has to organically belong. Sometimes I do the shot in the dark, and sometimes I do it against the light. Depends as to what the mood is. But a close-up is a very, very practical thing too, because you can tell so much. If you *can* tell. If I have an actor or actress that doesn't give me anything, then I don't do it.

CC: I was watching *Witness for the Prosecution* last night, and in it is a great example of silent filmmaking. Right in the center of the movie, Vole [Tyrone Power] is outside the window and he's complimenting the hat of the woman who's going to be murdered. It's just a wonderful silent moment.

BW: A silent moment where he had to pick up a woman, right? For what he wanted to do. It was a very elegant moment. I did it with cars kind of reflecting, and I liked the idea of him picking her up by becoming her fashion advisor. "This is no good," he says. [*He acts the moment, making a sour face over the hat.*] "Thank you so much, young man. What is your name?" And then he picks her up.

CC: These days, I think, the studio system is too anxious for you to pull out any silent moments. "Just pull it out, pull it out. Get the movie playing faster!" It's wonderful to see silent drama, silent humor live on in your pictures.

BW: Yeah, and there's always a little music there underneath. Yeah, that was easy, the pickup there. We had to have a widowed lady with money and some collection of African art, that was just right for him. Tyrone Power was an actor who loved those silent things, you know, because his father and his grandfather, they were also in show business, you know. He just wanted to have a good part.

CC: The way you filmed *Witness for the Prosecution* was deceptively simple. It's very sly. You spotlighted Charles Laughton by placing him alone in the shots, just filling up the frame.

BW: And God, could he do it! He could do it very well.

Gloria Swanson as
Norma Desmond preparing
for her close-up

CC: Yes, and the other people you shoot in groups, or you play them in master shots. But Laughton stands apart, powerfully. How much of that was planned with your cinematographer?

BW: Not much. I just had the script, not quite finished. We were still working on the last scene, as we always do. We knew that this was the payoff—she kills him with the confiscated knife. I told you that when we had a big scene coming up the next day, Laughton would come to my room, and he would do that big scene, and know every word. Then he would do it differently. Then he would do it another way, twenty times. And he was better and better and better. [*Shakes his head; he is still somewhat awed by the actor's talent.*] I just had to choose.

CC: Would you shoot it twenty different ways?

BW: [*Immediately:*] No. We had rehearsed it the day before, and by then were kind of happy with version number twenty, let's say. Then he came to the studio the next morning, and said he had an entirely *different* idea of working up to the big line ". . . Or are you not a LIAR?!" He had the idea of staying quiet, working up to it. So we did it, we kind of combined twenty and twenty-one. The whole thing we did in one close-up. You could see the whole up-and-down, the scale of the actor. . . .
　　[*Wilder pauses. Almost forty years later, Laughton's performance is still so pleasing to him. Laughton, it seems, is the quintessential Wilder actor—powerful, professional, creative without being obtrusive, always serving the character with a light comic touch. The director is searching for a way of expressing his highest praise. He settles for understatement, four words said with great respect.*]

That was very good.

And then his wife [Elsa Lanchester], she played the nurse. Both are dead now, unfortunately. [*Pause.*] I had a hell of a lot of fun with that picture. It was somewhat easy, forty days.

CC: The interesting thing is, as he drinks the brandy out of his thermos, you appear to have done something special with the key light in his eyes, to give him more of a twinkle. It really does appear that he's starting to get drunk.

BW: I did it with the light? No. He just knew where the key light *was*. He was just a very, very good listener and a very, very good inventor. Very, very good. Didn't get any awards, though he got a nomination [for *Witness*].

CC: But the public must have loved him in the movie.

BW: Yeah, they loved the movie. But it was very, very strange, because people said, "What the hell are you going to do? Are you going to do the whole picture in the Old Bailey?" And I said [*a sly smile, knowing the power of Laughton*], "No, I'm just going to do a little something. That's where the third act plays."

CC: I have some questions about *Kiss Me Stupid,* if that's okay.

BW: It's not okay, but ask them.

CC: [Laughs.] Martin Scorsese is planning a film biography of Dean Martin, based on the biography *Dino* by Nick Tosches. What should be in a portrait of Dean Martin, to capture who he was? Besides Sinatra, he was a key member of the Rat Pack.

BW: Yeah, sure, and he was the funniest one, to me. Dino was a first-class guy, a first-class talent. It was not a good picture, but he was the best in his class. Too bad that he became, with Jerry Lewis, the extra wheel on the chariot. He was a very funny man. I remember he—this was after lunch, we always had visitors after lunch, because they go for lunch in the commissary, and then they stand around—he would stand there, very close to the visitors, hands in the pockets, rifling through the pockets of his pants, and suddenly he said, "Plums? Where did I get these plums?" [*He stands and demonstrates the joke—Martin wildly groping around in the crotch of his pants.*] So that was a standard, big joke—"Where are the plums?"

CC: In the book *Dino,* Ray Walston gives an interview discussing the filming of *Kiss Me Stupid.* He says, "As was typical of Wilder and Diamond, there was no definite ending when we started the movie—"

BW: Yeah.

Tyrone Power and the hat in *Witness for the Prosecution* (1958): Power talks to the woman who's about to be murdered about her hat; "I liked the idea of him picking her up by becoming her fashion advisor." Charles Laughton in *Witness:* "When we had a big scene coming up the next day, Laughton would come to my room, and he would do that big scene, and know every word. . . . Then he would do it another way, twenty times. And he was better and better and better."

CC: "There was a lot of yelling and screaming and shouting on the set, but Dino always had Billy Wilder laughing most of the time."

BW: Yes. That's true. I laughed a lot. But there was much more, 90 percent more, to him than just the jokester. Yeah, I am a sucker for Dean Martin. I thought he was the funniest man in Hollywood.

CC: Another thing Walston says is: "Wilder came up to me and said, 'Something is going to happen in movies, more than you ever dreamed of, things on the screen you never expected to see. . . . Movies are going to be changing in the future." Of course you were right, but Walston said he wasn't sure you and Diamond expected the uproar that happened over *Kiss Me Stupid*.

BW: Well, the shabby thing that happened over that picture was that the Catholic Church said they would okay it if I cut down one scene. This was in the olden days, the *half*-olden days of pictures. They had their objection mapped out. I made the cut, and then the church still did not cease to object to that picture. They wanted me to cut out that scene [altogether]. There was a complex love scene [between Dean Martin and Felicia Farr], that was the scene.

I always played an honest game with the censors. Sex is in my pictures, but it is dramatic, or it is funny. Well, for instance, the scene between Marilyn Monroe and Tony Curtis on the boat. That is just one laugh after another. That, the censors forgave me, because it was funny. I once saw a picture in the very beginning, and—here's how they went around censorship—the guy is saying, "You son of a bitch." It's not allowed, but it was allowed as "If you had a mother, she'd bark." When you kind of put a little something funny in it, you know. They just let it go. I am very, very careful with . . . *that thing*, the censorship board. I was fair with them, and they were fair with me, except one or two exceptions like *Kiss Me Stupid*.

CC: Is the pain of *Kiss Me Stupid* that you replaced Sellers incorrectly, or that the film was never understood?

BW: It was not very good, I think. It was a costume play in Italy, a big success, and had the original idea of a guy who is a great cocksman. That was in costume, and that I think it should have been. It should have stayed an Italian play. In period.

CC: You mean a period piece?

BW: Yes. [*Dispassionately:*] I never liked that picture very much. I would not have liked it better with Peter Sellers, because he was too British. But I had him, and I was looking for something, and that was the decision. So, in other words, give it one page.

CC: [*Forging ahead:*] There's a beautiful thing you do in the beginning of the film. The score of the piano lessons that Walston is giving becomes the score of the movie.

BW: Yeah, it was quite good, that was good.

CC: Is that the scene you filmed with Sellers, the piano-lessons scene?

BW: [*Briskly:*] Yeah, that was the scene that I was doing with Sellers, and then he did not show up on Monday. He had borrowed some money from

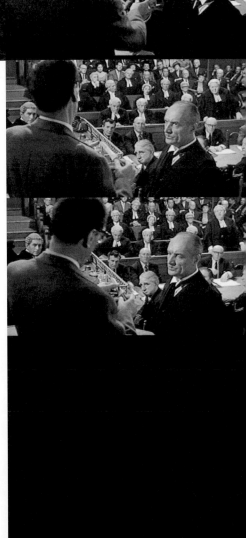

me, because he wanted to take his kids to Disneyland. And he was at Disneyland. And that's the last I saw him, giving him the money, it was two hundred or three hundred dollars, nothing. And then he was not there. And then the heart attack. It was a mistake. I replaced the English actor. It worked in Italian. It was an Italian play. But not in English.

CC: Was Kim Novak doing a takeoff on Marilyn in that performance?

BW: No, not once. I would not know what "doing Marilyn" would be. I never knew. I never knew what Marilyn was going to do, how she was going to play a scene. I had to talk her out of it, or I had to underline it and say "That's very good" or "Do it this way." But I never knew anybody who . . . except for a dress that blows up and she's standing there . . . I don't know why she became so popular. *I never knew.* She was really kind of . . . [*Simply:*] She was a star. Every time you saw her, she was *something*. Even when she was angry, it was just a remarkable person. A remarkable person, and in *spades* when she was on the screen. She was much better on the screen than not on the screen.

CC: Did you sense that the other actors didn't take her seriously?

The knife (right) in *Witness for the Prosecution:* "We knew that this was the payoff—she kills him with the confiscated knife."

BW: Did they not take her seriously? [*He offers a vivid look that says quite the opposite.*] Yeah, but there was Monroe, and that took the breath away. Whatever was said later, here is what they were thinking: "I'm with Monroe, and I'm gonna stand *next* to her."

CC: It's true, isn't it? In the photos you see, whoever is standing next to her usually has a deer-in-the-headlights look: *I'm standing next to Marilyn Monroe.* And next to them is Marilyn, always *presenting* herself.

BW: And whatever she threw away, we printed it, and it was very good. It was very, very good. If she got the character. Which, ultimately, was always the same character. That's the way she wanted it.

CC: I read the Humphrey Bogart biography written by his son. He quotes Bogart as saying about Audrey Hepburn: "Yeah, she's great, if you can give her twenty-six takes."

BW: [*Surprised:*] Twenty-six takes? Audrey Hepburn? Twenty-six, no. That was Marilyn Monroe, before we could get the line straight. Just a little line, like "Where's that bourbon?" She couldn't get it. That was eighty takes or something. You have to remember, when a man muffs a line, and they do it again and again and again, then you replace him, because he plays a small part. Marilyn was the star. She does the takes because it's gonna be in the picture.

CC: In the finished film, the "Where's that bourbon?" line is played on Marilyn Monroe's back. Did you never really get it?

BW: [*Wilder laughs at the specificity of the question.*] Maybe we did it two ways. I just remember that we had about fifty-plus takes, and there was the whole afternoon trying to get it, because she cried after every take, because she didn't get it, and then she had to be made up again. And then also we lost the morning because she didn't show up, and we lost the afternoon because she didn't remember the line. And I had to get the line in that location, because a close-up [shot later] would stick out like a sore thumb. Then again later, for instance, in the scene on the beach with Tony Curtis in the blazer and cap, where he is the co-owner of Shell Oil, there she had a three-page dialogue scene, which we had to get quickly because there were marine planes taking off at ten-minute intervals—she got it the first take. That went in three minutes; we had the shot. She almost fainted.

CC: But normally you wouldn't spend that much time on a line like "Where's that bourbon?" if you knew it could be played on her back.

BW: Then maybe I was just stupid. I was just kind of totally impressed with the thing [the line], or totally convinced that I had to have it on her forehead, or in her brain, and she had to say, "Where's that bourbon?" I don't really know, but you don't have to be that accurate, because this was not the only line that she missed in the two pictures. We spent quite a few

On *Kiss Me Stupid*: "It was a very bad picture . . . but I liked Kim Novak very much." Wilder on Dean Martin: "Yeah, he was the funniest one, to me."

takes getting "It's me, Sugar!" I had signs painted on the door: IT'S. ME. SUGAR. "Action" would come and she would say, "It's Sugar, me!" I took her to the side after about take fifty, and I said, "Don't worry about it." And she said, "Worry about what?" [*Shakes head.*] The fiftieth take, that was, and then there was the fifty-first, and the fifty-second.... As I've said before, I've got an old aunt in Vienna who would say every line perfectly. But who would see such a picture." [*Laughs.*] She missed a lot of [lines, but] then again, when I have a three-page dialogue scene—*boom!*

CC: It's quite a story, how you found out that she'd passed away. You were on a plane from New York to Europe. The reporters told you when you got off the plane—

BW: —in Paris. We got off the plane, and there was kind of an amazing plurality of reporters who jumped at me and asked me things about her. And I said to myself, "Why the hell are they at the airport, why is it so urgent?" Then, on the way from the airport to the hotel where we stayed, Hotel Lancaster, that's when I saw it on the afternoon papers. I saw the EXTRA! MARILYN MONROE IS DEAD! Then I said, "For chrissakes, those shits, why didn't they have the good taste to tell me?!" This is ridiculous, you know, because you ventilate your heart, and you say certain things that you would not have said if they had told me she was dead. Monroe is not too bad. I said, "What did she do now?" And they said, "She didn't do anything." But they didn't tell me she was dead....

It is just so odd, you know, that she should have died at the moment of the greatest brouhaha in her life. Namely the thing with Kennedy. She was screwing Kennedy . . . she was screwing *everybody.* She went to New York, and she sang "Happy Birthday" with her interpretation . . . the Strasberg interpretation of "Happy Birthday." [*Wide-eyed and blinking into an imaginary spotlight, Wilder does Marilyn singing "Happy Birthday."*] And then she killed herself.

Thirty-five years after her death, it is now quite clear that of all the actors to contribute signature performances in Wilder's films, Monroe has done the most to mint the legend of Wilder himself. Wilder's memories of her are sometimes flecked with melancholy, but always present is an almost quizzical form of respect, as if lightning did indeed strike him twice.

CC: What was the genesis of *Some Like It Hot*?

BW: The genesis of the idea was a very low-budget, very third-class German picture [*Fanfares of Love,* 1932] where two guys who need a job go into

blackface to get into a band . . . they also dress up to go into a female band. But there was not one other thing that came from this terrible picture. We had to find, I thought, the key to why they go into that band and what keeps them there. If the gangsters who are chasing them see them as women, only as women, then . . . once they are seen as men, they are *dead*. It's life and death. They cannot come out into the open. It's a question of life and death. That triggered everything. So we began to have a picture. But that German film was absolutely terrible, absolutely terrible. Deliriously bad.

CC: Were you daunted by the tone?

BW: Not really. I was asked by Selznick what I was working on. I told him it was a comedy set in the twenties, in the era of Prohibition, based around the St. Valentine's Day Massacre. He said, "Oh my God, you're not doing a comedy with *murder*? They're going to crucify you. They're going to walk out in *droves*! It's just going to be *embarrassing*." I told him, "I'm going to take a little chance here." We would be careful and delicate about it, but . . . that's the picture. It was set around the massacre, and that's the way it was. We did some comedy at the top, then St. Valentine's Day, the massacre, and they swallowed it because they were with me already. The two guys, Lemmon and Curtis, up on the stage playing those instruments . . . that set the mood that allowed us to spill a little blood.

We were pretty sure it would be a good comedy. What we did not know was that it would be a great comedy. That we did not know. But that was really the genesis. We wanted to do a comedy out of the St. Valentine's Day Massacre. Then the question of Marilyn. We just wanted any girl, because it was not such a big part. Mitzi Gaynor was who we had in mind. The word came that Marilyn wanted the part. And then we *had* to have Marilyn. We opened every door to get Marilyn. And we got her.

CC: What were the early film tests like for *Some Like It Hot*? Did you have to adjust Lemmon's and Curtis's looks much, as women?

BW: Not much. The early film tests . . . we did a day or two, just enough to find them acceptable as women. We worked on the differences between the two women, so that they would be different personalities.

CC: You are famous for having dressed Jack Lemmon and Tony Curtis in drag. Have *you* ever dressed in drag?

BW: [*Incredulous:*] Never.

CC: Not even to demonstrate the proper technique to your actors?

Working with Kim Novak during *Kiss Me Stupid*

BW: Never! I told them what to do and they did it.

CC: How did you come up with the title *Some Like It Hot*?

BW: Out of nowhere, the title came out of Diamond. He said, "But, you know, the title has already been used for a Paramount picture, *Some Like It Hot,* with Bob Hope [1939]." He says, "Well, we're going to do the picture for Paramount, so let's call it *Some Like It Hot.*" It sounded good. It sounds good, right? And then, we twisted the dialogue so we could use it for the title. Tony Curtis says, "Well, you know how it is, *some like it hot.*"

CC: Did the kissing scene on the boat in *Some Like It Hot* go easily?

BW: That went very, very easy. We never had more than two or three takes—that was good, that was solid. But other scenes, they did not go that well. Because, I don't know, she had some type of block . . . or it reminded her of something. She could not control her thinking apparatus. So we had many, many takes there, always over the shoulders of the guys [Lemmon and Curtis], and they had to be standing on those high platform shoes. That hurts if you're not used to it.

CC: Marilyn Monroe's exterior shots were always mobbed by fans. How many fans were there the night you filmed the subway-grating shot from *Seven Year Itch*?

BW: Thousands. Thousands of people, and there was a very kind of delicate situation, because there was Walter Winchell with Joe DiMaggio standing there, in the crowd. I could see in Joe DiMaggio's face, you know, how wrong the marriage was. I knew the marriage was not going to work, very clearly, from the beginning. But especially during that one scene outside that theater. Every time her dress blew up, he

JACK LEMMON

turned away. I finished the scene on a sound stage, with a very big close-up of her single figure, and a little dialogue. We couldn't do it on Lexington Avenue. It was too loud.

CC: Did you ever talk to DiMaggio about the scene?

BW: No, we did not talk about it. We talked about baseball.

CC: Joe DiMaggio publicly expressed displeasure about the scene. But what about Marilyn?

BW: She was thrilled. She was absolutely thrilled. The scene was silent, right? They walked out of the movie house, I remember, but then came *the thing,* that cold air came up. But that was absolutely fake. The air that really comes out of that is hot. It is much hotter. Total fake, but people believed it. Nobody cares. But then it became something so much bigger, it became everything . . . it sold the picture.

But Marilyn generally did it the way she thinks she's gonna do it, and then I talked her out of it. And then we rehearsed and then came that *blah,* you know, when you have a female star blow a line. "That's all right, you do it again. You have enough celluloid there." But Monroe started to cry, and that's a big brand-new makeup job that had to be done, you know, when the first three or four times did not work. And then we were suddenly in the forties [take-wise], with the makeup and so on. And then she got angry with herself. Yeah, she was quite somebody. But then came the part of the girl in *Some Like It Hot.* The big parts were the two men who have to dress as women, and we relied on that. But then came the added thing. "Marilyn Monroe is well, and she is ready to take that part." And we then just took Monroe. And I knew that I was going to go crazy at moments. And there were such moments, half a dozen such moments. Well, but you always tell yourself, "I'm not married to her, right?" [*Laughs.*] And then you come home, you have no dinner, you take a sleeping pill, and you wake up in the morning and you start again.

C C: Was it easier to work with Monroe on *Some Like It Hot* than *Seven Year Itch*?

B W: She had more life behind her; she was easier. But not quite *that* easy, you know. The question was, How do you get her into a mood? Not to have that wall, not to hit the wall.

She had a kind of elegant vulgarity about her. That, I think, was very important. And she automatically knew where the joke was. She did not discuss it. She came for the first rehearsal, and she was absolutely perfect, when she remembered the line. She could do a three-page dialogue scene perfectly, and then get stuck on a line like "It's me, Sugar." But I was a little upset—not a little, *quite a lot* upset— [at] her not showing up. I waited for her, and I swallowed my pride. But if she showed up, she delivered, and if it took eighty takes, I lived with eighty takes, because the eighty-first was very good.

C C: I read an interesting comment by you in an earlier interview. You mentioned that Monroe had a fear of the camera?

B W: She had a feeling for and a fear of the camera. Fright. She was afraid of the camera, and that's why, I think, she muffed some lines, God knows how often. She also loved the camera. Whatever she did, wherever she stood, there was always *that thing* that comes through. She was not even aware of it.

C C: How about the musical sequences in *Some Like It Hot*? "I Wanna Be Loved by You"?

B W: The orchestra, yeah, that went pretty easy. That, she sang a little bit, Marilyn, the girls. . . . It was the music of the twenties.

C C: Marilyn seemed very relaxed with the musical numbers. It doesn't appear that you had to do ninety takes for those scenes.

B W: No no no no. Whatever had a rhythm is whatever carried her. She doesn't carry the rhythm, the rhythm carries her. She did not muff a line there. But she sang to a playback. She just mouthed it.

C C: Last thing about Monroe for today: some people say the secret to the shimmer that her face had on film—the "flesh impact," as you've called it—

BW: Yeah.

CC: —was a light layer of facial hair, a soft kind of down, that caught the light.

BW: Could be. I don't know. I never went to her dressing room, looking at her while she was being made up. There was a love affair between the camera and her. And she stood out.

CC: And she knew it?

BW: She knew it. There was another girl in the band [in *Some Like It Hot*] who had blond hair. And she said to me, "No other blonde. I'm the only blonde."

CC: *One Two Three* is unique among your comedies in that the flow of jokes is absolutely nonstop.

"I Wanna Be Loved by You" in *Some Like It Hot:* Wilder explains, "Whatever had a rhythm is whatever carried her . . . She sang to a playback."

BW: Yeah. We knew that we were going to have a comedy, we [were] not going to be waiting for the laughs. But we had to go with Cagney, because Cagney was the picture. He really had the rhythm, and that was very good. It was not funny. But just the *speed* was funny. The speed was very good, how Cagney figured it out. The general idea was, let's make the fastest picture in the world, and give the actors, in order to make it seem fast, some slower scenes too. But that went very, very well. I think it's a kind of sporadically good picture. But overall, it's a plus. In Germany especially, after the Wall came down, it was a sensation, you know. Years and years later. They released it again.

CC: There's visionary stuff there. Coca-Cola helps bring down the wall. It's all come to pass, exactly as you predicted in the film. I also wanted to ask you about the sheer volume of jokes about Europe, or Europeans, and life behind the Curtain. I have an idea of you and Cagney on the stage, working at breakneck speed, careening through all those jokes: "Let's go, let's go!"

BW: Yeah, we were very, very fast with that script. And yeah, we did not wait, for once, for the big laughs. We went *through* the big laughs. A lot of lines that needed a springboard, and we just went right *through* the springboard. We just did it—*brrrrrp*. We just did it, nine pages at a time, and he never fumbled, he never made a mistake.

CC: So Cagney determined the rhythm of the picture.

BW: He is an actor that was born to play that part. There was a good actor in Germany when they did the original play. The play was all different, but it had an actor who played the part that Cagney played who was the greatest German actor of all times. Max Pallenberg was his name, and he was a sucker for horse races. He once flew to Prague for a horse race—this was in peacetime—and he died in a plane accident. But he was absolutely sensational, and if he could have spoken English—well, to begin with, if [he had been] *alive*—he would have been just absolutely phenomenal. That was a good picture. Good. That was a 7 plus, out of 10. Or 8 minus.

CC: One of the great lines from *One Two Three* is when Cagney, in describing himself to the Russians, says, "I'm not one of these suburban *jokers.*" The line has an autobiographical ring to it. Any particular resonance there?

BW: No, it was just a line. It's just Cagney talking about who he is. Just seemed like the right line. It was not a suburban comedy.

CC: Did you ever tell Cagney that he was yelling? Because he's so *loud* sometimes.

BW: I didn't tell him anything. We rehearsed a scene once, and he then says, "All right, when do we go?" And if it's a long speech I say, "This is going to take us a day, a day and a half, two days." And he says, "No. Why should it? Just don't tell me how long it is. It's in my memory. Let's do it." And he did it. This is like the speech of Edward G. Robinson in *Double Indemnity,* when he describes the possibilities of suicide from a train. They just do it.

CC: But there are some times in the film when Cagney is just literally *yelling.* You can almost see the spit coming out of his mouth, he's so loud.

BW: I don't know . . . is he really very loud? Or was it your projectionist?

CC: [*Laughs.*] Maybe so. There are also a lot of movie jokes in *One Two Three*—jokes about Preminger, *La Dolce Vita,* Sinatra, *Battleship Potemkin,* even Cagney with the grapefruit. In fact, modern film references run through all your movies. Were you ever worried that—

BW: —somebody's gonna sue me?

Ahead of its time, *One Two Three* was shown again after the Berlin Wall came down, and became a big hit in Germany in the eighties.

CC: That might be a better question than the one I was going to ask. But were you curious if all the movie references would date your films?

BW: No. They were movies that were well known and that were not easily forgotten. They are things that would have occurred to the characters. They did not talk about assistant directors.

CC: At the beginning of *One Two Three* there is a beautiful sequence with the balloons. And I thought, as I watched it, "This is very atmospheric." Almost an art film opening, and I'm thinking, "I have not seen a shot like this in any of Wilder's movies—"

BW: We just didn't regard it as an artistic shot. Just a shot that belonged. Maybe it sticks out now.

CC: And then I see the one balloon come up that says, YANKEE GO HOME. And I thought, "He's doing story."

BW: Story.

CC: So it's always story.

BW: Yes, and that was not the thing I'm too proud of. It was too complex—you know, "Go Home, Russkies." But it was a good picture for when you knew Berlin, and when you knew Coca-Cola. [*Indicates small poster from Germany, the credits for* One Two Three *in the shape of a Coke bottle.*] And we could never have that ad, because the shape of the bottle was patented.

We filmed in Berlin. We shot only the very ending in Hollywood at the big garage for the planes. We shot that there—it took me two days, that was the end of the picture. Because Mr. [Horst] Buchholz, he got drunk and had a car accident in Munich. He was in the hospital, and he could have died, and we had the best surgeon. We wound up everything we had to do in Berlin, and all the actors that I needed had been brought back here. Insurance there. And we shot the last, the last thing we had . . . we were shooting here in a hangar. That was the only thing. And the final joke was, that he goes to a Coke machine, you know, and suddenly the bottle he gets is Pepsi-Cola.

CC: One other question about *One Two Three.* You get off some pretty good jokes about rock-and-roll singers. The rock musician, Choo Choo, is the complete spineless fool of the movie. [*Wilder nods.*] Was there any rock and roll that you ever liked?

BW: [*Instantly:*] No. I never can even remember the first line of a modern song that has won the Academy Award. I don't know what there is to listen to. There is nothing like the songs we had to choose from. . . . There was Hammerstein . . . and Ira Gershwin. I'm talking about lyric writers. They were just absolutely wonderful.

CC: Do you ever watch MTV?

BW: No, I never heard of it.

CC: When you're switching channels at home, it's the one with the rock bands.

BW: I hate that. [*Laughter.*] I hate the rappers, I hate all of those things. When you're young, that's all right. There's not enough wit to it for me.

CC: Did you ever meet Elvis Presley, working on those studio lots?

BW: Presley, no. Presley was working then, I think it was a picture at Paramount, but I did not like Presley. However, nowadays, I am forced to remember that great icon. [*A humorous look of resignation from Mr. Wilder.*]

CC: A few of your statements about writing, I'd love to throw some of them back at you right now for your comments. "The audience is fickle. Get at their throat and keep them the entire movie."

BW: Yeah. That's a line of mine. You grab them by the throat, their heart is beating, and you never let go. You just apply more and more pressure. Then at the end, as they're going for the last gasp, you let them go, it's over, and the circulation starts again.

CC: "The more subtle and elegant you are in hiding your plot points, that's how good you are as a writer."

BW: Yeah. I just think that you have to be very, very careful so that you smuggle in a very important piece of action, or dialogue, whatever, so they don't know when they've swallowed the premise. So, you know, *no premise*. You just catch them in the theater, you've got them, now you've got to keep them. You don't want people to get up and say, "I've seen that trick before." Yeah, the structure is very, very important because everything you built up in act one comes back to haunt you in act three. If you do something for which you don't have payoffs in the third act, then you've failed.

CC: Were you nervous the day before starting a new film?

BW: [*Immediately:*] No.

CC: No?

BW: I was nervous when confronted with an empty page, with nothing on it . . . and a schedule for shooting in front of me. I was nervous at the preview. I saved my nervousness for those occasions.

CC: When you had previews and showed your movies early on to test audiences, did you find this to be true—that at the beginning an audience is so full of love, they're like a little baby, they just want to be amused, and they love you. They give you the world at the beginning, but if you squander that trust, and you lose them, there's a point where they turn—and they can be brutal. Then they give you nothing.

BW: Yes. Of course I've had that. For example, in the first reel, you can give them too much action. The picture then becomes disappointing, not what they expected. So by act two they dislike you, and by the end of act two they stand up and walk out. Sure. You have to know how to distribute your plot points. What is there to be remembered? What is there to be remembered that leads indubitably into the third-act situation, which they did not quite know existed? But now they'll remember. And now you play your cards openly if you want to. Because that's what they want.

CC: How did you keep from getting cynical about the whole process? You still seem so full of excitement talking about the movies, so full of affection for the audiences who love your work. How did you keep from becoming one of these directors who grew away from your audience and said, "I make movies for me, and that's it. If nobody comes, I don't care."

BW: I kind of think that overall, audiences are pretty smart. Sometimes they are a little cruel; sometimes they are too nice to you. But as soon as you say, "I don't give a damn whether they come to see me or not, what's the next picture?"—then there *is* no next picture. If you do something that is totally artificial, that is unbelievable, it might be good for the plotting, but you don't want to see "plots." You want to see

stories *develop.* Overall, I think audiences are much smarter than what they are getting. Mostly, they are being talked down to.

CC: They say the Bible is the Greatest Story Ever Told. Just on a pure storytelling level, what do you think of the Bible?

BW: The Bible. It's a *thousand* stories. Sure—it's been tried and tested ever since the Bible was constructed with the Apostles and everything. They just rewrote it all the time, you know? Like ten times in a century. I don't think that the Bible is very censurable. There are some stories which are, but it's a wonderful thing. The Bible. I or you, we can say, "I don't believe [in] the Son of God, I don't believe the whole theory," but if you take it as fiction, it's a wonderful thing—wonderful thing.

CC: Another quote from you on screenwriting. "The second-act curtain launches the end of the picture."

BW: Yes, but not just the end. You'd better have another twist in the third act—like the twist in *Witness for the Prosecution.* There's another end, you know? You expect that it's all over. No. Now comes the *end.* In *Double Indemnity,* I followed everything very logically. I did not have any other possibility. It was not a detective story, where you follow the detective and you know everything he knows. I played with open cards. In *Witness* we did a complete switch, right? And they went for it.

CC: In *Witness for the Prosecution,* Marlene Dietrich seems to tear into her part with a vengeance. Was that actually the case, or was it just another part for her?

BW: No, she wanted that part. As a matter of fact, the picture was done for Eddie Small, with the producer, Arthur Hornblow. And she said, as they approached her—

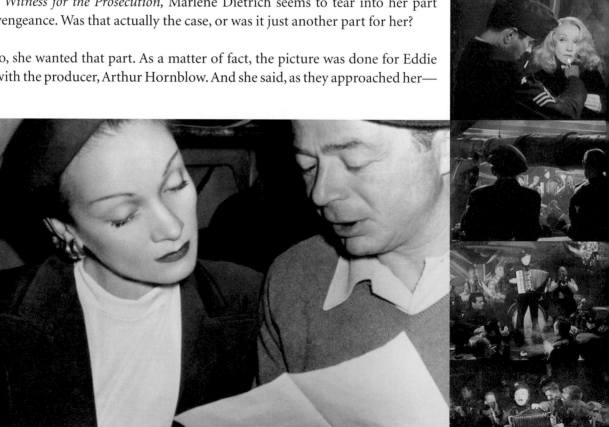

I was not in the company, I was just a freelancer—she said she was gonna do it, but they have to get me. Why, I don't know why. So they got me. I knew her, of course, from *Foreign Affair*. That was long before. For her to play a Nazi, she was very much afraid, but she did all right. [*Shrugs, with typical understatement.*] She was always Marlene. She was a good actress. But sure, you have to go for acting skills. Then there was Marilyn. She did it automatically, you know.

KL: The character Marlene plays in *Witness for the Prosecution* is one of the most unsympathetic roles a woman could have played—until the end. Getting an actress to do that must have taken some persuading.

BW: Yeah, it took some, but that she liked. She likes to play a murderess, she likes to do anything that is action. She was, I think, a little bit embarrassed when she played the love scenes. I think that she was a little bit embarrassed for her privacy because she just thought, "I would not do it." I would *do it,* but not for people. I don't know, she was just strange. But she kind of captured the audience with the way she was—

the way she wore clothes, for instance. She was some *model* there. But I don't think she was as good an actress. Then again, I didn't think that Garbo was a great actress. She just always did the same, kind of half-asleep thing. Never angry. She was always holding the arm like this. [*Does Garbo.*] But it was *Garbo.* I just think that Marlene played [the part] quite well.

CC: You don't see any of her plot moves coming.

BW: No. If it were an American, or it was just another actress . . . [*Shakes head, as if to say, "It would be a much different story."*] But those stars, they don't exist anymore.

CC: With Tyrone Power's character, Leonard Vole, you see his twist coming, because he's so virtuous at the beginning of the picture. But still, you're shocked.

BW: Yeah, and it was good that Marlene was her age. That she was not younger.

CC: You've said that Audrey Hepburn had a quality that jumped onto the screen, but you didn't necessarily feel it standing next to her.

Marlene Dietrich (opposite) with Wilder, whom she asked for as director on *Witness for the Prosecution*, produced by Arthur Hornblow; (above) Wilder directing *One Two Three*

BW: Yes. You never feel it standing next to somebody who is an actor. You very rarely feel it. Or, he's a bore, because he's an actor and talks like an actor, you know. Nothing, in private life.

CC: Was there anybody, actor or actress, who did have that great feeling in the audition . . . in the rehearsal too . . . and then when you shot with him, it just wasn't there?

BW: Sure. Nine out of ten. [*Laughs.*] Sure, and there you've made the mistake. You've had an exuberant morning, for some reason or other—we have retaken Paris or

something—and so you hired the actor. Then you bring the actor in that particular day to film. In a happy moment, you have overestimated. Now what you have is nothing, just a handsome man or a handsome woman. It is just very, very difficult to cast a picture. Very difficult to get it right, to capture that thing you felt on the day you hired the actor. And now we have a starless situation. Especially female stars—it's a starless epoch we're in. Audrey Hepburn was something special because she was not "pretty." She was very beautiful. But she was just average when you looked at her when she wasn't acting. And she was very good. Her death, that was a big blow.

CC: Did you stay in touch with her?

BW: Sure, I talked to her all the time, all the time. My last conversation, she knew she had cancer. She was being put on a plane and going to fly back to die in Switzerland. By touching something inside her dress, she gave herself morphine in order to survive.

CC: Did you say a proper goodbye to her?

BW: Yes, I did. [*Her privacy is safe with Wilder.*]
    We had big jokes, and she was funny. She was always looking with wide eyes at the happenings in Hollywood. She just did not know—she thought that she was a beginner, that she was just starting to act. She was very good.

CC: What would be a joke that you had with Audrey Hepburn?

BW: With Audrey, just . . . just jokes that happened. [*He looks at me thoughtfully.*] Lots of laughs. She was kind of a little frivolous, you know, in her jokes. She was not all Virgin Mary. It's just that when it came out of *her* mouth, it was twice as funny.

CC: Was her affair with William Holden an open secret on *Sabrina*?

BW: I never heard of it. I never saw anything like that. I saw it in a book, and I just said, "What the hell . . . ?" There's no way, no way. *That could not be.* She was still married to [Mel] Ferrer, and I still don't believe it. Do you believe it?

CC: I didn't really consider it, one way or the other, until I read the Bogart biography. And there is Bogart from the time of *Sabrina,* quoted by his son, worrying that their affair is weighing the chemistry of the movie against him.

BW: Absolutely crazy. He was crazy, Bogart was. He thought that the picture stunk. But peculiarly enough, when I knew that I was on his list of shitheels . . . when his illness was cancer, and he was lying there, he became very docile, he became very nice. And I felt for him, for the first time, because he was, after all, an anti-Semite who married a Jewess. How can I do better?

CC: You say time mellowed him. What about you? What do you think people who knew and worked with you forty years ago think when they meet you now?

BW: They are all dead. That's the trouble, you know, because the shitheels, they die too. If I'm in the hereafter, I'm always so afraid that I'm going to run into those people again. I'm gonna see the shitheels again, they're gonna be there! They'll all be sitting up there in that coffeehouse. That's the only thing that I am afraid of. I don't believe in the hereafter . . . but sometimes I just make myself believe. And I just say, "What will I talk to them about? What will I say?"

CC: Do you feel you've mellowed with time?

BW: I see fewer people now. That's the way I have mellowed. I see fewer people. I try to see only the people that I like. And I don't have to see an actress or an actor that I saw in my business. I am not in business anymore. I am out of business. For instance, I would not have a dinner date with an agent. I would not have dinner with people I don't need and I can gently maneuver around. [*Wilder studies a letter on his desk.*]

CC: Were you capable of being a bastard to an actor, or a crew member?

BW: A bastard to an actor? Yeah, sometimes you have to be a bastard to an actor, because the person likes to be treated like a bastard. You learn that very quickly. So you have to have a different pattern of behavior, from one actor to another actor, to an actress in the same piece. Because once the picture is over, it's over. You're not married to them, as I've said before. Sometimes there is a son of a bitch that I took for a picture *because* they're a son of a bitch. Because I want him to be a son of a bitch.

And look, it should be worth everything in this world to have an actor or an actress or a cameraman or *anybody* who helps you with your picture. It's gonna be over one day. But while you are working with them, you take abuse, or you take some niceties which you know are not sincere—you take it to go on. Come the next day, you're gonna be on that stage again, you're gonna continue this scene, or start a new one. You have to massage their ego, or you . . . If I knew that Mr. Bogart was an anti-Semite—and I knew it—I still took him, because I needed him for the picture. The picture means a great deal, a *great* deal, to me at least. And it's very difficult, but to take somebody who is unpleasant, and who has got no talent, *that's* a tragedy.

CC: So casting is the most important part of the directing process.

BW: It is important. Especially the parts where a character comes in for three important scenes. They have to make an impression; they have to make a stand. You find out about his background in advance. Then you have to give them confidence. You have to have the actors there before the scene, and you read it, and then you read it again—then when some weak spots show up, don't shout at him with the word

"RELAX!" You have to do it very discreetly, you know. For instance, one likes to have his ass kissed; the other likes to be screamed at. There is a director's chair—I sat in it for a total of forty or fifty years—I never sat down there for longer than three minutes, ever, and sometimes not even once.

CC: Was there much that you regretted in your own behavior on a set?

BW: Yeah, sometimes I go [off] a little bit too . . . I shout around. Yeah, sometimes, that's the way I am. I cannot do everything pre-scene, you know? If I have to, I will, to get that *thing* out of him, or out of her.

CC: What would be something that would make you shout on a set?

BW: If it's not quiet on the stage. During the playing of a scene, people somewhere in the corner, they're *tch-tch-tch-tch*. I hear that, I get very tough. But at the end of a picture, I am always very nice. I am very nice because it's over and I will not have to see them anymore. Although often I did. Three pictures every two years, that was the rhythm we had.

CC: Another writing question. Do you believe your best material has come from real life? Something you've seen and experienced yourself?

BW: Obviously. Yes. But there are certain things that I've seen that I cannot reproduce, cannot redo. But yeah, I don't think that people behave very much differently in my pictures than they do in life.

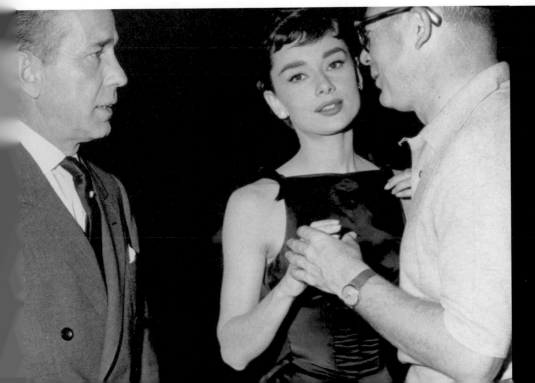

(Opposite) Watching rushes on *Sabrina*. "I was completely unaware that anything was going on between Audrey Hepburn and Holden. I'm still not sure." (Left) "Bogart thought the picture stank," and was not pleased with Wilder but in the end forgave him.

Billy and Audrey Wilder in his convertible Cadillac on their wedding day, 1949

6

CC: Were you in love a lot in your life?

BW: No, very rarely just in love. I always knew my situation, how it was. In other words, was I never carried away by a love affair of mine? No, I was very much in love. I was very much in love when I was young and I had arrived from Vienna to Berlin. And in Berlin I had two or three love affairs that kind of were not very good for a young newspaperman who wants to make a go of it. I was fired very often, and then I wrote, and then I became a dancer, and I wrote my experience in chapters, to be continued. And then I went back to be a newspaperman. Yeah. It took some doing to make me serious.

CC: So would you say that Audrey Wilder is the great love of your life?

BW: She is good, she is intelligent, I cannot lie to her. [*He offers a small, wondrous smile.*] She is to me . . . she is kind of . . . 80 percent.

CC: [*Laughs.*] By Hollywood standards, if not by anyone's standards, you've been a very popular and enduring couple. You've been together—

BW: Forty-eight years. Yeah, she's very good. She has many many first-rate qualities. She is very generous. She just spends a little bit too much money.

CC: You've written so many wonderful romantic scenes—not sentimental scenes, but scenes rooted in romantic realism—I wondered about the scene from your own life, the moment when you knew you were in love with Audrey Wilder.

BW: That feeling grew on me. I don't know, just a moment happens. I was divorced. A moment happens when you just, you just say it: "How would you like to be married?" [*Beat.*] And she says, "Let me think about it." No, she did not say that. She thought about it, and it was very, very good.

CC: The phrase "I love you" is thrown around so much in movies. It's squandered, I think, in so many modern movies.

BW: Yes.

CC: But it doesn't happen very often in your films. Deeper ways, more interesting ways, are found to say "I love you." Is that true in your own life?

BW: Yes, it is. The first time, I was married for seven years. And that was kaput after two or three years. Now, I've increased in my love for Audrey. No, she's been absolutely . . . absolutely . . . 80 percent *perfect*. [*Laughs.*] What the other 20 percent is, I cannot tell you.

CC: What percentage would she give you?

BW: I don't know. I never asked her. I'm no fool.

CC: As a younger man, did you ever get silly in a romantic way? Did you spend much time under the trellis, so to speak?

BW: No, never. No guitar, no serenading. It just happened. She repaired my opinion of marriage. I'm very happy that I married her. Especially now that I am ninety-one, it's very good. It pays off.

CC: I have to ask you this question—you're not going to answer it—but do you remember losing your virginity?

BW: There are some blurry memories. It's seventy years ago, right? Or seventy-five years ago. I was very young. There was a kind of a mishmosh of girls. I don't quite clearly remember my first mature affair, but I remember certain girls from my youth. In Vienna, in Berlin, in Paris . . . I don't know. I don't believe in virginity, as a whole. [*Laughs.*] How far did I go? I don't know. I just slowly made my way without having a tutor, an elderly woman who taught me things. [*Proudly.*] I figured it out all by myself.

CC: Your first furnished room in Berlin was on Pariserstrasse, and you fell in love with a dancer in the review of girls, named Olive Victoria. Is that right?

Mr. and Mrs. Billy Wilder shortly after they were married

BW: She was a dancer. They were going from show to show—London, Berlin, Paris, and so on. Olive Victoria was her name, yes. . . . Poor girl, she must now be in her eighties or nineties.

CC: And what did she think of the news story you wrote about her?

BW: I wrote a poem for her. I don't know. [*Shrugs.*] I just was in love with her, and I just lost three or four jobs. I did not show up. I was just kind of haunted by her.

CC: What was haunting about her?

BW: What was haunting was, she spoke very good English. I think that she slept with Eddie Polo [the actor who would later appear in the film of Wilder's first script, *Der Teufelsreporter* (1929)] and not with me.

CC: That's haunting.

BW: [*Smiles.*] That's haunting.

CC: Are there fleeting images of women in your past that you remember often, like the girl in the white dress that Bernstein discusses in *Citizen Kane*?

BW: Yeah. Sure, sure. Images from my youth. There was one such moment when I was fleeing Berlin, the day after the Reichstag fire, when they dissolved the Parliament. And there was a girl, we escaped to Paris together, and we lived in that hotel [the Ansonia, a haven occupied by other refugees who'd worked in the budding German film industry] forever, for eight months or so. Then I came to America, and I wrote her a love letter. "Why don't you come over, why don't we get married?" Then war broke out, and she stayed behind. She was in a concentration camp.

CC: And she died there?

BW: No, no, no. She came here, after I was married for ten years, for a visit. But before that she was my love. She was just a girl then. Her name was Hella.

CC: Do you know what happened to her?

BW: The last time I saw her was in Paris, about twenty years ago, and never since. Never saw her, never heard of her. Did not have any common friends. The ones that we had were dead, had died.

CC: Was Hella one of your great loves?

BW: Hella was a good love. Hella . . . Hella Hartwig. She was German. She came to visit us, me and Audrey. Good girl. She's still alive.

CC: Can you pinpoint the moment when you decided to leave Berlin?

BW: The moment, I can exactly tell it to you. That was 1933. Hitler had taken over. I did not know to what degree, but then we had that crazy Dutchman, Holbein or somebody. [Hitler] had snuck him into the Reichstag, the Parliament, and he started a fire, and he left. So now, the Reichstag being burned, obviously by Communists—who else would do a thing like that? All the parties became illegal, only the National Socialist Party remained. The fire was still burning . . . that's when I went to the hotel. I packed my things. And I went to the station with the girl named Hella. And we went to Paris. I could go to Paris. I didn't have a German passport. We left. They were already putting SS men in the railway stations. That was exactly when I decided.

CC: You were with Hella when you decided to leave?

BW: Yes.

CC: So you turned to her and said, "We gotta get out of here."

BW: Yes, that's exactly it. "Gotta get out of here." Because by this time, it's one party. The National Socialist Party. It's like communism—one party, no other parties are permitted. So I just said, "Now we have to go. This is going to get ugly."

CC: Was the train ride to Paris romantic, scary . . . ?

BW: I sold all my furniture—all my money was in this little pocket here. One-hundred-dollar bills. About two thousand dollars—we put it in there and we left. When we arrived in Paris, we went to a hotel which was recommended, Montparnasse, overlooking the cemetery, and we didn't like it there very much. It was out of contact with other people. The next day we walked through the whole of Paris, the whole goddamned Paris, and then we found a hotel, the Ansonia. And then other refugees also came to that hotel. The hotel was loaded with people.

CC: And then it became a party?

BW: No party. It was sad. We were sad. Paris was quite beautiful, but summer was coming. And then I found out one day that I was a rich man, for the time being. I didn't have to work, because Hella brought with her a thing made out of cloth, a money purse, with gold coins in it, which her father, who was a pharmacist in Frankfurt on the Oder, gave her. She and I used to sell one gold coin at a time. I was writing then; we were writing. There were two or three writers there, and we sold a story, and then I directed it [*Mauvaise Graine*, 1934]. With the help of Mr. [Alexander] Esway, a Hungarian, who was a born director. I was a dilettante, but I directed it.

CC: That was after *People on Sunday,* right?

BW: That was years. *People on Sunday* was 1929, Berlin. This is now five years later.

(Above) Wilder discusses the monocle in *Witness for the Prosecution* (1958)

CC: How did you say goodbye to your parents?

BW: Goodbye to my parents? They had stayed in Vienna, and when I left Vienna to go to Berlin, I said, "I probably will never come back again, because Berlin is where I want to be." Then I corresponded with them. In 1928, my father went to America to visit my brother Willie, who had a big business in New York. He was there a few months, and he was returning to Vienna to pick up my mother and bring her back to America. He returned by boat, and on the way back he stopped in Berlin to see me. He died in Berlin. He died of intestinal obstruction, a problem he had ignored. We were together when he had an attack. The doctor came and packed him up, put him on a stretcher. I was with him in the back of the ambulance when he died. He died before he could bring my mother back to America.

My mom was a mom, and she was a good cook, and we ate at home always, only once in a while in a restaurant. I was never as close to my mother as I was to my father. I never met the husband, the new husband. Mr. Siedlisker. And they all died. People who were with her then. She was taken to a concentration camp with her mother, my grandmother, and with her second husband. And I tried to correspond, but there was no way. And nobody had any idea. In 1935 when I came back from Europe—I went to Europe to see my mother—nobody had any idea that Hitler, who had taken over, would even contemplate an idea like the purge, the concentration camps idea . . . that the Jews have to be eliminated from the traffic.

My mother never saw me successful. My father, of course, never saw me successful, because he died in 1928, just about the time that we were shooting *Menschen am Sonntag* [*People on Sunday*]. They never saw me successful. I regret that very much, because they would have been proud of me. I never saw her after 1935.

CC: I think we all have defining images of our parents, little moments we remember and carry in our memory. What are the images that come to mind when I mention your mother?

BW: The image of a small, little, overweight, German-speaking woman. She spoke very few English words, [even though] she, as a girl, sixteen or seventeen years old, came to America to be with my relatives here. And then she came back [to Vienna] and then she got married. But she was a very good mother, very. She could punish me pretty good, beat me up, sure, when I was a small boy of eight or ten years old. And then one day I just grabbed her hand. I don't know what kind of stick she had there, but I grabbed her hand and looked at her, and she knew that she could never beat me again.

CC: Do you remember your last conversation with her?

BW: Not specifically. I last saw her in Vienna in 1935. It was a short visit. I did not stay at home, I stayed at the Austrian Court Hotel. A short visit, but that was fine. She was all right. I never met Mr. Seidlisker, my stepfather. She married after my visit. They stayed in Vienna.

CC: What was the atmosphere in Vienna as the war escalated?

BW: They were living there in panic, you know—what was Hitler going to do?—but nobody moved. And Austria did not ask for the Anschluss, for the bringing together of Germany and Austria. The German army marched in . . . and the Austrian Republic was overturned. The Germans who moved to Austria were absolutely in jubilation. And the Austrians were beating up the Jews, and the German troops, they had to separate the Jews from the Austrians. [*Shakes his head.*] And now Austria says that they were

the first ones who were occupied by Germany! Occupied! Then they were *begging* to be taken into the great German Reich. That was in '38, yeah. And shortly after that, Czechoslovakia went, Sudeten Germany went. And the jubilation in Austria and Vienna, when Mr. Hitler came! He is an Austrian, you know. They were very proud of him.

CC: How did you find out your mother had died?

BW: I found out by letters from the Red Cross. Nothing official came to me, just letters from people who knew her. They knew a little something, and told me. That's the way I got it. I never got any letters [from her]. Just from others. That's how I knew she was dead. They told me she had died at Auschwitz.

CC: Is it true or false that you were nicknamed after Buffalo Bill?

BW: I don't know. My mother just said kind of little family jokes. Kind of like Buffalo Bill . . . and I was Billie, and my brother was named Willie. [*Wilder takes a phone call from his wife.*]

CC: You've described *Witness for the Prosecution* as a Hitchcock-style movie. What do you think you did that Hitchcock would *not* have done?

BW: Well, I told my story. Which was not exactly a Hitchcock situation, because he dealt with other things. I think Hitchcock would have had a few more tricks up his sleeve, which he did very, very well. But there was an element of truth that I don't think was the strength of Hitchcock.

CC: I like how you stay on the master shot for the stabbing. Also, during the trial, when Laughton is playing with the pills, lining them up, or drinking, you photograph him from the upper balcony, looking down. You never push the audience's face into anything.

BW: Yeah, I was a little bit soft on them. But the end had to be violent. I wanted that knife there on the desk, the knife with which the old woman was killed. It is there on the desk. There is Marlene, there is

Tyrone Power, and there is Laughton. And when the truth comes out, I wanted him to put on that monocle. And there is a *little reflection* off that monocle. He had the reflection earlier in his office, when Marlene visited, when she pulled the curtain. But now, the moment when the truth comes out, when Tyrone Power reveals the girl he lives with—I wanted Laughton to point out that knife with the reflection, for Marlene to use. But that would not have been permitted.

CC: Why not?

BW: Because that will tell them that a member of the legal profession points something up to the murderess, who is not a murderess, to get to the guy she was supposed to be in love with. What's in there now is close, but it's subliminal.

CC: Yes, Laughton is looking down. He is playing with the monocle, and the reflection is an accident. [*Pause.*] Was that in the play?

BW: Nothing was in the play. No monocle. Kind of a tricky idea, but it went all right without it.
   Now, I will see you tomorrow?

10:56 a.m. I arrive several minutes early at Wilder's Brighton Way office. He greets me at the door, wearing a blue-and-white shirt, extraordinarily high-waisted pants, and a white hat, cocked to the side. "Hi, how are you?" he says. Ready as always, he takes his seat behind his desk and reaches for one of several boxes of Tic-Tacs. He is sporting a light beard; it gives him the appearance of a well-dressed painter. The desk is filled with paperwork from far-flung film festivals and cinéastes with obscure requests. The light hits his whiskered face. He slits open some mail with a letter opener. Behind him, a small stained-glass United States of America medallion hangs on the window. I look at the clock on his wall. I now realize it is several minutes fast, which makes me, by his standards, barely on time. Wilder now brings up the unspoken issue. Today, he is happily contentious.

BW: You were on time. You were here at eleven o'clock, as you should have been. And we are going to do this in two hours?

CC: I hope to make today easy. I have a lot of silly questions.

BW: All right. Very fine. There are no silly questions, there are only silly answers.

CC: For a number of years, I've followed various college polls where students are asked about their dream occupation. For some time, the number-one choice was president. Then it was rock star. This year, for the first time, the number-one ideal occupation is film director.

BW: Yeah, because they kind of see the finished product, and they don't know the sweat that goes into it. They don't know that a director, at the end of the day, he's *had it,* you know. You think it may be a good picture, but when you're stuck in a bad one, it comes out. . . . They only see the word "director." They just think the guy sits in his high chair and points—"Print!" One peculiar thing is that very few directors also write. Very, very rarely is it that a director decides, "I want to write too." But it is very plausible that a writer wants to become a director, because he directs it on paper, as it were.

But the director is a very important job, because you commit yourself. It is more or less the way it's gonna be at the end, unless you have a thousand shooting days, and then you can do everything better, right? But as the director, you are committed, and not only are you committed, unlike the director of a play, you

cannot change it anymore, that's it. You choose the best of what you have, and it's in the picture. Yeah, but if a young man just puts down he would like to be a director, he sees only the glory of it. He does not see the trouble, the fights, the things he has to swallow, the shit—that's very, very . . . [*Wilder offers the look of a man who has just swallowed vinegar.*]

You feel like a very small, small man.

CC: Did you have a good relationship with Truffaut? Godard? Or was it contentious?

BW: No. I was very friendly with Louis Malle, and I knew Truffaut. The whole bunch of them, I knew them. That was a thing, they thought that they found something new. It was not all that new, but it was very good. For instance, Mr. Truffaut's picture *Day for Night* [1973]. That's a real masterpiece, I think.

Really funny, and really good. I told him so. Just before he died, fortunately. I don't know, it was just a new way of making pictures, but it was not quite a new way, because certain pictures were already *nouvelle vague* before them. I don't like Godard. I think there behind the mask of the sophisticated man, there hides nothing but a dilettante.

CC: Did they look at you as "Hollywood"?

BW: As Hollywood, yes. Well, with a certain respect for the money that was spent.

CC: What about Godard's *Breathless* [1960], which Truffaut wrote?

BW: *Breathless,* that was the only good one.

CC: I'm a great admirer of Truffaut. I loved his ability to capture the poetry of everyday life. [*Wilder nods.*] And, of course, Renoir.

BW: Renoir, the old Renoir? Not the grandfather, who was [Pierre] Auguste Renoir, the painter—

CC: No.

BW: —whom I don't like, by the way.

CC: But you owned a Renoir.

BW: Just a drawing of his. But I just don't like him. Too pink.

CC: Too *pink*?

BW: It's all like the cover of a chocolate box, isn't it?

CC: I like him. [*Wilder shrugs: it's a big world.*] And Jean Renoir's sensibility, his work with his actors, were a big influence on me. I keep asking you about *Rules of the Game* because it has a certain charm that reminds me of your work.

William Wyler advised Wilder to make this scene from *Love in the Afternoon* silent.

BW: Yes, I enjoyed *Rules of the Game*. Sure. René Clair also. He absolutely vanished in the memory of people. He was very good at the very beginning, you know . . . *Sous les Toits de Paris* [1930]. But then he started, you know, with the thing [filmed] from up above. Some people are putting poison out, and only people who are very, very high can survive it. They are in an ivory tower, so they can survive? Crap.

CC: I want to read you something from an article in the *World Policy Journal* given to me by Karen Lerner. It's an essay by David Kipen called "The Death of American Film."

BW: [*Immediately:*] Ah, good.

CC: The theory of this is that we've lost national character and culture in film. And the writer goes back and he talks about some of the great American film portraits. He writes about 1939, a year which is now looked back on as one of the great years of American film. He writes, "Greed is nothing new in Hollywood, they made *Ninotchka* and *Mr. Smith Goes to Washington* as business ventures, and saw handsome returns on those investments. But meanwhile, Lubitsch, Wilder and Capra were busy defining America both to itself and to the world. Never mind that their quintessentially American comedy sprang from the brains of three guys from Berlin, Vienna and Sicily, these films had a certain cynical optimism, a headlong speed and love of vernacular, American English as impossible to deny as it is to resist. Trying to copy America, they helped create it."

BW: I don't even think in those big terms, you know. "American Film" and so and so. [*Waves it away, makes a sweeping noise:*] Shshshsh . . .

  I just make a picture and I hope that it's going to be good, that it's going to entertain people and going to show them something which they have not seen yet. But to think that "this is going to be the greatest film noir" or "the greatest comedy," or "In world terms, what is the importance of this?" . . . It's good, it's very good; it's nice that someone says something like that, for us old directors . . . the resigned directors, the directors who are not going to be saying "Action" anymore. But you can only judge a thing after it's done. And a director cannot live on lofty concepts, he must photograph definite ideas . . . and show them subtly, not [like] Capra. Capra was very good, I tell you, very good for its day, but he then got into the afterlife of people, and this is a . . .

CC: Sentimentality?

BW: Yeah, sentimentality. Broad sentimentality. Yes. But he was a very good, very popular director. Very, very good director for things that he did. He hit the times right on the head. There was just nobody but

Capra [for a long time], before that there was DeMille a little bit, you know. The DeMille pictures. These were two very popular, very powerful directors. Today there are few directors who tower over the times—just Spielberg.

CC: How about the work of Preston Sturges?

BW: Oh, very fine. He was the first writer who became a director. Then he left, started a company with Howard Hughes, across the street from Paramount. Raleigh Pictures. After that, I don't know, he never did anything that made any sense. [*He seems slightly mystified.*] Then he left the country. He was kind of bilingual. He was very good in French, because as a kid he was brought up by a French nurse, in France.

The last I saw of Preston Sturges, he was in a coffeehouse across the street from Fouquet. They had coffeehouses on every corner, but that was his one—the Café Alexandre. And he was watching for someone. That was Avenue Georges V, and all the Americans, they stayed at the Hôtel George V. They would always kind of walk by, and he would bum a brandy from them, you know. That was terrible, it was absolutely awful. And he had the first and only Rolls-Royce station wagon. How and why I do not know. But he drank that brandy all the time, and he died very early. But at his best, he was very good.

CC: What was one of the better comments another director made to you about your work? Did your friend Fellini comment to you about *Some Like It Hot,* for example?

BW: He would be very generous. He would call me "Maestro." He was seventy-five or something like that when he died. But I was to him "the Maestro." But there was nothing wrong with *La Dolce Vita*! If I am "Maestro," what would I call *him*? I learned something from good pictures, and from bad pictures. From good pictures, it's very difficult, because there are very few good pictures, great pictures, memorable pictures. [William] Wyler was a close friend of mine. He would be very critical. He would say, "I don't think that Audrey Hepburn should talk to Gary Cooper as he was taking the train at the end of *Love in the Afternoon*." The train was going, and now she was telling him once more the lovers she'd supposedly had. Wyler said, "Make it silent." But I couldn't, because her lips were moving.

CC: Would you have made it silent if you could have?

BW: Yes. I would have had her start to follow, and then he leaves, then she runs parallel with the train, and then he grabs her. But I had too many words there.

CC: I love her dialogue there, it's heartbreaking. To me, that takes it out of the realm of a simple running-after-the-train ending.

BW: Yeah, but she's already said goodbye to him. She should shut up at the moment and should just keep running, and then he *grabs* her.

CC: Tell me more about your relationship with Wyler.

BW: The relationship with Wyler . . . Wyler was a phenomenal man, because he never read anything. He absolutely never read *anything,* except the script of a picture he might do. He kibitzed as a nonwriter who was getting to direct, so he had time to get together with the boys quite often. He had plenty of time for cards. But there was no book ever printed that he would pick up. [*He is humorously baffled.*] Absolutely, just *did not read.* Did not need to know what was happening. Also, I must say, he had a wonderful war record. He had a wonderful kind of feel for a town, you know. He was a little bit corny, but very good. Audrey Hepburn and Gregory Peck in *Roman Holiday*—that was a good picture.

CC: So you dismiss the notion that it took a man from Vienna to capture America on film.

BW: No. It was making pictures in Europe about Europeans that gave me trouble. Although I did a picture in Berlin, with Jimmy Cagney. I faked that pretty good. But I don't like pictures that are in a foreign language. For example, I did not like *Irma la Douce,* because Lemmon cannot be a French policeman. [*Laughs.*] The whole thing was too American to be believed. I don't believe it . . . and neither did they. The picture was a flop in Paris, in France. But it was a big hit here. In Germany, they loved it because they thought that they could understand the French better. [*Laughter.*]

Wilder wrote *Ball of Fire* (1942) in Germany and then sold it to Sam Goldwyn. He found working with Howard Hawks difficult. Hawks (opposite) and Barbara Stanwyck (right)

CC: Was Howard Hawks a significant influence on you as a director?

BW: [*Immediately:*] No. Hawks was very good for what he did. But he did not influence me.

CC: Who did?

BW: Lubitsch. For many years, I had that sign on my wall. HOW WOULD LUBITSCH DO IT? I would *always* look at it when I was writing a script or planning a picture. "What kind of track would Lubitsch be on? How would he make this look natural?" Lubitsch was my influence as a director.

CC: Let me read you something from a book that Peter Bogdanovich has written, *Who the Devil Made It?* And this is an interview with Howard Hawks, who says: "Sam Goldwyn called me in, and Brackett and Billy Wilder told me the story of *Ball of Fire,* and I said, 'Okay, I'll do it.' And then I went fishing with Hemingway for three weeks. I came back and said, 'How are you guys coming with it?' And Billy said, 'We're not coming good.' 'What's the matter?' I asked. 'Well, we don't know what it's about,' says Billy. I said, 'Well, it's *Snow White and the Seven Dwarfs.*' And Billy said, 'We'll be done in a couple weeks.' Of course Brackett and Wilder were both superb writers. They could make almost anything good."

BW: It is not very good. It was a childish idea that I brought with me, written in Germany before Hitler. I had a thin idea of the screenplay, like twenty pages. Then we were working for Paramount, and Paramount made a deal with Goldwyn. Goldwyn [who then had a contract with Cooper] would get Bob Hope and the team of Brackett and Wilder for a picture. For that they would free Gary Cooper to be in Hemingway's first big picture, *For Whom the Bell Tolls* [1943], for Paramount. So that was a swap deal, right? Goldwyn made a picture with Bob Hope [*They Got Me Covered,* 1943]. The Goldwyn girls, they were dancing there. Terrible.

Then Goldwyn got the next Cooper picture, which was *Ball of Fire.* Now Hawks was one of the greatest liars in the world. [*Laughs.*] I remember very well, it was the Hôtel Prince de Galles, that's right next to the George V. And I was sitting there with a writer who lived there, in the lobby, and we were having some martinis or something. Down the elevator came Howard Hawks. He seemed to be in a very good mood, we invited him for a drink. And he says, happily, "Today I have gotten the papers all signed, I am the general representative of Mercedes for America! Secondly, I have sold parts of my oil wells in

"Drum Boogie": this swinging musical number from *Ball of Fire* is one of Wilder's first and best. "We invented this when we got Krupa."

Mississippi. The money just comes rolling in, I cannot tell you." He drinks the martini and says good-bye—*and goes away.* We're just sitting there, looking. The reception chief at the hotel comes up to us and says, "Who's this gray-haired man you know? He hasn't paid his bill for eight weeks."

That was Howard Hawks. Then when we wrote that picture, *Ball of Fire,* he came one day at a quarter of twelve, and he had in his hand a tablet with yellow sheets. And he says, "Well, boys, I couldn't sleep last night. I have the entire second act, third act of the picture here. This is just wonderful, I tell you." And he puts the tablet there on the desk, and now he sits there, and we wait for him to tell us what it is. Not one word. Then he says, "I have a horse racing at Santa Anita, in the first race. Let me just go and wash my hands, and then we'll go to see that first race." And he went, he washed his hands, he left with the two of us, left that tablet unopened there. And then we were at the races. We came back, we had the cars there, we ran upstairs and looked. There was nothing, not one word was written on the tablet. Not one word. [*Grinning, looking baffled.*] He did absolutely nothing.

CC: But you did watch Howard Hawks shooting *Ball of Fire,* and that helped you learn about economy in filmmaking. True or false?

BW: Half true and half false. I just listened how to say "Action," how to say "Cut," how to say "Print number seven."

CC: You supposedly hung from the rafters and watched that film being made.

BW: Yeah, sure, I was there all the time, the whole picture. It was not a very good picture. I did not like it. But *however* . . . I met Gary Cooper, yes.

CC: And Stanwyck, both of whom you would use later.

BW: Barbara Stanwyck. That's right, that's how I met her.

CC: You weren't happy with the finished product of *Ball of Fire?*

BW: No . . . [*Shrugs.*] It's all right. It was much better when it was fresh, when it was new, when it was in

Germany. Then I could go a little deeper into the various issues that people were tackling there. The professors are working together, it is all very silly to have them under one roof, everybody writes his stuff, history or geography. It was all so silly, and then there was so much slack in there. I don't know; I just did not like it. It was not very good. But I wrote that in Germany and I sold it here, to Mr. Goldwyn. Gary Cooper, Barbara Stanwyck.

CC: Was "Drum Boogie," the great dance number with Barbara Stanwyck, in the script?

BW: That we invented here because we had [Gene] Krupa. That's Krupa.

CC: Let's talk again about *People on Sunday* [*Menschen am Sonntag*], your famous and famously rare second film, from Germany. Today it exists as one of the only visual records of Berlin at the time, and it is studied as a historical document. Also, it marks the first work of Fred Zinnemann and many others. Here's another interview from the Peter Bogdanovich book, a conversation with Edgar Ulmer, one of the assistant directors on the picture—

BW: Ulmer, yeah.

CC: "Fred Zinnemann was the camera assistant, and Billy Wilder wrote the script on pieces of scratch paper in the Romanisches Café." Is that accurate?

BW: Yes.

CC: Do you feel ownership of *People on Sunday*? Do you feel it is truly one of your pieces of work?

BW: Well . . . "pieces of work" . . . it was a silent picture, twenty-five pages. . . . Robert Siodmak directed it, we all directed it, we all placed the lights. It was everybody's first official picture, except the cameraman [Eugen Schüfftan]. It was kind of vaguely true,

almost documentary. That was the first picture my name was on as a writer. I have found the script now, which you mention, in German, and I am going to write to the people, the Motion Picture Academy in Germany, and see whether they want it. And I am going to send it to them. It was a silent thing, where we talked while we were shooting, we told them what to do. I mean "we"—I was the writer, with Curt Siodmak. It was after an idea by Curt Siodmak, and the screenplay was by me. He was there too. Everybody was there, Zinnemann was there too, and we were schlepping the camera, we got no salary, we got like about—let's see, we got about a hundred dollars a week. We just did it, did it out of love. All the actors were new. They did not continue to be actors. [*Laughs.*] The cameraman was the only guy who was a pro, who had done pictures before. Very, very well photographed, I must say. He [later] made pictures in Hollywood. His name was Schüfftan, and he was the only guy who knew where to put the camera and what kind of lens to use. He later won the Academy Award for *The Hustler* in 1962. We borrowed the camera; we had the camera only on the weekend. But the weekend, you know, was not Saturday [and] Sunday. The weekend was on Sunday. There was no "Shops are closed on Saturday" or "Open until noon." It was a six-day work week. We were shooting for four or five months. Just on Sunday when we had lots of people for the background.

CC: If you could see *People on Sunday* today, would you?

BW: I would not see it. I don't know—I think it was just kind of a freelance experiment of a picture. It never quite got into much depth. But we had, for instance, things like the ways people spent Sunday. There was, among other things, a scene where a guy was chasing a girl, two guys and two girls, through the forest, and then she trips, and he falls on top of her, and they do it.

   Now *how* do they do it? We had a scene of a pro tennis championship, and the people in the audience there, a big stand with thousands of people—five thousand people. And we just shot it, people looking at the ball, we had hundreds of heads [moving back and forth], and we intercut *that thing* with the guy and the girl in the forest. [*Wilder is still proud of the move.*] Just by cutting, lots of shots of people doing it, on water bicycles, in the lake, and people on the bicycle, we had lots of fun. People are meeting, people are doing it, people are eating like crazy, playing sports, whatever you want. And then most of the

(Above) Stanwyck on the set of *Ball of Fire* with Hawks and Sam Goldwyn

people, they say goodbye and that's it. So that was the idea of it. I think it's possible to see it in Berlin.

CC: Do you feel that you captured the Berlin of your youth in *People on Sunday*?

BW: Yeah, I got that on film. Because we had scenes at the crowded lakes—there are so many lakes around Berlin, I think a thousand lakes. We concentrated on one lake, and then the people coming, going, cars, sex, whatever we wanted to do, and then always cut back to the Leipzigerstrasse, the main drag in Berlin, with the Bourse [stock exchange], absolutely empty, a cat would be running across. Everybody was there at the lake, so you know that on Monday they're going to be thrown back to the traffic. That was quite dense, a city of four million people. Not too many cars. But we had kind of a good time—it was a good picture for that purpose. You look at it now like it was a newsreel.

CC: What about the nightlife in Berlin?

BW: That was wild, that was crazy. That was a wave of dope taking. Berlin in the twenties was the town of Europe.

CC: "Dope" meaning marijuana?

BW: Dope taking—hashish, and opium, every known [drug], heroin and morphine. Then it kind of disappeared a little bit, it went underground. But there were a lot of cases of "poison" taking there. In coffeehouses, like for instance the Romanisches Café—the Roman Coffeehouse. That was the headquarters.

CC: What was it like to sit inside the Romanisches Café?

BW: It was a refuge. We lived in there, especially the bachelors. There were writers who wrote there, newspaper people, chess players, and card players. If it rained or shined, you took refuge there. We lived there more than in our own houses. It was a second home, a first home really.

CC: Just young people?

BW: No. Very civilized and very old people, too. It was warm there in the winter. We had long winters in Berlin. We were all there together. It was just enormous, what happened in that one coffeehouse. I wanted to make a picture about that, but then I got sidetracked. It was never captured in film, this feeling. It was home to us.

CC: When were you going to make that picture?

BW: Oh, in 1930, '31.

CC: Are you sorry you didn't do that?

BW: Certainly I'm sorry, but that would have been a documentary. Sound came in, and that kind of pulverized our plans.

CC: Does *Cabaret* [Bob Fosse, 1972] come close to capturing what it was really like at the time?

BW: *Cabaret* was very good, I must say. They came to me, they wanted me to do it. And at that time, I just didn't want anything to do with Germany, with Nazis. I didn't want to go there. They didn't go there either, they just did it here. Very good, though. From the novel by Mr. [Christopher] Isherwood. Good book, [but] the script was better. The picture was made by an American, and I tip my hat. Bob Fosse was a fine director, and he went much too soon. I admired Fosse very much. Big loss.

CC: How would your version have been different?

BW: I might have been more journalistic.

CC: So in the early days of Berlin, were you part of the freewheeling lifestyle, did you get into smoking the hash . . . ?

BW: No, I did not get into the hash. No. I was too young there . . . I was about nineteen or twenty [when I arrived]. I did not have the money to get it. I probably wouldn't have anyway. I don't believe in dope. Stupid. Just absolutely idiotic, and unnecessary for me.

CC: You've rarely discussed your early scripts, the ones you wrote, both in Germany and in America,

Some early German films written by Wilder: (above left to right) *Scampolo: Ein Kind der Strasse* (1932), *Emil und die Detektive* (1931), and *Das Blaue vom Himmel* (1932)

Wilder helped write and direct *People on Sunday* (right and below left); he also wrote the script for *Der Teufelsreporter* (below right) but claimed "it was a lousy picture"; (opposite below) the Romanisches Café in Berlin, 1926, where Wilder wrote the script for *People on Sunday* on pieces of scratch paper

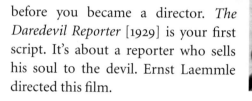

before you became a director. *The Daredevil Reporter* [1929] is your first script. It's about a reporter who sells his soul to the devil. Ernst Laemmle directed this film.

BW: *Der Teufelsreporter.* It was a lousy picture.

CC: Do you still have a copy?

BW: No, and I would not want to see it either. It was just an idea I had. I came up with the script.

CC: Did you use some of your own personal experience as a reporter to write it?

BW: [*Immediately:*] No.

CC: Does *Music in the Air* [1934], your first script produced in America, bring back many memories to you?

BW: None. That was the very, very beginning. Except I remembered [Gloria] Swanson later for *Sunset Boulevard.*

CC: *Bluebeard's Eighth Wife* [1938]?

BW: Yeah, that one was for Lubitsch. The first one that Brackett and I did for Lubitsch. Very, very funny. It was one of the weaker Lubitsch pictures, but one of the strong ones for me.

CC: This is the movie that features one of the great "cute meets." Gary Cooper and Claudette Colbert meet over a pair of pajamas. She takes the upper, he takes the lower, and you imagine, along with the characters, what they each look like half-dressed.

BW: Yeah. That's right.

CC: Did you first approach your scripts with certain tentpole scenes in mind—boy meets girl, boy loses girl, etc.?

BW: With *Bluebeard's Eighth Wife*, there was a kind of skeleton story that was there. We knew that the meeting had to be worked out, and that the machinery was going to be hidden behind good scenes, funny scenes. But we always knew where we were going. Otherwise, it's just pointless. Not every story has a third act. We had the first act, second act, third act. And then we improved it. We threw some stuff out and brought some other stuff in. But the original story, the story itself, was intact. We just knew that's the picture we're gonna make. And how we're gonna make it, we don't know yet.

CC: The element of boy-meets-girl, when man meets woman, is usually a magical event in your movies.

BW: Yeah. That's right. The moments where they meet, or the moments where they see each other clearly.

CC: Both of those actors would come back to work well with your writing later, Colbert in *Midnight* [1939] and *Arise, My Love* [1940], and Cooper in *Ball of Fire* [1941] and your own film *Love in the Afternoon* [1957]. Looking back at your early pictures that you wrote and didn't direct, it seems a little like you were studying the farm team, making notes, thinking, "Okay, Gary Cooper, he does my stuff well—I'll use him later when I'm directing."

BW: Yeah. But I did not think I would be a director in those early days when I was writing. It was only later, when we were writing the last picture at Paramount [*Hold Back the Dawn*, 1941, directed by Mitchell Leisen], where I was under contract, that I thought that. It was only after directors had fucked up things in the script that I took any great interest in staging them myself.

Before that, I never thought I would make it as a director. When the director came to inspect the script—when we were half or three-quarters finished—you know, there was respect, always. Only later on, when I found out that I was going to direct, did I allow myself to lose a little bit of my respect for Mitchell Leisen.

CC: What was the best work Mitchell Leisen did based on one of your scripts?

BW: *Midnight*. That was a good picture. Also, the leading man was Don Ameche, believe it or not. When they gave me that dinner at the [American] Film Institute, they invited everybody who had been in a picture of mine, and there was Don Ameche. He said, "I was invited here because of Mr. Wilder, but I've never met him." *He didn't know why he'd been invited!* So *en passant,* as I was walking by, I said, "Yes, you've met me with Mr. [John] Barrymore on the picture called *Midnight* that was directed by Leisen." He did not quite believe me. "I would have remembered if I was in that picture!" he said. But I remember very, very well. Hornblow was producer, he was sitting there with Brackett and me . . . and Barrymore came to check the costume or something, and Hornblow said, "Mr. Barrymore, do you know Mr. Don Ameche?" And Barrymore said, "Of course he knows me, we're sleeping with each other!" A little joke Barrymore made. Ameche didn't remember. And he was very good in that picture, I must say. I ran it about three or four years ago. It was very, very well done. Because Barrymore was too drunk to write his own scenes. [*Laughter.*] Leisen, he was a very good direc-

tor, but he did not want to have a writer on his back who would protest against things that were done. The next time, after *Midnight,* that I went down to the stage, I was not let in. There was a policeman there.

CC: How about Leisen's *Arise, My Love*?

BW: We were called in and told, "Look, the picture is about a pilot, in jail, and we would like you to write it for Colbert because she's gonna play it." That's it. We just wrote it [as a contract job]. A lot of Leisen's pictures survived; they were pretty good. But *Midnight* was an out-and-out smash. I am still always asked about that picture.

CC: How do you rate Claudette Colbert as someone who worked with your material?

BW: I worked with her only as a writer, also in *Bluebeard's Eighth Wife*. She was a good actress, who was not excited when she got the part, and she was not excited when she *didn't* get the part. She was a good, funny actress, a professional who never missed a line—but on the other hand, there was nothing surprising about her. Monroe was *always* surprising. You never knew what would come out of her. Monroe had a wonderful inborn feeling, "This is funny," or "This is when I start to cry." That, she did beautifully. Even when it took many takes, you knew it would be something surprising.

CC: Did you compliment Monroe like this at the time? [*Wilder pauses and truly considers this question.*]

BW: No. She was always crying.

Music in the Air (1934), was the first script Wilder wrote in America. He remembered Gloria Swanson when he made *Sunset Boulevard* (1950); (opposite) *Hold Back the Dawn* (1941), with Charles Boyer and Paulette Goddard. "It was only after directors had fucked up things in the script that I took any interest in staging them myself."

CC: Were you ever tempted to work with John Wayne?

BW: No. Did not do any pictures with horses. I am afraid of horses.

CC: You've written some memorable American heroes. Tarnished heroes, bittersweet comedic heroes . . . all very American. How much did America inspire your material? Do you think that your films would have had just as much bite if you'd never come to this country?

BW: I think so. About two or three years after I came to America, I had learned enough dialogue so that I could construct a little. Then it went on and on. But I never could lose my accent. You can lose your accent if you come over from Europe as a kid, if you go to school here. But at the age of twenty-eight, it was too late. It was too late for Lubitsch, and he was here since 1923. He was a little bit older when he started here. He was about thirty.

CC: It's so often written, or said, that your mother's fascination with America, and your ability to observe American culture as a European, allowed you to see it more clearly than many American writers.

BW: [*Expansively:*] Let them, let them. It's wonderful. It's wonderful.

CC: What's *your* theory on the subject?

BW: It's subconscious. I don't know. The American pictures, the background and the plotting, were different from the plotting of the German pictures that I wrote. With the German pictures . . . it was too sentimental. It was not my picture. It was just a picture which I wrote, because they liked the story that we told. But automatically, you know, you absorb something in your system. You automatically become an *American*. So I don't know. I just never thought that somebody would point out a scene and say, "This is great, now look, this is Wilder criticizing America" or ". . . flattering America." No, nothing. I was just a person who lived with Americans.

CC: *Rhythm on the River* [1940] starred Bing Crosby and Mary Martin as ghost lyricists to the hitmaker played by Basil Rathbone. You wrote the story with Jacques Théry.

BW: That was a screenplay, or rather a screen story [treatment], that I wrote in Berlin before I came to America. It was a good story, and I sold it, but then they used just one little detail. And that was it.

 The full story was of a man in New York who was kind of a Cole Porter. He did the words and the music; he was the number-one man in the country. We see now, through the backstairs, there comes a young man and he brings the music. He is the ghostwriter for the music. Then we see a girl, who comes later, without knowing the man. She brings him the lyrics. In other words, the Cole Porter character has got two people who are ghostwriting for him, because he's suffering from writer's block. The boy and the girl meet and find that they're working on the same man's songs. [*Wilder pops a mint.*] But now, now that they know each other, they're going to stay together and make a name for themselves: "Goodbye, Mr. Porter." And now the two get married, and she's pregnant, and they cannot get a job—because they're good ghostwriters, they keep their mouths shut about what they did previously. And now nothing, no matter what they write. They cannot sell anything. They sound too much like Cole Porter!

 Now the third act was—which they did not use—about a great writer, an Irving Berlin type, who comes up to see them. Destitute, the two of them, husband and wife, lyrics and music. And Berlin just takes his coat off and sits down, and he becomes the ghostwriter for the two. That was the story. They made *Rhythm on the River* out of it.

Ace in the Hole: Wilder on location with his cameraman, Charles Lang. "Lang sort of walked around, always, with the same look on his face. Squinting, filled with thought, as if he were looking at the world, not just the movie, and thinking, what kind of exposure is this? What exposure is the *world*?"

CC: Black-and-white versus color?

BW: There was a period when color was just too ice cream. A little raspberry juice, a little lemon juice—it was very hideous, you know. Because we were doing it in "color" instead of just *doing* it, shooting a picture in color without knowing it's in color. I just said, "Let's not do that. It's going to be all black or all white." I was just against color.

It's very difficult to shoot in black-and-white, you know, because you've got to create your own shadows. You have to kind of invent a thing, which then gives you a *thing*. In color, now, you can put the camera there and you just shoot, very natural. Not that heavy color, though. You've never made a movie in black-and-white?

CC: I'm tempted. There's just such a great texture to it, it seems to lend itself to storytelling.

BW: Yeah. But if there's a picture of mine that should be in [true] color, it's *Some Like It Hot.* I think it should have been done in color. Sure. The right colors were not available, the process was just not there. Just slip the colors in, no big deal.

CC: Interesting. I vote for black-and-white on that one.

BW: It's very hard to get them to let you shoot a picture in black-and-white these days. For television, they don't want any black-and-white pictures. But if you put in a little work, it's very good.

CC: How about cinematographer Charles Lang, who did *Sabrina* and many others with you?

BW: Charles Lang was very good. Charles Lang—"Junior." He's two or three years older than I am! He's still very, very strong. He was a very fine man. Lang sort of walked around, always, with the same look on his face: squinting, filled with thought, as if he were looking at the world, not just the movie, and thinking, "What kind of exposure is this? What exposure is the *world*?" He was in the upper class of photographers, along with LaShelle. He was on time, a wonderful collaborator, and I loved him.

CC: Any advice for shooting a picture in black-and-white today?

BW: Get yourself an aging master cinematographer.

CC: One of your greatest shots, the most bravura shot in all your films, is the final shot of *Ace in the Hole*. Kirk Douglas, stabbed with a pair of scissors, falls dead on the floor into a close-up. Spike Lee, who did an homage to the shot in *Malcolm X*, asks how you came up with that.

BW: [*Smiles.*] I like Spike Lee. He's a good, lively filmmaker. The shot was always in my mind, but it wasn't a part of the script. I never put much camera direction into the screenplays. We dug a hole and put the camera there. We were sure he was going to end up in the hole himself. We knew he was gonna die. *How* he was going to die—that came in the writing of the thing. The shot we had as we wrote the script. The camera is down low because something's gonna happen. It's gonna pay off. And then Kirk Douglas falls into the close-up. I wanted something powerful, and that was one of the few times I went for a bold shot like that. I needed it, but I never based a scene around a shot. Never an outré shot. That was outlandish. Never to astonish people. It was logical there. Instead of—he falls down in a long shot, then we cut to the close-up. No. I didn't want to do that.

CC: Were you a big one for lenses? Knowing what lens you wanted to use for what scene?

BW: Yeah . . . yeah. I always go for a thirty-five or forty. I just say, "Give me a wide lens," because I need a long shot. I don't have lenses. I don't have blue glasses. [*Gently contemptuous:*] Nothing. I don't. Doesn't make me a better director.

CC: Similarly, how did you decide if you were going to shoot a picture in wide screen? Movies like *The Fortune Cookie* and *The Apartment* were in wide screen.

BW: That was not the extreme version [of wide screen] that they had at the time. The love story of two dachshunds, that was the only thing it was good for . . . but a great big new thing. It was Fox who had that thing—CinemaScope—and it was gonna revolutionize the country. And I said, "It's not gonna revolutionize nothing." Because unless you always have panorama shots of the grandstand at the races or something, it's gonna be a lot of empty stuff. When you have a close-up, you cannot do it always in the center. There's nothing there. It's like the invention of a triangular screen, or Smellorama . . . that stuff, it's absolute nonsense.

CC: A question about comedy. Why do you think comedy is still undervalued as an art form? Why do you think even an overheated drama is always more seriously regarded than some of the greatest comedies?

BW: With comedies, people think that actors come on the stage and they invent those things, those little jokes. A serious thing, you know, of course, they are in *awe* of it. Some comedies have won the awards, like for instance *It Happened One Night*. It was a kind of runaway hit. It won everything. I don't know. Lubitsch never got an [Academy] Award; he got an *honorary* award. Because a serious picture weighs more?

CC: Did you ever feel militant on the subject, that this was something that had to be changed, or did you just accept it?

BW: I accepted it. It all changed, you know, constantly, because I always wanted to do something new. Something new in *Ace in the Hole* was to kind of show the newspaperman racket. When they have a story, they keep it to themselves. But when I started a comedy, I was just looking for a comedy. It seemed to me that it's much more rewarding to sit in the audience and hear them laugh.

CC: Do script pages exist on the Marx Brothers comedy that you and Diamond once planned [around 1960–61] about the Marx Brothers at the U.N.?

BW: No. We never had script pages. It was just an idea. We had an idea of doing a Marx Brothers picture set against the background of the United Nations. They were the four representatives of a republic. And that is always good, because the Marx Brothers were at their best against a very serious, pompous background. They were very good in *A Night at the Opera* because it's very pompous, the opera. They were also quite good at the race track, in *A Day at the Races*. But other things they did, they were not so good because there was nothing good to poke at. I wanted to do a Marx Brothers picture, but then Chico died, and Harpo was very, very unstable. But Groucho was a genius, absolutely a fabulous, fabulous man. They were at Metro. The movie would have been a combination of at least six of their top stars of the early sixties. Zeppo was the leading man. Zeppo as lead was incredible, absolutely incredible. When you went to see *Night at the Opera*, you were not disappointed. Thalberg was very smart, you know, because he treated it like a serious picture.

CC: Did you have a comedy rule about people reacting to the jokes within the film? In other words, which jokes were for the characters to acknowledge, and which jokes were only for the audience to acknowledge?

BW: Most of the time, the characters should not acknowledge the jokes. Sometimes you let them have it. As long as the actors are not in motion, you can prolong or shorten the joke. But it's a very smart idea not to put your actor in a long shot for everything. You have to be able to cut. But God help you if you leave a joke there because you thought it was a tremendous laugh . . . but in the next theater, suddenly it's a very short laugh, because there were only a

hundred people there. I figured that out, how you do it. It's just timing, and editing. But it's very important, how the actors react to the joke. Even in a two-shot: how do they react?

CC: There is a lot of your own work that is still unissued on video. Do you have conversations with studios, or archivists, about refurbishing your films so that they can be seen by future generations? Is that a concern to you?

BW: No. They've remade them . . . and remade them, so they don't want people to know [where they came from]. [*Laughs.*] For instance, *Double Indemnity* was remade five or six times. Always under different titles. And never, never any better. I think that also if the picture is fifty years old, the leading people there—Stanwyck, Robinson, MacMurray— they don't mean as much to the young audience, the middle-aged audience. They don't mean as much as an actor who could have barely played a small part in one of my pictures.

But fifty years, that is a long time. On the other hand, there are people who were born fifty years ago, forty years ago, thirty years ago, twenty years ago, who would enjoy to see that picture once more, or for the first time. But to rerelease the old pictures? The agents are against it, because they're not gonna make their fortunes.

CC: And yet, there's television. The last time we were here, you were signing photos for the people who'd written you—and those people all saw your work on television.

BW: They do know the picture of mine that they like very much, or the picture which they still see every week once . . . all sorts of nonsense is gonna be done to those pictures [when they are remade]. What am I gonna do now? Nothing. I'm just gonna sit and wait. I'm curious myself how it's gonna end.

CC: Do ideas for your films ever come from dreams?

Wilder (above) with cameraman Charles Lang; (left) Audrey Hepburn on location for *Sabrina*

BW: For a film, not yet. At a hundred, I'm going to get the great dream.

CC: Many directors just lose the edge. They film their dream project, and it fails. Then they slowly begin to compromise, they chase a hit. . . . There are so many ways a director can get soft, particularly trying to make it in the Hollywood system.

Or you can give up—"I'm not going to fight that fight"—and look for independent financing.

BW: Yeah. But that financing runs out, you know.

CC: How have you managed to stay sharp?

BW: For ninety-one, I'm sharp. But for nineteen, I'm not so sharp. [*Laughs.*] Yeah, I am always conscious of the work that you undertake as a director. It is, my God, the first day of shooting and then you have to have another seven weeks! [*Pause.*] But nobody has come to me and asked me whether I wanted to direct a new picture.

I got a job in the eighties with United Artists. Mr. [Jerry] Weintraub, and he hired me for my judgment on properties. But what I completely didn't realize was—what if he has a bucketful of stories and all of them stink? He had already invested money in them, quarter of a million, half a million. What can I do except "I'm very sorry, I cannot handle it"? If he had come to me first, before he had bought these properties, I would have said, "Let me read them." I may be wrong, but overall I'm gonna be right. I can definitely say, "This will not make a picture, this will not work." But it was too late. There was not one thing that he bought that made me say, "This is a picture." It was just dreadful.

The very day when [CEO Kirk] Kerkorian took the same elevator that I did, going down, he told me, "It's so wonderful that you're with the organization, blah-blah-blah . . . and good luck to you." And I said, "It's my last day—I'm gone. I've been here two months, and it's no good." The only good thing, Streisand directed it—*The Prince of Tides* [1991]. That was that. I had nothing to do with it, but even this could have been a better picture. I was there as a kibitzer—as a man who is enthusiastic about a project or says, "Don't buy that." But he bought it. He bought everything.

CC: Why did you take that job? Was it in lieu of directing?

BW: I just told myself that I would find something there, one picture out of twenty projects that they bought, *something*. And maybe I can help the writer, maybe I can concentrate on one thing. But it was a very, very lousy time for me. I could not get out of it. I just got very good money, five thousand dollars a week, to say, "This is no good," "This is bad," "This I would pursue." They did not have to take my word for

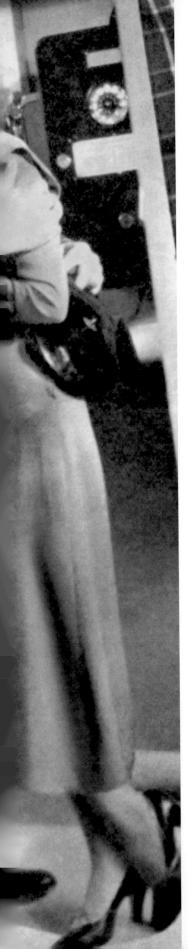

it. But there was nothing there. There was not one good picture that came out of that. As a matter of fact, there was not one good picture that they shot.

CC: Something that I think about in terms of the future of comedy is that human nature, and human personality, is still so mysterious and odd and embarrassing and funny that there's still comedy to be written if you work hard enough.

BW: Of course, of course. And you don't want to get an award.

CC: At ninety-one, do you feel that human nature is still as mysterious and odd and funny and embarrassing?

BW: It's very odd, the new inventions. We're discovering more and more, and we know less and less.

I ask him about the top news story of the day.

CC: Did you get a thrill from the Pathfinder photos from Mars?

BW: Yeah, but not if I see them every night! [*Laughter.*] You see the stones, and the one rock looks like the other rock, and they applaud. But it's a very, very fine thing to have shot a camera up there—for how many thousands of years it will be there. But I think we are going to go deeper and find out we know less and less. We know absolutely nothing. Nothing new since the days when Galileo, Copernicus came up with "The world is round."

CC: I wanted to bring up the subject of time capsules. You know how they bury time capsules, for future generations? I think TriStar recently sent a capsule into outer space with a copy of the script of *The Last Action Hero*—

BW: To see what lousy pictures they could make?

CC: [*Laughs.*] And this is a difficult question, but I would love, as part of our conversations, for you to say something to the future generations of filmmakers. A message that we could send to the people who read this interview, long after we're gone. I know it's a tough question.

BW: Yeah, it's a tough question. Maybe I have to send you a telegram with the answer. [*Laughs.*] I am not anchored there at some observatory, you know. I think that we're living in very, very important and interesting times. I think we're going to get used to the new inventions, but they're not gonna be as interesting as it

Das Blaue vom Himmel (1932): Wilder wrote the screenplay for this eighty-two-minute operetta directed by Viktor Janson.

would seem. If we concentrated on the United Nations, and worked on a prospect that there's gonna be no more wars, no more atomic wars, no more poison gas—that would be much more important than that thing [up on Mars]. But we're not even close to having an assured peace in this world. And it usually lasts only seventy years that you are capable of doing something about it. And then the next generation comes.

But I don't know. I'm just very curious. That's the one thing that keeps me alive, is curiosity.

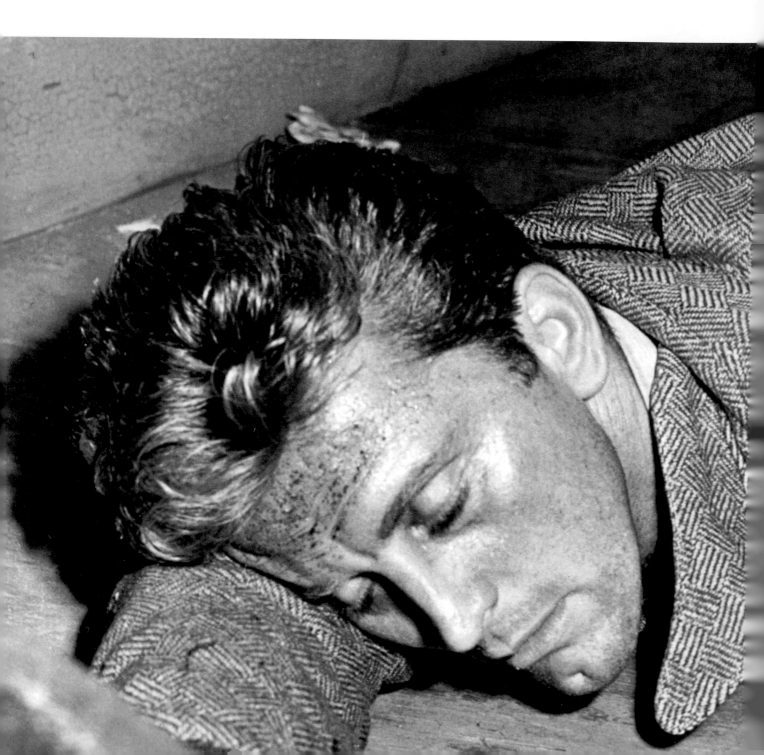

In the unforgettable final shot of *Ace in the Hole* (1951), Kirk Douglas falls into a low-angle close-up, dead. It's the single most bravura camera move in the career of a director who famously preferred camera work to be invisible. "I came up with it on the day. It's the first or second take. We stood in a hole with the camera."

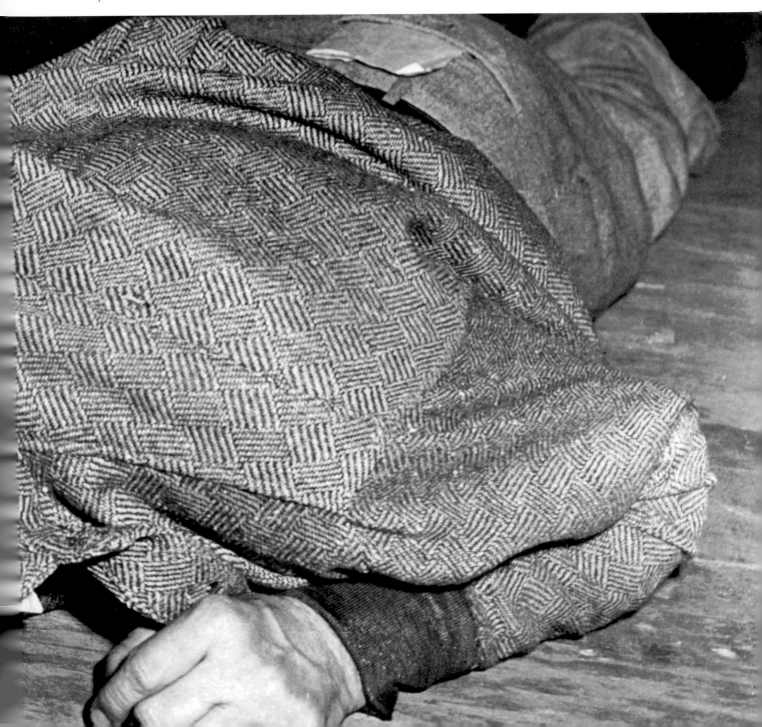

On the set of *Sunset Boulevard* (1950): Wilder in the Paramount office of
William Holden's girlfriend

CC: What should a score do for a film?

BW: It should be invisible, of course. Sometimes not. The score, for instance, of Richard Strauss, the opening, with the monkeys and the clubs in *2001: A Space Odyssey* [1968], that was absolutely sensational. That was wonderful, just great. But I think that music can also provoke. It provokes such feelings, such love, such hatred, just such excitement. The excitement is usually better than what's been shot. The score is very, very important. You need all the help you can get. I had my favorite composers, they were [Franz] Waxman and [Miklos] Rozsa . . . and sometimes I had Mr. [André] Previn. But Waxman and Rozsa, two Europeans, provided my best scores. They knew my work, knew it intuitively.

CC: In 1993, Fernando Trueba accepted his Best Foreign Film Oscar for *Belle Epoque* [1992] and endeared himself to all Wilder fans when he said: "I'd like to thank God, but I don't believe in God, so I'd like to thank Billy Wilder." Did he call you to warn you?

BW: [*Still charmed:*] No, no. Absolutely not. I was watching at home, because I only go to the Academy Awards when I win, or when I am giving. Either giving or getting. Then, if I'm at home, naturally I'm watching it. And then that guy came up there, and he says, "I don't believe in God, I believe in Billy Wilder." I was fixing a martini, and I let go of that very thin glass. I thought, "Did I hear right? Is the guy crazy, or what?" I talked to him afterwards. He came to see me.

Nice man. He surprised me.

7:50 p.m. Mr. Chow, Beverly Hills. I arrive for dinner early with my wife, making what I feel is a thrilling statement, a tone-setting move for tonight's dinner with Audrey and Billy Wilder.

"May I help you?" asks the hostess.

"Yes," I announce, rather expansively. "We're here a little early for dinner with the Wilders."

"Oh, good," she says. "They're already here." Sitting on stools at the bar are Audrey and Billy Wilder: Billy in a dress suit, Audrey in Chanel.

"We got here fifteen minutes early," Wilder explains. "We're just having a good time."

I introduce my wife, and we adjourn to the table for dinner.

The waiters dote on the Wilders, seating Billy first at his favorite seat at the usual table. It is an evening that never drags, nor does the conversation. Billy speaks engagingly, dazzling our newest dinner guest. His mood tonight, like his greatest work, is brisk and delectable.

We discuss his archives, most of which survived an early office fire. His papers and scripts were untouched, as was the famous Ninotchka *preview card reading, "I laughed so hard I peed in my girlfriend's hand."*

"This was before I met you," he says to Audrey.

"I was in high school," Audrey replies.

"Please," says Billy, "we don't need to know this much."

As always, he inquires about Tom Cruise's ongoing experience filming Eyes Wide Shut *in England with Stanley Kubrick. His interest is fixed on any detail concerning Kubrick's newest film. "He*

7

has never made a bad picture," says Wilder. "Each picture he trumps the trump."

I mention that it is the twentieth anniversary of Elvis's death and the news reports are filled with tributes. Wilder shrugs. "I did not get it." He says this respectfully, almost scientifically. "But he died at the right time. Where else was he going to go? Now he is a deity." Wilder admits liking the Beatles a little, only when pushed. "They had a personality, as a group. The other music . . . there is nothing to remember." His eyebrows rise; he shrugs a little. "What is rock music?" he asks, staring at me.

It is not a rhetorical question, and he is waiting for an answer.

I smile and nod. This is maybe one subject I have on him. As a former rock journalist, I proceed in the briefest possible way to share the history of rock and roll with Wilder. I begin with Robert Johnson and the blues, continuing through Elvis, the British Invasion, the rise of English hard rock, American pop, the arrival of punk, and am even able to finish by referencing the unplugged version of Eric Clapton's "Layla" now playing in the next room, bringing it all back to Robert Johnson in less than two minutes.

Wilder thinks about all this for a few moments, weighing the concepts. "I can live without it." He shrugs happily.

Such is the banter throughout dinner. I ask how Audrey's brother is. "He's fine. I saw him today for lunch," she says. "I'm not sure she has a brother," Wilder says, in a comic aside. He takes a sip of beer. His poker face is priceless.

I ask him about the looks in his movies. "Ginger Rogers was great." He does her look. "The great ones know how to do it." He offers a look of surprise. "Or to be curious"; he does the Curious look. And then the pièce de résistance, the look of an impish schnook. Each one a cinema staple, each one believable comedy from the man who says he is not an actor. And then Wilder does another look, a look of enchantment. Sabrina would be proud. He returns to his noodles.

Audrey and Billy evaluate the meal for a moment. They do not flaunt their affection, but it is clear in their

(Opposite) A view of the Hotel del Coronado in San Diego from the beach; Wilder used it in *Some Like It Hot* (1959).

almost collegiate chemistry. Audrey talks of Wilder, as he sits there quietly studying the last of his dinner, feigning only mild interest. He has never signed his name on any love letters or any notes to her, says Audrey. "He always used a pseudonym, a character like 'Colonel Johnson.' Never his name!"

Wilder looks up suddenly. "I didn't want to leave a trace!"

"I only got him to sign a marriage contract," she points out, dryly.

And then something dazzling, in its own small way. Wilder's eyes open wide, he turns to her: something about her comment utterly charms him. He lights up with a surprised look of wonder, and I realize what this is—this is Billy Wilder laughing.

Our wives go off to the bar for a chat, leaving us alone. Wilder asks about my next project, anxious to discuss any current problems. "Do you have a third act?" he asks pointedly. Structure, he says, is never easy. "It always takes time. For me, a year per script."

The talk turns to our interviews. "Do whatever you like with it," he says, dispassionately. It seems important to him that I know he finds the art of self-promotion rather inelegant. "Whatever you do with it . . . magazine or book publisher, do what you wish." I suspect I'm being paid a compliment. "Do whatever you like with it." He turns away. "Or just keep it for yourself."

The interviews continue the next morning, at Wilder's office. The door is ajar. I find him at his desk, shuffling through mail. The window slats are pulled open behind him; trucks rumble through the alley.

"Did you sleep well?" he asks.

"Yeah, I did. Did you?"

"Yeah, I slept," he answers. "I slept. I wake up every once in a while and orient myself, where I am." We proceed.

CC: I have a question about the Hotel del Coronado, in San Diego. I grew up in San Diego. The legend is that the hotel was the most magical part of the filming of *Some Like It Hot,* that Marilyn Monroe felt relaxed there.

BW: Yeah, that was fun. We had a good time there. We had a good time. I was just looking for something that looked like a hotel in Florida. And I was shown the hotel, and that was it. That was the style. Marilyn remembered her lines, everything was fine. Everything was going according to schedule.

CC: So you have good memories.

BW: Yes. Very good.

CC: And the exteriors were done there too, in the water, when Joe E. Brown was coming out of the boat?

BW: Yeah. Did about two weeks of shooting there.

CC: Marilyn seems fully engaged in those scenes.

BW: Yeah. She has that quality. She can do that.

CC: There's a story that Marilyn came to see a preview of *The Apartment,* and it was at that preview that you discussed her playing the lead in *Irma la Douce.*

BW: Yeah. There was a preview, and then there was a dinner, a party at Romanoff's. I think I very rarely listened to what she had to say. It was all kind of stilted.

CC: Why did you end up not using her for *Irma la Douce*?

BW: I don't remember. A commitment, I think. I just . . . maybe the wound was too fresh, you know? I needed a little bandage there. So I did *One Two Three,* which I did completely in Berlin and Munich.

CC: Just a quick photo to show you, it's a famous photo. I believe it's on the set of *Some Like It Hot,* she's wearing the "I'm Through with Love" dress. It's you and Marilyn . . .

BW: I don't know. Maybe I'd kissed her ear.

CC: What do you think you're saying here?

BW: "Show them a little bit more. Show them a little more character." Or "Show a little bit more bosom"—or "... a little bit *less* bosom." It was just a little sideshow I always had with her. Maybe it was a little something that she did, nobody's business but hers and mine.

CC: One of the reasons you've said that Marilyn enjoyed the Hotel del Coronado sequences in *Some Like It Hot* is that she had an audience there on the beach watching her. Is that true? Were there, again, a lot of people lined up, watching the filming?

BW: She had an audience. She always had thousands in New York, but at the beach there, hundreds. Yeah, she's a show-off.

CC: So they would be cheering and screaming and yelling?

BW: Screaming and yelling. But then when I wanted it quiet I had her say "Shhhh." They listened to her.

(Above) Marilyn Monroe liked to perform in front of an audience; (right) "I'm not sure what I'm whispering. Probably 'Show a little more.' Show a little more character, a little more bosom ... or a little *less* bosom ..."

CC: I'd like to talk a little bit more about the clothes in your films. The importance of clothing in completing a character.

BW: Yeah. The best example there is the clothes that Sabrina wore, and then the clothes that the remake of it had. That was just nothing. It depends on the actors, too. For instance, I had a special little niche for Givenchy. He did the clothes for Audrey Hepburn. There was always that style, you know. Of course she did not wear the clothes when she was with her father washing cars [at the beginning of *Sabrina*]. She was barefoot. So that I have distance, you know. She has some way to go there. So when she wore the clothes that she brought from Paris, Givenchy kind of gets all the fireworks.

Wilder answers his office phone. Someone is inquiring after the rights to one of his older films. "Yeah," *he says, politely and firmly. "But I don't own the rights." The caller persists. Wilder dials down the politeness. "Yes, but Mr. Wilder does not own the rights. Goodbye."*

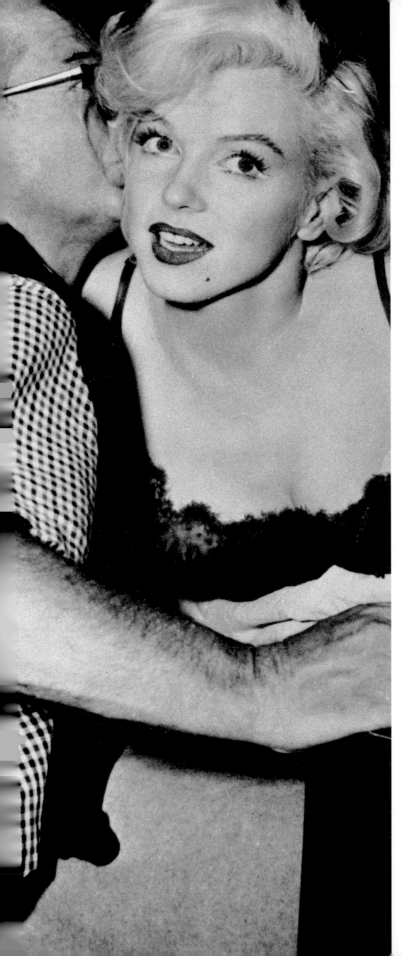

BW: Yeah, Givenchy. He was one of the best. And he kind of felt the girl she was underneath that dress. And that was Audrey Hepburn. She was simple, but stunning.

CC: So this was a big decision, when you decided to go with someone other than Edith Head for Sabrina's look after Paris.

BW: Givenchy? No, I knew that Audrey had first-class taste. And I knew that she knew the character, and I let her go, and she never disappointed me. She was delighted by Givenchy. He was a great friend of hers. It was wonderful. They were just way up there in the sky, you know, and I'm sure if he dies, he's gonna look her up. That was Audrey Hepburn. She was a thing made in heaven. It was obvious from her first Hollywood picture, *Roman Holiday*.

CC: Did William Wyler, who directed *Roman Holiday*, introduce you to Hepburn?

BW: No, there was some agent that brought her around. We first saw a test that was made with her. She looked like a princess. I got ahold of her after that, and then I got ahold of her once more.

Wilder's phone rings again and he answers. I can immediately sense from his strained cordiality that Wilder has just made the day of a show-business bottom feeder who has dialed his number and hit the jackpot. Though Wilder begins begging off shortly after "Hello," the caller refuses to go away easily. I can hear the sales pitch over the phone, four feet away. The great Wilder is getting hustled on the remake rights to Sunset Boulevard. *Suddenly all galantry disappears. The hustler's time is up. "I do not own the rights!" Wilder says sharply. "Call Paramount!" He hangs up, and the receiver rattles on the cradle.*

Orry-Kelly designed the diaphanous dresses Marilyn Monroe wore in *Some Like It Hot*, including the black see-through one for the number "I Wanna Be Loved By You." "It was a very good dress and it fitted her as a band singer. It was very well accepted," adds Wilder with typical understatement.

BW: [*Confiding:*] "Would Elizabeth Taylor be a good substitute for a new version of *Sunset Boulevard*, filmed against a fifties background?" *I have no idea!!* I'm sure she would be no better or worse than the actress who played Audrey Hepburn in the remake of *Sabrina*.

CC: [*Laughs.*] So . . . there's a wonderful sequence in *Sabrina* that brings together character, clothes, performance, and story, all in a shot. Sabrina's chauffeur father has just called her a "displaced person." Now you cut to her spinning in that chair at the head of the table in Linus Larrabee's conference room. She is perfectly at home with herself.

BW: Yeah.

CC: And you pull back with her collapsing like a swan on the desk in that great black dress. And that . . . that is to me one of the great little gifts that the right costume can bring you. It's the wonderful—

BW: Yeah.

CC: —last piece of the puzzle.

BW: Clothes were important to her, you know, and she always drifted towards Givenchy. Givenchy, who was there, for instance, that evening when they gave her that homage at the Lincoln Center. We all were there. I was there, Stanley Donen was there . . . Wyler could not be there, because he was dead, I think. Everybody made a little speech. Gregory Peck was there, because he was her first leading man, in *Roman Holiday*. Yeah, that was a fun time, you know, because there was never a loud word spoken.

CC: Were you a very big part of the costume design? Would they bring you every gown far in advance?

BW: Sure, they would bring me the gowns. I always liked everything [Givenchy] did, and I was very much surprised that it all worked. But the credit went to Edith Head because she got [credit on all the pictures at Paramount].

CC: And when they brought you Marilyn Monroe's gowns for *Some Like It Hot*, was that her own designer that you were working with?

BW: Who was that? That was Marilyn Monroe. No, she was not interested in costumes. She was not a clotheshorse. You could put anything on her you wanted. If it showed something, then she accepted it. As long as it showed a little something.

CC: Those diaphanous dresses she wore in *Some Like It Hot*—

BW: Those were designed by Orry-Kelly. [Orry-Kelly won the Academy Award for his work.]

CC: The flesh-colored "I'm Through with Love" dress was a stunner. It's almost not there. And the "I Wanna Be Loved by You" dress did the same thing, in black.

BW: [*Responds clinically, almost prudishly, with massive understatement:*] It was a very good dress. It kind of fitted her, as a band singer, and she also played the ukelele, and it was very well accepted.

CC: What did you think of *Tootsie* [1982]?

BW: There was an interview in the *New York Times* with Mr. [Sydney] Pollack where he said, "I developed something that is kind of brand-new. When Dustin Hoffman decides to become a woman, we did not do that dull thing, you know, where he goes and borrows a dress here, and tries the hairdo, and he slowly becomes Tootsie." He said, "I just cut and there was Tootsie." [*Wilder, who is not prone to such credit taking, feels strongly about this one cut. He continues, earnestly. He wishes it on the record.*] I did that in *Some Like It Hot*. I had that years ago. In other words, when Tony Curtis says over the phone, already mimicking the voice of a woman, that he and his friend are open for the touring date . . . the next cut we see the two dressed as women. The two guys decide to go with the ladies' band, because that's the only job they can get. They're gonna be dames. And I cut, and there they were. Wherever they got the dresses—from a girlfriend who forgot to put it back on, whatever—we just *omitted* that. We just had a sharp cut, and big laugh, once we see the two of them dressed as women, coming down the train platform. Walking. And we had such big laughs with the walks. . . . We had, like, two or three railroad cars on the MGM lot, maybe they're still there. So we cut and we saw the two walking, and the laughs kept coming and coming. They were bigger and bigger, so that I went back and I used the beads and the shoes and the stuff, always cheating, because we only had three wagons.

CC: A very modern cut.

BW: That was a modern cut, because there was no dissolve, no nothing, just *bang*—cut. From the two big heads in the telephone booth to the shot of their legs walking along the railroad platform. Not one word. It could have been so dull, you know: "Let's see whether we can do a

hairdo." Nothing. We did nothing. We just cut when the guys are on the phone, and when Mr. Curtis says to the agent that he's a woman, you know? And now the problem is solved. And they are women.

Tootsie was very good, but they tried to make it a little too serious with that element of actors looking for parts and not getting them, or whatever.

CC: There are so many films that are now called "Wilderesque." You read a lot of interviews with directors who say, "We were trying for a Billy Wilder tone." And I wondered—this may be a tough question for you to answer—but was there any recent movie you've seen that made you say to yourself, "This guy gets it. This is the kind of thing I would have done with Izzy Diamond."

BW: [*Pause.*] There are lots of movies I would like to have made—some wonderful movies. Some serious movies, some very funny movies. For instance, I would have loved to have made *M*A*S*H* [Robert Altman, 1970]. That was a first-class movie. Forgotten today. That was our kind of picture. The story, the actors—wonderful.

CC: It's too bad that the studio backing wasn't there for you and Diamond to make more films in the eighties. There was so much to write about—the rise of Reagan, the era of greed—

BW: —the disappearance of the importance of the director. You don't know any director, or just a very, very few. It has diminished with the power of the star, [getting] ten million, fifteen million . . . this is absolutely outrageous. And the producer—six producers on a picture! It's not anymore the medium of the director. You will need only two or three or four fingers to count the directors who are very well known. The directors have lost their power. It will come back. It always comes back. There were the directors, and then there were the producers . . . maybe even the writer will become important. He's important in the theater.

CC: There has also been a disappearance of the light touch. So many movies now are designed for a global audience, everything is hit with a hammer.

BW: It is, I think, that we are fed too much stuff for nothing, on television. We are too [satiated] . . . we don't want that dinner anymore, because we had that dinner. We had that dinner, Monday through Sunday.

CC: I'm curious. For many years, there was so much popular culture in your films. You felt very connected to pop culture for a long time.

BW: Yeah.

CC: There's jazz, there's "hip" dialogue, all very current. . . . I wonder when you started to feel that popular culture was parting company with you.

BW: It was the end of jazz. It was always that I was a guy who was trying to speak to as many people as I possibly could. I was not a guy who was writing deep-dish revelations, or writing a play like *Waiting for Godot*. That did not interest me. It interested me to lift the taste of the average person, just lift it a little bit. With some pictures, people leave the theater and it's forgotten. If people see a picture of mine, and then sit down in a drugstore in a neighborhood or have coffee and talk about it for fifteen minutes, that is a very fine reward, I think. That's good enough for me.

CC: And fifteen minutes is enough for you?

BW: [*Pauses, reconsiders.*] Fifteen minutes is the *minimum*.

CC: [*Laughs.*] But can you remember a moment when you started to feel disconnected from popular culture?

BW: Yeah. That was the moment, you know, when I saw the kind of pictures that were coming. And it was all action. You have to have action, you have to have somebody moving, and so on. But it was all right down the toilet. There are well-made action pictures. For instance, I liked *Jaws* [1975] very much.

CC: We're talking about the seventies, right? The release of *The Godfather* [1972] . . . the increased violence in movies?

BW: No, *The Godfather* was a first-class picture, one of the best pictures ever made. I like it. I just kind of knew at a certain point that we had sold out to the guys who were making special effects. That has happened and that has stopped me from going to nine-tenths of the pictures. It started slowly, and then in half a season, everything was special effects. It was higher and higher for the car to fall into the river, from the twenty-fifth floor. Then they made it the fiftieth floor. It was just a . . . I knew what was going to happen, and it was just too much. And then the caricature sets in—without them knowing it, they make caricature. With that town underwater, you know? With New York underwater?

CC: You've been very complimentary about the Kennedys. What's your theory on the Kennedy assassination?

BW: I just think that there's less to it than people make. It's just a guy. I bitterly regret that [Oswald] was shot when he was being led there by the police. That was . . . that was bad. I also had the feeling that Kennedy was on his way to becoming a very important president. There was a space for him on Mount Rushmore.

CC: Do you remember your conversations with John Kennedy at all?

BW: No, I just actually saw him two or three times. Once I saw him in the house of his sister who was married to Peter Lawford. And he was just getting out of his tennis clothes and putting something on. And Aud was wonderful because he was then the president, and it was on a Sunday, at the beach, and the *New York Times* had arrived, so she went to work on a crossword puzzle. [*Rapturous, he finds it the coolest move ever.*] There's nothing that she had to say. I talked to him . . . we didn't talk politics. We had a kind of chat.

CC: He knew your work?

BW: He knew my work. [*Matter-of-fact:*] I had made pictures with Marilyn Monroe, so he should have seen them. I kind of had an imaginary picture, that he was staying at the hotel in Century City—he had a suite there—and a helicopter came from Air Force One, came to pick him up . . . and the moment the girls saw the guy was about to land, you know, everybody was sitting, running the water in the bidet— you know, everybody was getting ready for who he wanted.

CC: [*Laughs.*] You don't remember which pictures you discussed with him?

BW: No, we just didn't talk about the pictures. We talked about Malibu, the people that were there, about power, whether I preferred Long Island to Malibu. We were just talking nonsense. But I had a more interesting talk about politics with Robert Kennedy. That was in the house of Ernie Kovacs. He was there for dinner. And he was very open, very intelligent. He *just* talked about politics.

The conversation turns to my newest project. I tell Wilder what he may already have guessed, based on my many questions about how personal his films really are. I've been writing a somewhat autobiographical screenplay—perhaps it will be my next film. He nods with encouragement, then immediately inquires about the structure. They are tricky pictures to make work, he says, noting he'd shied away from such a project himself because "it would only have been of interest to my mother and father." We discuss the autobiographical works of others.

CC: Along with Louis Malle's *Murmur of the Heart* [1971], Truffaut's *The 400 Blows* [1959] is one of the great autobiographical films. They are both signature films for the directors who made them. If you had made an autobiographical film of your childhood, what would it have been like?

BW: [*In the swift manner of a story editor, he examines the details of his life.*] It would have been kind of an autobiography of a disturbed guy who goes to the gymnasium—the high school there—and does not know what he's gonna be, what he's going to do.

CC: Why "disturbed"?

BW: I was disturbed because I put my values on the wrong things. I had no idea, in the gymnasium, of what I'm gonna be. I just fought the idea of my father to become a lawyer. That I didn't want to do, and I saved myself, by having become a newspaperman, a reporter, very badly paid. And with [bandleader] Paul Whiteman going to Berlin to give a concert, I latched onto him, only to go and to write about the concert that he gave. But first I was a newspaperman in Vienna. And then I just went to Berlin to write about that concert. But I got stuck. I rented a room and I was a bachelor who was kind of throwing his importance around.

Introducing Marilyn: Monroe had pressed for a special entrance in *Some Like It Hot*. Wilder (opposite top) demonstrates the move. After remaining offstage for the first ten minutes of the picture, she appears bustling down the railroad platform as steam from the train gooses her; (opposite bottom) at Peter Lawford's house at the beach. On Kennedy: "We talked about Malibu . . . we were just talking nonsense."

My father was no help to me, my mother was no help to me. My brother, two years older, left for London, and then for America, years and years ago. I did not know what I was going to do; I just knew it's going to be *something*. My father wanted me to become a lawyer. But that did not work out, on account of me.

I started with crossword puzzles, and I signed them. Then I graduated. I could have gone to the university, but I did not.

CC: It's in several of the extended pieces written about you that you left the university to become a newspaperman.

BW: No. I never went. I had the right to go to the university, because I made the final exam in the gymnasium—it's called the *Matura*—and I passed it. And then came a scene with my father, and I just said no, I would not go and become a lawyer. I just said, "I'm gonna become a newspaperman." And I did, through a lucky circumstance. I never went to the university. But people go by the old interviews. Which they made up. No, I never went. I got my foot in the door of a newspaper that came out at noon, the noontime paper [*Die Stunde*]. Then I started writing about football, and about movies. Little things.

Then Whiteman came to Vienna on a visit. He did not know Europe, so he went to see Vienna. He gave concerts, in London, in Paris, in Berlin, and in Amsterdam. I made an interview with him. In Vienna, in the hotel where I made the interview, he had a black man who he only used for winding up the Victrola. [*Smiles at the image.*] In my broken English, I told him that I was anxious to see him perform. And Whiteman told me, "If you're eager to hear me, to hear the big band, you can come with me to

Berlin. . . ." He paid for my trip, for a week there or something. And I accepted it. And I packed up my things, and I never went back to Vienna. I wrote the piece about Whiteman for the paper in Vienna. And then I was a newspaperman for a paper in Berlin [the *Berliner Nachtausgabe*].

I was a very lazy newspaperman, because I was in love with three or four girls, and I would not show up. I was fired, I was rehired, I was hired by another paper. But I then went into the direction of writing for movies. I was a ghostwriter. And those were very tough days, because there was many a night when I slept in the waiting room of a railway station. I had my clothes with a landlady who rented my room. The rent was about twenty-five dollars a month. No laundry, no nothing. I was rooming with a friend for a while. I just wanted to give it up. The writing was "black"—no credit listed. That was in the days when scripts were twenty-five pages. There was no dialogue, nothing. I tried to stay happy, to not let it depress me. Then I got the [newspaper] job again, and I rented a room for myself again. But I couldn't live one week today under those conditions.

CC: It's been theorized that you got part of your sense of humor from trying to make your mother laugh. What about your father?

BW: My father was a rather easy laugh. My father had kind of everyday humor. He, for instance, would construct a joke. He would come out of the bathroom and I would say to him, "Dad, you forgot to button your pants"—in those days we had buttons—and he looked at me and said, "I have not. There is a law that you don't know, my son, which says, 'Where there is a corpse, the window must be open.' "

CC: [*Laughs.*] Was it a painful childhood?

BW: I was chastised. Once in a while, I was whacked a little bit by my mother. My brother left immediately after the war. He went to some relations we had in London, and then he went to America to some other relations. So I just saw very little of him. I got along fine, I was essentially an only child.

CC: Were you beaten for no good reason?

BW: There were some good reasons. For instance, I didn't go to school for a week. I played football.

CC: Were you a rebel?

BW: Yeah, and I answered back, you know, when I was accused of something which I did not do. Or which I *did* do—I denied that too. But I got my comeuppance. There was none of that "Don't beat the children" then. There were little pains, and there was joy in my family. Of course I wish my father had seen me have success in movies. But there is no culminating event on which to base [an autobiographical picture]. It was not an O. Henry family.

CC: What's the key image that you remember of your dad?

BW: My father and I, we had a kind of secret bond. We never told it to each other. For instance, I remember one day I came home from school and the mail was in the anteroom. I saw a postcard that seemed to be incriminating as far as my father was concerned. [It] said, "Would you like to come to the graduation of your son, *blah blah blah,* to get into the gymnasium?" [This certainly didn't apply to Willie or to me,] and I had no third brother. So I knew that he had an illegitimate child. His name was Hubert. And I grabbed that card, I had enough sense, and I put it in my pocket, and when I was alone with my father I said, "Here. It must be somebody else."

CC: Did he take the card?

BW: He took the card and put it in his pocket.

CC: Did you ever meet Hubert?

BW: No. I did not have his address, didn't have anything.

CC: But I'll bet you remember your father's face, to this day, when you gave him the postcard.

BW: When I gave him the postcard? Sure.

CC: What was your secret world like? What were the things you did that nobody else knew about—shoplifting, things like that?

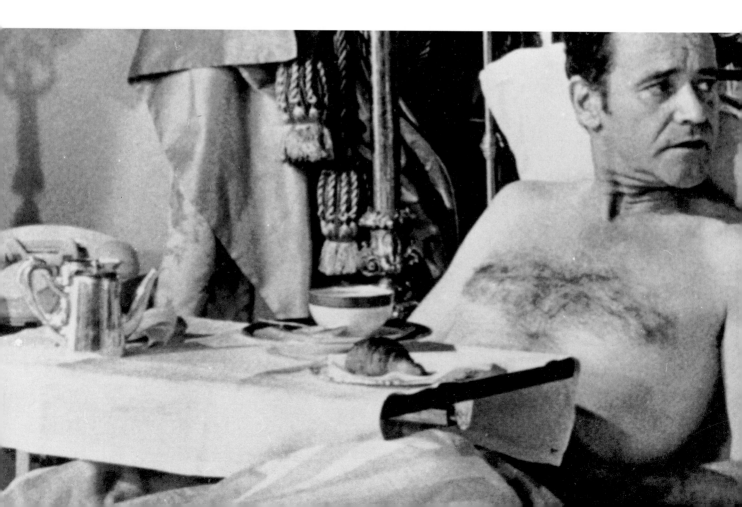

BW: No shoplifting. I lifted from a friend of mine, he was with me through these times. He had some stamps, a stamp collection, and I thought, "I'll [take] that, why not?" And the guy caught me, and that was the last time. No police.

[*Thoughtful:*] I don't know what my interest was in America. I had everything Mark Twain ever wrote. I followed, subsequently, Hemingway, in German, Scott Fitzgerald. I read their work in German; it taught me English. I learned from a guy by the name of Karl May. He was a very well-known writer in Germany, around 1900. He was never in America, this man, but he had characters, for instance, the Old Cowboy [who] had come to America—he was a German, naturally. He was the hero of a whole series, twenty books, and [May] called him Old Shatterhand. And he had a friend by the name of Winnetou. Winnetou was an Indian, an American Indian. They had adventures in the West. Everybody had a Karl May library. And he never was in America. Karl May. I learned a lot from him.

CC: Do you feel like you were loved by both your parents?

BW: I think that I was loved by my parents. But that was something entirely different then. That was ninety years ago. You know, the kids grew up on the street. When I got a bicycle, I was absolutely thrilled. But I don't think I got one from [them]. I got one secondhand [from] a friend of mine. And I took some bottles of wine and poured the wine off, and got some money for the empty bottle, the return. Good German wine! And with this money, and some other money that I got from something, I forget, I bought the bicycle. I got a Rosebud sleigh from my grandmother. She gave me something. But look, it

Jack Lemmon and Juliet Mills share breakfast in bed in *Avanti!* (1972).

was an old-fashioned upbringing, you know. There were days, you know, when they liked me a little bit better, and there were days when they beat the hell out of me. They beat me.

CC: Beat you?

BW: Sure. When I picked up bad notes, when I got bad grades from the teachers, they'd box me around a little. At that time it was very hard for my father, it cost money. But I was sly. I would, for instance, go home from the first class of the gymnasium. I was kicking a stone, and [it] hit an irregularity in the asphalt, or something, and it jumped and it broke a big window in a shop. I tried to run away, but they got me. Now I said that I'm going to pay it off. [But] I had [only] pocket money, and it was going to take me three years. Now how am I going to get the money? I'm not going to tell this mishap to my parents, because they would beat me. Or they would say, "Get out of it yourself."

I found a trick, you know. I told my father I'm going to take lessons in stenography, so that I could be very good, so that I can hear the teacher. And that money that I got for [the classes], I paid off what I owed for the broken window. Except one day, on a Sunday, I am sitting reading a book, and my father comes and says, "You took stenography, didn't you? Come help me, I need to dictate a letter." That's when I got caught. He had to laugh, I must say.

CC: Were you more assured of your mother's love than your father's love?

BW: Well; I was closer to my father than to my mother. It was not a tightly knit family, you know. I loved

The Major and the Minor was a darkly comic spin on pedophilia disguised as a piece of fluff.
(Above) Wilder with Ginger Rogers, Ray Milland, and Rita Johnson; (right) Wilder with Lela Rogers

my mother, but she was the strong one. My father, I helped once with that postcard, you know. And I had something on him. But I didn't have anything on my mother.

CC: You never mentioned the postcard incident until late in your life.

BW: Yeah, I didn't mention it, because I knew it would come into gross hands. They would whack at it—they would just . . . kind of draw conclusions from it.

CC: But does it have a lot of significance for you?

BW: At that time, naturally.

CC: So you had this bond with your father over the postcard, and somehow your mother seemed slightly more remote from you.

BW: Yeah, my mother, she was running the house, she was cooking. She thought my father was richer than he was.

The conversation soon returns to movies.

CC: Little is known about the dismantling of *The Private Life of Sherlock Holmes* [1970]. Nobody has discussed it publicly, but apparently there was a disastrous preview—

BW: Yes, the preview. It went poorly, and I . . . I sloughed it off. I was not too much interested in a perfect rendition of the picture. It was an unhappy circumstance. The only instance where I abandoned a picture. It was shot in London, and I could not go back and fix things and reshoot. I had to walk away for another picture.

CC: What was the movie that you left to do? I don't think you ever made the film.

BW: I left to do *Avanti!,* I believe. Or another picture that fell apart in Europe. I left [*Sherlock Holmes*] in the good hands of my editor and my pals the Mirisches and they murdered it. The cutting was

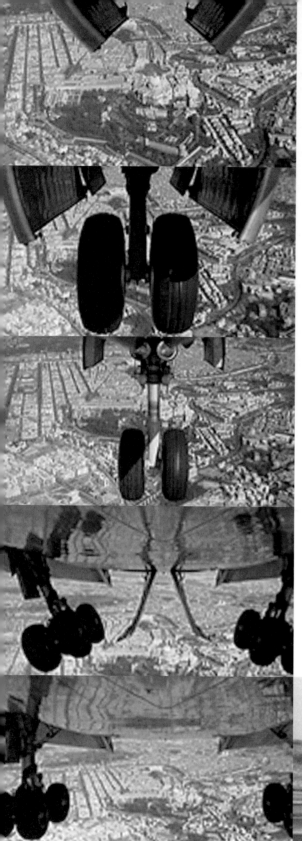

done by an English editor [Ernest Walter]—I had to have an Englishman.

CC: It's meticulously photographed. Was it a tough movie to shoot?

BW: Tough movie. Very tough. And episodic. And never do a picture with episodes, because some of them can be cut out. Episodic is no good. You know, like twenty minutes can go out. And the [editor and producer] had preferences in which sections to cut, preferences different than my own. I don't know, we just had a tough time. Harold [Mirisch] died before we started filming—that was a shame. I loved the movie. It got screwed up.

CC: Your work with Shirley MacLaine was always very strong. For me, she was a real inspiration in the casting of Renee Zellweger in *Jerry Maguire.* Later, Shirley MacLaine came to one of our early previews, I met her, and she was very supportive. I kept trying to talk with her about *The Apartment,* and finally she laughed and said, "Honey, that was three lifetimes ago. Let's talk about *your* picture."

BW: She is a good actress. She is a pro. She can play comedy; she can play something serious. [*Confides:*] I just cannot visualize, I still cannot see the pairing of Lemmon and Shirley MacLaine. To *me,* you know, to me that cannot be a real love thing, between the two. But who knows? She's pretty, and the audiences believe her, and she's a good actress.

CC: Was Shirley MacLaine your first choice for *The Apartment*?

The stock airplane-landing shots (above) from *Avanti!* used in *Jerry Maguire* (1996)

BW: Yeah. She had just made a picture with [Vincente] Minnelli . . . *Some Came Running* [1959]. Marilyn Monroe would not have worked. I just think it would have been a little too much, that she was an elevator girl. Everybody would have wanted to jump her, including the three guys who had the primary rights to the apartment of Mr. Lemmon.

CC: A few questions about *The Major and the Minor* [1942]. Is it true that after a good take, you would say, "Champagne for everybody!"

BW: Yeah. Just on the first movie. In the middle of the picture, I started to stand up and say, "Champagne for everybody."

CC: Before shooting your first film, Lubitsch also gave you some reassurance—

BW: Yes, sure. I went to Lubitsch. I said, "Look, you have made fifty pictures. I have made none. This is gonna be my first picture, what can you tell me?" And Lubitsch said, "All I can tell you is, after sixty pictures, I still shit in my pants on the first day."

CC: So let's count this as your first American movie, *The Major and the Minor*. And I want to talk about your first shot. Your first shot, making an American picture as a director, was Ginger Rogers as Susan Applegate, walking the streets of New York, East Forty-seventh and Park. Was there significance to it at all, you knowing this was the first studio shot in your first studio picture?

BW: Yes. I could see it on the screen, and this is all very, very exciting to me. And she did it very well. And I just had that feeling of . . . "This is wonderful." And she walked and walked and walked and walked. And we used that one part there. That was very good. It was so wonderful to me, because she had just won the Academy Award for *Kitty Foyle* [1940]. Right after this, she started with me, with *The Major and the Minor*.

CC: Was Ray Milland's part, the part of Major Kirby, originally intended for Cary Grant?

BW: Always was for him. Every part.

CC: You had him in mind when you wrote it?

BW: Sure, but Mr. Milland was under contract to Paramount, and then subsequently did *The Lost Week-end* [1945]. He was very good for *Lost Weekend*. He had no comedy in him, and that was good for the part. There was no laughing in Milland.

Summer morning, Beverly Hills. Wilder answers the door of his office, greets me, and shuffles back across the floor to his desk. He wears a fedora hat, and suspenders over a blue shirt.

CC: How was your morning?

BW: It was desperate. [*Sighs.*] Facing a new day. It's hot outside there, it's miserable. Okay, sit down, where would you like to start?

CC: I remember going to see *Avanti!* [1972] with my parents when it was first released. And even then, I think I was fourteen, I was mesmerized by that scene in the morgue with your great character actor Pippo Franco, who plays the Italian bureaucrat handling the business of the death of Lemmon's father.

BW: [*Lights up.*] Yeah, the crazy Italian super bureau man.

CC: And he's got all the stamps and the bureaucratic tools in his pockets, he's whipping them out with maniacal precision. I watched the film again last night. It plays even better with time. And I was watching your airplane-landing shots and they suddenly looked very familiar to me. Then I realized—I bought those landing-gear shots from a film house, and one of those stock shots appears at the beginning of *Jerry Maguire*. So, like it or not, you are in my movie.

BW: I beautified one of your pictures.

CC: So, now that we're co-conspirators in *Avanti!*, do you mind talking about the picture?

BW: No. I don't particularly like that picture, but I'll talk about it. What I really wanted to do with this picture—this is like, I always have a version which

Art director Ferdinando Scarfiotti found the morgue in *Avanti!* on Ischia.

is far superior—is that the father of Lemmon, right, he dies in Italy?

cc: Right.

bw: He died there with the mother of the girl beside him. Now what I really wanted to do was, the father is a homosexual, and he had a *bellhop* with him. [*Wilder smiles proudly.*] That was the first thing that I thought of—wouldn't it be funny if an elderly man who goes every year to take the baths is actually having an affair with the bellhop? But of course they talked me out of it.

cc: Who is "they"?

bw: The Paramount people, the Mirisch people. They talked me out of it.

cc: But you certainly had a lot of cachet with the Mirisch people. I mean, they would have let you do it. They were essentially working for *you*.

bw: Yeah, sure, but I myself was not so sure. Not so safe, that there is a man who had a son, a grown-up son, who's married too, and that he is a homosexual, but he does it only in Europe—only in Europe, in the four weeks that he has. [*Sprightly:*] But that's all right.

cc: You worked with [Ferdinando] Scarfiotti, one of the world-class production designers, on that film.

bw: Yes, Scarfiotti.

cc: Did you have a good relationship with him?

bw: No. He was not a [true] designer. He's dead now, of AIDS. But he was not a designer. He found *locations* and then [offered them as they were]. . . . Everything that he had—in this picture, and also in other pictures that I saw of his—was a found thing. He couldn't build a goddamn thing. He always had two little assistants. Little? They were aged men. You wanted a hotel, but he had to find it first. But then how do you find it, and where do you put the lights, and the third day they're going to throw you out of the hotel, but . . . this was "Scarfiotti."

cc: But the morgue was a beautiful found set.

bw: Yes, that was a found set on Ischia. On the island of Ischia.

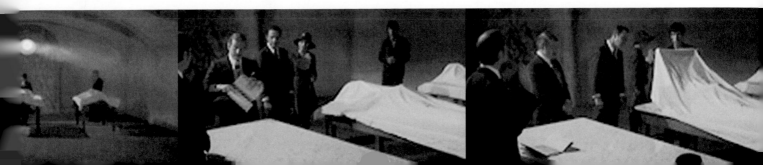

cc: And you had a director of photography that you only used once, on that picture [Luigi Kuveiller]. I thought he did a great job. The lighting in the morgue for example, had a beautiful Vermeer quality.

bw: Good quality, yeah, because that was in the air, you know. He could not help but to photograph it and make it look real. Because usually you do something with a set, and you would like to make it real; but they already made it real, for three hundred or four hundred years. That's wonderful.

cc: How much did you involve yourself in the lighting of a picture?

bw: I always look at it. Always, but I never make [the cinematographer] feel that I control them. I just say something like, "I think it should be later afternoon in the light." And I go, and the next day it's done.

cc: The movie has a great romantic melancholy. And I loved the performance that you got from Lemmon.

bw: Yeah, Lemmon was good. But he was not the right man. He should have had some love life in his own life. And he is the one, you know, who understands it, that the father had this affair. Now comes the time where he's going to get a girlfriend too. Yeah, Lemmon was good, but it was not particularly a Lemmon part.

cc: You've said that Lemmon was your Everyman, but that the one thing he couldn't do was play a lover.

bw: Yeah, without being funny about it.

cc: And yet you did this in *Avanti!* and it worked.

bw: [*Loves saying the title:*] *Avanti! Avanti!* Yes. It worked. The whole picture did not work. But we made him as romantic as possible. It was not a love story, but it came out as one. But that was our approach—to make him as romantic as possible.

cc: Still, it seems you and Diamond massaged the part into being a kind C. C. Baxter, later in life.

BW: Yeah, we did *that thing,* we did that for Lemmon. We knew it was going to be for Lemmon. Then we looked for a girl who was very fat—very, very fat—and we couldn't find one that was attractive enough, that you could say that it would be possible with that girl.

CC: Why would she have to be fat?

BW: She had to have some defect. I did not want her to limp. Just a girl that if she wanted to, she could lose twenty pounds. Juliet Mills was kind of sinewy, but absolutely possible in the part. She ate and ate but couldn't gain more. She's a good actress, the only part she had in the last twenty or thirty years. I wanted her to be real fat, so that you don't feel sorry for him because he goes back to his wife.

CC: There's also a kind of reminiscence of *Love in the Afternoon* in *Avanti!,* when Lemmon is talking into a tape recorder. He's working on the eulogy for his father—he goes back and revisits it in the hotel room. And watching it, I was thinking, this is another device you've always liked—using Dictaphones, tape recorders, and memos to show the change in a character. It's wonderful.

BW: It's wonderful that you saw more in this picture than *I* did. [*Laughs.*] I just kind of dropped it rather quickly. I did not fight for that thing, but it had some qualities. It smelled that it was shot in Italy.

CC: You've made quite a few jokes about psychiatrists, and they certainly run throughout *Avanti!*

BW: [*Immediately:*] Dogs too.

CC: What was your attitude toward psychiatrists? Did you ever have friends who were shrinks?

BW: Not many. With the exception of Mr. Freud, who threw me out. At the same time, I talked to Richard Strauss. And I talked to [playwright Arthur] Schnitzler. And other reporters took other ones.

(Above) Lemmon talks into a tape recorder, working on a eulogy about his father, a device Wilder used in other films to show a change in character; Jack Nicholson and Candice Bergen (left) in *Carnal Knowledge* (1971), which Wilder said "got to be a success because it was a dirty picture."

CC: Were you intimidated by the figures you interviewed back then?

BW: No, I could not be. I was up against it, you know. Because, for instance, I had to do it all by bicycle. On a bicycle, or on a trolley car. The trolley cars started at seven in the morning, so I was up and around, ringing the bell to apartments where the son of the lady there was arrested for murder, and I had to ask for a photograph. Because we didn't have photographers. And I would have to ask her if she had a picture of her son. And she said, "Get out of here, you son of a bitch!" I ran into that situation all the time, getting pictures for the paper.

CC: But Paul Whiteman, your ultimate interview subject in Vienna, was friendly to you.

BW: Yeah, Paul Whiteman was very friendly. His black valet was only about the first or the second person that I saw that was black. When he took me to Berlin, I saw and heard his concert, brand-new things—*Rhapsody in Blue* by Gershwin. We had no orchestras where I grew up. That was in the Grosserstrats Spielhaus. That was the theater of [Max] Reinhardt—five thousand people. And I said goodbye to him in Berlin, and I stayed on in Berlin.

CC: Did you ever go to a shrink yourself?

BW: No, never.

CC: Mike Nichols's *Carnal Knowledge* came out the same year as *Avanti!* What did you think of that film?

BW: Mike Nichols is a very fine director. I like him very much. I miss the days when there were more directors of import like Nichols. You looked *forward* to their work. *Carnal Knowledge* was a good pic-

ture. That was with Nicholson—peculiarly enough, Nicholson playing a college student. And then he had that crazy guy who was kind of a songwriter [Art Garfunkel]. *Carnal Knowledge* got to be a success because it was a dirty picture. I don't know how he got away with it, going to a whore, and she does it to him, then a dancer . . . it was kind of about playing with oneself, you know. All kinds of weird things, interesting things—but it was a good picture. It just had no plot, so it *had no plot!* Just a combination of things that happen to people.

CC: Seeing how it could work, were you ever tempted to do an unplotted picture like *Carnal Knowledge* . . . or even *La Dolce Vita*?

BW: I always need a plot. I think I need a plot, because I don't like pictures where you can take half an hour out and it's only better. But I don't go out wildly speculating, that I must keep things in an order, so that boy loses girl in the end of the second act, and then the third act. . . . No, I never think about that. It's automatic, I think.

CC: Structure seems to be missing from most movies now. There's a lot of shock value, but so much of it is just skimming the surface, like TV.

BW: Yeah, I always tell myself that I will do a picture that is interesting character-wise, not just something *atmospheric*. The atmosphere, that I photograph. But I am careful to find an original set if I can, an original erection of that set, so that I know where I'm going to put the camera already. I write with the camera, but not *too much*. The picture succeeds because of the story, the characters, and the actors. I'm not looking for an original camera move that doesn't go with the story.

But a funny thing was that I wanted to photograph Holden after he had been shot and killed

Scenes from *Stalag 17* (1953): "It was a very dry, dry picture. It was good. It was more of a suspense picture, of escaping, than it was an escape picture with laughs"; (opposite) Holden, Nancy Olson, and Wilder, during the filming of *Sunset Boulevard*

by Gloria Swanson. He was
floating there in that pool. I
wanted to photograph his face in
the water, right? Dark, but still
you see him, and the eyes are
open. You couldn't photograph through water then. You had to
have a mirror on the bottom, and you photograph the mirror
image. You could not photograph through water unless you were
outside the water. So we built a mirrored bottom to the tank, tested
it out on a rubber duck, photographed it, and got it.

CC: Is that a photo dummy, by the way, or is that Holden floating
in the pool?

BW: Not a dummy, no. Holden was very good. Physically, he was
first-class. He was wonderful, for instance, in a picture like *Sabrina*. He had that scene where he sees Sabrina downstairs on
some steps leading into the garden. By this time he knows it's Sabrina; he'd given her a ride to his own
home. Now he sees her down below, in that wonderful white dress that was sort of glowing in the dark.
And he says, "Sabrina!" and he jumps over the five steps, over the railing.

   Now I, like an idiot, I said, "That's very good, Bill, but could you drop a little *slower*." And he tried,
but he could not do it, because he's got the weight of his own body. But he always had the joke with me:
"I know, I know . . . you want it exactly like this, but a little *slower*."

CC: Given the choice of comedy, charisma, or dramatic prowess, which do you value most in a leading actor?

BW: The comedian. The comedian can sometimes be serious, but the serious actor can rarely be comic.

CC: Let's talk about comic rhythm. Let's say you have written a beautiful speech, for example, and it's
funny. And now it's the day of filming. There's the actor rushing through it—he doesn't have the
rhythm, the comedic timing that you always had in your head. What was your favorite thing, that last-
chance piece of direction that always worked?

BW: I just tried to make absolutely sure that this guy or this dame was funny to begin with, that they had the gift. Once or twice, I got an actor who wasn't an actor. He was just a funny man around the living room. I had someone like this for one of the guys in *Stalag 17*, and after the first half a day, I knew he's not going to be able to do it. So I fired him. With certain people, you can get some comedy out of them. Certain people are *antihumorous*. They just try and try and try, this way and that way, and it does not work. Then the best thing is, just fire him. And I got another guy, absolutely terrific. They were dancing together there, [Robert] Strauss, "the Animal," and the other was the little guy with the black hair— [Harvey] Lembeck. He was absolutely perfect. I took some people from the stage [version] and gave them new dialogue. Others were film actors. It was a very dry, dry picture. It was good. It was more of a suspense picture of escaping than it was an escape picture with laughs. There were elements that were very strong, like the Germans—the German spy outside—having heard the order that they're going to shoot the guy. They think that they're shooting the guy who escaped.

Stalag 17: Wilder has the stocking-footed colonel put on his boots in order to make a phone call to headquarters.

There was another good gag in that picture, one of my favorite gags. I don't know whether everybody got it. It got a laugh, but it didn't get that big a laugh. There's a colonel there, in *Stalag 17*, and he is in his office with his orderly. And he does not have his boots on. He walks in stocking feet. Now he says to the guy, to the orderly, "Get me Berlin, headquarters *ruh-ruh-ruh-ruh-ruh.*" 'Cause now he's going to brag that he captured, single-handedly, the German lieutenant that they've brought in. And now, the colonel does the following thing. He says, "Get me that number in Berlin, that always takes five minutes to get through to headquarters!" And now he sits on the corner of the table and he has the orderly put on his boots! And he only puts them on for the phone call. He's clicking his heels after each line. Then he hangs up. Now comes the real joke. He sits back again, the same spot, and has the orderly take off the boots.

CC: The feeling of Lemmon's father permeates much of *Avanti!* Did you find in making the film that you thought about your own father much?

BW: No. Maybe subconsciously. Because I had too many things to do, to worry about. Maybe if the father was alive in the picture, I would have. I also had a father, Mr. [Maurice] Chevalier, in *Love in the Afternoon.* I made him sweet, made him nice. He goes to Mr. Cooper and says, "She's such a small fish, throw her back in the water, it's not proper." He appeals to the propriety of the thing.

CC: Last time we spoke about the relationship you had with your dad. And you told me that story about the postcard that you found.

BW: Yes.

CC: How old were you when you found it?

BW: I was ten. I was about nine or ten years old.

CC: This had to be a big event in your life.

BW: In my life? To have a brother whom I never met—

CC: Yes.

BW: —who must now be an old man? I don't know. I didn't know whether he had a son, when I was—

The phone rings, and it's a cursed interruption. Wilder talks a few moments. Then:

CC: Did Hubert ever try to find you?

BW: No, never. Never knew the full name, never knew nothing. I just knew a postcard that seemed to be from somebody, and was in amongst the mail. And I just gave it to him, and we looked at each other, and we understood each other better.

CC: Did you ever talk about it?

BW: No. Never.

CC: But you knew that *he* knew.

BW: And he knew that I had the tact of not talking about it. What was I going to ask him? Like I was a spy for the mother? But I think that those things happen. But that's a good thing, that she didn't see it, because that would have been a kind of very unpleasant situation, that she may have left him.

CC: Was your father ever worried that you might tell your mother?

BW: No. Never, because I said, "I think you will find that interesting—put it away in your pocket." He knew that I was ten years old. I was just entering gymnasium.

The phone rings again. After a warm and rather lengthy conversation in German, Wilder seems genuinely bemused.

BW: A friend of mine from Berlin. He calls me and tells me about the weather.

CC: We were talking about that incident with your father, and you know, a historian might say that this was a defining moment in your life.

BW: Just let me remember that, because it was about eighty years ago. I speculated, "Did he father the son? Yes, he must have, because it said, 'Your son is graduating.' " I just forgot about it. It was the only thing I could do.

CC: Did it hurt you at the time?

BW: No. Absolutely not. [*A thoughtful pause.*] As a matter of fact, I *envied* my father. [*He has danced out of reach and left me with a joke.*]

CC: I watched *Mauvaise Graine* [1934] for the first time the other night.

BW: Oh my God—I haven't seen it in sixty or seventy years! I shot this in Paris, with no transparencies. We were everywhere with those cars! It was the very first picture that I ever directed. I had flown from, I had disappeared from, Berlin, as did a lot of other people. But I had that plot, and then two other guys came by, and they also contributed to that picture, which made me very happy because they got a little money too. And then I said, "I would like to direct that picture." A very small company, and almost the whole picture was shot indoors, was all shot in a garage. In a big garage and—

CC: It has a very vital, fresh feeling. You did it all on location; your backdrop is the city. There you are in the car, blasting around Paris.

BW: Yes. The Place de la Concorde, and the boulevards. The lead actress [Danielle Darrieux], I heard, when I was in Paris, during the war, was very friendly with the Germans. She was very alluring, very young in the picture. She's like sixteen or seventeen years old.

CC: And once again, you have costume design working for you, because she's got that amazing dress.

BW: She has an amazing dress, that was her own dress, because no designer could be paid. It was like doing a picture in Hollywood for five thousand dollars.

CC: But you got great production value for the money that you spent. And there are signature touches throughout. It's wild and reckless and a wonderful first film. And it's also hilarious, because that garage is so cold, you can see the breath coming from their mouths.

BW: Yes. I knew that. But it was a *sound* film, you know? The dialogue must be terrible, right? *How did you see this film?*

CC: You can find a bootleg video copy if you root around a little.

BW: Yeah? I never saw the picture after Paris. I never saw the picture after 1934.

CC: Would you like to see a copy?

BW: No.

CC: There's also a great sequence where your leading man is walking and you [*laughing*] just have a close head shot, and behind him you keep running the same little piece of film of the car turning a corner, going back, and turning again.

BW: That's all we had!

CC: But it works. It's just very modern. I felt like it was something that would be done today on the independent film circuit.

BW: That was well before the modern French *vague*. The *vague* pictures. All I can tell you is most of the *nouvelle vague* was not born yet when I was making that picture.

CC: Did they ever comment to you about that picture?

BW: Never. I knew Truffaut; I knew him quite well. No, I didn't want to bring it up, because it's shit, I thought, and it is.

CC: And yet, here on your office wall is the same Michelin doll that appears on the garage wall in *Mauvaise Graine*.

BW: No, no. It's not the same doll. I bought that in Paris at the Thieves' Market two or three years ago.

Wilder and Franchot Tone in the dunes outside Yuma, Arizona, for *Five Graves to Cairo* (1943)

CC: Newspapermen often appear as characters in your films, and I wanted to ask you a little about your relationship with the press. A lot of this comes from *The Front Page* [1974], because I watched *The Front Page* again, and not to torture you with movies you may or may not like, but—

BW: [*Brisk, grim:*] Yeah.

CC: —*The Front Page* had a very real sense of what it is to be a newspaperman. That was my background too.

BW: I tried for that. But I don't know. That was the only time I did a remake. . . . They always have in their memory the picture that they praised, that they think is a masterpiece, better than it actually is. When you look at *The Front Page*, the very first one [1931], [it does not hold up]. Then they did it once with a girl instead of with the boy [*His Girl Friday*, 1940], and then I did this thing. I wish the critics had seen the old picture. You say *The Front Page* and they say, "Oh, God." You remember that you saw it as a rerun forty years ago. And the times were better, or we were a little bit more naive—we laughed easier. It just did not work.

And Miss Pauline Kael, in her [*New Yorker*] review, she was so absolutely right. She was so correct. She said, for instance, there are things that would never happen. A character like Matthau, who was the chief editor, does not go to look up the girl that Lemmon is going to marry. He's never going to do that; he wouldn't have time. He's going to do it on the phone, if that. Going [to visit her], and then she plays the piano and sings? It was just bad. In that she was absolutely correct, and ten other things that she said. So she was right. She was good.

CC: So you do put some stock in what Pauline Kael wrote about you.

BW: Oh yes. I like Pauline Kael. She never had a good word to say about my pictures. Maybe a little bit . . . *Sunset Boulevard.* But she was more often right than wrong, and she was always very positive about what she thought was bad. And she just said it. I never met her. But she was so crazy about *Last Tango in Paris*—she said we others, we might as well just stop making pictures! And this [film] was a brand-new thing, she compared it with a piano virtuoso, a composer, who wrote atonal things that were on another level of modern music. And that it was the best picture ever. [*Curious:*] Today, Bertolucci has difficulties making his pictures.

CC: There was a time in the sixties when some reviewers chose to label your work "crude," almost like you weren't dressed properly for their party of higher-brow directors. Today many of them have recanted, or upgraded their opinions; it's all forgotten. But Pauline Kael was never easy on you. Her review of *One Two Three* said this: "Wilder hits the effects hard and sure; he's a clever, lively director whose work lacks feeling or passion or grace or beauty or elegance. His eye is on the dollar, or rather on success, on the entertainment values that bring in dollars. . . ." What was it like to read a review like that at the time?

BW: I have no idea. All I know is that she always wrote bad reviews [of my work]. Maybe one or two slightly laudatory. It was no fun living with her, but it was fun reading her.

CC: Because you did respect her, did you ever take her words to heart? Late at night, staring at the ceiling . . .

BW: Yes—that one example, for instance. There were many others where she was right, absolutely correct, but in other things she was not correct. But then again, if she had not written it at all, that would not have been better for me. It was better for me that she wrote it.

CC: Was that true, that there was a time when your eye was on the money?

BW: No, never. I was not interested in money, but I was being paid very well. I just never had any discussion about money. My agent did that.

CC: *The Front Page* was made during the period when *The Sting* [1973] was very popular. Did you ever say to yourself, you know, "I've worked with Lemmon and Matthau enough. They're great. We're all friends. It's wonderful. But give me Redford and Newman." Did you ever think about trying out younger leading men? You could have gotten them.

BW: [*Slightly offended:*] No, I was always happy to have Matthau and Lemmon. Matthau didn't do anything wrong. Lemmon didn't do any wrong; I gave him the wrong direction. But I love the guys. I would like to make pictures with them all my life. They're a great, great, great pleasure to work with. Robert Redford and Paul Newman? I would have not gotten the laughs, such as they were.

Maurice Zolotow's book Billy Wilder in Hollywood *is a largely anecdotal account of Wilder's life, written in the mid-seventies. Central to the work is a Rosebud-style search for the clue to Wilder's unique wit and perspective. In the end, Zolotow decides that Wilder's life and work were defined by a broken young love affair with a girl he didn't realize was a hooker.*

CC: What did you think of Maurice Zolotow's book, and the theory he presents about why you've written a number of hooker characters over the years?

BW: It's stupid. That I was in love with a whore or something? Absolutely stupid. It was a plot that I used in *The Private Life of Sherlock Holmes,* this thing of being in love with a girl but he did not know that she was a whore. So that was his big, big analysis. Stupid.

Wilder (opposite) directs Walter Matthau and Jack Lemmon in *The Front Page* (1974), a remake of the Ben Hecht–Charles MacArthur play; (below) Matthau and Lemmon under arrest in *The Front Page.* Wilder agreed with Pauline Kael's criticisms of the film.

CC: That never happened to you personally?

BW: [*Incredulous:*] No. That book, it was a mixture of truth . . . and 80 percent of it was invention. The solution that he brings forth is just idiotic, you know. That I'm in love with the girl who was a whore is just stupid. Well, when you saw him, he was so haggard you wanted to cry. He was in AA. He wanted to make a drunk out of me. No way I can drink more than two martinis. I don't know, I just threw him out of my office after the first two weeks. Then he came back. But fortunately very few people read it, and once they read it, they didn't believe it, because I'm not like this.

CC: Who was Ilse, the woman he writes about?

BW: I don't know.

CC: Really?

BW: I don't know. I have no idea. He writes that I loved her, and then I found out that she was a whore. There is no such thing—no whore, no nobody. Oh, there are girls—there were dozens of girls before I got married. He just fell into a trap, you know, of thinking that he has the key to my character. I have no character! Yes I do. I do, yeah—but this was just *idiotic,* you know. And then he omitted so many good laughs. And then he had it cross-filed, you know, and I just didn't want to have that book around me. I just hated it.

CC: Let's talk about a couple of your famous "lost sequences." In *Double Indemnity,* why didn't you use the gas-chamber ending you'd scripted and shot with Fred MacMurray and Edward G. Robinson?

BW: I did not need it. I knew it as I was filming the next-to-the-last scene. The story was between the two guys. I knew it, even though I had already filmed the gas-chamber scene. Here was the scene I didn't use. It was a close-up of Robinson and a close-up of MacMurray. The looks. There was a connection with his heart. The doctor was standing there listening to the heartbeat when the heartbeat stopped. I had it all, a wonderful look between the two, and then MacMurray was filled with gas. Robinson comes out, and the other witnesses are there. And he took a cigar, opened the cigar case, and struck the match. It was moving—but the other scene, the previous scene, was moving in itself. You didn't know if it was the police siren in the background or the hospital sending the doctor. What the hell do we need to see him die for? Right? So we just took out that scene in the gas chamber—cost us about five thousand dollars, because we had to build that thing. It was an exact duplicate, and there are always two chairs there—two chairs, in case of a double mur-

der and they executed them together. So one chair was empty. It was a very good scene. But we'd said it. Again, we were guilty of duplicating a thing.

CC: It was a bold move, robbing yourself of the shocking ending in favor of a quieter scene.

BW: There was no greater significance than this—we'd said it.

CC: This one is for Wilder fanatics everywhere. Why wouldn't you release this sequence on laser disc or DVD with the alternate ending? Have you thought about it?

BW: Yeah, but I don't talk to Paramount, and Paramount doesn't own it anymore. Because it is now being owned by Universal. They bought that group of pictures, and I don't know who to go to. The guy doesn't even know what I am talking about. I am talking about a picture which got lost fifty, thirty, forty years ago, like *Lost Weekend*. I don't even know who owns it now. Maybe it is owned by Universal, maybe it is owned by RKO, which then sold it to Goldwyn, which sold it to [*hand gesture*]. I don't own them, I don't control them; I'm not sure who does anymore. I don't even make money on the old pictures. Every once in a while, a check from *Seven Year Itch*, because of an arrangement that was made with MGM to own the rights.

CC: Right, but if someone sorted it out one day, would you approve the release of this material? There are many who would love to see it. Same with the Sellers footage from *Kiss Me Stupid*.

(Above) *The Private Life of Sherlock Holmes* (1970): from left to right, Colin Blakely as Dr. John H. Watson, Genevieve Page as Gabrielle Velladon, and Robert Stephens as Sherlock Holmes. This film was cut while Wilder was in Paris making another film, and 30 percent of the footage was lost forever; (opposite top) Wilder during the filming of *The Private Life of Sherlock Holmes;* (opposite below) with Audrey, visiting his father's grave, in Berlin

BW: *Kiss Me Stupid*. That was not good. I was pretty ill at ease with it. [*Shrugs.*] Sellers did not work, but then I took a worse choice for somebody else to play the part of Sellers. Sellers did not belong in that little town, could not hide the English accent.

CC: Where is the footage?

BW: I have no idea.

CC: It's not destroyed, is it?

BW: [*Shakes his head.*] I have no idea where 30 percent of *Sherlock Holmes* is. Because I left, I had to go to Paris to make a picture, and they cut it themselves. They promised me they'd cut it. I had the cutting rights, but I didn't want to do it myself. It was too late.

CC: If the footage resurfaces, if they find it in a warehouse one day—

BW: They lost the *Sherlock Holmes* footage. They have been searching for it for years. They did not find it.

CC: But if they find it, would you like it restored?

BW: [*Wounded ambivalence:*] No, it's forgotten. I don't want to make an ass of myself and then it is no good. It's forgotten. Don't bring up things anew. You bring things up, you do a thorough job, which is right, but—

CC: You don't want to be the one crying for the restoring of "my film, my film!"

BW: [*Mimicking tortured artist:*] "It was good, it was good, it should be in there!"

CC: The face you're making right now is hilarious. Someday, though, I hope we're able to see the original end of *Double Indemnity*.

BW: It can be seen. Also, the ending of *Sherlock Holmes,* because they were separate episodes. Also, you could see . . . we cut out the opening of *Sunset Boulevard*. But you can see it. I don't know who has it now.

You can see the whole thing. Sure, I think they have it. The first time we previewed the picture, we did it outside of Hollywood, because it was a Hollywood picture—we didn't want a Hollywood crowd. We went all the way east to Poughkeepsie for that preview, where they're not used to those things. And the picture starts with the opening, with the corpses, a kind of slight little fakery, we made it kind of eerie, because you looked through the canvas—you know, the sheet which they put on the dead people, right? They are lying there, under the cover. We superimposed over them something sort of white, murky.

People are telling each other episodes, the things that led to their death. One guys says he is sixty-five and he is being pensioned off, and he now goes with that money he's saved from an avocado ranch, and he has a heart attack and dies. Then there is an episode of a ten-year-old boy who drowns in the ocean, and they find him. And the third one was, I think, Holden. He says, "You know, I was in pictures. I was a writer, and I came away from Des Moines, or someplace, and the one thing in the world I wanted was a swimming pool. And I got a swimming pool, and then I *died* in the swimming pool." People were laughing as soon as we slipped that tag on his toe. People didn't know whether they were going to see a comedy or a serious picture. But I was in that theater, with the preview cards all handed out. They're laughing, and now the picture begins. It was a very difficult picture to start with, to go into the monologue of a dead man. So I thought that that was a good idea, you know. But then people got up and left. I left too. I went down some steps, leading to the toilets, and I looked up and there was a lady with a spring hat on, in her sixties, and she turned to me, and she said, "Have you ever seen such shit in your life?" And I said, "Frankly, no." [*Laughs.*]

That was that. And then already between Poughkeepsie and Evanston, Illinois, where we had other previews, I was convinced that had to go, the beginning had to go. I just took it out. No new footage was shot. I just cut it. The first five minutes are very important. I didn't need it. We had one more preview in Westwood. We left it completely alone.

CC: There is a famous story from the first Hollywood screening of *Sunset Boulevard*. Louis B. Mayer was standing on a stairway, railing about "how dare this young man, Wilder, bite the hand that feeds him?" What did you say to him, when you overheard all this?

BW: "I am Mr. Wilder, and go fuck yourself."

CC: What did he say to that?

BW: He was astonished. He was standing with the great MGM bosses who were below him, there at the studio . . . Mr. [Eddie] Mannix and Mr. [Joe] Cohen. And that so astonished them that somebody had the guts to say "Why don't you go and fuck yourself" because I knew that I had a good picture there.

CC: And you had just seen Barbara Stanwyck kiss the hem of Gloria Swanson's dress over the performance, so you must have felt especially good.

BW: And then I was going out, and they were down below the steps of the projection room, and Louis B. Mayer had a group of his cohorts next to him and he was lecturing them. "That Wilder! He

Louis B. Mayer, the head of MGM for twenty-seven years, with his wife, Lorena. After the first screening of *Sunset Boulevard* (1950), Mayer came out talking to his cohorts: "That Wilder! He bites the hand that feeds him!" Wilder said, "Mr. Mayer, I'm Mr. Wilder. Why don't you go and fuck yourself."

bites the hand that feeds him, *ruh-ruh-ruh!*" I said, "Mr. Mayer, I'm Mr. Wilder. Why don't you go and fuck yourself."

CC: And your paths never crossed again after that?

BW: No, not so long after that he was out of MGM. That was a year later.

CC: *Buddy Buddy* [1981] is one of the earliest films in a genre that has now come into its own—the hit-man comedy.

BW: [*Unenthusiastic:*] Yeah, maybe.

Wilder instead selects Some Like It Hot *as a greater example of the so-called genre, citing the St. Valentine's Day Massacre subplot.*

CC: But in *Buddy Buddy,* Matthau's hit man is the protagonist. Long before *Pulp Fiction* [1994] or even John Cusack's *Grosse Pointe Blank* [1997], you and I. A. L. Diamond faced the very difficult tone challenge of basing a comedy around a hired killer.

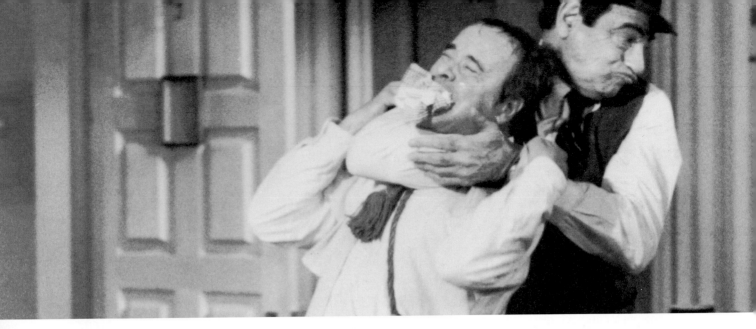

BW: Yes. Tone is always difficult in a picture like this.

CC: What advice would you give a director attempting black comedy today?

BW: You've got to have a talent for it. Get a good story. *Buddy Buddy* was not my kind of experiment, not the kind of comedy I had an affection for. I did it once. Here is the problem. The audience laughs, and then they sort of resent it. Because it's negativity. Dead bodies and such. If you hold up a mirror too closely to this kind of behavior, they don't like it. They don't want to look at it. Same with me. But I would not especially call *Buddy Buddy* a black comedy, more like a *broad* comedy.

CC: Were you ever close to directing anything after *Buddy Buddy*?

BW: I kind of pooped out by the end of the picture. Nothing came along. Diamond then died. I wanted to quit. I wanted to quit when I was eighty. I quit when I was eighty-two.

CC: What did you think of Woody Allen's *Annie Hall* [1976]? For me, this was the groundbreaking romantic comedy of its generation.

BW: I loved it. Very personal, very good. I am a great, great follower of Woody Allen, when he's at his best.

CC: It still holds up—it's wonderful.

BW: Yes, but he does not make films, he makes kind of little episodes. Somehow he does not even know how to cut them. He has dialogue where two people are walking, walking, talking, funny stuff. It's dead footage, if you know what I mean. The camera follows them as long as it can, it now runs out of the planks of wood it's rolling on, and they are still talking and going on. Yeah, he's a very, very cunning, sly guy who I wish would not act. A wonderfully funny person in life, but he's not funny in the picture. I don't think so. Do you think so?

CC: I do.

BW: Then I think so too, because he's said so many nice things about me. He says that *Double Indemnity* is the best picture ever made in America, in the world! In the *world!* For that I have to thank him, right? So I just don't say a word against him. I loved *Annie Hall,* and I loved almost every picture he did.

CC: [*Laughing:*] And every picture he's *going* to make.

BW: He's making three a year.

CC: Do you remember the first time you met Audrey, your wife?

BW: She was under contract to Paramount, and I was a director. They sent her to the set to play a small part as a hatcheck girl. I said, "Stand here, hand him [Ray Milland] his hat." I was directing a scene in *Lost Weekend* where Ray Milland goes into a nightclub and he gets boozed. And then he also sees a purse lying next to him, belonging to a lady who belonged to a man. And he steals some money from *that thing,* because he has got no money, and they get him, they catch him. The strongman, you know, in the nightclub. Then I saw the arm of the hatcheck girl come in, with the hat of Ray Milland. They throw him out, then they take the hat and throw it out with him too. And I only saw the arm, and I fell in love with the arm.

  Then we started seeing each other. I was going through the early stages of my divorce, and I had a girlfriend. And then came Audrey. She was a singer. And then we started going out, but she was leaving for Mexico City, to sing in a nightclub. They had her at Paramount as an actress, but she was a singer with Tommy Dorsey. Once she was in Mexico City, she called me back in Beverly Hills, and she said, "I hate it here, I've got to get out. I need some money." So I sent some money. I told my business manager that I have to send some money—two hundred dollars, that was the amount. And she came back. And my business manager said, "My God, you give money to girls to get *out* of town, not to get *back* to town. Don't do that." And I said, "Well, I have to do it." I did, and then she came back, and a month or month and a half after that, we got married—very simple.

CC: What's your definition of love?

The arm: Audrey Wilder was under contract to Paramount. Wilder was directing a scene in *The Lost Weekend* (1945). "I saw the arm of the hatcheck girl come in with the hat of Ray Milland. They throw him out, then they take the hat and throw it out with him too. And I only saw the arm, and I fell in love with the arm."

BW: Oh, now you come with the big howitzer! . . . Love has many, many visages, many aspects to it. That is, love for a boy, love for a woman. . . . If you love a woman as much as you do on the wedding night, if you love her five years later, then that's real love. Then you have done the tough part, you know—to fall in love and to be in love. She's a very good girl, Audrey. She's a funny girl.

10:59 a.m.: one minute early. The session occurs at his office on Brighton Way.

CC: I know you saw *Midnight* again a few years ago. The script is a beauty, and very funny. Of all your scripts that you didn't direct, the finished movie *feels* the most like one of your films.

BW: Yeah, maybe. Maybe. I don't know.

CC: So it's open to argument. To me, the performance by Claudette Colbert is fantastic. In the opera sequence of *Midnight,* she falls into a chair better than any comedic actress I've ever seen. She gets more out of that chair than most actors get out of an entire movie. Today's actresses should all watch Claudette Colbert in this part, just to see how high the bar really is in romantic-comedy acting.

BW: It was her favorite, of all her movies. She's very good in this, and also in, first of all, *It Happened One Night.* She did not like *It Happened One Night.* She liked *Midnight* best. What did she know?

CC: You never worked with her as a director yourself.

BW: I liked her. I never worked with her. I never had the correct part.

CC: She's very much in tune with your writing in *Midnight.*

BW: With *our* writing.

CC: Yes, exactly. You and Brackett. The exposition is so elegant in this script. It's a great example of what we've talked about. If you cover those story points well enough, the audience never knows they've swallowed them.

BW: Yes, that's right. That's the whole idea, just like taking medicine. You just say "Stick your tongue out," and there's a little something there. And then you swallow it and you don't even know that you have done it. But if you can make the exposition, the rules of the game, clear and yet obtuse to the onlooker, he just does not know what's happening to him. He does not know that behind that laugh, there hides a story, a plot point.

CC: There's a wonderful moment with Claudette Colbert

when you establish that hat—you know, the wet newspaper that she wears as a hat. And she says, "I forgot my hat." And she reaches for the newspaper. And later that's going to come back, with Don Ameche and so forth. And they fall in love over that hat. Was that always a priority, in your collaborations with Brackett or Diamond, the matter of "We have to get that moment where they fall in love"?

BW: The softer, the funnier the plot points . . . if you can make the plot points entertaining, they swallow that medicine. But tell them it's going to be wonderful, tell them that it's going to be better than Pepsi-Cola. Just take it, drink it. [*Laughter.*] You should not do it two or three times in a row. That is too much. Then they notice. So you see, you can hammer on it, but if you make them swallow that, then you are okay. But you have to have some funny stuff in *between,* naturally.

CC: There's also some skillful exposition at the top, when she just says a single line getting off the train. The single line takes the place of an entire explanation of her background. All she says is: "So this is Paris. From here, it looks an awful lot like a rainy day in Kokomo, Indiana."

BW: Yeah. That's medicine that went down easy.

CC: So in one line, you know who she is, where she's from, and where she's going. Did the train to Paris have a little poetry for you, in that movie? Didn't you escape to Paris on a midnight train?

BW: Le Train Bleu. That was the only thing to go on. In those days, maybe some planes were flying, but it was this and the Shanghai Express—the big train going to Mongolia. Those were always very romantic things. Think of *Shanghai Express,* with Marlene Dietrich—that was the only train on which people dressed for dinner. They dressed for dinner!

CC: The year of *Midnight,* 1939, was a big year for the movies.

BW: And only five were nominated. There were at least ten worthy.

CC: What did you think of *Gone With the Wind,* also from that year?

BW: I think it's much, much too late to ask me this question. It was then a marvelous picture. It wound up the exact opposite of what movies think, that they have to have a happy ending. This may be one of the very important pictures—it has an unhappy ending. What was Gable's last line?

CC: "Frankly, my dear, I don't give a damn."

BW: That was the picture. And more people have seen that picture than any other one. No matter how big *Titanic* is. I just think it's a very good picture. It holds up, in spite of the fact that they never solve the character of Scarlett. Is there any solution to Scarlett? No. She's crazy. Just nutty. It had some wonderful things.

CC: Did Mitchell Leisen, the director of *Midnight,* get as tired of you as you got of him, as time went on?

BW: Sure he got tired of me, because I very often contradicted him, and I wrote something entirely different. And he just did not even look at it then. [Arthur] Hornblow, the producer, was sort of a middleman. But as always the director was the captain, you know. He was running the boat, and he shot it or didn't shoot it. Very often, he didn't shoot it. Or shot something entirely different.

CC: But the film of *Midnight* is very faithful to your script, isn't it?

BW: Yeah.

CC: And you were there quite a bit of the time for the shooting?

BW: Yeah, I was there. Then I was writing another one with Brackett, *Arise, My Love* [1940], and then I did *Hold Back the Dawn* [1941]. Once I had become a director, Leisen talked entirely differently to me. [He] never liked me very much. He said I spied on him, just because I'm on the set and watching how he's going to develop the scene.

CC: Also, I felt your writing voice coming through very strongly in that movie.

BW: You couldn't write them anymore like this. The plot is not valid now. That was the idea that shocked Barrymore in it, that he would like to have a dame to show off to his wife. And *blah-blah-blah.* It amused people when they saw it. And they saw it very often. That's the one old picture they bring up all the time.

CC: Leisen very obviously comes from set decorating. Suddenly the shot

Peter Lorre with his wife, Celia Lovsky, in 1936. Wilder roomed with Lorre at the Château Marmont when he first arrived in Hollywood.

will feature a statue or a staircase in the foreground, and the actors are barely in the background. You think to yourself, as a director, he's still a set decorator.

BW: [*Correcting:*] He was a window dresser.

CC: But do you think it's inevitable that films take on the personality of the director?

BW: Sure. A musician plays with an inner echo of stuff that he has conducted before. A doctor works in the manner from which he was trained. Of course it takes on your personality. As with Leisen or as with me, you bring your sensibility and hope that people will show up. [*The phone rings. Wilder chats for a moment or two with a caller.*]

CC: Do you feel an affinity with Sunset Strip, the street? You've certainly made it famous in film, but when you drive Sunset Boulevard, what does it feel like to you?

BW: All kinds of things occur to me, because there are various parts of Sunset Boulevard, all with different character. It's a very long street. It starts at the railroad station downtown, which is mostly Mexican, not very often used, because there are not that many trains . . . then it goes through a neighborhood of blacks and Latinos . . . then it gets to be more elegant, then there are kind of ranch houses, then there is Pacific Palisades. It's all different. But the Sunset Boulevard that we've built up since the war . . . all the high-rises that were started, they were once meadows. It starts and stops all the time. You can buy a piece of property on Sunset Boulevard for a few hundred dollars, also for a million dollars. But I don't think of that picture, though it's in everybody's language out here.

CC: And you lived at the Chateau Marmont?

BW: I lived at the Chateau Marmont. That was here about 1915.

CC: Tell me about Peter Lorre, another European refugee, who you roomed with in the early thirties.

BW: We were friends. I later found out he was a dope addict. In 1935, I was going to Europe and I found that Lorre and his wife were going on the same boat to Europe, before the war. So we took the same train [to New York] . . . we had dinner, amusing ourselves . . . "I'll see you tomorrow morning at nine at the table." His wife arrived at the table at half past nine and said Lorre was very sick. The medicine he took, the bottle had broken, and he was scrambling around. I sent a telegram to a town in Arizona and I put the prescription in it so the doctor could bring it to the train. Meanwhile Lorre was absolutely insane. . . . You cannot open windows in an American train. He was going nuts. The doctor met us at the train in Tucson, carrying the typical bag of a doctor. I said, "Here, here, Doctor, come here." The doctor said, "I cannot fill this prescription. The prescription you sent me was pure morphine." The train started again, it was a crazy scene. We sent another telegram to have an ambulance meet the train, and he left for a hospital in Albuquerque. Four days later, the boat was leaving from New York, and Peter Lorre and his wife are there. Now he's in a good mood; he's got a big bottle of that stuff. He died young. That's the story of how I found out he was a dope addict. We roomed for a short while at the Château Marmont, sharing Campbell's soup for dinner. We were friends, but never as close after that episode.

CC: It is said that the film *Sunset Boulevard* gave the street a grandeur that it didn't previously have. Do you agree?

BW: Yeah, because I only took a certain portion of it. When I came here, Sunset Boulevard was in the country. It was not even asphalted when I came here in 1934. People went for weekends to the Beverly Hills Hotel. Fairbanks and Pickford built a house and a big estate up from Sunset Boulevard, up north to the mountains, and they regarded it as their weekend house. People lived around Vine Street, and Santa Monica Boulevard and Hollywood Boulevard.

CC: What was your feeling watching Sir Andrew Lloyd Webber's stage musical of *Sunset Boulevard* for the first time?

BW: I was impressed. And I was very happy that it was made into a musical. But if you take a picture and make a play out of it, this was the worst example of material that could be easily transported to the stage. There were too many cuts. Already the picture, which could jump anyplace, with the voice of a dead man . . . it was very, very much for the screen. But he tried what he could, and for somebody who didn't see the picture, then, this was good.

CC: What did you think of some of the other show-business-themed films, Joseph Mankiewicz's *All About Eve* [1950], Alexander Mackendrick's *Sweet Smell of Success* [1957], or even Cukor's *A Star Is Born* [1954]?

BW: Great. Wonderful. Mankiewicz had a very fine style. Absolutely wonderful. Then

Peter Lorre had starred in Fritz Lang's first sound film—the classic *M*, about a child murderer—in 1931, before coming to the United States.

he sold his own private company, which was also working for Fox, called Figaro Productions, and then he sold his soul down the river. Mankiewicz was a writer, a newspaperman first, in Berlin, about my time. Sigrid Schultz, chief correspondent of the *Chicago Tribune* for Central Europe, was his boss. But he started there and he came to Hollywood. His brother, Herman, was here already, and he started as a writer. One early script, which I saw in Europe, was about the Olympic Games. It was 1932, something like that. Then he wrote other pictures; then he became a producer; then, ultimately, he said, "I'm going to direct now." And he had a very good record. *All About Eve* was a masterpiece. Beat us for *Sunset Boulevard*.

CC: Paul Schrader, the very skilled screenwriter and director, has a theory. He says you should only have five *great* lines in any one screenplay. Otherwise you dilute the power of any one of those lines.

BW: It's a theory.

CC: Mankiewicz, of course, violates this theory. His scripts were so dense with very written-sounding zingers—

BW: Yeah.

CC: —that by the third act, you're almost woozy from an overload of great lines.

BW: Yeah, you just think, "My God," because everything else is pale. You establish a mode of writing which is very difficult for you to sustain.

CC: Because you never want something to sound too "written."

BW: That's right. It should come naturally, so that it flows from the characters' mouths. Yeah. You have to keep the level up as high as you can. It has to have a style. It has to have one voice.

CC: Structure is the toughest. You seemed to have had an innate knowledge of structure, to have grown up understanding it.

BW: It's just learning it. That took a long time. Not to say things three times. Not to bore people, that's number one. Then, how to be economical. You have to be very economical. You know, pictures are now longer than they were. They were once an hour. Now they're two hours, two and a half hours, you know. There are certain things that people say—that my scripts have got a hundred and twenty-five pages. They do, and somehow it often comes out two hours and three minutes, one hour and fifty-seven minutes. Except, of course, big long things which don't quite work. *Sherlock Holmes*—in that case it felt longer when they made it

The phantom tank with dead bodies, rolling through the desert—the dramatic beginning of *Five Graves to Cairo*

shorter. It should have been a three-hour picture . . . or relegated to television, six or eight half-an-hour shows.

CC: What did you think of *Triumph of the Will* [1935], the famous Nazi propaganda film?

BW: Leni Riefenstahl. I just saw excerpts of that thing. Just a wonderful technique of shooting. Wonderful amount of extras, right? [*Laughter.*] More flags, my God . . . more people. There were more people there than even in *Cleopatra* [1963]. Everybody was in that picture. They ran *Cleopatra* for Jack Warner for the first time when they came back from Egypt, and he looked at it and finally he said, "If every person who's in the picture comes to see it, we're gonna break even."

CC: Let's talk about *Five Graves to Cairo* [1943]. It's the one picture we haven't spoken a lot about. It's a tight, confident film. And also, the surprising thing is that it's so much like what Spielberg and George Lucas later did with Indiana Jones.

BW: I did not notice it. No.

CC: You worked so well in that action-adventure genre, and you never did it again. How did you like making that kind of film?

BW: Fine. We just shot it as one of the small pictures at Paramount. It was made at the beginning of the war. I was delighted that I could get Erich von Stroheim, whom I adored from my high-school days. And you know, there's that joke, when I am in the desert shooting exteriors, and I come back, and they tell me that Mr. Stroheim just arrived, and he's up in the wardrobe department. So I was just running up the stairs, and I say, "Good God, this is fantastic, you know—that little I . . . that I should be directing you now, directing *the great Stroheim!* You were *ten years* ahead of all of us—*ten years* ahead of the industry!" And he looked at me and said, "Twenty."

CC: [*Laughs.*] Did you like the Indiana Jones movies?

BW: I liked them. That was kind of a *wham-bang* thing there. Very good, very good.

CC: And there is such a great beginning of *Five Graves to Cairo:* the phantom tank, with all the dead bodies, rolling through the desert.

BW: Where the guy falls out? Yeah, we had fun with the openings of the pictures. Yeah, I have fun. I just have to find a style, and then I write or rewrite the opening. And sometimes we didn't shoot it, or show it—like, for instance, *Sunset Boulevard*.

CC: Do you find that an audience accepts anything in the beginning of a movie?

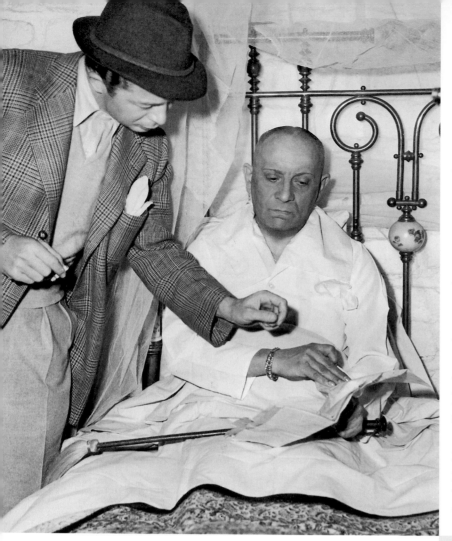

BW: No, I find that we fight them. Because they don't know what they're going to see. It's not like a famous play that they know about. Most times they go into the theater without knowing whether they are in the mood for a comedy or for a serious picture. Some people get up and leave in the first few minutes. So you have to have something arresting, telling them what they're going to see. The first five minutes are very important.

CC: Brackett made a comment some years ago, he felt that *Five Graves to Cairo* hadn't aged well. But you watch the movie today, I'm telling you, it feels like an Indiana Jones–level action-adventure.

BW: That's wonderful to hear, but the pictures were made to play for a week, when we were lucky . . . and two days or three days when we were not lucky. Then

it was gone, it was gone. No repeat, no nothing. I don't know how you got all these pictures. You must have worked really hard at getting them.

CC: In the future, I hope they'll be made more available.

BW: That's good. That I hope is the truth.

CC: Do you still feel ownership of these movies, even though the studios control them?

BW: Yeah. I do feel kind of an ownership, if you want. But the bad pictures, they are not mine.

CC: [*Laughs.*] Also, the title treatment on *Five Graves to Cairo* was great. Did you work much on that, on the titles of the films? They were always stylish.

BW: Oh, sure. A director has to take care of all that, the overall view—that it's properly advertised too. I forget the titles of *Five Graves to Cairo*. We worked hard on all of them.

CC: The preview of your fourth film, *The Lost Weekend,* didn't go well. This time you didn't know how to fix it.

BW: Well, we did not know. The first preview we had in Santa Barbara—it started with 1,250 people, it wound up with 50. They did not know the novel. They did not know it was going to be a picture about drinking and that it's going to be a serious picture. I was sitting there in the car with Brackett and with Henry Ginsburg, the head of the studio. And I said, "There's not much we can do, and I'm going to Washington tomorrow." And he says, "What for?" I got an offer to enlist in the army, because for the future of German pictures, the war was not quite over yet. We knew that we were going to defeat Mr. Hitler, and that there must be a kind of a rule as to who is allowed to make pictures, who was a Nazi and who was okay, and who was in America or France, or someplace else, hiding out. To get them together and get the Nazis out of the industry. So I left. I left the picture with Brackett. I said, "There's not much you can do with it. And I'm going."

CC: You went off to war thinking that you'd failed?

BW: I thought I'd failed. And I was now in Frankfurt, Bad Homburg exactly, I was doing the rules and regulations in German. I was writing the book on how to release pictures in Germany—who is allowed and who is not allowed, and I am getting letters from people who had seen *The Lost Weekend,* and they liked it. People were then going to see a picture that was made from a best-selling novel. But at the time we made it, it had just been published.

Until this time, a drunkard was a comic in pictures: he got drunk in a bar, bumped into things, put on the wrong hat, backwards, then came home asking his wife, "Where is my satchel, because I have a brain operation this morning." That was always the comedy of the drunkard. So I got these letters, and continued working on the book. Then, when I got out of the army, when I got back in 1946, the picture won an Academy Award. People heard that it was a good picture, and came. They came. Yeah, I thought I'd failed. But it grew into some picture.

CC: What did you think of Mike Figgis's *Leaving Las Vegas,* a serious movie about drinking which also won the [Academy] Award for Nicolas Cage?

BW: Yes, I love that. It was wonderful, his style was just completely invisible, you did not know they were even shooting a picture there. They made this picture very cheaply, out of poverty, and it was absolutely wonderful. A great picture.

(Opposite above) Wilder with Erich von Stroheim on the set of *Five Graves to Cairo;* (left) with Franchot Tone on location in Arizona

CC: Last question about *Midnight*. Barrymore is in fine form here, an elegant disaster—

BW: Yeah, very good.

CC: And if he was drinking, it certainly didn't harm his rhythm, his comedic delivery, especially with lines like "Jack's family makes a very superior income from a very inferior champagne."

BW: [*Nodding, a distant fond memory:*] Yeah—

CC: He delivered them beautifully.

BW: —I remember that line.

CC: So was he drinking at the time?

BW: Sure, all the time.

CC: Was there a lot of drinking in the afternoons, making pictures?

BW: There was a lot of it, and a lot of very romantic drinks: Sweet Sue, and all the Mexican names. Toad-in-the-Something. And when you saw a bar, let's say in the St. Regis, there were a hundred different drinks poured. Now nobody drinks anymore. They drink vodka, they drink gin, they drink scotch, that's all, and then once in a while they drink tequila. But before there were . . . sidecars. That was the name of a drink.

CC: It wasn't looked down upon, to have a drink at lunch? While making a movie?

BW: We did not make a big thing out of it. I was not drunk, but I would have a martini. [*The phone rings. Wilder takes a quick call.*]

CC: What are your memories of your first marriage?

BW: First marriage was a marriage that was all wrong. She was a married woman who divorced her husband. She had a daughter with her first husband, and then we had twins, and the boy died. He was about eight weeks old. I don't know, I just did not think that I was made for marriage. But then again, I'm being proven a liar in my new marriage, which has lasted now just about fifty years. She was a very, very fine lady; she was not a Hollywood type at all. Whereas Audrey is a Hollywood type, but she's a *good* Hollywood type.

   She was interesting, but, I don't know . . . it just went wrong there someplace. And that was also one of the reasons why I went to Europe to be with the army, because that was a clean cut, you know. When I came

Midnight (1939): the tango line (right) and John Barrymore and Claudette Colbert (opposite)

back, I did not move back into the house. Then when we got the divorce, I got the house again, and then she moved to another house. And it was all very clean, and there was no bitterness, no fight over money or stuff like that. It was a seven-year experience. The Seven Year Itch.

CC: Is she still alive?

BW: Yes, she's still alive. She's eighty-some years, and she is married again. The husband died of cancer, and she lives with my daughter, in the upper chambers of the house which they have in San Francisco. She always gets a hefty sum for Christmas and on her birthday. I like her very much; she is a good person. But we did not fit together.

CC: You know how some people have a taste for the person that they know is going to wreck their lives—

BW: Yeah.

CC: —they love to pick the person that's just going to tear their entire being apart? I gather that was never you.

BW: No, not at all.

CC: Some of the critical reviews from the later sixties really took you to task for your women characters. It's funny to read them now. You always wrote women in a very clear-eyed fashion. Sometimes they're flawed, or manipulative, sometimes they're hookers . . . but they're all truthful modern women. It wasn't often done in most of the other pictures at the time. Usually there was a heroine who was all sweetness and light, and not interesting.

BW: They all had a character. The woman characters, we just tried to make them real. What was a modern woman? How did she act, and what did she wear, how would she really be? Shirley MacLaine was very much like the type of girl she played. Modern, you liked her. They can write anything they want

to—because people forget. I've been around a little beyond my years, a little long, and the older I get, the less I care. The pictures last longer than the reviews.

CC: Do you feel you were ever deserving of the label "misogynist"?

BW: [*Scholarly:*] I have no idea whether I am or am not.

AUDREY WILDER: [*From the next room:*] Yes!

BW: I'm not! I don't think so!

AW: He is!

BW: Okay, then, I am.

CC: The lack of self-pity in Fran Kubelik from *The Apartment* is the best thing about her character. I watched it again and thought how wrong it could have been if the character felt sorry for herself: "Oh, woe is me." Even when she takes the overdose, she's not crying for herself.

BW: Yeah, well, I did not want to have a depressed girl in tears, you know, because the man is not gonna marry her. I don't know what the hell it was, but it was just a girl of today. I think this is the way a girl would behave, unlike a girl in an English novel. [*Laughs.*]

CC: For me, it's one of the reasons the films stand up so well. Because your women aren't cutout cardboard characters. The women are living, breathing people.

BW: They are? [*Slight smile.*] Yeah, well, that is a lucid writer's description. But you have a great big advantage, because you are a scriptwriter yourself. And you get yourself into the role of writing somebody's life. Right? But you are a picture writer too, foremost now, and I think that helps a great deal. You know the trials and tribulations of a motion-picture person.

CC: If you're able to present a living, breathing human being on screen, people will respond. Do you believe that?

BW: Absolutely. Even if a person *becomes* somebody, just the becoming, that is the important thing.

CC: Now, this is a question I asked you early on, but one of the great gifts of our interviews here is that we've been able to debunk some of the myths that other men have huffed and puffed and tried to come up with an answer to over the years. But here's something I just want to ask you again. Great writers, they say, tend to revisit a specific place or time in their lives. They continue to write about it, examining it in different ways. I wondered if that was true of you.

BW: You mean geographically?

CC: Geographically, philosophically . . . creatively.

BW: Yeah, I was very curious to find out how I was going to feel when I went back [to] Vienna. And it was all very placid, and it was not as much of a turmoil as I thought it was going to be. And I wanted to revisit my school, but all of the guys who went to school with me are dead, every one of them. It all flattened out, you know. The big events, you know. It all flattened out. I was very, very interested to see Kärtnerstrasse, which was the big street in Vienna in November of 1918, when Austria became a country. A country of fifty-six million—it became a country of seven million, overnight. Everything dropped off, Czechoslovakia, Hungary, Poland, and it all flattened out.

I can see that the world will go on. It will drag on, with all the mistakes that we make. Maybe another war, but I hope not, because it's going to last one week. I don't even wish I was younger, and I don't wish that I would have made something different out of myself. Everything became, naturally, good or bad, you know.

It had to be, it had to be.

I had that great desire to see Berlin again. And I saw it right after the war, because I went there from Frankfurt, I went to Berlin for a week, and there was no Berlin anymore. But everything came out pretty good. I mean, I lost my parents, my friends, my smaller family, they are all dead. . . . Either it was cancer or it was Auschwitz. But I swallowed it, I sorrowed, I wept a little, but I'm still here.

cc: The theme in your work of the masquerade, of people playing roles—

bw: That did not occur to me. I was not playing roles. That did not happen in my life. I was playing all the cards open. [*Pause.*] Look, the fact that you should be here asking me those questions,

that makes me very proud. Yeah, that is a victory, no matter how it comes out, no matter what happens to it, it is a victory because I know it's going to come out fine. But life will go on . . . it's going to go on, I hope a little better.

CC: I'm still surprised at how often the word "cynicism" comes up in discussing "the great wit of Billy Wilder—the great cynical, acerbic wit." Correct me if I'm wrong, but to me the pictures, if you take them all—and I've been looking at them a lot, as you can tell—they boil down to a basic joy of life, in all of its silliness, humor, romance, and pain. There's a joy of life there.

BW: There is, I hope so, even in a picture about an alcoholic . . . even in a war picture . . . even in *Sunset Boulevard.* Those [films] are tests and preambles for bigger things to come, but they are to be used, I hope.

CC: In the end, is love the most interesting subject to write about?

BW: One of the strongest. Love between people who are married, or who are getting married, or love, the father or the son or the mother—this is a very strong emotion. It comes into many stories. But to just set yourself out and say, "I'm going to make a picture now about love"—that's so big a project, how can you dramatize that? I have made pictures without any love—for instance, *Stalag 17.* There are other films—thank God, not too many—that have nothing to do with love.

CC: I could present an argument to you that even *Stalag 17* is about love. For example, when Holden says, "If I see you again, let's pretend—"

BW: [*Loving the line:*] "—let's pretend we never met."

CC: That's a great "I love you."

BW: Yeah . . . love between men too. Sure. Friends. That's very important. But when it has emotion, and good action between them, you get away without a love story. You just kind of breathe a little sigh of relief and say to yourself, "Prisoners of war. I did it." [*Laughter.*] But then again, he pretended he danced with Marilyn Monroe, that guy in the underwear. A little drunk, because they made the alcohol there, and he just thinks that he is . . . that this is a little bit of love. [*Laughter.*] Without sex, that's possible too, but with sex is better.

CC: [*Laughs.*] It's said that the play *The Guardsman* was one of your early inspirations for using disguises and role playing in your scripts. Is that true?

(Opposite) Scenes from *The Spirit of St. Louis;* (above) Holden in *Stalag 17,* saying, "If I see you again, let's pretend we never met."

BW: That's absolutely true, *The Guardsman*, and it is carried to the very end. You never find out whether it is the husband or whether it is another one. Another very good man there, [Ferenc] Molnár, a Hungarian, a very good writer.

CC: Were the pictures like emotional diaries for you at the time? In other words, were you in a romantic mood when you did *Love in the Afternoon* . . . and in a sharper mood when you did *Ace in the Hole*? Could a case be made for all the pictures being autobiographical in a way?

BW: Yeah, sure, and most of the time I'm the *opposite*. When I start the picture, I have to be very humorous, very, very bright. Kind of playing the clown if you want to, if I do *Witness for the Prosecution*. On the other hand, I have to be very much in love when I do *Sunset Boulevard*. The opposite. In other words, I'm at my best when I'm writing against my mood, in that particular period of time.

CC: Why is that?

BW: I don't know. It just happens. I think funny, to get myself away from the sorrow of losing a lover.

2:30 p.m. Thirty seconds late. Naturally, Wilder seems to notice. He has moved across the hall to a sunny new double-sized office. The office before had been a temporary lease. This new one, on the other side of the hall, now looks out on a colorful Brighton Way. Though Wilder is in some physical discomfort today, he insists we continue with our program of conversations. We are a long way from the days of his wary sidelong glances at my tape recorder. These days he's downright encouraging. "Is that okay? Is that working? What can I tell you?"

CC: How would you and Izzy [Diamond] begin a new idea? Would you pick situations from the newspaper and pitch them around?

BW: Well, we had kind of a drawerful of situations, you know, which could have happened and could be made into a good scene, for any picture that we were doing. We were always kind of taking things out of that drawer, but only if it fitted. If it did not fit, then it's no good. Then you wait for the better moment.

CC: What happened to your book of ideas? The book you've discussed in interviews, where you kept ideas for future projects, like *The Apartment*?

BW: Well, I have it. It was not burned in the Goldwyn fire. I was just with Iz then. We were twenty-five years together.

CC: I want you to know that I've now seen the last movie of yours that I hadn't studied completely, *The Emperor Waltz.*

BW: Ohhhhhhhh. *Ach, ach.* [*Mimes great pain.*] That was 1946, when I had my fortieth birthday. It came out of a bravado gesture that I made in a meeting of the front office. They did not have a good picture for

Bing Crosby. And I just said, "Why don't we just make a musical!" But it was not really a musical, because a musical is a thing where people, instead of talking, they sing to each other. The songs are plot scenes, and they sing. And I started kind of fumbling around there for a plot, and that was kind of, well, the dog—

CC: That is a good joke in there, the RCA dog.

BW: The dog, and it was just kind of *ach*. We had to go to Canada with *that thing,* for the Alpines. It was supposed to pass as the Austrian Alps, except there were many villages in the Austrian Alps. In Canada, there was just snow. And we were not very happy with Joan Fontaine, she didn't have the part . . . [*Struggles to find a positive, but gives up.*] We had nothing. I was just kind of improvising there. The less time you consume in analyzing *The Emperor Waltz,* you know, the better. There's nothing to explain, there's nothing to read into *that thing.*

CC: It probably has the least bite of all your films, but there are still those great jokes fighting to get out. There's a wonderful joke about Freud analyzing the dog.

BW: Joke, yeah. That was Sig Ruman [playing the doctor].

CC: Crosby's song "Plain as the Kiss in Your Eyes" really works in the movie. And his acting was some of his best. Did you have a solid working relationship with him?

BW: Yes, very good. But the picture was just . . . nothing. We were doing kind of little tricks that a good magician would have maybe been able to get something more out of than I did. I just had come

Love in the Afternoon (1957): "I'm at my best when I'm writing against my mood . . ." Audrey Hepburn and Gary Cooper play at romance in Paris.

back from Germany, from the war, from the job that I was doing there. And I was in the mood kind of to do something gay, and when they brought up Crosby, I jumped in with this idea. . . .

His physical discomfort gets the better of him. Reluctantly, he pulls the plug on our session and reaches for his cane. I walk him to the door. He slips on his suit jacket and locks up in short order. I walk alongside him down the steps. For months I have admired his steadfast desire to always use the steps, methodically, one at a time, never the elevator. Today, I find out the real reason. "I never use the elevator because it might get stuck," he confides. "And I would be here the whole weekend."

Out in the daylight, Wilder moves purposefully to the sidewalk. Just across the street is his car, and he's anxious to get home. It is at this moment that Wilder is recognized by a boisterous Italian tourist of about thirty-five.

"Mr. Billy Wilder!" he says. "I am a great fan. Mother, this is Billy Wilder!" The fan pulls his equally energetic mother directly into Wilder's path.

"Hi, hello, how-are-you," the director answers. He nods briskly to mother and son and waits for a pause in traffic.

The young man and his mother now begin speaking to him in Italian, a language Wilder doesn't speak. He stares at them through thick glasses. The only recognizable phrase I can pick out of their impressed and respectful chatter is "Some Like It Hot." Wilder nods his head politely. The fans, flushed by a genuine Hollywood encounter, move with him. "Thank you for recognizing me," he says. "Do you want an autograph, is that what you'd like?" They respond enthusiastically. "I cannot do it now, but you can come tomorrow."

"Thank you, Mr. Wilder."

"If you see me in the window," says Billy Wilder, "I am here."

The bright new office would herald a cheery phase in our concluding conversations. And sure enough, on most mornings, if you look above the storefront, just above the high-energy street traffic, you'll find Billy Wilder in that window—rustling through sports pages, taking calls, conducting the business of being Billy.

Saturday morning, 11:05 a.m. I'm five minutes late. Audrey Wilder greets me at the door to their apartment and points me to the dining-room table, where Wilder is reading the New York Times *over coffee.*

"Hello, Cameron," Wilder says cheerfully. He indicates the seat to his left. The remnants of breakfast, a few papers from the Directors Guild of America, and a screening cassette of In the Company of Men *(1997) rest on his table before him. I have his good ear. On my other side is Audrey Wilder. We begin on the subject of Billy Wilder's friend the director William Wyler.)*

BW: His work is very good—very exacting, very detailed. [*Wilder turns to me, quite comfortable here at his dining-room table. He discards the paper and continues with a tone of great fascination.*]

He was a guy who tried to do his very best work, and he was a director of many takes. He would have points, like for instance, he would have twenty-six takes to see what he liked. With Laurence Olivier, in *Wuthering Heights* [1939], he said "again" and "again" and "again," and after take twelve, Olivier came up to him and said, "Just tell me, what do you want? What did I do wrong?" And Wyler says, "I don't *know* what I want. But if I get it, I know that I'm going to print it." And he did print it, and it was, naturally, first-class. Because he was a trial-and-error director, he had to have a lot of tries before he said,

"Okay, print this here." He was a very, very peculiar man, who played cards, who did everything he did—motorcycle things he did—and was very, very open and free. But when it came to directing, he took it very, very seriously. He sensed that something in the script was wrong and he'd say, "Do it again" . . . "Do it again" . . . "Do it again." And when they did it right, and he said, "Okay, this is it," then that was it. For instance, his wonderful picture *The Best Years of Our Lives*. First-class. But there was two years of working with the writer, of trying to condense his thinking, which was very big, you know. But when there was something good, he would stop, and he would just then talk it over again and again with the writer. And then when he said, "This is it" . . . it was.

CC: Did that cause a lot of frustration with the actors?

BW: Of course. But they knew that it was Wyler, that he was a very strange man, and when he undertook a picture, he did it beautifully. He had no original ideas, but he did them to perfection. His direction was just very unassuming, he was very quiet on the set, very quiet, because he lost the hearing of one ear during the war. He was photographing one of the missions, and—

Paramount did not have a film for Bing Crosby, so Wilder offered to make a musical, which they shot in Canada. "The less time you consume in analyzing *The Emperor Waltz*, you know, the better," said Wilder.

Wilder answers the phone. It's a call from his bookie. For a few minutes, Wilder meticulously picks the games for tomorrow. He then hangs up and we continue. He is really quite enjoying this Saturday morning.

CC: I read that people used to confuse the names Wilder and Wyler. And one of you said, "Manet, Monet, what's the difference?"

BW: And they're both very good. That's right. I said that. [*Correcting the order of the joke:*] "Monet, Manet. . . ." [*Nods.*]

CC: I watched two movies last night, and one was *Best Years of Our Lives,* because I wanted to revisit it.

BW: Very good.

CC: Yeah, and what it reminded me of was something we haven't really talked about—sentimentality. Shirley MacLaine says in one of her interviews that you gave her one of your best talks ever, about avoiding sentimentality. And even Wyler in that movie really skates on the edge of it. But there's a tough sentimentality that's wonderful about the movie. For instance, when the actor [Harold Russell] reveals the first hook on his hand. And then he steadies the paper and reveals his second hook—

BW: Yeah.

CC: And that to me is beautiful sentimentality.

BW: Sentimentality in a *good* sense. I remember that I cried there. In the very first scene, I started to cry. And that was the scene where the three guys come back from the wars. The first one to get out is the guy without the arms, and he stood there, and in the background you saw the parents who are waiting for him. They come and they run up to him, and he stands there with the back towards the camera, with his hooks, his hands are gone . . . that's in the beginning of the picture, right? I started to cry there, and nobody could stop me. It was very good. It was funny in the right spots. Fredric March, you know, dancing with the waiter. But it did not . . . did it lose any power now?

CC: No. Not in the slightest. But what is it about most sentimentality that does not wear well and causes a movie to seem dated?

BW: Sentimentality, or "sentimentality," in quotes, is to show one's sentiment—to be affected by a scene which makes you sit back and react in a way you cannot help. You cannot help it. That can be a wonderful thing. But then there is false sentimentality, obvious sentimentality, and that you reject, that you hate. It's better if the picture just goes on, you like it, you don't like it. Some directors are very, very sentimental, and they get away with it. Some others, they try for it, they try for it, they try for it . . . they try to keep levelheaded and impartial, but they cannot.

Good sentimentality, for instance, was a picture called *Bright Victory* [1951]. A picture of a man who has been in the wars, and he's blind. He has a girl, a woman he loves, who does not know that he is blind. The audience does not know, either. I think that is the way the scene worked. He opens the door for her; he makes her sit down. He has counted the steps it takes him to go to the fireplace . . . he makes a drink, has counted the steps to the table. And then we worry about how he's gonna succeed. That was a very, very fine thing. But then *that thing* was copied, reshot, and things done to the story, many times, where it was revealed to the audience in advance that the person was blind. The audience was brought in on the story, and that was very sentimental, and you didn't like it at all, it was over the edge. But it was a good trick in the beginning, a very good, very effective scene. That's good sentimentality.

CC: The thing that angers or bores you as a writer watching false sentimentality, I think, is that it's just so *easy*. The easiest road to take as a writer is to just slather an idea with sentimentality. You know, suddenly, "The baby is lost! The baby is lost!"

BW: You just kind of sweep people up, you sweep them up by being *truly* sentimental. Just a little bit will go a long ways. To not reveal it to the audience first, that's true sentimentality. The blind man is a good example.

Wilder had a good relationship with Crosby (left) but felt that "a good magician would have maybe been able to get something more out of [the film] than I did"; (above) Olivia de Havilland and Charles Boyer in *Hold Back the Dawn* (1941)

CC: Yes. It is. It's like crying in movies. There are many, many movies where the actor is weeping, trying to get *you* to weep. But it's always more powerful if you see the character trying *not* to cry.

BW: Yeah.

CC: You know they're dying inside.

BW: That's right. That is all in the style of the director. And you know Wyler was very good at comedy. He made comedies with Margaret Sullavan, and he was married to her. And then she married the agent Leland Hayward. But those comedies—very, very good.

CC: There are some great character touches in *Hold Back the Dawn*. Paulette Goddard has a good time with the dialogue. And I loved her line about "a woman wants a *man,* not a radiator cap."

BW: Yeah.

CC: And like Boyer in the famous unfilmed cockroach scene, you were in that situation too in Mexico, waiting to get your own visa in 1934.

BW: Yeah, I was in the situation. But I got off easy. I didn't have my papers. I went across the border to Mexico to enter the country with an immigration visa. So I went there, and I came to see the consul, to get the immigration papers. But I didn't have the proper paperwork with me, to show that I was not a criminal. I came here to America, and I had one paper, my birth certificate. And I said, "I'm sorry, but I cannot go back to Berlin to get my papers, which I need, the police record and things, because they will not do it for a

Jew." It was 1934, 1935. "They would just keep him there, if he is stupid enough to go to get his papers. They will just put him away." So I haven't got the vital statistics, the vital papers, to prove my behavior, that I did not have a sexual disorder or something. The guy looked at the papers, they were so poor. There were two or three things. And he was walking around the desk, studying, studying me. And then he said, "What do you do, in your private life? How do you expect to make a living?" And I said, "I am a writer. A screenplay writer." With that he smiled, he twisted my papers around, and gave them a stamp, *dock-dock-dock-dock,* and he said, "Write some good ones." And I was in like Flynn. [*Thoughtful pause.*] He didn't have to let me in. He could have taken back my original papers, and I would not have been let back into this country.

CC: It's interesting looking at the credits of *Hold Back the Dawn,* which Mitchell Leisen directed. You have Edith Head, you have Doane Harrison—

HOLD BACK the DAWN

VICTOR FRANCEN
WALTER ABEL

DIRECTED BY MITCHELL LEISEN
Written by Charles Brackett and Billy Wilder
From a Story by Ketti Frings
A PARAMOUNT PICTURE

BW: Yeah.

CC: You have, really, your gang, which would later come and be with you on *The Major and the Minor,* when you first directed on your own.

BW: That's right.

CC: How did you get them all on your side?

BW: Well, Edith Head was the head of the department of costumes, and she just automatically was on every picture. Some more, some a little bit less—she gave it to an assistant. Doane Harrison was a cutter already, for Mitchell Leisen. And who else was there? The cameraman? Leo Tover? Yeah, I got the best, you know, because they expected *Hold Back the Dawn* was going to be a hit, and they wanted to make it, so they spent a little bit more money on it. More money! I mean, a million and a half. As much money as now the advertising for a picture over one weekend in Los Angeles. But they were all rooting for me, yes. Except Mitchell Leisen, maybe—he was not rooting as much. As directors go, he was all right. You could get to be an old man writing just Mitch Leisen pictures. Sure, but then you don't have any pride, you know, that it is *your stuff* that they are shooting. You have no right to say no. On Broadway, yes. The writer sits there and is king, yes. But still not yet in the pictures.

CC: Ginger Rogers said in her later years that—and tell me if you think this is true—she told one interviewer, "Well, I helped Billy Wilder with his career more than I ever got credit for."

BW: She got enough credit. I don't know what she wanted. She was the first credit on *The Major and the Minor,* with Ray Milland. . . . And I always spoke very well of her. I did not read that comment, or call her on it. When I saw her [at a New York Wilder retrospective], it was very warm. Yeah, very warm. And it was always "MFD," My Favorite Director—that's what she called me. I did see her once or twice between the picture and other pictures which I then made, and she was very, very sweet, because she had agreed to do the picture exactly at the time when she won the Academy Award for *Kitty Foyle.* That was the very first picture [she did afterward], and with a very new director. She did not know me. And she agreed to it because she read the script and she liked it. But I think that she agreed to do it because she was screwing her agent, who was Leland Hayward.

CC: Leland did get around.

BW: Leland Hayward. So it was kind of in the middle of a screw. He just told her that he would like her to be in that picture because it was very good—he was my agent too.

CC: Here's an overall question about genius. In your work, did you find that genius is something that can be learned, or are you born with it?

BW: Oh, you're born with it . . . you're born with it. But I don't know. Neither am I a genius nor do I know how to define a genius. I just know that you cannot learn it. But you can learn a lot and you can fake it. There is no such thing as a man making only good or only genius product. There is no such thing as a constant result. For instance, George Bernard Shaw wrote about fifty plays, of which there are seven or eight well known today, still being played in the repertory. But the other ones were just plays. And he was a genius.

CC: What was the first time that you heard an audience laugh at something you'd written? Do you remember that?

BW: Tiny little silent pictures, with an orchestra. There was not even a tape made of that music. No, there was an orchestra, and they played these things that the audience wanted—to everything, to

something funny or something tragic, the same music! But I remember the pictures, kind of very vaguely.

CC: Was it *People on Sunday*?

BW: No. But *People on Sunday,* they laughed there, too. There I wrote the script and had my name on the screen. The other pictures that I did, I was a ghostwriter for two guys. There were some laughs there—sure, there were laughs—but not *enough,* because the director interfered.

CC: You had a couple periods in your career where you allowed yourself to become depressed over the public reaction to a movie. We won't spend too long on this. *Sherlock Holmes* was one.

BW: Yeah, because that was butchered.

CC: The other one was, I believe, *Ace in the Hole.*

BW: Yeah, that was the other one. I was hoping that it would find an audience. Because it was so self-evident why people behave the way they do. And they didn't get it at all, lots of them. Some discerning critics lauded it up and it was their favorite picture of mine. But many at the time did not want to face that people are sensation-grabbing, and any time you see an accident, you know, you see people coming and staring at it. They love to see . . . to *see*. They can be smug about Princess Di and the paparazzi, but then they sit in the theater and say, "All right, entertain me." But this was not exactly the entertainment they wanted to see.

CC: The other day you mentioned *Shall We Dance?* [1997], the very elegant, very soulful film from Japan.

Wilder's first leading lady, Ginger Rogers—here on the set of *The Major and the Minor* (1942)—used a special nickname in inscribing this photo to him. It stands for "My Favorite Director."

BW: Oh, I loved it. [*Rapturous:*] Beautiful picture. So elegant. I just loved it. I just . . . it's the exact opposite of all the other pictures, you know. The jealous wife. She hires a detective and she follows the guy, she finds he's taking tango lessons. Tango lessons! It was like an Italian movie. It was just exactly kind of . . . it was absolutely hilarious, and I loved the way that the man gets more and more beautiful, he dances so well, right? It was just absolutely clean, you know, but good and clean. A small movie with a beautiful idea at the center.

Wilder on the set of *The Apartment* (1960)

9

CC: You know, one of the great things that you've been credited with is that you embraced the American new-wave film movement of the late sixties—Hal Ashby, Jack Nicholson's films. You were early in saying that good work was being done by these new directors. And I wondered what it was like for you to begin to see these movies in the late sixties.

BW: I had already made some pretty significant pictures, like, let's say *The Lost Weekend,* and I had made *Double Indemnity. . . .* But I was on the side of Ashby. He died since then. He was a sniffer. Cocaine, I think, or something, that killed him. But he was a very good director.

CC: Underrated these days, and due for rediscovery.

BW: It is important not to listen to the voice, which is always there, of the gray-haired executive who warns us not to go too far. A good picture is always made when you have a director or a creative producer who has a vision. You give him the money and you let him go. But that was in the golden *golden* days of picture making.

CC: So much has been written about the sixties and what that whole decade meant. You worked pretty consistently throughout the entire sixties. What were the sixties like for you?

BW: I didn't even know they were the sixties.

Nearby, Audrey collapses in laughter.

BW: I didn't know, they could have been the forties or the fifties. I just thought that we had deepened the dimension of what we'd allowed pictures to be. But we always fall back on something trivial, and something that is photographable. It's important that we not spend all the money making *Air Force One* [1997] and *Waterworld* [1995], just because they have some action. Somehow, we've left the smaller pictures to television.

CC: Yes, that's true. But every once in a while, people show up for a movie about human relationships. James L. Brooks's *Terms of Endearment* [1983], I think, was an example of that. A great, personal movie, and large numbers of people showed up.

BW: A very good picture. This is a section of the public that sometimes shows up. They find out that it hasn't got a big battle, a hundred-car explosion, driving into each other, they come out to see that picture.

But I just don't pay any attention to this 1950, 1960, 1940. I just make a picture which is different from anything that I have ever done, and I hope to God that it's going to work. But then again, myself, I get somewhat scared that "no, I've got the money now, I've got to do it a little bigger, a little better. . . ." So I'm just sitting on my fat ass for the last ten years, and I envy the young directors for their energy, even if the picture's bad.

CC: What is the best unproduced idea that you never got to, as a director? Anything you regret not making?

BW: There were some ideas that I fought through, and I wrote it, wrote it with Iz, and they didn't come out. They did not have an interesting enough, or a capturing-enough, quality. So I could go to the next one.

CC: So are there any scripts in your drawer?

BW: No. No scripts. I never wrote anything for which I was not paid.

CC: You never wrote anything and decided with Izzy or Brackett that it wasn't good enough and just put it away?

BW: Maybe an idea or two, but there was this talking, talking, talking for weeks, and then deciding not to do it. And then there's nothing left.

The wrap party for *The Seven Year Itch* (1955) given by coproducers Billy Wilder and Charles Feldman in the upstairs room at Romanoff's: (left to right) Charles Feldman and Clark Gable look at the table decoration; Billy Wilder, foreground, and behind, Monroe dancing with Clifton Webb; Darryl Zanuck, Jean Howard (Mrs. Charles Feldman), and Gary Cooper; Clifton Webb and Clark Gable in conversation in the foreground and Marilyn Monroe behind; Darryl Zanuck dances with Lauren Bacall.

CC: When did you get your best ideas?

BW: It depends. Sometimes when I'm sitting on the toilet, sometimes when I'm in the shower, sometimes during eating. Just various places. If I knew what was I doing when these ideas occurred to me, then I would always put myself in the same position.

CC: [*Laughs.*] Driving is always good. But it's very dangerous, driving and writing at the same time.

BW: I just have to be disciplined. I have to get up early in the morning and know that I'm going to be doing something. Sometimes it comes out, and sometimes it doesn't. Sometimes it comes from seeing another picture, like *Brief Encounter* inspired *The Apartment.* . . .

CC: Do you still get ideas for films?

BW: Sure. I figure out the three acts, I write it all down, and then I don't make them. I haven't made one in fifteen years, but I still might.

CC: Tell me one of your ideas.

BW: No.

CC: You're not in any of your movies, are you? You don't appear anywhere.

BW: No.

CC: Ever tempted?

BW: No. Mr. Hitchcock was noticed, even in a wig, right? He's in every one of his pictures. I'm in none of my pictures.

Wilder sees me to the door of his office, his shoes tapping along the floor. "No one has talked to me for so long," he blurts at the doorway. I tell him it's going well, and he seems surprised to agree. Commenting on his interviews, he says: "Usually they start out strong and collapse in the second half. But I'm holding up pretty good." He shuts the door.

Dinner with Billy and Audrey Wilder at Mr. Chow. A casual evening out. The conversation turns to Oliver Stone, a sometime lunch date of Wilder's. I ask him what he thinks of Stone's films. He has studied them. "They are bewilderingly simple," he says with fascination. "He makes too many of them." Wilder considers his words. "Maybe I made too many pictures. I made two every three years."

CC: I hear there's a movie coming out inspired by *Ace in the Hole*. It's called *Mad City*.

BW: I did not know.

AW: What's the difference between "inspired by" and a "remake"?

BW: "Inspired by" means no credit.

Wilder discusses Paul Diamond, the screenwriting son of I. A. L. Diamond. "I put him together with the Spanish director who did Belle Epoque. *He was the one who won the Oscar for Best Foreign Film . . . the one who mentioned me at the Oscars."*

"And then there is Satyajit Ray . . ." Audrey prompts, mentioning the great Indian director.

"Yes," says Wilder.

"We were watching the Oscars one year, and on comes an interview with Satyajit Ray. He's in a hospital bed in India, and he says, 'I write Billy Wilder but he does not write me back.' I said, 'Billy, write him back.' "

"And I did," says Wilder simply. "I got it back in the mail. It did not reach him in time." He shrugs. "The address was so long. . . ."

Wilder asks about Tom Cruise, still in England on the Kubrick movie. I tell Wilder that Cruise often asks about him.

"Yes," says Wilder, "he flatters me, but when I call him for my next movie, he will say yes, but for three or four million!"

I explain to Wilder, delicately, that Cruise might, but he'd be doing it as a favor. "Especially because he gets twenty *million per picture now."*

Wilder smiles into his meal. "Oh. I see."

Audrey discusses picking up Billy at the office the next day. "You've got to put up the shade," she says, "so I know you're there."

"It was down," he says, regarding the day before. "I wasn't there."

"So you'll put it up when you're there?" asks Audrey.

"Yes."

"Good. We have a plan."

11:15 a.m. Wilder's office. I am fifteen minutes late. Today he is friendly but guarded with his time. He agrees to ten minutes. He wears a white cap and is chipper. The sports section is open, his glasses on the paper. His two windows on the world are flung open; there is a brightness in the room.

BW: Now, what do you want to ask me?

CC: Did you feel any affinity with Las Vegas and the Rat Pack, any of that gang?

BW: No. I was not a member of the Rat Pack, and they were intellectually way below me. [*Laughter.*] Now I don't say that I'm an intellectual, that I'm "way above." But I don't think that they *ever read a book.*

Wilder stays behind his sunlit new desk, wearing his white cap. As I'm leaving, standing in the doorway, he comments on money. "Money is boring. When you get to my age, you don't know what to spend it on. When I was your age, I was 'money, money, money' . . . 'save, save'. Now, what does it matter? She will get it all. She's a good girl.

"So I will see you soon."

(Above and on page 292) In *Kiss Me Stupid* (1964), cinematographer Joseph LaShelle captured an era that is now long gone—the Rat Pack era of Vegas. Where others focused on the garish display of colored casino lights, Wilder chose black-and-white.

One day a few weeks later, I call Wilder at the office at 10:45 a.m. His voice sounds clouded and smallish.

"Hello," he says. I announce myself. "Hello, how are you?"

"Good." I find myself asking the question I try not to overuse. "How are you?"

"Oh," he says, "I am not well . . . but you know . . . I will make it!"

I tell him to enjoy the World Series.

"HOW CAN I ENJOY THE SERIES?" he booms. "WE GOT CLOBBERED!" (Wilder is referring to the Dodgers.)

We agree to meet another day, soon.

It is Audrey Wilder's seventy-fifth birthday, and we are gathered at a restaurant in Century City called Jimmy's. I am seated between Audrey and Billy, and the others at the table are a collection of old friends. There are the Wilders' longtime friend Leonard Gershe, Audrey's brother, Stratton Young, and Karen Lerner. Wilder sits next to me and orders an entree of kidneys.

Leonard Gershe tells a good story from an Oscar party some years back: "It was after midnight and Billy just announced that the evening was over. 'It's over!' Jimmy Stewart was there, the Lemmons, quite a few people. Suddenly, surprised at the abrupt ending to the evening, they began filing out. The next day I talked to Billy. 'Next time, you might just say goodnight and go to bed, and everybody will get the idea.' Wilder looked at me. 'What,' he said, 'and appear rude?' "

"How is your steak?" Wilder asks me.

"Great." I unwittingly supply him with his setup line. "How are your kidneys?"

"Not good!" he answers.

There is one person more punctual than Billy Wilder, and it is my own mother. I had begun to feel pangs, I had missed my encounters with Mr. Wilder, but I was on my way to San Diego for an extended Thanksgiving visit. My mom had said one thing before I left town to visit her:

"*Do* not *be late.*"

I promised to be in San Diego by three. From previous experience, I knew that being more than twenty minutes late made for a tone-setting disappointment that could last the entire visit.

On the other hand, there was Wilder. He had asked to meet him at ten a.m. The drive to San Diego was two and a half hours—on a nonholiday. I had two hours and no more to spend with Wilder. It was a battle between two very powerful, very punctual forces in my life.

Ten on the nose, I knock on the door to the Wilders' apartment. My appearance creates a small panic for Billy and Audrey. Wilder has double-booked the time, forgotten a previous appointment with his physical therapist, and not written down our engagement. "Always better to make the appointment with me," Audrey instructs, as she leads me toward the back TV den.

Wilder's time with the physical therapist, I now see, is rather sacred. He suggests we talk until the therapist arrives, and then, ever the problem solver, we will continue while he does his physical therapy. Wilder is extremely apologetic, but it's all fine with me. I turn the tape recorder on as we walk to the backroom.

CC: Should I let you sit down?

BW: Yes, but I will get up pretty soon, because he's coming. We do it in the bedroom, always, the exercise.

CC: How's the new office?

BW: The new office is half-finished, but the other half I cannot finish because I need a truck for the [move]. . . . But it's gonna be a race between my death and fixing the office.

The matter-of-fact mention of his death is new in our conversations. I laugh quietly, which I suppose is the proper response, but I am unsure if he is offering his mortality up for comic value. He settles on the corner of his sofa in the den, his power position for reading and watching Jeopardy!

BW: Let's go as far as we can.

What follows is a conversation about the working method of Diamond and Wilder while filming. According to Diamond's wife, their working method was the stuff of a longtime marriage. While Wilder walked the room, pitching dialogue and shaping scenes, often while holding a riding crop, Diamond always consulted the legal tablet. It was Diamond who served as the keeper of the document that they had labored over those many long hours in the office, and this role continued on the set, where he policed every line of their dialogue.

CC: Overall, does Izzy Diamond get enough credit, or just enough?

BW: Gets enough credit, gets all the credit that a collaborator has. I was the lead horse, because I also directed. But Diamond absolutely deserves all the credit he can get. I loved having him on the set too. He was right there, if a line was muffed or not said clearly.

CC: When you were filming, was Izzy allowed to talk to the actors?

BW: No. He would not do it. That was never discussed, and he would never do it. He would talk to me on the side, and he would just whisper to me, but he would never talk to the actors, because then it's codirection. If it was no good, or a line was muffed, or it was not clear—if he had anything to say, any observation or something that was wrong—he would come up to me and whisper to me. When I thought I had a print, I'd look at him. And he does like this [*an imperceptible nod*] and that means that no words had been left out, and it made sense. It was good, yeah. But if something displeased him very highly, he would just kind of make a little movement with his hands or with his eyes. I would see that he was unhappy about something, and then we will discuss it. And then we will do it right or we will leave it as it is. He was never loud. I never heard him loud. It was always, the better the joke, the softer he is. It was just understanding, you know, really collaboration.

CC: Do you remember your last visit with Izzy?

BW: Yeah, I went to see him the day before he died in 1988. He said one dirty word. That was the only dirty word he ever said. He saw me there, and he just looked up at me, and he said, "Oh shit." That was the dialogue. Because he knew that he was a goner.

His illness started in . . . I think it started in Munich. We were there on a picture. *Fedora* [1978]. He just was on the phone all the time, to his doctor really. And he says, "Well, I've got the shingles." Very secretive, "the shingles." Then we came back, and he went to the doctor right away, and he told him that he had cancer, that he's going to die. It was not curable. He did not tell me until six weeks before he died. [*The phone rings. It's the downstairs doorman.*]

That's my doctor.

Dr. Marks arrives at the front door, and enters the den.

AUDREY WILDER: Jeff is here, Billy. Cameron Crowe, Jeff Marks.

Izzy Diamond and Wilder on location: "If it was no good, or a line was muffed . . . any observation or something that was wrong, he would come up . . . and whisper to me"; (opposite) Ray Milland and Howard Da Silva in *The Lost Weekend* (1945); the set is a recreation of P.J. Clarke's in New York.

I shake hands with Dr. Marks. Marks is clearly ambivalent about sharing his time with Wilder. These physical-therapy appointments are far from drudgery for either doctor or patient, and I soon find out why. While Jeff Marks works Billy out in the bedroom, they use the time to compare their weekly football picks. My presence has thrown the whole rhythm off. But I too am reluctant to surrender my time with Wilder. Marks and I size each other up. Silently, we agree to work together.

BW: [*Directing us:*] We will be talking while we're counting to ten, twenty, and thirty!

AW: You mean you're going to exercise and talk?

BW: I'm going to the bedroom.

AW: Everybody into the bedroom!

I follow them through a large adjoining bathroom adorned with many photographs framed and standing on the counters. The photos are a scrapbook from a well-traveled and cosmopolitan marriage. I move into the bedroom, tape recorder in hand. Wilder invites me to take the seat near the door, facing the bed. His wife takes a similar position to Wilder, lying on the other side of the bed. Wilder assesses our positions in the room. Assured of all our motivations, he eases back onto the bed. Wilder smiles a lot with the therapist; their accomplishments brighten his mood.

BW: [*To Dr. Marks:*] How silly we were to discuss that half a point in that football game on Monday.

JEFF MARKS: Yeah, I took Denver.

CC: I took Oakland.

BW: [*Settling on bed:*] Okay [*as in "Action"*]. You ask me the questions in between.

The Wilders' smallish bedroom is a homey collection of art pieces, knickknacks, and photographs. Wilder performs calisthenics on the bed; on the other side Audrey practices the same exercises. The dominant painting is by Raphael Soyer, who was from the ashcan school of artists.

JM: Okay. One knee up to the chest. Grab it with both hands and pull it up.

BW: You can ask me questions, Cameron. Go right ahead.

CC: Did you ever read *The Catcher in the Rye*?

JM: Both knees.

BW: Both knees? [*Wilder is on his back, and the doctor helps with his legs, pressing them into position and straightening them out again.*]

AW: This is some kind of scene, but I don't know what. [*Laughs.*]

BW: Of course I read *The Catcher in the Rye.*

Wilder does arm bends now. The blood is flowing, his heart is pumping, he is comfortable with his audience. This is one of the more animated conversations I've had with him. He is the energized center of the room, and he is flat on his back.

BW: Wonderful book. I loved it. I pursued it. I wanted to make a picture out of it. And then one day a young man came to the office of Leland Hayward, my agent, in New York, and said, "Please tell Mr. Leland Hayward to lay off. He's very, very insensitive." And he walked out. That was the entire speech. I never saw him. That was J. D. Salinger and that was *Catcher in the Rye.*

JM: Take a rest. Take a rest. Take a rest.

BW: That's a good thing that you told me, because I would have dropped dead here.

CC: So discussions were already in progress for you to direct *Catcher in the Rye.*

JM: Arms over your head.

BW: Yeah. Leland Hayward, that was my agent at the time, and I said to him, "That's a hell of a book." Naturally, we all knew, we all knew who Mr. Salinger was. We just didn't know Mr. Salinger. Maybe the people at *The New Yorker* knew him. But there was no way of getting into a conversation with him, of being confronted with him.

CC: How would you have adapted the book?

BW: I would have been true to his words. But it never got far enough along. I would have protected his view of things. He was completely unique. The way he showed the stories in the life of that family [the Glass family]—wonderful. I was very much taken by the book. When you have a book like this, that sort of captures the world, you know, you have to be very careful. Because the letters would keep arriving saying, "Why didn't you do *this* scene, and *that* scene?" [*Pause.*] And whatever happened to Salinger? Where is he?

Wilder looks on as Ray Milland begins his five-day binge by trying to make an impression on Doris Dowling.

JM: Lift your bottom up.

CC: I also wanted to ask you about a book in which you and your work are mentioned, Frederick Exley's *A Fan's Notes*. He talks about going to a place called P. J. Clarke's in New York City—

BW: Yeah. Fifty-fifth Street.

CC: In the book, he writes about it as the *Lost Weekend* bar. Did you film there?

BW: I filmed a few scenes there, and a few scenes after . . . because in those days there was the elevated train going down Third Avenue. And I used that for when he goes trying to hock his typewriter. Because it's Yom Kippur, everything is closed.

AW: Lift your foot up, Billy!

BW: Yeah, I shot that area. Of course there were some interior shots, but I shot against the live background. In the window you can see the traffic. You could see people walking. A good location depends on the action, the milieu of where you are. The perfect picture of a New York bar—if nothing happens, it gets to be pretty dull after half an hour.

CC: When Lubitsch directed *Ninotchka,* how protective was he of each line in the script?

BW: Nothing, absolutely nothing was changed. The script was finished. No invention, no nothing. Just very, very rarely did he find something new, but—

JM: Take a rest.

Wilder turns his body, looks up at the ceiling. Happily flushed with adrenaline, he continues. He is energized by the therapy.

BW: —he explored everything. He read the scene. He acted the scene with us. He acted it out with the secretary. This was the very funny thing, because he dictated from the yellow [work] pages that he had to a clean sheet with the secretary. He dictated six or eight pages to her, a scene from *Ninotchka*. He then came to us in the room and said, "We have failed. There is not one single laugh in the picture. The secretary did not even smile!" Very depressed. Then the next day he came in and he said, "Do you know why she didn't laugh? Because she had braces on her teeth." [*Laughs.*] Lubitsch protesting: "I knew it was very funny! I knew!"

AW: [*Dryly:*] I don't want the maid to see the messy bed, from all these people.

CC: Billy, who were your rivals back in the forties, fifties?

BW: Preston Sturges, who was the first writer who just freed himself and became a director. Joe Mankiewicz. Then Norman Krasna—he did comedies. Then Claude Binyon. There were [other writing] teams, you know, but not [with one] as a director. Some of them tried it. But then they said, "Oh shit, this is too tough and this is no good." Some of them made it, some of them did not make it.

JM: Up and down with the toes.

CC: Did you feel competitive with them?

BW: No. We were very open, we talked about it. There were very few. Some found it difficult to get into the dialogue, but it was fine. There were 104 writers under contract at Paramount at the same time. There was a Writers Building, a Writers Annex Building, and a Writers Annex *Annex* Building. There were many scripts that were never made, you know. Finished, but they were never made. We made fifty pictures a year then. But we wrote a hundred and fifty.

We now move into the outer area of the bathroom for some stand-up exercises. The therapy continues as we stand near a sunny windowsill, on which rest four large glass vases carefully filled with individual denominations of pocket change. Constantly turning his head, sometimes answering my questions while looking at the doctor, sometimes looking at me while answering the doctor, Wilder continues our conversation.

CC: A quick question about *Sherlock Holmes*. What was your relationship like with your leading actor, Robert Stephens?

BW: Stephens. He was a wonderful, wonderful man. He came from the theater. Also, he was married to Maggie Smith. I never quite knew if he was a homosexual or not. Then he, during the shooting of the picture, he attempted suicide. Then we had to wait until he recuperated. He died about five years ago. He was a very fine actor. He looked very much like, I thought, like Mr. Sherlock Holmes looked. But he was a very, very friendly, nice man, who took direction like a fish does to the water. He was very, very good, except for those weeks when the picture was half-done and we were worried whether the script was ever going to be finished. We worried that the picture was never going to be finished.

Garbo and Melvyn Douglas in *Ninotchka* (1939). According to Wilder, "This absolutely crazy hat is the symbol of capitalism to her."

JM: Arms forward, both sides.

Wilder pauses to survey the lively atmosphere around him. The doctor manipulating him, Audrey exercising nearby, me holding a microphone. He has clearly missed the beautiful chaos of a movie set. With barely disguised glee, Wilder encourages our behavior, but commands us to specific places in the room. Suddenly the room pops with loopy syncopation. We all feel like characters in a Wilder film. And he knows it. He stands watching the successful scene he has just staged. His face melts into a rare look of complete creative satisfaction. It's just a small smile, a simple expression of deep bemusement, but it's the most revealing glimpse Wilder could offer any biographer. This is who he is. This is his bliss.

BW: [*Ever the director:*] This is a nice scene, with the dialogue, and with you wondering whether I'm speaking the dialogue to you or the doctor. . . . A lot of funny stuff could happen here. Ask me another question!

JM: Arms to the sides, like you're flying. Now . . . up on your toes.

CC: Stephens wrote a book and said he was unnerved by the experience of shooting *Sherlock Holmes.*

BW: Yeah, because he had to start the engine every morning, right? Instead of starting it every afternoon and going through the whole play. I never read his book. Was he very unhappy with me?

CC: I sense that the experience came at a tough time in his life. What was the relationship like from your perspective?

BW: Stephens? I loved working with him. I just adored it. Because he was a really learned, professional actor. And he used to go and go and go with the dialogue forever. I was finished, and he would just *go,* another four pages.

JM: Sit down and take a rest.

Wilder sits down in a seat near the bathroom door, an adrenalized warrior. For a few minutes, the conversation turns to Wilder's picks on the weekend football games. Then, continuing the therapy, Jeff Marks and Wilder go walking around the apartment, down the hallway and back. Audrey stays behind in the outer area of the bathroom, where she shows me a framed note from Billy. It reads simply, in small script: "To My Love."
    It is unsigned.
    "That's the only time Billy has ever written anything to me." She laughs heartily. "This was for my last birthday—but you see, he didn't sign his name." She continues, laughing. "But every time he sent a cable or something, never something in longhand. And he'd sign it 'the Prince of Liechtenstein' or 'the Baron of Münchhausen' or something. But never his name, and never handwritten."
    "Didn't you ask him to sign this?"
    "No! I'm just lucky to have this!" She laughs again. She resembles nothing so much right now as a char-

acter from Wilder's own pen: the girl who cleverly allows a very married husband to still feel mysterious and free. She laughs again. "Never signed his name once!"

BW: [*Returning:*] All right, I'm finished here with my therapy. More questions? [*We retire to his den, Wilder now huffing lightly like a postfight boxer.*]

Show me photographs. [*Audrey enters and lets him know a lunch date with a friend is still on. I have only a few more questions today.*]

You said it was going to be twenty minutes.

CC: I know, I—

BW: Your twenty minutes are always an hour!

CC: Here is just a great picture of Gloria Swanson as Norma Desmond. And it inspired a question in me. That these characters that you've written, in this case with Brackett, are so larger than life. . . . Norma Desmond is more famous than most famous actors.

BW: Yes.

CC: Having created Norma Desmond, what did it feel like making the movie? Was she a living, breathing person to you?

Robert Stephens and Colin Blakely in
The Private Life of Sherlock Holmes (1970)

BW: Yes she was, yes she was. Yes, absolutely. Suddenly there is a person there, not just on paper. She was a real character, who had lived, who could be living on Sunset Boulevard. Not on the stage thing—that was enormous. And she had an affair with the monkey. I always told Swanson, "Remember that your lover is in the garden."

CC: Did she laugh at that?

BW: At first she laughed. But then she . . . [*He offers a look of stunned horror.*]

CC: Again, it's an odd question, but what are the characters that you've created that you actually enjoyed spending time with? Missed, when the movie ended?

BW: You mean fascinating characters? One would like to sit down with DeMille, one would like to sit down with Stroheim, or would like to sit down with Bill Holden, for sure. Or even the little pale reader from *Sunset Boulevard*. [Nancy] Olson played her, I think. So the characters, I knew every character, I knew everything was working except one thing, and that was that Stroheim did not know how to drive a car. And so we had to pull him through, we had to put a chain on something, and out of camera, we had to pull him, and yet he ran into that gate, and we had to have it fixed.

CC: But in terms of all the movies, were there other characters that you sort of hated to see leave your life when the movie ended?

BW: Sure, there were characters—not necessarily expected characters. I liked the lawyer, Walter Matthau, in *The Fortune Cookie*. I liked C. C. Baxter [Lemmon in *The Apartment*]. I liked almost every character. I loved Holden in *Stalag 17*. I loved [Otto] Preminger in that one little scene, a very good scene in *Stalag 17*. Came off good. And all the characters were good in *Stalag 17*, because they'd lived with the play. I didn't have the play, but I had the *feeling* of the play. My love will always be with Mr. Holden.

CC: Well, this brings me to another of these photos. I love this photo of you dancing with Audrey Hepburn, and I guess you're showing her what the scene will ultimately be.

BW: Yeah.

CC: Was she a good dancer?

BW: Great. She was almost a dancer, she was almost a ballerina. She was a good *everything*. And everything came to her so easily, you know. It was her second, her third American picture.

CC: What goes through your mind when you see this picture [of you dancing with Sabrina]?

Wilder examines the photograph. He holds it carefully, soaking in the image, seemingly studying it more for composition than for nostalgia.

BW: Well, I forgot that I was showing her how to do it, because she did it very well herself. She was guiding *me*, I wasn't guiding her. And I thought that I was at the ball, I was in a restaurant dancing with her . . . I was completely forgetful, and then I thought, "Oh my God, the camera! Where would the camera be?"

CC: So it's like what we talked about earlier in these interviews. You wrote these movies, really, to live all these different lives, to experience the things you weren't able to in real life. And here you are, dancing

(Above) "Bogart does the scene . . . and I say, 'Oh, that's not as good as mine'"; Wilder (above right) dances with his creation, Sabrina.

with your own character, played by Audrey Hepburn. [*Wilder is still examining the photograph.*] Until, of course, Bogart steps in and actually does the scene.

BW: He does the scene . . . and I say, "Oh, that's not as good as mine."

I show him an old class photo from the early days in Vienna.

CC: And this?

BW: This is me, here. [*He points himself out, as if it weren't obvious that he was the one just to the left of the center, wearing a ten-year-old's version of the same lopsided grin he's wearing now.*]

CC: Any particular memories jogged by that?

BW: No. Except one: that every one of them—those are most of the class—all of them, with the exception of me, are dead.
    Are we leaving now?

He means me. And as usual, while I pack my tape recorder, he leaves me with a gem.

CC: Okay, last thing, from your American Film Institute interview, one statement you made that's stood out: "I don't do cinema. I make movies."

Wilder (above), on the set of *The Apartment,* shows Jack Lemmon how to drop the razor blades from his cabinet into his pocket; at the 1961 Academy Awards: (opposite top) Mr. and Mrs. Billy Wilder; (opposite bottom) Elizabeth Taylor with Wilder, who won Best Director, Best Screenplay, and Best Picture for *The Apartment*

BW: "I don't make cinema, I make movies." Yeah, that's right. I make movies, for amusement. That's the difference between a bound book and a thing to be continued every week in the *Saturday Evening Post*. In other words, you just do it for the moment. It is not to be bound. There are only a few pictures [worthy of that], here and there, from other people—Eisenstein, or Mr. Lean, David Lean. I just do not like to think in kind of inspired language that we're not making pictures, we are making [*with grand accent*] CINEMA!

CC: And yet your movies last, and they can't seem to remake them. For example, Costa-Gavras's new film, *Mad City*. Almost every review said, "You can't remake the great Billy Wilder's *Ace in the Hole*."

BW: Where was that? In what paper?

CC: The *New York Times*, the *L.A. Times* . . .

BW: Is it really that similar?

CC: Similar enough. And many of the reviewers caught it, and just said, "Look, nice effort, but it's not *Ace in the Hole*." I think it was the *L.A. Times* that said, "It doesn't have the corrosive wit of Wilder." And so these movies do hold up. [*Convinced that this attention is real, Wilder screws his head backwards a bit and blinks at me behind his glasses. He grins goofily.*]

BW: Oh, goddamnit, it's wonderful!

I head for San Diego to my next—late—appointment.

Football season is a pleasant time for Billy Wilder. Monday Night Football

is a ritual at his home. I have been invited to watch tonight's game with the director, and I arrive early, before game time. Wilder is sitting in his study. He has a martini in a small glass in front of him, no olive. He has bet San Francisco, and the return of a rehabilitated Jerry Rice to the team, giving up three and a half points.

The study is lined with books on art, history, and film. On a stack of books next to him are Eric Lax's book on Woody Allen and Neil Simon's autobiography, Rewrites, a heartfelt inscription inside. "His book is first-rate," comments Wilder. Nearby, a photo of Groucho Marx is also signed: "Billy—Here is a picture that adds nothing to your collection. Groucho."

During a commercial, I ask Wilder about the famous New York doctor Max Jacobson, also known as Dr. Feelgood. "He was my doctor in Berlin," Wilder recalls. "Dr. Feelgood, yes. Max Jacobson. He was a good doctor, very bold. I was making Sabrina and I was sick. I called him. Sam Spiegel was with me. He came in and gave me a shot with the longest needle. Spiegel fainted. He would also give cocaine. On a long needle that he stuck up your nose, and it was on the very tip. Kennedy was one of his patients. They called him before the subcommittee. He is an old man. He's 110 now. However, he's dead."

The game resumes. He likes the impressionistic black-and-white Miller Genuine Draft commercials. He dismisses the many other more high-octane advertisements. "Too many cuts, though, too many setups . . . it's more powerful with less setups."

Audrey flits into the room from time to time, smoking Eve cigarettes and checking on the drinks. Her martini is classic and definitive. We each have two.

Billy gets up to have dinner during half-time, as is the Monday-night custom. We move to the dining room, with the Greta Garbo martinis made by Audrey, and reposition ourselves at the table. In the corner, there for reference, the football game plays on a small television. Over dinner, Wilder comes alive discussing art. On Edward Hopper: "Very original, very American. My friend Richard Cohen has his greatest piece, Man Awakening at Early Morning . . . a man with a naked woman behind him. He has slept with her on the sofa. Why did he sleep with her? Why there, on the sofa and not a bed? Will his marriage end? He was maybe the greatest American painter. I never met him. He was an honest man, he painted what he felt."

Audrey exits into the kitchen. Finished with his meal, Billy gets up from dinner in the third quarter, steadying himself as he moves back to the den. He stops for a moment; his balance shifts dangerously. And then, inch by inch, he tips over. I see this in slow motion, from the other side of the table which separates us. He lands on the floor with a soft thud, managing to curl his shoulder and take a sportsmanlike fall. His glasses skid across the floor. He lies on the ground, silent and surprised.

"Aud!" he calls out sharply.

I reach him as the Wilders' maid flies out of the kitchen first, traumatized, then Audrey. It is Audrey who helps him to his feet. "I'm fine!" says Wilder. Nearby, the maid still looks shaken. Audrey and I steady him. "I'm fine!" I compliment his fall, which he executed even more delicately than Jerry Rice, who is already reinjured and out of the game. Wilder appreciates this comparison as he replaces his unbroken glasses. "Yes," he says, "I took a soft, rolling fall."

And that is the last we mention of the after-dinner mishap.

My own great-grandfather had been a practicing lawyer into his early nineties. I had grown up with this lore, always thinking, along with my sister, that there was some kind of a human dinosaur in our family line. What could he possibly have been like, still lumbering the earth at that great advanced age? Knowing Wilder now, having made the acquaintance of a man in his nineties, as an adult, I feel let in on a much simpler truth. As Captain Pringle might have said in A Foreign Affair, it's a short distance, baby, and we all

travel on the same shaky trolley. I sit with Wilder watching the broadcast, discussing our winning bets. The game turns out to be a rout by San Francisco. The fifty-plus years between us feel exceedingly short.

Before I leave, Wilder inquires about my own next screenplay, asking, as always, "How is the third act?" I tell him I am trying to solve a few problems. "If you have a problem in the third act," he offers, like a fellow writer, "the problem is gonna be in the first."

"Bye, pal," says Audrey.

Wilder stands with her in the doorway on his den, shaking my hand and saying goodbye with a wave. I am reminded of Karen Lerner's early description to me of Wilder, the private Wilder—brave and gallant, not just tough.

"Come back again," he says with a slight bow. "I will crumble before you."

Working with Wilder has filled me with a joy of filmmaking. Over the next month, I work on my own script and these transcripts in rotation. Each benefits from the other. There are few filmmakers who wouldn't benefit from a steady diet of Wilder, and so it has been. I have given Wilder himself the month off from our interviews. Late in the month, I talk to Karen Lerner, who has spoken with Wilder.

"Where is my collaborator?" he asked her. "What happened to him?"

Three minutes late. The door is open. Audrey is in the office; Billy is pulling up the shades. He wears a cap, and a brown sweater over dress trousers. The office is fully made up, with long rectangular lithographs of Henri Matisse's and Miró's signatures, . . . along with a framed nude posterior photograph of Naomi Campbell hanging on the wall, just to the right of the desk. To the left of his desk is a large dictionary folded open on a wooden stand. The most prominent word on these opened pages, quite aptly, is "logic." In the middle of these two worlds, the carnal and the cerebral, sits the man himself. He and Audrey are discussing the flowers in the pot just outside his double windows overlooking Brighton Way. It's been raining heavily all morning, but Wilder is bouncy as he hunches by the window to look out.

"We won't take more than two hours," he wonders. He makes an arrangement to meet Audrey at noon.

Audrey suggests we go out this week. She pulls on a smart-looking Italian blazer. "We'll go someplace swell," she says. Then, as she leaves, she notes, adding up the visual picture of the now-finished office, "Billy—there are more bare-assed women on your walls. . . ."

He chuckles, and we dive in. I pull out my large notebook manuscript. Wilder eyes it. Today's session is for clarifications and corrections.

"We have work to do," he says, with the brisk professionality of a man who has seen many a bulky manuscript that needed to be reduced. We talk initially of Ernst Lubitsch. I am still trying to isolate the Swedish silent film by Mauritz Stiller that first inspired Wilder's mentor to begin making the elegant comedies that shaped Wilder's own cinematic voice. I run through the names of several early Stiller films. Wilder rejects them as possibilities. I pledge to keep looking. The conversation continues as we adjust some names and dates.

CC: James Lipton on the *Inside the Actors Studio* series asks his guests this question: "What will you say to God when you arrive at the gates of heaven?"

BW: Will I know it's God?

CC: Yes.

BW: I will know it . . . definitely? I'll just look around like it's a hotel room and let the manager show me around. But I will be comfortable there.

CC: What things do you see clearly now, living such a long life?

BW: Now? It's just a question of longevity. How old can I get? Can I make it to 2000? Can I make it to a hundred? That's something I want to do. I'm the oldest living director, I think. Maybe there is someone older, hiding somewhere in the suburbs of Hollywood . . . but not too many. What do I see clearly at my age? I have a good wife.

CC: In the recent *American Masters* special on you, Diamond comments that even years after the movie was released, you still thought quite a bit about giving Jack Lemmon the physical handicap of a club foot in *The Apartment*. Do you remember that?

BW: Vaguely. But that was forgotten. The film was a big success, it won an award, it won everything. I forgot about it. I just don't dwell on old pictures. I don't redirect, or rewrite, or re-anything . . . especially now, in my nineties, you know?

CC: Why were you worried that Lemmon needed more?

BW: I don't know why, but I thought so. People kind of accused me of making a happy ending to *that thing*. Or that it was "dirty." That kind of story happens in every big outfit, and it happens always tragically. You know what I mean. The boss, or bosses, who do their afternoon extravaganzas. The picture was only dirty to some because they didn't listen to one line, to one very important line, about how Lemmon became a superior at the company. One of the higher-ups came with the suitcase, and he said he was going to the opera that evening, and could he change his clothes in the apartment, and Lemmon said, "Of course you can." And then he was stuck. Suddenly there are three guys taking advantage of him, and he's got to maneuver. . . . I was worried how to stick him with the dilemma. I think that was the problem—I don't quite remember, which is good. Then others won't, either, and they'll think it all came spontaneously.

So now you have everything . . . that's good.

"Goodbye, my friend," he says simply, as I leave. And I have heard his side of enough phone conversations to know the rareness of that goodbye.

Dinner at Mimosa on Beverly Boulevard. The Wilders are seated at opposite ends of the table, and in the middle are their friends Richard and Barbara Cohen and Jerry and Ann Moss. This is the Wilders' regular dinner-and-movies gang. The restaurant is a beer-and-wine establishment. I sit across from Audrey, who has smuggled in small airline-size bottles of vodka in a black Chanel makeup bag. She covertly prepares vodka-and-water drinks for some of her guests. At the other end of the table, wearing a sharp hat and a silver moustache, is Wilder. It is a noisy dinner crowd, and Wilder can't hear those of us at the other end of the table, but we all enjoy an evening in the outskirts of his glow.

Audrey pleasantly sits at the outskirts herself, proudly sharing him with her guests. As I have come to know, all those who love Billy love Audrey equally. Corralling the waiter, keeping the evening going, speaking loudly to Billy when he needs to make an entree choice, Audrey enjoys the evening out.

Out of his hearing range, but still regarding him across the table, she talks of meeting Wilder for the first time. She had her eye on him and they had dated three or four times before she'd left on a road tour. She didn't know him well, but it was Wilder whom she called from the road. She called him at home, where he was in the early stages of divorce, still sharing the house with his wife. There was also a girlfriend (Doris Dowling) in the picture. Wilder accepted her collect call. Girlfriends had whispered advice of playing hard to get. She ignored them. She asked Wilder to send her money for a plane ticket back to Los Angeles. She wanted to see him. He sent the money; they dated regularly. Audrey recalls that she proposed to him, but Wilder had told it differently, giving that credit to himself. "His first wife didn't like the business," she says matter-of-factly. "She wanted him to move to Modesto. I met her once. What you have to realize is—" she regards her husband across the table, the stature of his talent— "you're always going to come second. That's the way it's gonna be." She says it proudly. "And once you know that," she confides, "then you're always going to be number one."

Early in their relationship, Wilder had said, "No more children—and don't trick me." Audrey agreed, and though "of course" she would have loved a child, "I wouldn't trick him," she says. She shrugs and smooths her blouse. "But we're closer because of that." Looking down the table at Wilder, who is hunched but somewhat swashbuckling tonight in the white moustache, she says a little wistfully, "We've stayed closer than if we'd had children. At least that's what they say."

I ask if it's true that it was Audrey who supplied the sumptuous career-girl coat Fran Kubelik wears in The Apartment. It is a shaggy coat that tells you everything about that famous character, her hopes and dreams—one of the great costume touches, unforgettable, even though its exact color will forever be an unclear shade of black-and-white. "Yes, it was mine," says Audrey. "It was lime green."

She tells me one more story from Oscar night 1960. Wilder was up for Some Like It Hot. He and Audrey did not go to the Oscars, but watched it at a viewing party. "He didn't want to go if he expected to lose," she remembers. "He knew it wasn't going to win. It was the year of Ben Hur. Billy had thirteen or fourteen martinis, the most I'd ever seen him drink. He was so embarrassed, he locked himself in the bathroom and wouldn't come out. 'Why won't you come out?' I said." Here she imitates Billy, a quiet and self-conscious ache in his voice, on the other side of the bathroom door: " 'I am drunk,' he said. And he would not come out. 'I cannot,' he said."

"Tony Curtis and Kirk Douglas started banging on the door. Finally he opened it, and they carried him out, carried him to the car. He was moaning, so embarrassed. He had to be carried up to our place by the

Scenes from Mauritz Stiller's *Erotikon* (1920)

doormen and put to bed. 'I've never cheated on you,' he said. And it wasn't like him at all, but that's when he told me."

The next year, Wilder had a better feeling for his odds at the Oscars. He attended and won the triple crown: Best Director, Best Screenplay, and Best Picture for The Apartment.

Audrey looks down at her husband. "I could never be with another guy. It's just been him. He was just different. He still is. He's still the same guy."

At the other end of the table, Wilder finishes his meal. The waiter, a respectful tone in his voice, asks him if the mushroom soup is okay. Wilder gives him an appreciative look of perfection.

As we stand on the curb waiting for our cars, I lean over to Billy. I whisper in his ear that I think I've found the name of the elusive film by Mauritz Stiller that first influenced Lubitsch. The name is Erotikon.

More scenes from *Erotikon*

Billy Wilder lights up immediately. It is as if I have found the obscure first single by his favorite band. "Erotikon! Yes! That's it! That's the name of it! That was when Lubitsch became Lubitsch. It's silent, you know." He pauses at the car door. "Not for today's audience!" Then a happy shrug, as he adds the kicker. "But who knows, it might come back someday! I will see you soon. . . ."

Two weeks later, I call Wilder's office to arrange our last big clarification session. It's Friday morning, around 11:20. My hope is to catch him at home over the weekend, where I can show him a compilation tape of some of his scenes, in hopes of jogging some new memories. As usual, he picks up the phone after one and a half rings.

"Hello," he announces in his lilting voice.

"Hi, Billy, it's Cameron Crowe."

"Hi, how are you?"

"Pretty good. How are you?"

"I am not doing so good," he says in a clear but disappointed voice.

I attempt to cheer him; my enthusiasm for the book spills out of me on this day.

"This is wonderful," he says.

I ask him for an appointment. He says he is taking the weekend off, to call in a couple of days. "I'm very weak," he says. And then he adds a simple statement of fact. His voice has surprise and wonder in it. "This is the end of me," he says.

I thank him for his time and the opportunity to work with his words. "I am rooting as much as you," he says. "Goodbye."

The sad, delicate tone in his voice haunts me for days.

6:28 p.m. Sunday night, the phone rings. My wife and I are cleaning the house; our hands are full. The answering machine picks up; an odd and dissonant outgoing message plays for whoever is calling. Beep.

His voice is full of power, all business:

"Cameron! This is Billy Wilder. We have a date for tomorrow morning, but make it at eleven instead of nine or ten. I have to go to a doctor. So I am going to see my doctor, and then I am going to see you. At eleven,

or eleven-fifteen. Thank you."

I call back and explain that the only thing that could have gotten in the way of one of our meetings has. I must take my wife to the doctor.

"I am going to the doctor too!" He pauses. "Good! We can all go to the same doctor, and then we can all be together!"

He is back.

We make a plan to see each other at noon the next day.

Our doctor's appointment ends early, so I speed to Wilder's office at eleven a.m., if only for the feeling of arriving wildly early. There is no answer at the office door. I peer in through the envelope slot. The office is dark. I go downstairs to wait for him, and sure enough, he and Audrey are walking down the street toward me. Both wear white overcoats, under one umbrella. They stroll together, looking very stylish, very snappy, very European on this rainy late morning.

"Hey, I'm early!"

There is no celebration. Instead we stand and order coffee in the downstairs shop. The Latinas behind the counter smile sweetly at him; the elegant curmudgeon is a favorite customer. The coffees appear, and we place them on the small white table. I hold the chair for Billy as he negotiates his descent into the seat. Plop.

"Have you seen Titanic?" he asks. He leans closer. "Have you seen *such* horse-shit?" Wilder looks down, his eyes peering above his glasses mischievously. He shakes his head. This is a parlor game he truly enjoys—taking shots at one of the most successful movies of all time. "I still cannot believe this. The money that is spent. One studio goes to another studio and says, 'Help us finish this movie'?" His eyes flash; he finds great ironic humor in the idea of a single movie nearly emptying the pockets of two studios. I remark that I enjoyed the chemistry of the leads; they transcended the script for me. "What script?" he deadpans, sipping coffee. "I'm telling you, if this wins the Academy Award, I will scream."

Audrey laughs and changes the subject. Soon Wilder finishes his coffee and reaches for his cane. It's time to go to work. "I will see you later," he says to Audrey. "Good*bye.*"

"See you later, hon."

He slips on his coat and heads upstairs, negotiating each step, never considering the elevator. We walk in silence.

He asks me if I have an ending for the book. Not yet.

Wrap party for *The Spirit of St. Louis* (1957), given by the Wilders and Leland Hayward at the Luau: (clockwise from opposite top) Richard Egan, Robert Preston, and Dana Wynter (Mrs. Greg Bautzer); Paul McNamara, David Niven, and Humphrey Bogart; Audrey Wilder and Humphrey Bogart; Spencer Tracy, Slim Hayward, and Dusty Negulesco; Billy Wilder and Jack Lemmon; Hjordis Niven and Gary Cooper; Slim and Leland Hayward; Kirk Douglas and Lauren Bacall

Carefully, he opens the office door. He shuffles to his spot behind the desk, and does not lift the shades on this rainy day. He looks at me, his nose pinched between the two large frames of his glasses. He is wearing a checkered hat, a yellow shirt with blue checks, and a light olive sweater-vest.

"We have work to do," he says, abandoning the cane and easing down into the seat with care. I set up my microphone, and he positions a box of Kleenex before him.

I show him a copy of the famous dress-blowing-up shot of Monroe from Seven Year Itch.

CC: It's interesting to look at the set photographs from some of your films. You are sometimes showing behavior, demonstrating scenes, as in showing Lemmon how to drop the razor blades from his cabinet into his pocket in *The Apartment*. And other times, you seem to be kibitzing with the actors to get the performance.

BW: Yeah, it is not a consistently *directorial* attitude that I have. Sometimes I run into a scene and something is missing. Or something will not come through, something will not be clear, because I am mostly a writer. And as a matter of fact, Diamond was on the set most of the time. I would say, "This is no good—we need an additional line to get somebody out of the room!" So I was kind of a writer-director all the way through, with Diamond, naturally, because I had to have his ears. Always, I would take a good idea wherever I could find one. I have nos only for the front office. Always "No, no, I don't think so." Always no. They had lousy ideas which they wanted us to do . . . and we didn't do them. But it was kind of . . . it was fun, I must say.

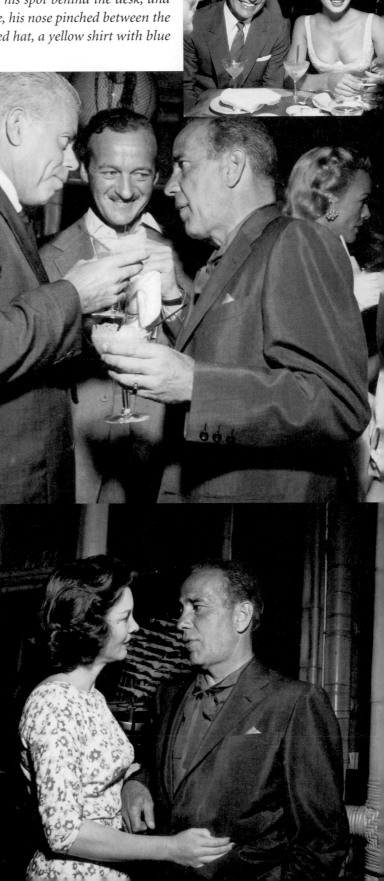

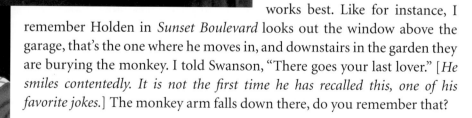

CC: I just like the idea that sometimes stern direction works, and sometimes a joke works with actors.

BW: Yeah, sometimes, in a serious scene, sometimes a joke works best. Like for instance, I remember Holden in *Sunset Boulevard* looks out the window above the garage, that's the one where he moves in, and downstairs in the garden they are burying the monkey. I told Swanson, "There goes your last lover." [*He smiles contentedly. It is not the first time he has recalled this, one of his favorite jokes.*] The monkey arm falls down there, do you remember that?

CC: Yes.

BW: "There goes your last lover!"

CC: Let me show this photo to you. This is you directing *The Apartment*. And it reminded me of the importance of rhythms, and you seem to be saying, "Now, you, catch up to her." Just getting the physical rhythms—

BW: Yeah. This was a rehearsal, without his clothes on. Because he was having a bad cold, and he had a trench coat, and I just rehearsed in the building itself. That was on Wall Street. He had the sniffles here, which was good. It made you like him.

CC: It seems like you are getting the timing of the scene right. And my question is, is it the responsibility of the actor or the director to get the timing right?

BW: I make it easy on myself, you know. If I had Mr. Lemmon and not Mr. Whoever, that helped a great deal. But that shot played in two takes, very good. They knew when to stop, they knew where the laugh comes in—and yeah, that's a lucky thing, that I worked with pros.

CC: But it's also interesting about casting—casting is so important. Let's take, for example, Kirk Douglas. If you had cast Lemmon in *Ace*

(From opposite bottom) Audrey Wilder and Gary Cooper; Billy Wilder, Anita Ekberg, and Gary Cooper; Bill Orr, Audrey Wilder, and Jennifer Jones Selznick; Alfred Vanderbilt, Frances Bergen, and Merle Oberon; Slim Hayward and Gilbert Roland

in the Hole, that's a very different movie; he becomes the poor schmuck who gets in too deep.

BW: Of course.

CC: And if you had Kirk Douglas in *The Apartment,* it's not funny.

BW: Not funny because it was not his part. He would have been uncomfortable; he would throw in some of his own laughs. It's no good, you know. You just cannot cast against the will [of the part]. I also knew that Shirley MacLaine was going to be fine—just leave her alone. And she was very good.

CC: There's a tough-mindedness about your films that some people confuse with cynicism. And we've talked about that. But I wondered how you were able to resist the temptation for schmaltz.

BW: For what?

CC: For schmaltz. Throughout your career.

Wilder offers a rare smile, as if I've just told a dirty joke. Have I misused the word?

BW: We never took the sentimental route, because in the early days—you know, silent days—when I was writing, we did everything that was filmable, you know. But then you got to be a little choosy. Then, when I started directing, I just said, "I'm going to make a picture that is going to be very popular, and they're not going to send me back now to the typewriter." The first pictures, we were two writers, Brackett and I, and I became a director. I lifted my content of pictures to more of a level of "This is going to be a fun picture, but not in a cheap way." That was the very first picture which I made, *The Major and the Minor.* And I kind of forced myself, you know, to not make a deep picture, but to be pretty close to the surface, you know. I built from there. I tried very hard, you know, to make the pictures original, to make them new, to make it so that people laugh, other people don't laugh, but they are *taken* by it.

I made it a little bit more difficult for myself with *Sunset Boulevard.* It was about the closest of things, you know, to make a picture about Hollywood, about an old star, falling in love with a young writer, and committing suicide, attempting suicide. Tough, and then, how are we going to end it? So we just had him shot. That was a tough decision to make.

CC: How so?

BW: He could have thrown everything away and gone back to Cleveland or wherever he was a reporter. That was not the solution. Because it came back to that line that we had discussed for a long time. He always wanted to have a pool. He got a pool. He died in the pool. That we hung on to. And they bought it. So she goes crazy, and the police are around there, they're very kind, and she thinks that it's DeMille. It was Stroheim. She's just going crazy.

CC: Was there anyone around who said, "Let Gillis live! Let him go back to Cleveland!" Did the studio ask why you had to shoot him?

BW: No. They were all for it.

CC: You brought up the producer Arthur Hornblow. He went out on a limb to support you as a director in the beginning, didn't he?

BW: He was the producer on the first movie, and the second one too. He was very good, very, very good. He was very learned—"learned" in the motion-picture sense. Not a deep philosophical thing there, but he had a good taste, and at no time did I want to contradict him. And I followed a little bit his thinking. I give him credit. He and Joe Sistrom, a minor executive, who brought the story of *Double Indemnity* to my attention. He acted as a producer on the picture, yet did not take credit.

CC: There is a theory that Mitchell Leisen actually played a key role in the rise of the writer-director in Hollywood. Preston Sturges says in interviews that because of Leisen's job of directing *Remember the Night* [1940], he knew he had to direct his own scripts. Which then paved the way for you.

BW: Yes. And I paved the way for Mankiewicz. There were quite a few who followed.

CC: So Leisen, in his own way, pushed some very important directors into the job.

BW: He died in the hospital for motion-picture people. He didn't like me at all, because of that thing with the cockroach [in *Hold Back the Dawn*]. He was an actor's director. Whatever an actor said, he took for granted it was a good idea.

(Opposite left to right) Anita Ekberg and Humphrey Bogart; Leland Hayward, Spencer Tracy, and Skip Hathaway; Cole Porter and Rosalind Russell; Anita Ekberg and Jack Warner; Doris Day and Lew Wasserman; Marty Melcher and Doris Day

(Top row, left to right) Leland Hayward, Jack Benny, and
Freddie Brisson; Slim Hayward, Cynthia and Jack Lemmon;
Joseph Cotton and Leland Hayward; Louis Jourdan, Quique
Jourdan, and David Niven; Mr. and Mrs. Edgar Bergen;
(center row) George Montgomery and Lauren Bacall; Kirk
Douglas and Ann Douglas; Spencer Tracy and Sam Gold-
wyn; David Niven and Anita Ekberg; Jean Negulesco and
Claudette Colbert; (bottom row) Audrey Wilder, Dinah
Shore, Slim Hayward, and George Montgomery; Robert and
Rosemary Stack; Dinah Shore and George Montgomery

CC: Here's a great picture from *The Major and the Minor*—the first day, I guess—and there's Sturges right there.

BW: Yeah, he was a friend of mine. He died in Paris, having done a picture there.

CC: So you weren't competitive with Sturges.

BW: Well, we were competitive, yes. When he was working he was above me. His things were very popular, but also on a good level.

Wilder examines a photo of his brother.

CC: Who's this, do you remember?

BW: That's my brother.

CC: Anything we should say about your brother?

BW: No, he was a fool. [*Wilder swivels slowly in his chair, turns and looks toward the dictionary as he discusses his brother. Somehow he manages to be both wistful and dispassionate.*]
    He lived in America many years before I even came here. I came here, really kind of pushed by Hitler. He was in the leather-goods business—he manufactured handbags. And then one day he said, "Well, if my brother can do it, I can do it too." He sold his business, he bought a house here, and started making pictures, one worse than the other, and then he died.

CC: Who was the relation that he stayed with when he first came to America. You had an uncle?

BW: Yeah, we had a relation in England, right after the war [World War I]. So he was taken there, where he learned English, and then he went to America, where I had another uncle—Reich was his name. He was a jeweler. And then I came over, my brother picked me up from the boat, the *Aquitania,* and I stayed there with him and with his wife, about three or four days. Then I took another three or four days to come by train—naturally by train. . . . In 1934, that was. But then he made up his mind, you know, things were going well with what I was doing, the Academy Award–winning picture *The Lost Weekend.* He said, "That's stupid, what the hell am I doing here? What the hell is the factory for?" He sold everything and came here and fell flat on his ass.

CC: What were your first impressions of America?

BW: I first saw America from the *Aquitania*. We were delayed half a day, we were up in the harbor. It was a snowing winter night. I stayed with my brother in his little house in Long Island. In the morning when I got up, I looked out the window. It was still snowing. And there was a big, black stretch Cadillac. Out comes a young boy with a stack of newspapers and he deposited one on the front doorstep. The weather was bad, and the newspaper boy's family was driving him in that big car. But to me, I thought, "What kind of country is this?" Newspapers delivered by Cadillac! It was stunning! I liked it! I *loved* it.

The phone rings, and Wilder speaks with a caller in French.

CC: I've asked you a few times about your opinions of modern comedies. Which ones stand out for you?

BW: Yeah, to begin with, Mankiewicz—*All About Eve.* Very, very clever. New, you know. The backstage thing, really explored and done magnificently. Sturges—you know, the opening pictures that he made, they were really something. And then he really just kind of washed out. I don't know, there are some pictures, for instance, pictures which I never could do. *Singin' in the Rain* [1952], that was a first-class picture. But if you had neither Mr. Kelly nor Mr. Astaire, you could not do a picture like that. Now both are dead, you could not do a musical. No, there are some good recent pictures—some very, very good pictures. Very simple, very direct . . . and they did not cost $200 million to make. The picture that I loved was *Forrest Gump* [1994]. *As Good as It Gets* [1997] is also a very good picture, nothing to be ashamed of.

CC: You've mentioned *Forrest Gump* quite a few times.

BW: A picture that I loved.

CC: Tell me why.

Billy Wilder, Akira Kurosawa, and John Huston make the presentation for Best Picture at the Academy Awards, 1986.

BW: [*His face lights up.*] It's very original. It's very entertaining. I just thought, there lived among us a very normal human being that is slightly on the minus side. Forrest was not retarded. He was honest, and good, and true . . . and a little slow. The world would be a better place if there were *more* Forrest Gumps. It's kind of . . . very original, this character. He is not stupid. He's not retarded. He's *naive*. He's a naive man who is thirty or thirty-five years old. A straight man to the world. And how the world looks through his eyes, that is just wonderful, I think. It is a picture about America that could have only been made in America. I love it. I also loved *The Full Monty*. [*Smiles.*] A wonderful picture about the lives and dreams of simple people, real people, who don't give a damn about rich people like us. I loved it.

CC: I've read all of the books and a lot of the articles. Your biographers always try to analyze your use of disguises . . .

BW: Yeah.

CC: And they all try to figure out where that comes from. If you were a historian writing about your own life, how would you deal with that issue?

BW: I don't know. But of the upper class of directors, of my era, I always changed my locale, I changed the tenor of the thing. I did a comedy, I did serious pictures. I did not develop a style of my own—with one exception, maybe: that I took it seriously whether it was a comedy or not. And most of the time I succeeded.

CC: But your fascination with characters pretending to be something that they weren't—

BW: No, that was necessary for certain scenes, but that is not a must that I wrote it. What it must have is this, you should not be bored. The old number-one thing. But if a disguise, or if anything of that sort, is helpful for the development of the picture, then I will do it. I will stoop to nothing but to excellence.

CC: And the romantic banter, good romantic dialogue, which is so rare, where did you get your taste for that?

BW: [*Poker-faced:*] That you have to be born with.

Monroe and Wilder at a party at Romanoff's; (opposite) at Charles Feldman's party for Cole Porter: Richard Burton, Audrey Wilder, Charles Vidor, Billy Wilder

We talk for another half hour, going over photographs for captioning, until Wilder announces that my time is up, his lunch date will be waiting for him. I have kept him longer than he wanted to be kept, but he is gracious and happy when I shut the tape recorder off. He eases on his overcoat, and we talk briefly about my current screenplay. He offers a simple, memorable directing tip.

BW: You have to be serious to direct a good comedy.

CC: Do you believe that the good comedies have a lot of pain in them?

BW: Sure. Pain, and then, in a comedy, a very rare victory for your leading man, one they did not expect. It's not always that you're gonna hit the bull's-eye, but somewhere in the vicinity of it—that's good enough.

Wilder moves to the door. We exit, and he stands with his keys, locking up. We move down the stairs. It is raining hard now, and Wilder is slightly late. He hands me his black cane. I hold it while he quietly adjusts the collar of his overcoat. I return his cane to him. We head out into the rain.
   "Call me and we will work some more," he says. He heads down the street at a brisk clip.

I call Wilder at his home. In a previous conversation, I had mentioned finally finding a video copy of the elusive Swedish movie that had run through many of our conversations. Wilder sounds excited. We again discuss the silent film by Mauritz Stiller, Erotikon, which had inspired Ernst Lubitsch, who in turn inspired Wilder. Wilder, who had often said he didn't like to "rummage around in old celluloid," then surprised me: he asked to see the video copy of the film he'd missed in the theaters as a schoolboy. I left the tape with the Wilders' doorman.

Several days later, I call. Audrey picks up the phone, and after a moment, an animated Billy Wilder jumps on the extension.

"I ran that picture," he reports, sounding like a young scientist. "Now, Lubitsch must have seen something in it—he told me so. He told me himself, he learned everything from this picture. After it, he did twenty pictures, all very much Lubitsch." Wilder now gravely details the analysis. "I watched it, looking for clues. I did not see any of the little jokes, or inserts . . . just close-ups and two-shots. There was just nothing there." He pauses curiously. "So. I have watched this picture, and after studying it for clues to the Lubitsch touch, I have to say—" he delivers the verdict with quiet triumph in his voice—"Lubitsch did it better!" And though he is announcing that our long search for the Holy Grail of elegant modern romantic comedy has turned up with fool's gold, everything that is deeply funny and deeply inspiring about Lubitsch's ninety-one-year-old protégé is present in the way he delivers the bad news with a flourish: "I was looking for something," he says, "and it was not there!"

Knee-deep in transcripts, I call Wilder at his home on a Sunday afternoon. I've been tipped that this can be a good day to call him. It is between football and baseball seasons. He is bored on Sundays, looking for excitement. True to form, he answers the phone with a cheerful expectancy. I present him with a handful of intricately new questions. He attacks them with a flourish, and I nudge harder with each inquiry, as he rummages through seventy years of memory, me pressing for moments that he had long since relegated to the back of his mind. Only when I am done, when I am telling him how close we are to finally completing the project, does he laugh at my serious tone.

"Let it go," he says, friendly and direct. "Just—just . . . let it go."

I stand in my kitchen, silently nodding my head, looking at the many yellow-legal-tablet pages of follow-up questions, detailed questions about detail, all scattered on the counter. I have burrowed deeply into the research. And within the burrows I have made new burrows.

"Just put it out," he adds. I laugh pleasantly, a little nervously, and I am wondering if he indeed has X-ray vision into my writing world. Then he adds a question he'd posed at our previous meeting. "Do you have an ending for this thing?" Before I can answer, he adds something new, with a bit of wonder in his voice. "Because the perfect ending would be that I died."

Now I am really lost for a retort.

There is nothing in his comment that indicates a dark joke, nor is there a trace of self-pity. And then it hits me. This is the writing-room voice of a celebrated story man, a fan of logic and brevity, and he is concerned about the power of our ending. In a very workmanlike fashion, Billy Wilder has just pitched his own death as a solution to a story problem.

We pause in silence to consider the ultimate last scene. It's a long two and a half seconds.

"I have an ending I like," I tell him. He is too good a writer not to read my subtext—I'd like him to see the finished book. "I like ending with our last session. The rain. The final questions. You walk away. That's it."

"Very good," he says quickly. "That's wonderful. That's good." He pauses. "But you have neglected your next picture long enough. Let it go. God bless you, and I hope to see you soon. Goodbye."

Oscar night. *Billy Wilder quietly sits at a front table at the* Vanity Fair *telecast party; next to him is Audrey. He watches the large-screen television angled toward him, the flow of images, and smiles slightly as the clips from* The Apartment *and* Sunset Boulevard *earn pointed applause in the room. Later in the evening, as* Titanic *is announced as Best Picture, he does not scream. Instead, he watches, very still, fascinated and transfixed, mouth slightly open. Silent. I wonder what he's thinking, how much he's able to listen to the proceedings in this noisy room. I soon get my answer.*

A tuxedoed partygoer positions himself directly in Wilder's line of vision.

"YOU ARE IN FRONT OF THE SCREEN!" Wilder suddenly thunders.

All eyes turn to Billy, who has naturally been studying every word of the broadcast. The partygoer looks mystified by the sheer power of this owlish man in the large black-rimmed glasses. Having received a sharp lesson in good manners from Billy Wilder, he vanishes on the double. Wilder contentedly continues watching James Cameron's acceptance speech. When the telecast is over, Wilder reaches for his cane. The Wilders swiftly leave the now crowded party, arm in arm, moving past the new faces of young Hollywood, bathed in white media light outside.

Another Sunday, a month later. The book is finished. Baseball season has begun again. I call Wilder at his home. He answers; the ball game plays loudly on a radio in the background. "Who is it?" he asks.

I tell him.

"Who?"

I say my name a little louder.

"Who is it?"

I now bellow my name.

"Hold on," he says cheerfully. He moves to the radio, across the room, turns it down. For a moment, all I hear is the clicking of his cane moving across the floor. He picks up the receiver. "I am sorry for the delay. Now, who is this calling?"

I tell him. He is happy to hear from me, he says, and pleased with the Dodgers too. His tone is exceedingly warm. In our first conversations, Wilder had asked if he could check his own words later. Unsure if the request is still in play, I offer the senior member of this collaboration a chance to look over the entire manuscript. Billy Wilder declines instantly. After all our discussions of the many movies and carefully tuned plots, the characters, the actors, the explanations of all things large and small, the details of a life well lived, and his emphatic denials of the Grand Importance of It All, he leaves me with the very thing he has left the world: a bittersweet and very true sense of humor. The Wilder touch.

"No," he says pleasantly. "I do not want to read it." He pauses. "That way I can always say, 'Well— he fucked it up.' "

THE MOVIES

Mauvaise Graine (Bad Seed)

1934

Directed by Billie Wilder and Alexander Esway
Screenplay by Alexander Esway, H. G. Lustig, and Max Kolpe
From a story by Billie Wilder

From the first moments of the clever title sequence, it's clear that young Billy Wilder's sensibilities were well in place long before he arrived in Hollywood. Wilder's debut as a director is both personal and intoxicatingly funny— it's a love letter to Paris, crime, and automobiles. Part of the fun in watching it today is spotting the clues to future Wilder classics. Then twenty-five, Wilder had fled Berlin with his girlfriend Hella and taken up in Paris, staying at the Hotel Ansonia with other refugees who had worked in the German film industry. He hooked up with two neighbors, Lustig and Kolpe, and began concocting this high-energy yarn about a ring of car thieves and their Mata Hari, a young Parisian named Jeanette. Jeanette, as played by the seventeen-year-old Danielle Darrieux, is the prototype for many Wilder heroines to come. She's a bad girl with a gleam in her eye and an unforgettable coat. Monroe, Stanwyck, and MacLaine would all later find their greatest successes playing variations on this theme. *Mauvaise Graine* also contains a banquet of styles—Lubitschian touches, clever cutting, assured camera angles, high-octane driving shots, characters with names such as "The Man with the Peanuts," and wild film dissolves the likes of which Wilder would never use again.

Though the picture was well received, it was not an easy shoot for the earnest team of filmmakers. Wilder found far greater joy in screenwriting than in wrangling actors and equipment on a shoestring budget. It would be nine years before Wilder would direct again, and his more elegant Hollywood debut came after years of honing his skills as a writer. But the brash and underseen *Mauvaise Graine* survives as his only independent directing job. Call it Wilder's *Reservoir Dogs.* Though Wilder himself usually dismisses the picture as fluff ("shot in a garage") he does tolerate—make that *encourage*—all theories pointing out that this run-and-gun style of filmmaking predated the French *nouvelle vague* movement by many years. The subversive and jazzy music is also a perfect fit. It's by Franz Waxman, who would later go on to provide Wilder with some of his most memorable scores, including *Sunset Boulevard* and *The Spirit of St. Louis.* And watch closely for the first appearance of the famous "compact mirror" shot that would surface so powerfully in *The Apartment.*

MIDNIGHT

1939
SCREENPLAY BY CHARLES BRACKETT AND BILLY WILDER
BASED ON AN ORIGINAL STORY BY EDWIN JUSTUS MAYER AND FRANZ SCHULZ
DIRECTED BY MITCHELL LEISEN

Midnight plays today like one of the better early Wilder films. Only one problem: Wilder did not direct it. Director Mitchell Leisen did the honors, and while he credited himself for wrangling the script out of Wilder and Brackett (whom he liked better), the movie resembles nothing so much as an expertly rendered Wilder script with a sensational comic performance at the center. Claudette Colbert came to play in this performance, and her characterization as Eve Peabody (great name) is the spark plug that every good movie needs.

Colbert's sensational performance is also proof that world-class comedy can be far sexier than the steamiest of love scenes. Check out her turn in the opera sequence, early in the film, when she tries to hide her true, plebeian identity from a clearly soused John Barrymore. As she squirms in her seat, Colbert instantly and effortlessly ranks herself as the single greatest comedienne who ever worked with Wilder's words. Sadly, she never worked with him as a director. No matter. She smokes up the screen, deepens the film with her performance, and even steals *Midnight* from Barrymore, who is at his pickled and hilarious best. And yes, that's young Don Ameche in the Don Ameche part. Years later, at a tribute to Wilder at Lincoln Center, Ameche ran into Wilder and wondered aloud why he was there. "You were in *Midnight*," said Wilder. "No I wasn't," said Ameche. "I would have remembered."

Hold Back the Dawn

1941
Screenplay by Charles Brackett and Billy Wilder
Based on an original story by Ketti Frings
Directed by Mitchell Leisen

The film is worth watching, mostly because it captures on celluloid the spiritual birth of Billy Wilder as a director. Watch closely the early sequence at the Hotel Esperanza, where Charles Boyer is stranded while waiting for a visa. In Brackett and Wilder's original script, Boyer delivers a soul-stirringly funny monologue to a cockroach. Contained in that scene is all the irony and deep humor that could have powered the story. Instead, Boyer protested to Leisen that the scene lacked reality. "Why would I talk to a cockroach," asked Boyer, "if a cockroach can't answer me?" All directors have their own methods for eliciting the performance they want. Leisen chose to listen to Boyer, cutting the dialogue. When Wilder learned of the episode in mid-filming, he vowed to drop Boyer from the third act of the screenplay, which he and Brackett were still finishing. Lesson for actors: don't piss off the screenwriter. Boyer magically vanishes and Wilder gives the film to Paulette Goddard, who earns it with her delivery of lines like "A woman wants a *man,* not a radiator cap." Another classic early Wilder line, delivered with relish by a bit player: "In Europe, we respect the institution of marriage!"

THE MAJOR AND THE MINOR

1942

SCREENPLAY BY CHARLES BRACKETT AND BILLY WILDER
SUGGESTED BY THE PLAY *CONNIE GOES HOME* BY EDWARD CHILDS CARPENTER AND THE STORY "SUNNY GOES HOME" BY FANNIE KILBOURNE

Wilder was lucky to land one of the biggest stars of the day, Ginger Rogers, to play the lead in his first film as a Hollywood director. Behind the camera, top-line Paramount talent, like costumer Edith Head and editor Doane Harrison, pitched in to help the not-so-neophyte neophyte on his first picture.

The film is no piece of fluff. Actually, it's *disguised* as a bit of fluff. *The Major and the Minor* works on several levels, the most effective one being a darkly comic spin on pedophilia. Ten years before the publication of *Lolita*, Wilder's directorial debut was a big hit with audiences who may or may not have been aware of how subversive the film really was.

Rogers plays a modern New York City girl who tires of Manhattan and decides to return to Iowa. When she doesn't have enough money for the train fare home, Rogers poses as a twelve-year-old to buy a half-fare ticket. Stashing herself in a compartment with Ray Milland, who would later star in *The Lost Weekend*, she proceeds to fall in love. The possible revelation of her true identity is the thread that Wilder keeps taut to the very end. Look for an amazing scene, rife with subtext, as Milland reads Rogers a children's story on the train. Perhaps Nabokov—and Stanley Kubrick—were watching.

FIVE GRAVES TO CAIRO

1943

SCREENPLAY BY CHARLES BRACKETT AND BILLY WILDER
BASED ON A PLAY BY LAJOS BIRÓ

Wilder wastes no time in trying a different genre, the action-adventure. Disguised as a B-picture, *Five Graves to Cairo* is in accomplished yarn about a British corporal (Franchot Tone) who battles the Nazis and loses the woman he loves in the course of the struggle. Disguises and deceptions all play a part, and the solid professionalism of the picture added quickly to Wilder's growing directorial prowess. Look for a haunting opening sequence where a ghost tank rolls through the North African desert, introducing Tone in a manner that would make Indiana Jones jealous. Brilliant opening titles, and an appearance by Erich von Stroheim as Rommel.

DOUBLE INDEMNITY

1944

SCREENPLAY BY RAYMOND CHANDLER AND BILLY WILDER
FROM A NOVELLA BY JAMES M. CAIN

Billy Wilder's first classic is a film noir made before the term "film noir" even existed. Fifty-five years later, it just gets better. Stylistically, structurally, and directorially, this is flawless filmmaking. Don't look here or anywhere else for a capsulization of the story—just watch it. And don't forget to study one of the greatest moments in Wilder's entire body of work, when Fred MacMurray does his nasty murderous business off-camera and the shot stays simply on the now-widow Barbara Stanwyck's face. In the words of Woody Allen, who isn't exaggerating much: "The greatest movie ever made."

THE LOST WEEKEND

1945
SCREENPLAY BY CHARLES BRACKETT AND BILLY WILDER
BASED ON THE NOVEL BY CHARLES R. JACKSON

Changing trains in Chicago, Wilder picked up this paperback as a time killer and selected it for his next picture. Wilder was unsure about the fate of this movie after several preview audiences responded oddly. ("In Santa Barbara, three hundred people turned to fifty.") This serious character drama about an alcoholic, well played by a sad-sack Ray Milland, was unique in its day. No easy laughs were to be had at the expense of the leading man's affliction. Shot on locations around New York, including P. J. Clarke's, the movie has a grit and reality that showed Wilder's talents in taking a potboiler of a book and turning it into a first-class film. He would not know the power of the movie until later. Wilder left Hollywood to join the service, where he devoted his energies to the editing of wartime documentary footage. When he returned, the film was nominated for several Academy Awards, including Best Director, Best Screenplay, and Best Picture. *Lost Weekend* won Oscars for Best Picture, and Milland for Best Actor. The film is also notable as the meeting ground of Wilder and his future wife, Audrey Young, who played the hatcheck girl at a bar where Milland is thrown out. "I fell in love with her arm first," recalls Wilder with a slightly raised eyebrow. But don't look for her: not even the hand is visible in small-screen video. Trivia note: The liquor industry offered the studio five million to "bury it," says Wilder. "If they'd offered *me* the five million, I would have." He is, however, decidedly proud of having made the first serious picture about an alcoholic.

THE EMPEROR WALTZ
1948
SCREENPLAY BY CHARLES BRACKETT AND BILLY WILDER

"The less said about this the better," says Wilder of this feel-good postwar musical. The movie depresses him to this day. It stars Bing Crosby and a number of dogs. It was a commercial disappointment. The director is unforgiving and has called it a favor for Paramount. ("No good deed goes unpunished.") The movie is fascinating today, almost riveting, in how aggressively un-Wilder it is. For that reason, it stands alone and apart from all his other work. And still there is a jewel: Crosby's musical number "A Kiss in Your Eyes."

A FOREIGN AFFAIR
1948
SCREENPLAY BY CHARLES BRACKETT, BILLY WILDER, AND RICHARD BREEN
BASED ON AN ORIGINAL STORY BY DAVID SHAW

The undiscovered classic. *A Foreign Affair* shows all the strong-suit characteristics of the assured young director. Wilder now had the directing reins firmly in hand. The photography is a feast of shadows and light. His characterizations were never sharper, or his undercurrents more darkly satisfying. John Lund is a revelation as Captain Pringle, who spouts line after line of outrageously multileveled romantic banter with Marlene Dietrich. "Berlin and Dietrich are one," Wilder has said. This film, in which she sings "Black Market," is cinematic proof. Watch for a brilliant scene where Congresswoman Jean Arthur gets a jeep tour of wartorn Germany and notices that there is much fraternization between Americans and Germans. Part of the fun is watching the crackling chemistry between the three leads, who barely got along on- or off-camera. Wilder's and Brackett's pens were sharp for this one. Lund handles some of their best dialogue in moments with Dietrich: "I'd like to build a fire around you, you blond witch." Or there is this sparkling exchange between Jean Arthur and Lund: "How do you know so much about women's clothing?" asks Arthur, as Lund adjusts her dress. "My mother wore women's clothing," snaps Lund. The entire movie is glistening with sexual subtext. Check out Lund whistling as he exits Dietrich's home.

The movie began innocently enough. Wilder wanted to do a film about Hollywood. It took a former *Life* magazine writer to help crack it; D. M. Marshman Jr. suggested that the young writer protagonist get mixed up with a silent-film star. Enter the sensational approach devised by Wilder and Brackett. The movie smells like musty red-velvet curtains, and Gloria Swanson's bravura performance as the faded film queen Norma Desmond is actually a wonder of pure and delicate artistry. With help from William Holden, who narrates from the grave, Swanson towers above the film with such wicked grace and humor that she even made her character's *name* a household name. Almost fifty years later, there are few stars as famous as Wilder's fictional one.

Casting is another delight. Erich von Stroheim appears as her long-suffering former husband and current valet. Mae West turned Wilder down, and Pola Negri almost took the part, but it was Swanson who was the Norma Desmond of destiny. Suggested perhaps by George Cukor, Wilder was able to use Swanson's own actual silent footage from *Queen Kelly,* an unreleased film produced by Swanson's lover Joseph Kennedy Sr. Kennedy had removed Stroheim as director, thinking him anachronistic in the new era of sound pictures. For Wilder, the ironies were too delicious—his story now *lived.* Even Wilder's old roommate Peter Lorre makes a cameo, as does Cecil B. DeMille. When the film was first screened in Hollywood, the effect was shocking and brash and hilarious and dark—just as the writer-director intended. At the first preview, Barbara Stanwyck kissed the hem of Gloria Swanson's skirt. Meanwhile, outside in the lobby, legendary big-shot studio executive Louis B. Mayer stood on the steps and said with bluster, "This Billy Wilder should be sent back to Germany! He bites the hand that feeds him!" Wilder overheard. "I am Mr. Wilder," he said, "and why don't you go *fuck* yourself!"

One of Wilder's most controversial movies, *Ace in the Hole* needed a generation's passing to be fully appreciated. Nothing about the film was easy. Wilder had split with longtime collaborator Charles Brackett ("The surface of the matchbox had been struck one too many times") and hooked up with new partner Walter Newman for his next movie. They turned to an idea of Newman's, the reality-based story of a newspaperman who capitalized on the tragedy of a young man who'd fallen into a cavern.

The original title of the project was *The Human Interest Story.* With the help of former journalist Lesser Samuels, the screenplay evolved into a real scorcher. Kirk Douglas plays Chuck Tatum, the hard-nosed reporter who thirsts for a big story and finds it. Douglas's performance is as unrelenting as the finished movie. Jan Sterling's turn as the jaded wife of the trapped man is equally hard-ass. When told by Douglas to go to church and show some concern for her husband, Sterling responds with a stellar retort credited to Audrey Wilder: "Kneeling bags my nylons."

There was a price to pay for such wicked fun. Released in the summer of 1951, *Ace* was Wilder's first true flop. With Wilder already directing a new movie in Paris, Paramount tried to tie a prettier bow around it, quickly retitling the film *The Big Carnival.* It didn't work.

As the years went by and the rise of tabloid television created a thousand Jack Tatums, *Ace in the Hole* increased in stature. Spike Lee wanted to remake it. Costa-Gavras did his own homage; and while the resulting *Mad City* [1997] never officially credited Wilder, opening-day reviews nearly unanimously hailed Wilder's original film. Forty-six years later, *Ace in the Hole* received the accolades that never arrived in its day. Watch for the final shot, a rare bit of bravura cinema from the man who still delights in shaking his finger at the complicated shots of other directors. "Just tell the story!"

STALAG 17

1953
SCREENPLAY BY BILLY WILDER
AND EDWIN BLUM
BASED ON THE PLAY BY
DONALD BEVAN AND
EDMUND TRZCINSKI

Wilder regained his footing in relatively short order. He found a hit play—set in a German prisoner-of-war camp—and radically adapted it to feature one of his favorite leading men. William Holden shines as the cynical loner named Sefton. With Holden in place, the shooting went easily and swiftly. Even today, Wilder twinkles at the memory of this film. One senses that Holden's Sefton is the closest thing to an alter ego that Wilder has put on celluloid. And Holden's final exit line is pure Wilder: "If I ever run into any of you bums on a street corner, just let's pretend we never met before." Television minted its own spoofy version of the film and called it *Hogan's Heroes.*

SABRINA

1954
SCREENPLAY BY BILLY WILDER, SAMUEL TAYLOR, AND
ERNEST LEHMAN
BASED ON THE PLAY *SABRINA FAIR* BY SAMUEL TAYLOR

"Once upon a time on the North Shore of Long Island, some thirty miles from New York, there lived a small girl on a very large estate. . . ." So begins Wilder's most romantic and lushest film, the tale of a chauffeur's daughter in love with the roguish son of the rich family they serve. Sabrina goes to Paris, returns in full bloom, and changes all the lives around her. The spell of the film is still as strong today. Beautifully composed and devastatingly acted by Audrey Hepburn, the picture is also a high-water mark of modern style. An issue of *Vogue* still rarely goes by without a referencing photo of Sabrina, and rightfully so. It is also the definitive display of Hepburn's beguiling strengths. Just check out the opening shot of her in the tree, gazing at the Larrabees' ball. In her second American film, Hepburn steps into Hollywood history with that single wordless portrait of yearning. Today, when many a newly arriving ingenue is heralded as "the new Audrey Hepburn," it is this moment Hollywood yearns to recapture . . . and never quite can. Edith Head won the Oscar for Best Costumes, although it was Hepburn's newly favorite designer, Givenchy, who did most of the work. History has later revealed that Hepburn mimicked the movie's plot in real life, carrying on a secret affair with co-star William Holden while filming. There is charm and elegance to spare in *Sabrina,* and this classic could not even be knocked off course by the sour disposition of Humphrey Bogart, who disliked the movie and its director. Bogart knew he was Wilder's second choice for the part. The character was originally written for Cary Grant, who, heartbreakingly, pulled out at the last moment. The movie was reshaped for Bogart, but it did little to ease his inferiority complex. Barbs flew through the filming. He reconciled with Wilder a couple of years later, shortly before his death. Says Wilder: "He always played the hero, but he never was . . . until the end."

THE SEVEN YEAR ITCH

1955
SCREENPLAY BY GEORGE AXELROD AND BILLY WILDER
BASED ON THE PLAY BY GEORGE AXELROD

Billy Wilder is not crazy about this one ("I never liked it"), although there is clear and certain appeal in watching the freight train of sexuality just below the surface of Marilyn Monroe's "innocent" performance as the Girl. Monroe easily elevates this somewhat dated adaptation of Axelrod's second-rate play, a snapshot of horny postcensorship America. *Seven Year Itch* suffers greatly in comparison to the elegant power of Wilder's previous film, *Sabrina*. Still, his genius pokes through even the problematic casting of Tom Ewell, who finds none of the deeper layers in Wilder's writing. The performance still bothers Wilder today, especially because the studio refused to approve his first choice, a young, unknown New York actor named Walter Matthau. Trivia note: In Matthau's screen test, the part of Marilyn Monroe was played by Gena Rowlands. Imagine Matthau and Monroe and you have a much different movie. And of course there is the throwaway moment that became legendary. Walking the streets of New York with Ewell, Marilyn Monroe cools herself over a drafty subway grating. Her white dress blows up, she smooths it downward, and the single most iconographic image of Hollywood was born. Just out of range of the shot were thousands of gawking New Yorkers, including Monroe's husband, Joe DiMaggio, who whispered something in his wife's ear and went home in a huff. Did DiMaggio's exit change Monroe's mood? "No," says Wilder. "She loved the crowds. She lifted a finger to her lips, they all quieted down, and we filmed some more."

THE SPIRIT OF ST. LOUIS

1957
SCREENPLAY BY BILLY WILDER, WENDELL
MAYES, AND CHARLES LEDERER
BASED ON THE BOOK BY
CHARLES A. LINDBERGH

Wilder's much underrated color portrait of Lindbergh's famous journey is a sumptuous biopic. James Stewart's trademark grace and humor is very much on display in this performance, set to a moving score by Franz Waxman. Wilder felt a little intimidated by the protective legend of Lindbergh himself. He was unable to even bring up the real-life subplot involving a waitress that Lindbergh supposedly slept with the night before his journey. They were friends, but very different men. At the time of the movie Lindbergh was one of the most famous men in the world, but he still took the public bus to visit Wilder in Beverly Hills. The kidnaping of Lindbergh's child was not covered in this movie, and little of Wilder's subversive wit was utilized in the picture. One exception is the sequence where a fly is trapped in the cockpit, allowing Stewart to carry on a running conversation with the insect. Many years after Charles Boyer famously refused to perform a similar screen monologue to a cockroach, Wilder finally gets his scene on film. Barely. Stewart reportedly disliked the idea, so the fly is set free early. Still, it's a bit of Wilder magic that reminds you who's at the helm.

LOVE IN THE AFTERNOON

1957
SCREENPLAY BY I. A. L. DIAMOND AND BILLY WILDER
BASED ON THE NOVEL *ARIANE* BY CLAUDE ANET

This gem, set in Paris, is the second of Wilder's two Audrey Hepburn masterpieces, and the beginning of his great collaboration with I. A. L. Diamond. Hepburn plays the lovestruck, cello-playing daughter of private investigator Claude Chevasse (Maurice Chevalier). Eavesdropping on the business of her father, she entangles herself quite literally in the affairs of a famous playboy, played by Gary Cooper. Filled with visual and musical poetry, the film is one of Wilder's greatest. The spirit of Lubitsch is very much alive in this one, as is all the romantic bite of Wilder at full power. Cooper's part was another character written for Cary Grant, and it remains one of cinema's greatest misses that Grant passed on the part. Too old for the character, and sometimes shrouded in shadows, Cooper gamely delivers all the necessary romantic power and more. His is an underrated and selfless performance, always serving Audrey Hepburn, who dazzles from beginning to end. Look for the genius of Wilder in the Hungarian string quartet, which follows Cooper everywhere, providing a romantic soundtrack for all his pursuits. The sequence where Cooper listens to a Dictaphone recording left by Hepburn, an account of her nonexistent laundry list of lovers, is an all-time winner. Cooper and the string quartet pass the liquor cart back and forth, from room to room, as the sad-sack Romeo begins to realize his growing affection for the young girl. Most directors would simply send the leading man to a bar. They are not Wilder. Trivia note: Look for Audrey Wilder as Cooper's date at the opera.

WITNESS FOR THE PROSECUTION

1957
SCREENPLAY BY BILLY WILDER AND
HARRY KURNITZ
BASED ON THE PLAY AND NOVEL BY
AGATHA CHRISTIE

Another sterling romantic comedy now under his belt, Wilder moves to a new genre—the courtroom drama. His original intention was to do a "Hitchcock movie." *Witness for the Prosecution* is that and much more. Hitchcock rarely left room for acting fireworks like this at the center of his films. Laughton's performance as the great Sir Wilfrid Robarts, one of London's most celebrated barristers, lifted him into the ranks of Wilder's favorite actors. Tyrone Power delivers a beautifully slippery performance, and, of course, there are few delights as sinful as Marlene Dietrich in a Billy Wilder film. Bold truths are dealt, plot turns abound, and Laughton delivers the craftiest and juiciest performance of his career. Yes, this is the movie where he shouts, "LIAR!"

SOME LIKE IT HOT

1959
SCREENPLAY BY I. A. L. DIAMOND AND BILLY WILDER
SUGGESTED BY AN UNPUBLISHED STORY BY ROBERT
THOEREN AND MICHAEL LOGAN

"It will be a disaster," Selznick said to Billy Wilder. "You cannot combine comedy with murder!" Not only did Wilder do exactly that, building his most famous comedy around the St. Valentine's Day Massacre, he also added Marilyn Monroe and cross-dressing to the mix. To hide from gangsters, whose handiwork they had accidentally witnessed, down-and-out musicians Jack Lemmon and Tony Curtis don wigs and dresses to join an all-female traveling band. Mitzi Gaynor was the original choice to play Sugar Kane Kowalczyk, but when Monroe expressed some interest, says Wilder, "we just had to have her." They won her for the part, and for once, a dream cast got dreamier: everyone is firing on all cylinders in this one. Monroe's happy-sad comic turn is her sexiest and most unforgettable. She was not popular with her co-stars, who often stood on high heels waiting through many takes for Wilder to be satisfied with her performance. But the last laugh is hers. Forty years later, a day rarely passes when her co-stars are not asked about the careless brilliance of Monroe's performance in this movie. (Watch for the line that took over fifty takes: "Where's that bourbon?") The last line of the film was the biggest joke of the movie. It was a Diamond throwaway that became the "Frankly, Scarlett, I don't give a damn" of modern comedy: "Nobody's perfect." Recalls Wilder: "The first [test] screening was at the Bay Theater in Pacific Palisades. It laid there. There had been a serious picture on before it. The next night we had a preview in Westwood, and we brought down the house." Trivia note: the original title was *Not Tonight, Josephine*. Another trivia note: Wilder briefly considered Frank Sinatra for one of the two cross-dressing lead roles.

The notion sat in Wilder's black notebook of ideas for years. Inspired by David Lean's *Brief Encounter,* the idea read, "Movie about the guy who climbs into the warm bed left by two lovers." As censorship eased, the time to actually make *The Apartment* finally arrived. Is there a better sadly sweet comedy-drama about contemporary American life? Years from now, the answer will probably still be no. Modern to the core, this "dirty fairy tale" is a social and romantic masterpiece about a little man in a big company. His apartment becomes a trysting place for philandering executives, and Lemmon, as inimitable C. C. "Bud" Baxter, dubiously moves up the corporate ladder, a kindhearted and unwitting pimp with a sniffly nose. He falls for the elevator girl, Fran Kubelik (Shirley MacLaine), who is secretly visiting in his own apartment with Fred MacMurray, the *über*-cad insurance boss J. D. Sheldrake. In 1961, Wilder won a rare triple crown of Oscars: Best Screenplay (with Diamond), Best Picture, and Best Director. As playwright Moss Hart presented the second of Wilder's three awards, he leaned over and whispered in the director's ear, "It's time to stop, Billy." The words would haunt Wilder, who knew even then that *The Apartment* would be hard to top. Trivia note: Lemmon and MacLaine lost best-acting awards to Burt Lancaster in *Elmer Gantry* and Elizabeth Taylor in *Butterfield 8.* There have been few greater Oscar injustices.

ONE TWO THREE

1961
SCREENPLAY BY I. A. L. DIAMOND AND BILLY WILDER
BASED ON THE ONE-ACT PLAY BY FERENC MOLNÁR

Where most of Wilder's comedies were elegantly sculpted and edited to allow room for laughter, this film is a steamroller. The jokes come fast and furiously, one on top of another. James Cagney, in his last leading role, helms the picture as C. R. MacNamara, sales executive for Coca-Cola. There are no lower gears to his performance; it's full-blast from the top. Ahead of its time, this film was subsequently screened again around the time the Berlin Wall came down. It was a hit again in Germany in the late eighties. Wilder's distaste for rock and roll is on glorious display, with a torture scene featuring "Itsy Bitsy Teenie Weenie Yellow Polka Dot Bikini" and his first and only pop-star character, the lamentable Choo Choo.

IRMA LA DOUCE

1963
SCREENPLAY BY I. A. L. DIAMOND AND
BILLY WILDER
BASED ON THE MUSICAL PLAY BY ALEXANDRE
BREFFORT AND MARGUERITE MONNOT

Wilder calls it a misfire; audiences made it one of his biggest hits. Shirley MacLaine sharply plays the title role, the quintessential hooker with a comic heart of gold. Lemmon gamely attacks the double part of Nestor, the French policeman working the red-light district while masquerading as Irma's client "Lord X." It's bawdy and colorful, fast and loose, more charming and sexy than the director chooses to acknowledge. His disappointment may stem more from a violation of a personal code: never play foreigners in a foreign country with an American accent. Trivia note: Brigitte Bardot begged for a shot at the title role. Wilder stuck with MacLaine, who has rarely been more alluring. "It should have stayed a play," Wilder comments dismissively. He is not looking for an argument on the point.

KISS ME STUPID

1964
SCREENPLAY BY
I. A. L. DIAMOND AND
BILLY WILDER
SUGGESTED BY THE PLAY
L'ORA DELLA FANTASIA BY
ANNA BONACCI

A critical and commercial failure, *Kiss Me Stupid* was dismissed in its day as a coarse and controversial sex farce, the cinematic equivalent of an old *Playboy* that belonged in the barber shop and not people's homes. Somewhere along the way, a nastiness invaded the picture that was uncharacteristic of Diamond and Wilder. The film was also plagued by bad luck. Scheduling problems caused the production to go with Peter Sellers, rather than Jack Lemmon, as the struggling, not-so-talented songwriter Orville J. Spooner. Wilder prefers his actors to stick closely to the carefully etched scripts; Sellers was an actor prone to improvise. Their rocky collaboration ended when Sellers suffered a heart attack four weeks into filming. Convinced the script was strong enough to handle an off-kilter casting choice, Wilder replaced him with Ray Walston, then famous from *My Favorite Martian*. Walston had done a nice job for Wilder in *The Apartment*. The fit was not so perfect here. And Walston's relationship with his screen wife (Felicia Farr, Mrs. Jack Lemmon) veers toward the sadistic from time to time. There were censorship battles over Kim Novak's cleavage, and a love scene featuring Farr and Dean Martin had to be trimmed to appease the Catholic Church. When the movie was released, the Church still attacked the movie. This is the movie on which Wilder and Diamond pushed the limits, and the limits pushed back. It was his first crashing failure.

All that having been said, there are riches to be mined from *Kiss Me Stupid*. Dean Martin is supremely comfortable as the Dean Martin–like entertainer, "Dino," who finds himself stranded in Climax, Nevada. "Shave and a haircut, the works, baby," he says, pulling into town. The film has a smooth, leisurely pace. The title sequence is historically significant as the definitive cinematic rendering of Rat Pack–era Las Vegas, shot in poetic black-and-white by the great Joseph LaShelle. Alexander Trauner, Wilder's greatest production designer, works wonders with the detail of these lives on the fringe of the Nevada desert. The lost footage featuring Sellers is "somewhere, I'm not sure where," says Wilder. He wouldn't mind it being seen; he just doesn't want to search for it himself. "It was just not a good time for me," he comments. "What is your next question?" Trivia note: Wilder's favorite name, Sheldrake, appears again as Dr. Sheldrake in the movie.

THE FORTUNE COOKIE

1966
SCREENPLAY BY I. A. L. DIAMOND
AND BILLY WILDER

One of Wilder's more poignant memories is his description of life with Diamond after *Kiss Me Stupid*. "We were like the parents of an idiot child," he has said. "Slowly you come back together and look at each other, and you wonder—should we make love again?" The great collaboration of Wilder and Diamond continued, of course, and the result is one of their funniest screenplays. *The Fortune Cookie* is the first joint appearance of Walter Matthau and Jack Lemmon, a comic duo still working today, always bringing with them a whiff of their Wilder magic. Matthau is transcendent in his Oscar-winning performance as "Whiplash" Willie Gingrich, the bottom-feeding lawyer brother-in-law of TV cameraman Lemmon, who is struck while filming a Cleveland Browns game. Lemmon suffers no serious injuries, but Matthau convinces him to wear a neck brace and bilk all participants of a quarter-million in insurance money. Ron Rich appears as Boom Boom Jackson, the sweet football player who runs Lemmon down and carries the guilt. It was one of the first major black roles in a mainstream Hollywood picture where color was not a story issue. In *The Fortune Cookie*, Wilder also uses the then-modern technique of cutting between television footage and film. Beautifully shot and composed, with visual similarities to *The Apartment*, it's worth screening a high-quality copy to appreciate. And Lemmon, now on his fourth film with Wilder, is clearly and proudly the director's primary cinematic voice. In a cruel reminder of *Kiss Me Stupid*, Matthau suffered a heart-attack during filming. The production halted for several weeks before continuing. A close look reveals a much-skinnier Matthau in several scenes.

THE PRIVATE LIFE OF SHERLOCK HOLMES

1970
SCREENPLAY BY I. A. L. DIAMOND AND BILLY WILDER
BASED ON CHARACTERS CREATED BY SIR ARTHUR CONAN DOYLE

Wilder's most ambitious film, *The Private Life of Sherlock Holmes* began as a long collection of richly detailed episodes in the life of the great sleuth. Wilder and Diamond's script was carefully tuned before filming began in the waning days of the sixties. Check out the rich photography of Christopher Challis, and the meticulous rendering of Wilder and Diamond's Holmes by Sir Robert Stephens. Do not be misled by the milieu, though. The film is flecked with Wilder's unmistakable humor. One solid running joke, for example, hangs on the question of Holmes's possible homosexuality. If only all the pieces were still together. It's hard to judge the film properly— huge sections were jettisoned after one disastrous preview in which an unforgiving audience found the picture too episodic. Wilder uncharacteristically left the film in the hands of editor Ernest Walter and traveled to Paris to work on a new project. Important questions still remain. Where is the lost footage? What was the project Wilder left to pursue? (He suggests it might have been *Avanti!*, but that picture was still a full two years away.) Holmes himself should be enlisted for the answers. The truncated final version assembled by Walter is far better than Wilder realizes today, but the director is understandably upset over the missing sections, which have apparently disappeared forever. Hopefully Wilder and Diamond's script will soon be made available so that one of his more important works can be imagined in its original form. Until then, the currently available version is an inspired riddle.

Avanti!

1972

SCREENPLAY BY I. A. L. DIAMOND AND BILLY WILDER
BASED ON THE PLAY BY SAMUEL TAYLOR

The prize of Wilder's later-period work, *Avanti!* is a melancholy classic steeped in the feelings of a man a long way from home, entering the third act of his life. Jack Lemmon's rich performance as the ulcer-stricken executive Wendell Armbruster is the first of his own celebrated midlife-crisis roles. It was pushing it only a little to call *Avanti!* a semisequel to *The Apartment:* there are clear similarities. The picture was a new peak in the collaboration of Wilder and the actor most tuned to his nuances. *Avanti!* has improved with age, and—with the exception of a hirsute hotel maid with a moustache—almost every supporting character deserves a spot in the pantheon of the gloriously Wilderesque. Lemmon plays the businessman called from the golf course by the early death of his father, vacationing in Italy. He must travel overseas to supervise the transfer of the body. One of Wilder's most masterful sequences happens early in the film, when Lemmon faces an Italian bureaucrat in charge of all aspects of the body. Armbruster soon meets the daughter (Juliet Mills) of his father's mistress, in whose arms his father died. Love ensues, as the married son plays out his father's peccadillos. Mills, playing the unfortunately named Pamela Piggott, does a nice job with a part written for a character far less attractive than herself. "I tried to find an overweight actress, because that's what we wrote," says Wilder. "We couldn't find one. But we hired Juliet Mills, and though she tried to gain the weight, she ate and ate and mysteriously couldn't gain a pound." At any weight, she is a wonderful foil for Lemmon. Clive Revill also shines as the Italian hotel manager. The end result is absolutely lyrical. Trivia note: After years of eluding censors with double and triple meanings, this is the first Wilder film to feature profanity and even some nudity. It's all delicately layered, and purposeful, but still a little bit like hearing your dad swear for the first time. Essential in many ways.

THE FRONT PAGE

1973
SCREENPLAY BY I. A. L. DIAMOND AND
BILLY WILDER
BASED ON THE PLAY BY BEN HECHT
AND CHARLES MACARTHUR

An authentic and top-notch period comedy set in the newspaper business, *The Front Page* ultimately feels like Wilder's best effort to stay current and employed in seventies Hollywood. He was the only one of his era still even *attempting* to stay meaningful. Superbly photographed by Jordan Cronenweth, the picture has depth and conviction. Today, Wilder wonders why he undertook the remake, even if it *was* a matter of reworking a film and play that were, he notes, overrated to begin with. Matthau and Lemmon play the crusty editor and the star reporter, and an out-of-tone Carol Burnett appears as Mollie Malloy, the hooker. It is all good fun, though, meant to capitalize a little on the nostalgia craze that had begun the previous year with *The Sting*. In many ways, it's more honest.

FEDORA

1978
SCREENPLAY BY I. A. L. DIAMOND AND
BILLY WILDER
BASED ON THE NOVELLA BY THOMAS TRYON

Wilder and Diamond's last great screenplay is a fascinating revisit to the territory of *Sunset Boulevard,* this time in color. Fedora is a Garbo-like star living in seclusion on a Greek island. William Holden plays the former assistant director who seeks her out. An ingenious plot turn is handled with grace, though Wilder is quick to point out that his original casting plan would have served the picture better. He is not wrong, though *Fedora* still has all the style and bite of a Diamond and Wilder classic. It's their last serious picture, with a master sense of structure, and a rich, mysterious air. Listen for the moving and personal voice of Wilder's writing, commenting on the state of new Hollywood ("They all have beards!"). If it misses the upper rung of Wilder's greatest work, it's only a matter of inches. Henry Fonda makes a brief appearance as himself.

Buddy Buddy is the *Godfather* of a genre that would take hold years later—the hitman comedy. Walter Matthau again pairs with Jack Lemmon in this dark and frisky tale of a world-weary assassin (Matthau) and the suicidal executive (Lemmon) who complicates his job. "I take no credit for this genre," says Wilder today. "I don't believe in genre." Production values are minimal here. *Buddy Buddy* is not the most visual of Wilder's films—the rear projections behind many of the scenes strip it of much lyricism—but it's lively, with an assured sense of its day. We are a long way from *Ninotchka,* however, when Matthau, who brings a kinetic deadpan energy to his role as a killer, tosses off surprising lines like "Are you out of your fucking mind?" Klaus Kinski appears as Dr. Zuckerbrot, a bizarre sex therapist who has entranced Paula Prentiss, playing Lemmon's ex-wife. One can only imagine the writing-room conversation that resulted in Wilder and Diamond's first pot joke. (The play on which it is based was also made into the 1974 French film, *L'Emmerdeur,* released in America as *A Pain in the A——*). And yet you're never far from a reminder that you're in the comic hands of Wilder and Diamond. Says Kinski in one memorable speech: "Premature ejaculation means always having to say you're sorry." The film ends on a freeze frame of Walter Matthau enjoying a cigar, facing paradise on a deserted atoll populated by gorgeous island women . . . and Jack Lemmon. Wilder's last film is also a love letter to his favorite comic duo, who attack their parts with real zest.

But one can only long for the movies he was unable to make in subsequent years. When Martin Scorsese passed on the rights to the book, Wilder pounced on the property that was his choice to be his last film—*Schindler's List.* He missed making this final and most personal statement by only days. Steven Spielberg committed to the project and, hearing of Wilder's interest, called the master and explained his own passion in making the film. Wilder gracefully understood and wished him the best. When the picture opened in Los Angeles several years later, Billy Wilder was at the first public screening. He marveled at the audience of young and old moviegoers, all weeping by the movie's end. "I would have made it differently," he says, "but I can't tell you that it would have been better. It's a hell of a picture."

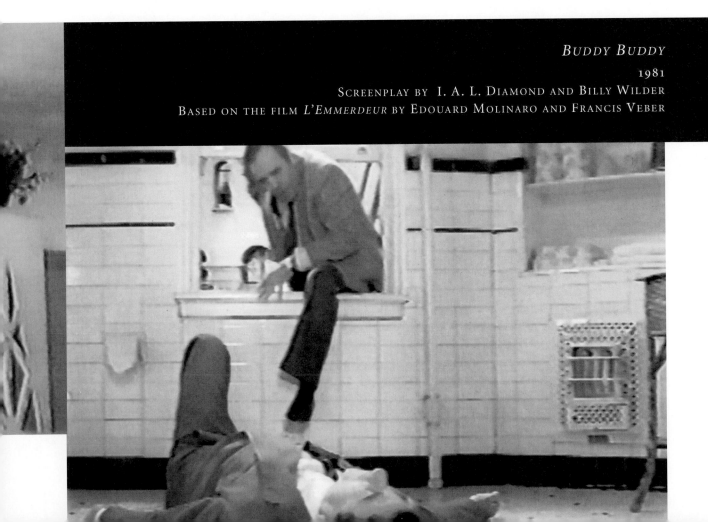

BUDDY BUDDY

1981

SCREENPLAY BY I. A. L. DIAMOND AND BILLY WILDER
BASED ON THE FILM *L'EMMERDEUR* BY EDOUARD MOLINARO AND FRANCIS VEBER

BILLY WILDER'S
EXPLOSIVE
NEW
COMEDY

ONE TWO THREE

STARRING:
JAMES CAGNEY
HORST BUCHHOLZ
PAMELA TIFFIN
ARLENE FRANCIS

THE CRE
FROM
BLACK LA

URE
HE
ON

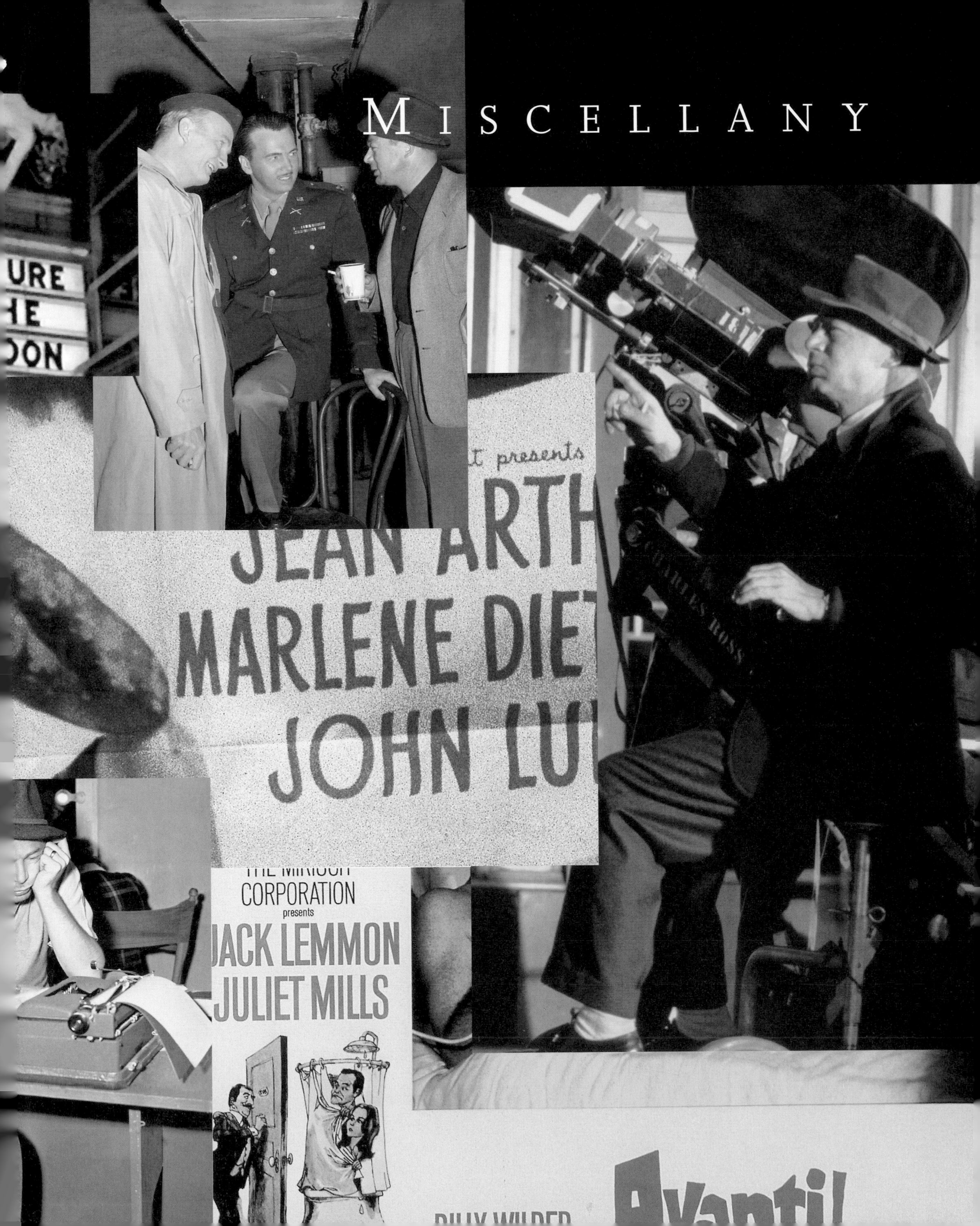

presents

JEAN ARTH

MARLENE DIE

JOHN LU

THE MIRISCH
CORPORATION
presents

JACK LEMMON
JULIET MILLS

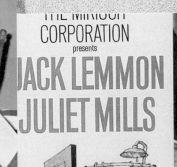

BILLY WILDER

Avanti!

WILDER'S TIPS FOR WRITERS

1. The audience is fickle.
2. Grab 'em by the throat and never let 'em go.
3. Develop a clean line of action for your leading character.
4. Know where you're going.
5. The more subtle and elegant you are in hiding your plot points, the better you are as a writer.
6. If you have a problem with the third act, the real problem is in the first act.
7. A tip from Lubitsch: Let the audience add up two plus two. They'll love you forever.
8. In doing voice-overs, be careful not to describe what the audience already sees. Add to what they are seeing.
9. The event that occurs at the second-act curtain triggers the end of the movie.
10. The third act must build, build, build in tempo and action until the last event, and then—
11. —that's it. Don't hang around.

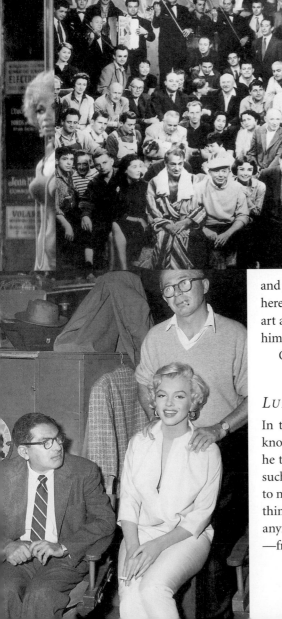

WILDER IN THE ART WORLD

Billy's late friend the businessman Richard Cohen described Wilder's taste in art as brilliantly eclectic. Like his films, they range from the classic, to the beautifully profane, to the mysterious and compelling. Many odd and hard-to-categorize pieces also struck Wilder's fancy along the way. Nothing was purchased as an investment, and all were acquired according to Wilder's taste. Over the years, in ways that he never could have predicted, or enjoyed as much if it had been his intention, the collection grew in value. With Cohen's assistance, a chunk of Wilder's collection was auctioned in 1989 and brought in a whopping $32.6 million.

"He rarely discusses his films with me," said Cohen. "Our relationship began over art. His eye is remarkable, and varied. And I'm often in awe of the way he conducts himself with artists, and people in the world of art. His father lost all the money in his family . . . and here he turned out to be an intellectual who took big chances, knew music and art and literature, and knew how to talk to people. He's never eager to discuss himself. It's always 'How are *you*? How is your son? How is your wife?' "

Cohen shook his head in admiration. "He just knew how to *do* it, you know."

LUBITSCH

In the summer of 1975, Billy Wilder looked wistfully out a window. "You know," he said, "if one could *write* Lubitsch touches, they would still exist, but he took that secret with him to his grave. It's like Chinese glass blowing; no such thing exists anymore. Occasionally, I look for an elegant twist and I say to myself, 'How would Lubitsch have done it?' And I will come up with something and it will be *like* Lubitsch, but it won't *be* Lubitsch. It's just not there anymore."
—from *Ernst Lubitsch: Laughter in Paradise* by Scott Eyman

A WILDER MOMENT

Well into his nineties, Wilder's famed wit still flourishes. Whether at his beloved front table at Mr. Chow, or at Spago, or even the fifties-style diner Johnny Rocket's in Beverly Hills, some of the great Wilder lines and bon mots of the eighties and nineties happened for the smallest audiences: his lunch and dinner companions. Here is one example of the layers of humor he could pack into four words.

At a post-dinner screening at the home of Richard and Barbara Cohen, Wilder sat on a large couch and watched the trailer attached to the main feature. The trailer was for a garish and unfunny comedy, and after the coming attraction passed, Wilder leaned over to Barbara Cohen and quietly commented:

"Thanks for the warning."

AUDREY WILDER'S RECIPE FOR THE PERFECT MARTINI

"I use a bitters bottle . . . and I do it by eye. I pour enough vodka for one or two martinis, then add the vermouth. These days Billy likes Ketel One vodka.

Noilly Prat vermouth is the key. I use seven or eight drops, stir, and pour it.

Originally we drank gin martinis. The martinis that Garbo drank were gin. After the war, vodka crept in. We started using vodka. But originally it was gin."

WILDER AT THE AFI

Speaking at the American Film Institute tribute in 1989, Wilder ended his speech with this statement to budding writers and directors, concerning the constant struggle with financing and studios. "Remember," he said, "they have the power, but we have the glory."

WILDER'S SPEECH WRITTEN FOR GARY COOPER
(FRIAR'S CLUB TESTIMONIAL DINNER, JANUARY 1961)

Ladies and gentlemen:

I understand in Las Vegas they were laying ten to one that when I got up all I'd say is "Yup." I don't know where I got this reputation—for being a sort of Johnny Belinda on horseback. It's not that I don't like to talk—it's just that I never had anything to say before. But after tonight I'll be known as the silver-tongued orator of the Golden West.

First, I would like to thank each and every one of you for this tribute—never have so many made so much fuss over so little. Frankly, I'm a little puzzled why you picked on me—but then maybe you people know something I don't. It's been some thirty-five years since I came to Hollywood. A lot of celluloid has flowed under the bridge—and it's all been fished out again for *The Late, Late Show*. A great many honors have come to me in those years—my footprints are in the forecourt of Grauman's Chinese, my name is on the sidewalk in front of the Pig'n'Whistle—and David Susskind called me a *personality*.

But seriously—as the comedians say—the only achievement I'm proud of is the friends I've made in this community. Just looking around this room makes me feel that my life has not been wasted. And if anybody asks me am I the luckiest guy in the world, my answer is—Yup!

COLBERT · AMECHE
in
"**MIDNIGHT**"
with
JOHN BARRYMORE · FRANCIS LEDERER
MARY ASTOR · Elaine Barrie

Directed by MITCHELL LEISEN
Screen Play by Charles Brackett and
Billy Wilder · Based on a story by
Edwin Justus Mayer and Franz Schulz
A Paramount Picture

ARTHUR HORNBLOW
AGATHA CHRISTIE'S

82ND AIRBORNE DIVISION
AIRBORNE

AA

HEADQUARTERS

LY WILDER · ARTHUR HORNBLOW

Italicized page numbers refer to illustrations and their captions.

Italicized page numbers refer to illustrations and their captions.

PHOTOGRAPHIC CREDITS

Front endpapers: left page all from Shooting Star except *Avanti!* poster from The Everett Collection; right page all from The Everett Collection

Back of front endpapers: left page from the Collection of Billy Wilder. Right page, top left from Archive Photos; bottom right from The Kobal Collection; all others *Sunset Boulevard*, Paramount, 1950

i left, top from Shooting Star; bottom from The Everett Collection. Right, top from the Collection of Billy Wilder; insets, bottom from *Some Like It Hot*, United Artists, 1959

iii large photograph by Peter Stackpole/LIFE Magazine © Time, Inc.; insets, *Some Like It Hot*, United Artists, 1959

iv from the Collection of Billy Wilder

v both from the Collection of Billy Wilder

vi from the Collection of Billy Wilder

ix from the Collection of Billy Wilder

INTRODUCTION

x, xii, xiv, xvi, xvii, xix © 1999 by Neal Preston; xv by Michael Montfort/Visages; xviii from the Collection of Billy Wilder

xx left, top to bottom, *A Foreign Affair*, Paramount, 1948; *Buddy Buddy*, Metro-Goldwyn-Mayer, 1981; *Fedora*, United Artists, 1979; *The Front Page*, Universal, 1974; *The Lost Weekend*, Paramount, 1945. Right, top to bottom, *Avanti!*, United Artists, 1971; *Double Indemnity*, Paramount, 1944; *Five Graves to Cairo*, Paramount, 1943; *Irma La Douce*, United Artists, 1963; *Love in the Afternoon*, Allied Artists, 1957

xxi left, top to bottom, *The Private Life of Sherlock Holmes*, United Artists, 1970; *Sabrina*, Paramount, 1954; *Some Like It Hot*, United Artists, 1959; *The Spirit of St. Louis*, Warner Bros., 1957; *Stalag 17*, Paramount, 1953. Right, top to bottom, *Sunset Boulevard*, Paramount, 1950; *The Apartment*, United Artists, 1960; *The Fortune Cookie*, United Artists, 1966; *Witness for the Prosecution*, United Artists, 1958; *The Major and the Minor* from The Kobal Collection

xxii–1 from the Collection of Billy Wilder

CHAPTER 1

2 from the Collection of Billy Wilder

5 from the Collection of Billy Wilder

6 *The Apartment*, United Artists, 1960

7 from Photofest

8 left, *Hold Back the Dawn*, Paramount, 1941. Right, from Lester Glassner Collection/Neal Peters

9 from Kotsilibas-Davis Collection

10 *Sabrina*, Paramount, 1954

11 top from John Springer/Corbis-Bettmann, bottom from Kotsilibas-Davis Collection

12–13 from Culver Pictures

14–15 left from Neal Peters Collection; right by Jack Harris/Culver Pictures

16–17 left and right from Neal Peters Collection; center from John Springer/Corbis-Bettmann

18 from Cinetext

21 *Trouble in Paradise*, Paramount, 1932

22 from Shooting Star

23 both from Kotsilibas-Davis Collection

24 from Archive Photos

25 from Kotsilibas-Davis Collection

26–27 left, center top, and right from Photofest; center bottom from The Kobal Collection

28–29 left from Photofest; center from the Collection of Billy Wilder; right from Culver Pictures

30–31 by Orlando/Globe Photos

32 from Culver Pictures

34 large photo from the Collection of Billy Wilder; inset from Culver Pictures

35 *Some Like it Hot*, United Artists, 1959

36-37 left to right, from Photofest, *Some Like it Hot*, United Artists, 1959, Photofest, the Collection of Billy Wilder

38–39 top and bottom from the Collection of Billy Wilder; center from Culver Pictures

40–41 by Ralph Crane/LIFE Magazine © Time, Inc.

43 from Photofest

CHAPTER 2

44 by Allan Grant/LIFE Magazine © Time, Inc.

46–47 left, from MPTV; insets, top to bottom by Mark Shaw

48 from The Kobal Collection

49 top from Photofest; center from The Everett Collection; bottom from the Collection of Billy Wilder

50–51 all from the Collection of Billy Wilder

52–53 top from The Everett Collection; center from The Kobal Collection; bottom from the Collection of Billy Wilder

54 top row, left to right and left row, center *Double Indemnity*, Paramount, 1944; left row, top and right from Culver Pictures; left row, bottom from Photofest

55 both *Double Indemnity*, Paramount, 1944

56-57 top and center row, *Sabrina*, Paramount, 1954; bottom left from MPTV; bottom right from the Collection of Billy Wilder

58 from the Collection of Billy Wilder

59 both by Richard Miller/MPTV

60–61 right and left Richard Miller/MPTV; insets top to bottom *The Apartment*, United Artists, 1960

62–63 *The Apartment*, United Artists, 1960

64–65 left from The Everett Collection, right from the Collection of Billy Wilder

66–67 *Some Like It Hot*, United Artists, 1959

68–69 left from The Kobal Collection; center from Culver Pictures; right *The Emperor Waltz*, Paramount, 1948

70–71 from Culver Pictures

CHAPTER 3

72 from the Collection of Billy Wilder

74–75 all from the Collection of Billy Wilder

76 musical score from *Kiss Me Stupid*, United Artists, 1964; insets left to right *A Foreign Affair*, Parmount, 1948

77 from the Collection of Billy Wilder

78–79 all from the Collection of Billy Wilder

81 from Photofest

82 top from Photofest; bottom from the Collection of Billy Wilder

83 from the Collection of Billy Wilder

84 from the Collection of Billy Wilder

85 from The Everett Collection

86–87 left and center from the Collection of Billy Wilder; right from Archive Photos

88–89 all from the Collection of Billy Wilder

90–91 both from Globe Photos

92 from the Collection of Billy Wilder

93 left from Archive Photos; right from Culver Pictures

94–95 *Stalag 17*, Paramount, 1953

96–97 left from The Everett Collection; right from Culver Pictures

98–99 top from Photofest; bottom *The Major and the Minor*, Paramount, 1942

100–101 both from Culver Pictures

CHAPTER 4

102 from the Collection of Billy Wilder

104–105 from The Kobal Collection

106–107 left and center from Photofest; right from Shooting Star

108–109 left and center by Orlando/Globe Photos; right, *Sabrina*, Paramount, 1954

110 from MPTV

112–113 from The Kobal Collection

114 left from The Kobal Collection; right from Photofest

115 *The Lost Weekend*, Paramount, 1945

116–117 second from right from Culver Pictures; all others *The Lost Weekend*, Paramount, 1945

118–119 left by Orlando/Globe Photos; right from Photofest

120 from the Collection of Billy Wilder

121 *The Fortune Cookie*, United Artists, 1966

122 top from Photofest; bottom *Love in the Afternoon*, Allied Artists, 1957

123 from Shooting Star

124 from The Everett Collection

125 both from The Kobal Collection

126–127 by Orlando/Globe Photos

128–129 left and right from the Collection of Billy Wilder; center from John Springer/Corbis-Bettmann

130 left from the Collection of Billy Wilder; right from The Kobal Collection

131 left, top and bottom *The Spirit of St. Louis*, Warner Bros., 1957; right from Culver Pictures

133 from the Collection of Billy Wilder

134–135 *The Apartment*, United Artists, 1960

137 from The Everett Collection

CHAPTER 5

138 from the Collection of Billy Wilder

140 from The Freud Museum, London/Sigmund Freud Copyrights

141 both from the Collection of Billy Wilder

142–143 right from Photofest; all others from The Everett Collection

144 from Culver Pictures

145 left from Archive Photos; right from The Kobal Collection

146 *Love in the Afternoon*, Allied Artists, 1957

147 from the Everett Collection

148 from Photofest

149 left *Love in the Afternoon*, Allied Artists, 1957; right from Culver Pictures

150 from The Kobal Collection

152 *Sunset Boulevard*, Paramount, 1950

153 from Culver Pictures

154 left top to bottom *Witness for the Prosecution*, United Artists, 1958; right from The Everett Collection

157 *Witness for the Prosecution*, United Artists, 1958

158 from The Everett Collection

159 from Photofest

160–161 top by Jack Harris/Globe Photos; bottom from AP/Wide World Photos

162 from Culver Pictures

163 top left and right from Globe Photos; bottom left by Bill Kobrin/Shooting Star

164–165 *Some Like It Hot*, United Artists, 1959

166 by Gjon Mili/LIFE Magazine © Time, Inc.

167 *One Two Three*, United Artists, 1961

168–169 left from The Everett Collection; center from Culver Pictures; right Gjon Mili/LIFE Magazine © Time, Inc.

170 left from The Kobal Collection; right, top to bottom *A Foreign Affair*, Paramount, 1948

171 by Jack Harris/Culver Pictures

172 left, top and bottom from The Everett Collection; right *Witness for the Prosecution*, United Artists, 1958

174 from Photofest

175 from The Kobal Collection

CHAPTER 6

176 top and bottom from the Collection of Billy Wilder

179 both from the Collection of Billy Wilder

180–181 from the Collection of Billy Wilder

182–183 top from the Collection of Billy Wilder; bottom left and right *Witness for the Prosecution*, United Artists, 1958

184–185 *Witness for the Prosecution*, United Artists, 1958

186–187 by Win Muldrow/Globe Photos

188 from Lester Glassner/Neal Peters Collection

189 *Love in the Afternoon*, Allied Artists, 1957

190–191 from The Everett Collection

192–193 *Ball of Fire*, Samuel Goldwyn, 1941

194 from Photofest

195 from The Everett Collection

196–197 left and right from Cinetext; center from Ullstein Bilderdienst

198 all from Cinetext

199 both from Ullstein Bilderdienst

200 from The Everett Collection

201 from Photofest

202 from Photofest

203 from Culver Pictures

204 from the Collection of Billy Wilder

206–207 top from the Collection of Billy Wilder; bottom from Archive Photos

208–209 from Cinetext

210–211 from Photofest

CHAPTER 7

212 from Marc Wanamaker/Bison Archives

214 by Steve Schatzberg/Globe Photos

215 from The Everett Collection

A NOTE ABOUT THE AUTHOR

CAMERON CROWE was an associate editor and frequent contributor to *Rolling Stone*. In 1979, Crowe wrote the book *Fast Times at Ridgemont High* and later adapted it as a screenplay. He wrote and directed *Say Anything, Singles,* the Academy Award–winning *Jerry Maguire,* and *Almost Famous* (for which he won an Academy Award for Best Original Screenplay). His film *Vanilla Sky* is to be released this fall. This is his second book.

A NOTE ON THE TYPE

This book was set in Minion, a typeface produced by the Adobe Corporation specifically for the Macintosh personal computer, and released in 1990. Designed by Robert Slimbach, Minion combines the classic characteristics of old-style faces with the full complement of weights required for modern typesetting.

Composed by North Market Street Graphics,
Lancaster, Pennsylvania
Printed by Quebecor Printing,
Leominster, Massachusetts
Bound by The Book Press,
Brattleboro, Vermont
Designed by Chip Kidd and Kapo Ng